DOUBLY ERASED

SUNY series in Queer Politics and Cultures
───────────
Cynthia Burack and Jyl J. Josephson, editors

DOUBLY ERASED
LGBTQ LITERATURE IN APPALACHIA

ALLISON E. CAREY

SUNY PRESS

Published by State University of New York Press, Albany

© 2023 State University of New York

All rights reserved

Printed in the United States of America

No part of this book may be used or reproduced in any manner whatsoever without written permission. No part of this book may be stored in a retrieval system or transmitted in any form or by any means including electronic, electrostatic, magnetic tape, mechanical, photocopying, recording, or otherwise without the prior permission in writing of the publisher.

For information, contact State University of New York Press, Albany, NY
www.sunypress.edu

Library of Congress Cataloging-in-Publication Data

Name: Carey, Allison E., 1969- author.
Title: Doubly erased : LGBTQ literature in Appalachia / Allison E. Carey.
Description: Albany : State University of New York Press, 2023. | Series: SUNY series in queer politics and cultures | Includes bibliographical references and index.
Identifiers: LCCN 2022044291 | ISBN 9781438493558 (hardcover : alk. paper) | ISBN 9781438493572 (ebook) | ISBN 9781438493565 (pbk. : alk. paper)
Subjects: LCSH: American literature—Appalachian Region—History and criticism. | Sexual minorities' writings, American—History and criticism. | Sexual minorities—Appalachian Region—Intellectual life. | Sexual minorities in literature. | Appalachian Region—Intellectual life. | Appalachian Region—In literature. | Mountain life in literature.
Classification: LCC PS286.A6 C37 2023 | DDC 810.9/974—dc23/eng/20221129
LC record available at https://lccn.loc.gov/2022044291davis

10 9 8 7 6 5 4 3 2 1

To Mom and Dad,
who fed my curiosity and my love of language and libraries.

And to Walter and Dash,
who make every day an adventure.

Contents

Acknowledgments		ix
Introduction		1
Chapter 1	The Elders of LGBTQ Appalachian Literature	13
Chapter 2	The Conversation Begins: Landmark Texts and Trailblazing Authors	49
Chapter 3	Visibility and Seeing: Photography in LGBTQ Appalachian Literature	81
Chapter 4	Silences and Storytelling in LGBTQ Appalachian Literature	119
Chapter 5	HomePlaceBody: The Pleasures and Perils of the Physical World	145
Chapter 6	Flight and Food: Transcending Life and Death in LGBTQ Appalachian Literature	173
Conclusion		195
Appendix: doris davenport Videos		199
Notes		201
Bibliography		241
Index		261

Acknowledgments

Early parts of this manuscript were supported by grants at my home institution, Marshall University. First, a 2015 Sarah Denman "Faces of Appalachia" Fellowship from the Center for the Study of Ethnicity and Gender in Appalachia, made possible by gifts to the National Endowment for the Humanities (NEH) Challenge Grant and NEH matching funds, provided me both time and funds to support the research. Then, thanks to a 2018 John Marshall Fall Scholar Award, with funding from the Marshall University Research Corporation, I was able to devote a semester to research and writing.

I owe a debt of thanks to colleagues at Marshall who talked through parts of the argument with me or otherwise offered advice or support. Thank you to Marshall (or one-time Marshall) colleagues Kristen Lillvis, Steve Underhill, John Young, Daniel O'Malley, David Cartwright, Sandy York, Olen York, Cat Pleska, Eric Smith, and Jeffrey Ruff. Thank you also to Dr. Robert Bookwalter, dean of the College of Liberal Arts, for his support of my work.

I couldn't have completed this work without the assistance of librarians and archivists at Marshall University and other libraries across the country. At Marshall, thank you to Dr. Monica Brooks, Lori Thompson, Gillian Sochor, Phyllis White-Sellards, Cathy Cover, Johnny Bradley, Kelli Johnson, Eleanor Anders, and Chris Hodge. At other institutions, I had assistance from Sarah Coblentz, Jay-Marie Bravent, and Reinette Jones at the University of Kentucky; Mandi Johnson (University of the South); Tim Noakes (Stanford University); Patrice Green and a host of people at the University of Georgia's Hargrett Rare Book and Manuscript Library; Rachel Vagts (Berea College); Anne Moore (University of Massachusetts, Amherst); Tina Monaco (historian with the Augusta-Richmond County Public Library System); Jeanne Kambara (Syracuse University Libraries).

For research assistance, I'm indebted to Lindsey Harper and Carin Wolfe. For help with copyediting, thank you to Dr. Michelle Schiavone.

For help in the English Department office, thank you to Jackson Armstrong, Amanda Fannin, Rebecca Fitzgerald, Amber Murphy, Kathryn Thompson, and especially Jillian Hovatter.

Thank you to the graduate students in my Fall 2020 ENG 632 course at Marshall University: our conversations helped me clarify my thinking and offered joy during the early months of the pandemic.

Thank you to Kate Black, George Brosi, Gurney Norman, Dr. Thomas Frazier, and Dr. Randy Mackin, all of whom patiently answered my questions about this literature and these authors. (Additional thanks are owed to Dr. Mackin, who shared with me research materials from his own archival research in George Scarbrough's journals.)

Dr. Jane Hill read and commented on an early draft of the manuscript. Thank you, as always, for the sage advice and perspective.

Thank you to Elizabeth Stephens, Jeff Mann, and Julia Watts, for their helpful conversations about their work.

Thank you to Dr. Cynthia Burack and Dr. Rebecca Colesworthy at State University of New York Press.

Thank you to Dr. Shirley Lumpkin for moral support and meals.

Finally, thank you to Walter and Dash, whose love, laughter, and patience sustain me.

Introduction

In Kentucky-born novelist Silas House's keynote address at the 2014 Appalachian Studies Association Conference, he noted that his Berea College students who identify as LGBTQ feel "invisible" within Appalachia, and that they cite this feeling among their reasons for moving out of the region. In this talk, House highlighted the challenges facing LGBTQ Appalachians, particularly calling attention to recent acts of anti-LGBTQ violence and discrimination. House called for the audience (and the reader, when the talk was published in the *Journal of Appalachian Studies* the following fall) to speak up against such hate, and he explicitly called out the Appalachian studies community for remaining unacceptably silent on these issues. House's remedy, his call-to-action for the audience, is framed in terms of speech as action: "we can fight this first and foremost through talking about it, by singing about it, by writing about it, through education, science, and research, and with conversation."[1]

My own preparation for that conference unearthed another case of invisibility and silence. While preparing my presentation on the young adult novels of Kentucky-native Julia Watts, I expected to find ample scholarship on Watts's 2001 novel *Finding H.F.*—a Lambda Literary Award winner, groundbreaking in its portrayal of young, queer Appalachians—and on LGBTQ Appalachian literature in general. Instead, I found only a few essays about individual authors and texts but not what I was looking for: a comprehensive study of the rich (and fairly recent, covering the last thirty to forty years) tradition of LGBTQ themes in Appalachian literature.[2] From that absence, that silence in the scholarship, the seed for this book was planted.

Four years later, at the 2018 Appalachian Studies Conference, House convened a session entitled "The Other in an Othered Culture: LGBTQ

Writers in Appalachia." This session, which featured readings by House as well as other LGBTQ Appalachian writers, Carter Sickels, Jason Howard, and Savannah Sipple, focused on LGBTQ Appalachian literature as well as on the challenges facing the Appalachian queer community. During the Q&A that followed, in response to a question by writer and *Oxford American* poetry editor Rebecca Gayle Howell about the future of Appalachian letters, House became reflective, noting that "there were many years when there weren't any gay Appalachian writers" and named Lisa Alther, Jeff Mann, and Julia Watts as groundbreaking LGBTQ Appalachian writers.[3] House's acknowledgment of these writers' impact was heartening, yet the situation was ironic: Mann and Watts were speaking at the conference but were not invited to be part of this panel.

This irony was a reminder of my original inspiration to write this book: although we are in the midst of a flowering of LGBTQ Appalachian literature, readers might easily believe that Sipple and other emerging writers such as Mesha Maren, Jonathan Corcoran, and Rahul Mehta are the first openly queer Appalachian writers, or that House is the first novelist to focus on queer Appalachians. Yet these writers walk a road paved by many others, including Alther, Mann, and Watts, as well as Maggie Anderson, doris davenport, Fenton Johnson, filmmaker Beth Stephens, and, in an earlier generation, poet George Scarbrough. Undoubtedly, there were other queer Appalachian writers—about whose lives we may never know more—who felt compelled to prevent any hint of scandal about their sexuality from emerging.

What, I wondered, unites queer Appalachian authors and their works, beyond issues of sexuality and an affiliation with a region? How do these texts grow out of or diverge from the Appalachian literary tradition, or from the tradition of LGBTQ literature in the United States? What are their common preoccupations, tropes, character types, and concerns? This book is my attempt to answer those questions. In it, I trace the history of this literature, preparing us to more fully appreciate the work of these emerging writers by understanding the origin story of LGBTQ Appalachian literature and appreciating how we arrived at this moment.

Only within the past forty years, beginning with the 1976 publication of Lisa Alther's *Kinflicks*, have openly queer Appalachian authors published works that directly address issues of sexuality. In *Doubly Erased*, I undertake a systematic inquiry into the work of LGBTQ Appalachians who are writing about LGBTQ themes and characters, focusing primarily on those writers (and one filmmaker) who produced a full-length work between 1976 and 2016. Authors covered by this research include some of the most influential and highly regarded contemporary writers and artists in (or from) Appalachia, including poet and essayist Jeff Mann; novelists Dorothy Allison, Lisa Alther, Julia Watts, Fenton Johnson, Karen Salyer McElmurray, and Silas House; graphic memoirist Alison Bechdel; filmmaker Beth Stephens; Affrilachian poet doris davenport; and others.[4] There are other LGBTQ Appalachian writers—including Nickole Brown, Ann Pancake, and Victor Depta—whose works could have been included here but were not due to limitations on space and time.

When these contemporary LGBTQ Appalachian authors and their works are placed in dialogue, common patterns, tropes, and themes emerge. LGBTQ Appalachian literature derives many of its themes—land, family, food, and social justice—from the Appalachian literary tradition. Yet a set of preoccupations is common to this literature as well: a focus on visibility and seeing, a persistent concern with silences, a love of place that figures the land both as refuge and threat, metaphors of flying and flying creatures, and representations of food linked to both love of family and loss of family connections. Moreover, these writers describe feeling voiceless in an already voiceless region, being outsiders-yet-insiders in a marginalized and stereotyped culture. The content of this literature—the controversial topics (treatment of Appalachians with AIDS, religion wielded as a weapon against LGBTQ Appalachians) and references to queer sexuality—made these texts less likely to be taught in Appalachian studies classes, discussed at conferences, or written about in journals. These authors and their work have been *doubly erased*: disregarded within the literature of the United States because they're Appalachian ("regionalists," "local color," etc.) and overlooked (or excluded from) the Appalachian literary tradition because they are queer.

The erasure of these Appalachian writers also exemplifies the invisibility of queer Appalachians and other rural queer people within popular representations of homosexuality in the US. Such representations are primarily dominated by images of urban, white, largely upper-middle-class queer subjects, a phenomenon that queer theorist Jack Halberstam has dubbed "metronormativity."[5] In Halberstam's 2005 study *In a Queer Time and Place: Transgender Bodies, Subcultural Lives*, he chronicles the elision of rural queer populations within representations of US queer lives: "Until recently, small towns were considered hostile to queers and urban areas were cast as the queer's natural environment. . . . While there is plenty of truth to this division between urban and small-town life, between hetero-familial cultures and queer creative and sexual cultures, the division also occludes the lives of nonurban queers."[6] Halberstam further argues that this occlusion has shaped the development both of LGBTQ literature in the United States and of queer identity, in the sense that many queer youth first seek models for their sexuality in the pages of a novel. Halberstam (referencing the work of historian Will Fellows) notes that "queers from rural settings are not well represented in the literature that has been so much a hallmark of twentieth-century gay identity. . . . Little of this literature has anything at all to say about rural life, and most of it ties homosexual encounters to the rhythms of the city."[7] Although this observation might be true of US literature overall, LGBTQ Appalachian literature has demonstrated a consistent focus on rural queer lives.

Regarding my terminology, throughout this book I will use "LGBTQ" or "queer" to describe people whose cultural and sexual practices diverge from heteronormativity. In adopting this terminology, I am indebted to Catherine Lord and Richard Meyer, coauthors of the 2013 book *Art and Queer Culture*, who wrote, in explaining their use of the word queer, "We have chosen the term 'queer' in the knowledge that no single word can accommodate the sheer expanse of cultural practices that oppose normative heterosexuality. In its shifting connotation from everyday parlance to phobic epithet to defiant self-identification, 'queer' offers more generous rewards than any simple inventory of sexual practices or erotic object choices."[8] My intent is not to exclude other identities (which are sometimes represented by additional letters or symbols) but rather to pitch a big tent in which a variety of nonheteronormative practices can reside. My thinking was also shaped by a presentation by Judith Butler at the 1995 School of Criticism and Theory, in which Butler outlined their forthcoming book, *Excitable Speech: A Politics of the Performative* (1997). Butler's discussion of the changing valance of the word "queer"—its shifting power to wound or seduce or describe—shifted my understanding of the term and its rhetorical and descriptive power.

Beginning in the mid-1990s, a few key texts within Appalachian studies began to acknowledge the existence of queer Appalachians, making them visible within the scholarship. Although lesbian and gay studies arose as an interdisciplinary academic discipline in the US in the 1970s–'80s, it was incorporated much more slowly into Appalachian studies, beginning with Kate Black and Marc A. Rhorer's 1994 presentation at the Appalachian Studies Conference (published as the 1995 essay "Out in the Mountains: Exploring Lesbian and Gay Lives"). As Black and Rhorer described the genesis of their project, they focused on the silence about this issue: "The idea for this project began when Marc wanted to do a research paper on lesbians and gays in Appalachia and asked Kate, curator of the University of Kentucky Appalachian Collection, about prior research on the subject. Kate said, 'There isn't anything.'"[9] For "Out in the Mountains," Black and Rhorer interviewed gay and lesbian Appalachians about "coming out experiences, homophobia, AIDS-phobia, and community building."[10] Several themes emerged: participants' feelings of isolation, fears of job loss or physical violence, and internalization of the homophobia that surrounds them. Black and Rhorer found that "while everyone readily identified themselves as gay or lesbian, we found that many people seemed to avoid directly addressing their Appalachian identities."[11] This same dilemma—how to reconcile one's queer and Appalachian identities—is a consistent theme for later writers.

Danny Miller's "Homosexuality in Appalachian Literature," a talk presented at the 1996 Appalachian Studies Conference, is the earliest foray into LGBTQ themes within Appalachian literary studies.[12] Acknowledging Black and Rhorer's essay, Miller echoes their criticism of the scholarly silence about "gays and lesbians in Appalachia" but notes that "their existence has been acknowledged in the fiction of the region for several years."[13] Miller goes on to examine the portrayals of gay characters in five Appalachian novels (including Dorothy Allison's *Bastard Out of Carolina*), thus making queer characters in Appalachian literature visible for readers (or scholars) who have overlooked or ignored them: "I hope that the foregoing discussion shows that homosexual characters in an Appalachian setting <u>are</u> a part of the fiction of the region and that literature at least admits their existence, in various personifications."[14]

Three years after Miller's presentation, in 1999, Jeff Mann published "Stonewall and Matewan: Some Thoughts on Gay Life in Appalachia," an essay in which Mann describes the balancing act for those who embrace their identities as both Appalachians and members of the LGBTQ community. Mann echoes Black and Rhorer's interview subjects in describing his early feelings of isolation as a gay teen in Appalachia, then his later rejection of Appalachian identity and relocation to an urban area. However, living outside of Appalachia led Mann to a realization: "I was an Appalachian." Mann describes himself and other Appalachian gays and lesbians as "balancing gay or lesbian and Appalachian identities," acknowledging, "It's taken me twenty years to achieve some kind of reasonable equilibrium."[15] Mann hopes that the increased visibility of queer

Appalachians will lead to greater understanding: "In the face of such honesty and courage, opinions shift: the newly-made friend or coworker is less likely to hate, the gay adolescent less likely to contemplate suicide in the face of Antarctic isolation."[16]

In the same year that Mann's "Stonewall and Matewan" was published, a documentary gave voice to queer young people in Appalachia, highlighting the danger and condemnation they face. *Through Their Eyes: Stories of Gays and Lesbians in the Mountains* (dir. Burke, Caudill, Cupp, and Rowlette) was produced by Appalshop (an arts and education center in Kentucky) and "was made by and features lesbians and gays living in Harlan and Perry Counties in Kentucky."[17] This short film comprises interviews with young queer Appalachians (and one older man). In the voices of these young people, we hear about their coming-out experiences with family and friends, their endurance of oppression and violence, and their desire for acceptance. One young man tells of his mother holding a loaded gun to his head because, as she said, "I would rather see you dead and know that you were in Hell than see you living a life of this sick sin," and a young woman describes the time period when her sisters "beat the hell out of me for three years thinking they could beat it out of me, that I'd like men afterwards." Yet most of the young people express their determination to stay in their home counties, find partners, and make lives there. In Kate Black's review of the film, she describes its message of activism and inclusion: "They aim to expose their own reality—and the heinous deeds of their communities—while simultaneously affirming their sense of place and their right to be a part of it."[18]

Earlier generations of queer folks—both in Appalachia and nationwide—faced these same obstacles, as well as job discrimination, police harassment, and threat of imprisonment or institutionalization. As Craig M. Loftin describes in *Masked Voices: Gay Men and Lesbians in Cold War America*, anti-homosexual rhetoric geared up in the late 1940s and peaked in the 1950s, as "investigations of homosexuals under national security auspices allowed McCarthyites to bolster claims that their political opponents were 'soft' on communism, thus jeopardizing national security."[19] Yet Loftin describes gay people responding with "adaptation and resilience," passing as heterosexual and thus donning a metaphorical mask, which "provided gay people with the necessary security that *allowed* them to consciously identify as homosexual and participate in a subaltern, camouflaged gay public sphere."[20]

A key example of such masking—and of the careful, gradual removal of this mask—within Appalachian literary circles is the career of novelist Silas House. Over the past decade (2012–2022) within Appalachian literature and Appalachian studies, queer themes have been made safe for discussion in large part because of House and his work. House has occupied a unique position within LGBTQ Appalachian literature, in that when he first became celebrated for his writing—most notably for his first novel, *New York Times* bestselling *Clay's Quilt* (2001)—his subject matter fell squarely within the confines of traditional Appalachian themes, and House himself had not yet publicly identified as a gay man.[21] In *Clay's Quilt*, protagonist Clay Sizemore comes to terms with the long-ago murder of his mother in a novel that addresses themes of family ties, domestic violence, the redemptive value of music, and the lingering fault lines in the Appalachian economy. Scholar Emily Satterwhite notes that the novel "reiterates major touchstones of Appalachian fiction, including coal mining (Clay's occupation), fiddling . . . , quilting, boozing, gambling, squirrel hunting, clogging, gospel singing, and Pentecostal religion."[22] In the two decades since the publication of *Clay's Quilt*, House has become a central figure in Appalachian literature and in Appalachian studies more generally; numerous awards, appointments, keynote addresses, and other acknowledgments have cemented his establishment position.

Thus, House had secured a distinguished literary reputation and an influential position within the Appalachian literary and scholarly communities before he began to write about LGBTQ issues and before he came out as gay. In a 2018 interview, House notes that he came out at age thirty-four; that would have been in about 2005 or so.[23] Even as this topic—LGBTQ issues—emerged in his writing, House often rhetorically distanced this material from its queer subject matter. For example, House has stated that his 2012 play *This Is My Heart for You* was inspired by, among other events from the summer of 2011, an incident in Hazard, Kentucky, when two young men were kicked out of a community pool for "acting gay."[24] Yet House maintained in a January 2014 interview that "this is not so much a 'gay play' as it is a commentary on how Americans have lost the ability to have a civil conversation with one another about political and social issues."[25] Later that same spring, in March 2014, House's Appalachian Studies keynote focused on LGBTQ issues, but the talk was framed in such a way that House's frequent uses of the first-person plural, "us" and "we," grouped him with fellow Appalachians or fellow academics, not fellow people who identify as queer, such as when House asks his audience, "Why do we quietly accept that this treatment is all right for members of the queer community?"[26]

The fact that House was a member of that queer community was not a secret: in an August 2014 interview, writer Jason Howard referred to House as "both my partner and an incredible writer."[27] However, House continued to be discreet about this issue as it related to him personally. In a September 2015 NPR interview about his perspectives on the Kim Davis case in Rowan County, Kentucky, House was identified simply as "novelist Silas House, who grew up in the region. He is a professor at Eastern Kentucky's Berea College."[28] There is no acknowledgment, in either host Steve Inskeep's questions or House's answers, that House might have a personal stake in this case other than as a Kentuckian interested in issues of fairness. When Inskeep, as part of his last question, noted that "it sounds like you disagree with Kim Davis' views in this case," House replied, "I just believe that what she's doing, I personally disagree with." House did not volunteer (nor was he obliged to do so) that he and his partner had themselves successfully applied for a marriage license earlier that summer in another Kentucky county.[29]

Yet only two years later, in a 2017 profile of House in *Spectrum South: The Voice of the Queer South*, he was being identified as "gay novelist Silas House" and "arguably the most prolific gay novelist in Appalachia."[30] In multiple interviews leading up to the release of his 2018 novel *Southernmost*, House discussed the challenges he faced in coming out and his long process of reconciling his sexuality with his religious faith.[31] By the 2018 ASA Conference, House was chairing a panel of LGBTQ Appalachian writers. And in House's June 2018 op-ed in the *New York Times*, "The Masterpiece Decision Isn't Harmless," House writes from the perspective of a member of the queer community, enumerating the many forms of legalized discrimination against queer people in the US and describing his 2015 wedding, in which he and his husband were married by a judge only "five days after the Supreme Court gave us that right," not waiting to be married in his church "because we didn't want to wait the three weeks it took for the banns to be published; we were too afraid the right would somehow be snatched from us."[32]

These details are relevant because House's careful self-positioning and his strategies for "coming out" as a queer Appalachian writer demonstrate the high stakes for an Appalachian writer—even now, even one who is a prominent, respected figure like House—whose life and work represent stigmatized identities. In other words, House surely took such care, so precisely executed strategies that enabled the mainstreaming of queerness within Appalachian literature and Appalachian studies, because he felt that such care was necessary. By the 2012 premier of his play *This Is My Heart for You*, House had a solid reputation among national literary circles and had become an establishment figure within the Appalachian studies community: among the signs of House's prominence were his selection in 2004 to complete famed Kentucky writer James Still's unfinished second novel (*Chinaberry*, published in 2011) and his 2010 appointment as NEH Chair in Appalachian Studies at Berea College. Yet events have demonstrated that queerness is a risky topic even for an esteemed writer like House: leading up to *This Is My Heart*'s 2012 premiere, House "received hate mail and death threats about my 'gay play.'"[33] In gradually introducing queer content into his work, House both demonstrates the need for this measured and diplomatic response and illustrates why earlier writers perhaps didn't develop the mainstream reputation they might have under other, less stigmatizing circumstances. Today, House uses his position within the Appalachian studies community to advocate for LGBTQ issues and similarly uses his position within the broader literary establishment to advocate for Appalachians.[34] Examining the evolution of House's career has shown us how hard House had to work to achieve this balance. Earlier queer Appalachian writers—especially from previous generations—would have felt the personal and professional impact that Loftin discussed in *Masked Voices*, and they would have suffered from the stigma, or carefully masked, or both.

A consequence of the kind of careful masking that LGBTQ Appalachians and some LGBTQ Appalachian authors have practiced is a sparse early literary history of queer writers, especially within Appalachia. In chapter 1, "The Elders of LGBTQ Appalachian Literature," we go in search of those writers, examining the life and work of three Appalachian writers who serve as points on the spectrum of openness. Tennessee poet George Scarbrough published poems about gay sexuality and came out in the 1990s, near the end of his life. Georgia poet and novelist Byron Herbert Reece never came out, although both his published work and his personal letters reveal positive portrayals of homosexuality (a rarity for the 1950s) as well as Reece's engagement in national conversations about gay literature. Finally, Kentuckian James Still, often called the "Dean of Appalachian Literature," adamantly denied being gay, but his friendships and his correspondence reveal a man comfortable with people of a range of sexualities and who was alert to society's biases. For all three, a closer reading of their work within this context reveals another (perhaps masked?) layer of meaning.

Beginning with Lisa Alther's 1976 novel *Kinflicks*, issues of queer sexuality began to be more directly addressed within Appalachian literature, and chapter 2, "The Conversation Begins: Landmark Texts and Trailblazing Authors," provides a chronological overview of the key texts of contemporary LGBTQ Appalachian literature and introduces the authors who did this important work. Many of these texts were notable firsts, like Fenton Johnson's 1993 novel *Scissors, Paper, Rock*—the first novel to address the AIDS crisis in Appalachia—or doris davenport's 1995 poetry collection *Soque Street Poems*: within davenport's portrait of her Affrilachian community in north Georgia are glimpses of queer Affrilachian relationships. From *Kinflicks* through Silas House's 2018 novel, *Southernmost*, this chapter explores the history—and critical reception—of the texts that opened Appalachian literature to LGBTQ themes, characters, and concerns.

Each of the subsequent chapters examines a different thread running through contemporary LGBTQ Appalachian literature. Chapter 3, "Visibility and Seeing: Photography in LGBTQ Appalachian Literature," explores this literature's preoccupation with seeing and being seen, frequently through imagery of photography or filming in such texts as *Kinflicks*, the poetry of Maggie Anderson, the essays of Carter Sickels, and others. Of course, within a Western philosophical tradition in which seeing is equated with understanding, these textual explorations of sight serve as inquiries into how we understand ourselves as well as others. In Alison Bechdel's popular graphic novel *Fun Home*, for example, Bechdel situates the issue of photography within epistemological dilemmas of how we can truly know our loved ones or ourselves.

Chapter 4, "Silences and Storytelling in LGBTQ Appalachian Literature," focuses on images of secret-keeping and silencing, including how questions of "voice," coming out, and staying in the closet have been framed within contemporary LGBTQ Appalachian literature. This analysis includes an overview of the early conversations within Appalachian studies about HIV and AIDS, one of the most prominent examples of a topic seemingly too taboo to discuss. The chapter's focus on silences and stories—in all their tangled complexity—includes those within Johnson's *Scissors, Paper, Rock*: silences about protagonist Raphael Hardin's HIV infection as well as the stories recounted by the Hardin family. In *Strange Birds in the Tree of Heaven* by Karen Salyer McElmurray, profound silences mark the alienation of gay man Andrew Wallen from his mother Ruth Blue Wallen, and dueling radio stations—one broadcasting popular music and the other hymns—signal the alienation of a young Ruth Blue from her father. Finally, through an examination of doris davenport's twin poetry collections *Soque Street Poems* (1995) and *madness like morning glories* (2005) whose individual poems are written in the voices of community members, we see the influence of the oral storytelling tradition as davenport gives voice to her Affrilachian home community and to queer Affrilachians.

Another key element of the work of many Appalachian authors is love of place, whether that place is the natural world or Appalachia's urban spaces. In chapter 5, "HomePlaceBody: The Pleasures and Perils of the Physical World," I examine how LGBTQ Appalachian authors Carter Sickels, Jeff Mann, and doris davenport—plus West Virginia–born filmmaker Beth Stephens—frame the Appalachian landscape as a refuge or liken it to the contours of a lover's body. However, as this chapter discusses, these texts often highlight the ways in which home is not always welcoming and not always safe; the chapter explores the portrayal of rural queerness as a logical impossibility within American culture, thus further othering queer residents of Appalachia. Other authors, such as Julia Watts, Karen Salyer McElmurray, and Lisa Alther, reveal the complexities of "Love of Place" for queer Appalachians, and make visible the complications and darker undercurrents of rural and urban Appalachian spaces. Finally, the chapter also explores, especially in the poetry of Jeff Mann and of doris davenport, the Appalachian landscape's embodiment of not only the beauty but also the vulnerabilities of the physical body. In fact, davenport's role as a performance poet makes her work particularly challenging to analyze on the page: the presence of davenport's physical body and her vocal delivery of the poetry are crucial, she has argued, for the appropriate "reading" of her work.[35] (The appendix includes links to videos of a few of davenport's readings and performances.)

Although these authors celebrate the beauty and pleasures of the physical world—the joys inherent in our homes, homeplaces, and bodies—they also seek transcendence of that world, rising above it through images of flight and symbolically conquering it through eating. Chapter 6, "Flight and Food: Transcending Life and Death in LGBTQ Appalachian Literature," examines the ways these authors move beyond the limitations of the material world. Both food and flight—including images of birds and other winged creatures—have deep symbolic ties to the transcendence of life's perils: freedom from enslavement, freedom from famine, freedom from death. McElmurray, through the winged things in *Strange*

Birds, and Alther, through the motherless birds in *Kinflicks*, explore our mutual yearning to rise above the boredom, pain, and struggle that yoke us to our physical existence. Others of these authors—especially Mann, Watts, and Johnson—explore the transcendence available through not flight but food, including Johnson's illustration, in *Scissors, Paper, Rock*, of the way that food helps us overcome the strictures of what can and cannot be spoken. Throughout, these authors explore the permeable boundaries between body and spirit, between this world and the next, and remind us of the pleasures and hazards inherent in all that makes us human.

1

The Elders of LGBTQ Appalachian Literature

Although this book focuses on contemporary LGBTQ Appalachian literature by writers who are of the Baby Boom generation and later—including Lisa Alther (b. 1944), doris davenport (b. 1949), Dorothy Allison (b. 1949), Fenton Johnson (b. 1953), Jeff Mann (b. 1959), and others—we should acknowledge that these were surely not the first queer Appalachian writers. Although contemporary authors have faced the dilemmas of whether to come out and whether to move out of Appalachia to a locale more welcoming to queer folks, earlier queer Appalachian authors would have had fewer options. Being "out of the closet" was generally not an option for earlier generations of queer Appalachians, or other queer Americans, for whom such openness could have meant being arrested and prosecuted under the many laws that enforced both sexuality and gender presentation.[1] (In Alison Bechdel's *Fun Home*, she references the New York City laws of the 1950s that required women to wear at least three articles of women's clothing.[2] There were similar laws all across the country; some were struck down in the 1970s, while others were on the books as late as 2011.[3]) Appalachian writers who were born early in the twentieth century (and before) would have felt intense pressure to conform, for the sake of family, safety, and legal standing.

Consequently, we lack a long and vibrant tradition of a queer Appalachian literary heritage. This chapter focuses on the work of three Appalachian writers: Kentucky writer James Still, Tennessee poet George Scarbrough, and Georgia poet and novelist Byron Herbert Reece. Still (b. 1906), often called "the Dean of Appalachian Literature," adamantly denied being gay until the end of his life, but his sexuality has been a topic of discussion among scholars. Scarbrough (b. 1915) became more open about his sexuality near the end of his life and published some openly gay verse. Finally, Reece (b. 1917) was closeted during his too-short life, but his poetry, novels, and correspondence hint at his sexual orientation (and his intense struggle to keep that under wraps). A closer look at the work by these three writers, and the trajectory of their careers and lives, will illustrate the stakes for Appalachian writers of earlier generations when their sexuality was called into question.

Asking these questions is not driven by prurience. Instead, in order to understand why we don't have a tradition of LGBTQ Appalachian literature until 1976, we must understand the pressures on Appalachians (and US citizens more generally) regarding gender and sexuality, as well as the personal and professional consequences that resulted from scrutiny by the FBI (or other government agencies), by postal authorities, by employers, or by neighbors. The consequences that Silas House suffered in 2012—hate mail and death threats for writing a "gay play"—would have been only part of what was in store for queer writers who dared to broach this topic, in Appalachia or elsewhere in the US, in the early to mid-twentieth century. Understanding this history is crucial to appreciating the authors whose groundbreaking work we'll examine in chapter 2, "The Conversation Begins: Landmark Texts and Trailblazing Authors," as well as to seeing the complexity of the possible subtexts, and why there would even need to be subtexts, for Appalachian authors of earlier generations.

An inquiry like this one is complicated by the scant documentation of queer lives in the traditional historical and archival record, at least for queer citizens who were quiet, cautious, and/or fortunate.[4] Most of the queer lives from previous generations that we've heard about are famous due to tragedy (Oscar Wilde, Rock Hudson) or flamboyance (Liberace, Truman Capote), not the lives of average, everyday queer citizens whose existence did not attract official or public attention. By and large, traditional archives are more official (and officious?) collections of documents and objects, typically the items that have been carefully saved and preserved and then passed along to libraries or historical societies. If someone donates their papers to a library's archives, they are unlikely to contribute content that could have earlier resulted in their being fired, ostracized, or persecuted. Little of that material is likely to be saved for the use of future scholars. (In some cases, disapproving family members might have selectively culled material before passing along a loved one's papers to a waiting archive.)

Scholars have explored the resulting gaps in queer history and the seeming absence of queer lives from the archival record. Ann Cvetkovich, author of *An Archive of Feelings: Trauma, Sexuality, and Lesbian Public Cultures* (2003), discusses the reasons for this absence: "That gay and lesbian history even exists has been a contested fact, and the struggle to record and preserve it is exacerbated by the invisibility that often surrounds intimate life, especially sexuality."[5] Valerie Rohy, describing the work of Cvetkovich and others, notes that "recent queer scholarship has sought to explore the blind spots of historical narrative, expose the fantasies at work there, and probe the affective and figural investments that inform views of the past."[6] As Alana Kumbier points out in *Ephemeral Material: Queering the Archive*, scholars of queer history "encounter specific kinds of discrimination around their object of study, as some would challenge the existence of LGBTQ subjects," noting that "records about sexuality, sexual lives, and sexual subcultures—written by participants (and not scientists and doctors analyzing them, or police surveilling them, or anthropologists studying them)—have been scarce."[7] Cvetkovich and others have written about the efforts of queer communities to establish their own archives, and to excavate what can be discovered within official archives. Cvetkovich observes, writing in 2003 about this impulse, "In the last decade in particular, there has been a marked historical turn as historians, documentary makers, and average citizens have been drawn to historicizing not just the politics of a gay movement but earlier generations of struggle that threaten to become lost history; they are affectively motivated by the passionate desire to claim the fact of history and acknowledge those who provided the foundations for the 1970s' gay rights movement."[8]

The decades that preceded the gay rights movement were an especially difficult and dangerous time for LGBTQ citizens in the United States. A congressional focus on homosexuals working in the US State Department began in 1946, gained traction and publicity through McCarthy's Red Scare in 1950, and expanded into a "Lavender Scare," leading to the harassment and firing of countless gay and lesbian government employees and the general demonization of queer people, who were represented as security risks akin to alcoholics, Communists, and the criminally insane.[9] Executive Order 10450, signed by President Eisenhower in 1953, barred homosexuals from working in the federal government and institutionalized employment discrimination against gays and lesbians.[10] Similar guidelines were applied in state and local governments as well; this system would remain in place for decades.[11]

One factor that intensified the stressors on queer citizens—and one that explains the caution exercised by LGBTQ people of previous generations even in personal correspondence, as well as why archives might retain only faint traces of queer lives—is the role of the US Postal Service in facilitating the FBI's antigay crusades in the Lavender Scare. As Craig M. Loftin explains (in *Letters to ONE*, his book about subscriber letters to the early queer periodical), private correspondence did not offer queer citizens refuge from scrutiny and persecution: "Antigay crackdowns by the U.S. Postal Service were of particular concern to *ONE* subscribers and correspondents. . . . Federal law . . . gave Post Office officials broad power to seize mail they considered obscene. For some postal officials, this could include anything pertaining to homosexuality."[12] In a famous case in the 1950s, "postal officials in Los Angeles seized all copies of individual *ONE* issues on obscenity grounds, once in 1953 and again in 1954. Postal officials reversed the first seizure after further review. *ONE* fought the second seizure to the U.S. Supreme Court, which, in 1958, ruled that the magazine was not obscene."[13]

The fate of Newton Arvin—a resident of Northampton, Massachusetts, where he was a distinguished professor of English at Smith College and a renowned scholar of American literature—illustrates the human cost of these policies, of this institutionalized homophobia, and of the postal service's complicity in its enforcement. In the autumn of 1960, a contingent of Massachusetts State Police raided Arvin's apartment to enforce a new state law that "recently made it a felony to possess obscene pictures with the intent of showing them to others . . . placing [Massachusetts] in the vanguard of a national crusade that was now cresting with the adoption of broad new federal powers to fight mail-order filth."[14] Arvin had come to the attention of the police thanks to "a postal investigation. Either federal authorities had got his name from a mailing list seized from a magazine supply house in St. Louis, they said, or else a package addressed to him had 'broken open' in the Springfield post office, revealing obscene pictures."[15] The police seized and read Arvin's personal journals, compiling more evidence as well as a list of other men to round up. Under questioning, Arvin provided police with the names of other men to whom he had shown the pictures.[16] With a growing list of names, the police raided more homes and interrogated and arrested more men. Two weeks later, a total of seven men were put on trial.[17]

The case received widespread press coverage; newspapers in at least twenty-five US states carried stories about the scandal. Sometimes the coverage was sensationalized, although the *New York Times*' "2 Smith Teachers Held in Vice Case" was relatively restrained. In addition to mentioning that Arvin's confession had led to the arrest of his colleague, the *Times* article also noted that Arvin had won the 1951 National Book Award for nonfiction for his biography of Herman Melville.[18] Arvin checked himself into the state mental hospital after the arrest and then checked back out for the trial, at which he confessed and pled guilty to an obscenity charge and "being a 'lewd and lascivious' person." He received a suspended (one-year) sentence, was fined $1,400, and was given two years' probation.[19] Arvin lost most of the professional affiliations that he prized. Not only was he was forced to retire from Smith, but he was stripped of his seat on the board of directors of (and even his membership in) Yaddo, a writers' colony in Saratoga Springs with which he had been affiliated since 1928 and which had always served as a refuge for him.[20] Arvin died less than two years later, of pancreatic cancer, in March 1963, having never regained the professional standing that he'd lost through this scandal.[21]

Although the cultural and legal conditions that had led to Arvin's arrest and public humiliation slowly began to change over the next decade, "America's unbuttoning arrived too late, of course, for Arvin."[22] In 1962, Supreme Court decisions regarding obscenity and police searches had, essentially, "invalidated the legal bases for the persecution of Arvin" and the other men tried with him.[23] Moreover, things began to shift in employment regulations as well, driven in part by changes in both public opinion and governmental priorities. David K. Johnson describes this shift in *The Lavender Scare: The Cold War Persecution of Gays and Lesbians in the Federal Government*: "By the late 1960s the CSC [Civil Service Commission] was beginning to acknowledge that, due not only to court pressure but changes in societal mores, it could no longer automatically fire all gay men and lesbians. . . . Other government entities were liberalizing their personnel policies. New York City, for example, began quietly hiring unwed mothers and homosexuals in 1966."[24] By the time of the Stonewall Uprising in June 1969, change had been happening in gradual increments for many years. As Loftin observes in *Masked Voices*, "In every corner of the country, significant numbers of gay people challenged their stigmatized status in creative—albeit limited—ways."[25]

Yet by the time of Stonewall, many Americans—including the three Appalachian writers whose work I discuss in this chapter—had lived the bulk of their adult lives amid the strictures of the Lavender Scare. Out of necessity, "lesbian and gay Americans negotiated the social, political, and cultural forces that threatened their livelihoods, reputations, and family relations."[26] By the beginning of the 1970s, James Still was sixty-three years old, and George Scarbrough was fifty-four. (Byron Herbert Reece had died in 1958 at the age of forty.) My intention is not to "out" any authors who chose to keep their personal lives private. However, scholars—as well as young Appalachians—will benefit from a deeper understanding of the work of these earlier Appalachian writers, perhaps enabling a renewed appreciation of—and, in the cases of Scarbrough and Reece, long-overdue attention to—their work. Byron Reece's poetry, for example, with its emphasis on the burden of carrying secrets and on the dangers (and pleasures) of illicit love could seem quite timely and contemporary to an Appalachian who is facing the dilemma of coming out. I hope the following discussions—including of the context in which this literature was formed and the intense pressures for conformity regarding gender and sexuality—will prompt a closer look at the work of these writers and will help to cast their work in a new light.

James Still: "No, I do not believe in that."

Although James Still (often called "the Dean of Appalachian literature") is perhaps not well known today except among scholars of Appalachian literature, in the mid- to late twentieth century, he was regionally celebrated and was an active and well-connected figure in national literary circles in the US. As Still's biographer Carol Boggess describes the trajectory of his career, "Like his masterpiece [the novel *River of Earth*], Still had had early success, then fell into obscurity, eventually to reemerge and approach celebrity status in the region."[27] A native of Alabama, Still relocated to Kentucky in 1933 to take a job at the Hindman Settlement School, and, aside from his time stationed in Africa during World War II, he lived and worked in rural Kentucky for the rest of his life, most famously in an isolated log house built in the nineteenth century. Between 1936, when he had his first major publication, and 1942, when he was drafted, James Still published three books (a novel, a collection of stories, and a collection of poetry) with a prestigious New York–based publishing house, was awarded fellowships at summer writers' colonies including Yaddo, Bread Loaf, and the McDowell Colony, and built connections and friendships among influential writers and editors. Still's correspondents and literary friends during those years included Katherine Anne Porter, Delmore Schwartz, and Marjorie Kinnan Rawlings, who reported to Still in a letter that Robert Frost was a fan of Still's poetry.[28] As George Brosi notes in his review of Boggess's biography, Still's life and career—his combination of the rustic and the urbane—pose something of a puzzle: "Was he a hermit or part of the literary mainstream of his time? . . . He traveled to 26 countries and was friends with many literary luminaries, almost all of whom he outlived."[29]

His novel, *River of Earth*, was published by Viking Press in 1940, the year after they published *The Grapes of Wrath*. Like Steinbeck's novel, Still's book portrays an American family enduring the Great Depression, this time in the hills and coalfields of Kentucky. The novel was favorably reviewed in publications with national reach (*New York Times*, *Atlantic Monthly*, *Time*) and was admired in literary circles (winning "the 1940 Southern Author Award for the most distinguished book of the year by a Southern author on a Southern subject"), but it was hardly a bestseller, and it was frequently pigeonholed as an example of regionalism, without broader impact or appeal.[30] Over the many decades of Still's writing career, from the 1930s through his death in 2001, Still became a chronicler of Kentucky's people, a master of its idiom, and closely associated with the literature of not only Kentucky but also the Appalachian region as a whole.

It is unknown—and ultimately unknowable—whether James Still should be included in an accounting of queer Appalachian authors. We can safely say that he appeared to have no heterosexual romances during his adult life, although he cultivated the impression that he had loved and lost a classmate from Lincoln Memorial University, Mayme Brown, who died young.[31] Moreover, I'm acutely aware of Still's own reservations about what would be written about him after his death. Among the pages of a manuscript he'd been working on in the months before his death, he'd copied out the following quote from Yiddish writer Sholom Aleichem: "When you die others who think they know you will concoct things about you. . . . Better pick up a pen and write it yourself, for you know yourself best."[32] Ultimately, it is no one's business what James Still's personal understanding of his own sexuality was.

However, I believe that scholars have disregarded ample evidence in Still's life and work that demonstrates his awareness of and appreciation for variance in human gender and sexuality. I believe that greater attention to this issue—the portrayal of gender and sexuality in James Still's work—could open his work for a new generation of readers who may think that the elders of Appalachian literature, perhaps especially the "Dean," were oblivious to the pressures regarding gender and sexuality. Moreover, understanding that James Still was friends with people of various sexual orientations and attitudes, and also knowing that he was deathly afraid, even in the last decade of his life, of being thought to be gay, could prompt us to take a second look at some of his work through that more complicated web of circumstances. Ultimately, this could lead to a much more nuanced reading of Still's work and, consequently, perhaps lead to a reenvisioning of the history of Appalachian literature, of which he is the "Dean."

This second look becomes significant when analyzing one of Still's signature poems, "Heritage," first published (as "Mountain Heritage") in the *New Republic* in 1935, and typically read as a celebration of Appalachia, a reflection of Still's "profound love for his adopted home."[33] Instead, I find that the language of entrapment that pervades this poem—"I shall not leave these prisoning hills" and "I cannot leave. I cannot go away."— almost overwhelms the poem's imagery of Appalachia's rich natural world and of the picturesque: "the new-born foal, / The lumbering ox drawing green beech logs to mill."[34] Much more prominent than images of beauty are the images of death and destruction: the threat of flood, the erosion of land, and the focus on the deadly part of the circle of life: "And one with death rising to bloom again, I cannot go." The speaker of this poem, who describes himself as "Being of these hills, being one with the fox / Stealing into the shadows . . . ," has much in common with the speaker of a Byron Herbert Reece poem, "If Only Lovers," that will be discussed later in the chapter, whose speaker insists that "Never a sorrow / Was born of two / Couched in the shadow / The whole night through." Readers will recognize this ambivalence about Appalachia in the work of Jeff Mann, Julia Watts, Carter Sickels, and other contemporary LGBTQ Appalachian writers: they too love Appalachia, but they know its dangers—both of its natural world and the threats that reside in its people—all too well.

In Carol Boggess's meticulously researched biography, *James Still: A Life* (2017), she structures this inquiry—into Still's romantic life—as though Still's heterosexuality is a given, writing of Still that "since he never talked about any courtships, the question can be explored only through his correspondence with women or with his other friends about women,"[35] thus effectively excluding any possibility that Still's romantic partners might have included men. Yet the subject of Still's sexuality is addressed in this biography, twice, albeit briefly: once to recount a rumor (about the rift between Still and his friend Albert Stewart) and once in a footnote to that passage (to describe Still's vehement denial of being gay). In her book, at the end of a two-page-long discussion of this broken friendship, Boggess notes that "at one time a vague rumor circulated that

Stewart believed he had seen Still approaching some man in Morehead in a sexual or romantic way."[36]

Boggess expands on this matter at length only in a footnote, where she recounts an occasion when Still raised the issue of his sexuality in conversation with her. I'll quote this important passage in full:

> If Still had homosexual interests or tendencies, he never admitted it. Once he emphatically denied it, while not giving the topic credence of a name. At one of his readings/conversations in the 1990s, a young man asked Still about his sexuality. Still would not repeat the question when recounting the incident, but he was upset and emphatically restated the answer—"No, I do not believe in that." The young man had raised a taboo topic and had asked a question that was boldly inappropriate and insulting to the old gentleman and would have been so for most people of his generation. Why did Still tell this incident? I was not present at the session and had no knowledge of or curiosity about the topic. At that time I was not his biographer but was merely driving him from place to place. Did he tell me this in veiled hints and angrily deny it because the insult was so great, or was he taking the opportunity to give me a definitive answer to a question I had not asked?[37]

Boggess is criticized for her very light coverage of this topic by George Brosi in his review of the biography, published in the *Appalachian Journal* in 2018. In this review, Brosi praises Boggess's book but states his criticism directly: "The one aspect of this book that bothered me was what I took as a strain to present James Still as heteronormative. He may well have been. All that is known is that he never had any open romantic relationships."[38] Missing from Brosi's published review are additional details that were in the submitted version of the review but were removed by the journal's editor. After the phrase "open romantic relationships," Brosi originally wrote, "and, at least since he was a college student, speculation has followed him. His classmates, Jesse Stuart and Don West, revealed to me that they assumed that he was gay."[39] According to Brosi, the journal's editor maintained that Brosi should not state this in the review if he had not shared it with Boggess when she interviewed him. However, in an interview with the author in 2018, Brosi maintained that he did in fact raise this issue with Boggess repeatedly, over the two decades that

Boggess was researching and writing this massive biography, and that he had asked Boggess how she planned to handle the topic in her book.[40] By Brosi's review, we can gather that Boggess did not do so to his satisfaction.

Notwithstanding Still's adamant "I do not believe in that" assertion to Boggess in the mid-1990s, James Still had maintained decades-long friendships and professional collaborations with men whom he knew to be nonheteronormative, even after they came out of the closet, and even when they (in some cases) suffered ridicule or condemnation due to their sexuality. His vehement disavowal of homosexuality to Boggess, while maintaining longstanding friendships with people of a variety of sexual orientations, suggests that while Still might have been accepting of queer sexualities among his friends, he was anxious not to be thought to be gay himself. For many people of Still's generation, a generation that had grown up steeped in the heteronormative biases of American culture, who witnessed the Lavender Scare of the 1950s and the continued imprisonment and institutionalization of queer citizens at least through the 1970s (not to mention the "conversion therapy" that is still available in many places today), it would be important both personally and professionally to not be thought to be gay.

By the time of Newton Arvin's arrest in 1960, James Still had been acquainted with Arvin for over two decades, thanks to their mutual involvement in the Yaddo writers' retreat. Arvin had been a regular at Yaddo since 1928; by 1939, the year of Still's first visit when he was polishing the final manuscript of *River of Earth*, Arvin had been made a trustee of the Yaddo Corporation.[41] Still went back to Yaddo in 1940, then again in 1950 and 1951, years when Arvin was still associated with the colony. In other years in the early to mid-1940s, Still and Arvin exchanged letters. Although their correspondence had trailed off by 1960, there's no doubt—between the national newspaper coverage and Still's friendships in literary circles—that Still would have been aware of Arvin's arrest, his guilty plea, and the professional losses that quickly followed.

One of Still's friendships that demonstrates both the hazards facing queer people of Still's generation as well as Still's long-standing comfort level with people who are not heteronormative is his friendship with New England–based poet Robert Francis (b. 1901).[42] Letters and postcards between the two men, and tales from Francis's 1971 autobiography, document a friendship that lasted from 1937 (when they were roommates at the Bread Loaf Writers' Conference) through Francis's death in 1987, punctuated by visits by Still to Francis's Amherst home and visits by Francis to Kentucky to visit Still and for speaking engagements at Kentucky colleges. Francis even arranged for Still to receive an invitation—"a reserved seat pass for you with your name written on it"—to the October 21, 1959, dedication of the Robert Frost Room at the Jones Library in Amherst, an occasion at which Robert Frost spoke.[43] (The postcard of thanks that Still later mailed from Hindman, Kentucky, reads, "Dear Robert, Thank you for food, shelter and good companionship on my journey to see the wizard. James Still."[44])

Especially relevant for the context of this discussion is Robert Francis's 1971 autobiography, *The Trouble with Francis*, which serves as a reminder of the pressures of America's heteronormative society, even for a gay man who was immersed in a literary/artistic milieu that one might imagine to be more progressive or accepting. In the chapter entitled "Eros," Francis wrote, "Since adolescence I had been drawn erotically to members of my own sex and to them only," nevertheless until 1958 (when he was fifty-seven years old), "my sex life was lived entirely within my imagination" due to "my timidity and my sense of decency" as well as his awareness that an overture to the wrong partner "would probably bring me intolerable disgrace."[45] As Francis describes coming to terms with his sexuality, which he insists that he embraces "without embarrassment or guilt," he nonetheless worries about how this news will be received in his small New England hometown: "What adds greatly to my problem is the persistent identification of the homosexual with sordidness, brutality, and crime."[46]

James Still, himself living and working in small towns, knew of Francis's autobiography, having written to Francis on August 14, 1971, "Cheers for the new book. I promptly ordered a copy. Nifty title. Anticipating its arrival," and he surely read it.[47] Despite Still's "I do not believe in that," Still maintained his correspondence with Robert Francis after the publication of this autobiography, at least through 1985 when Francis writes to compliment him on *Jack and the Wonder Beans*. The correspondence was clearly not one-sided: Francis thanks him (in a letter dated January 1, 1982) "for your beautiful greeting card showing your home with flowers in the foreground."[48] Francis ends this letter with "warm greetings from Bob who treasures our long friendship."

Still likely would have also been aware of a specific attack that Francis was subjected to based on his sexuality, one made public (and well known, in literary circles) by a discussion in a 1976 biography of American poet and four-time winner of the Pulitzer Prize, Robert Frost.

In retaliation for a perceived slight from Francis, in 1953 Frost wrote "On the Question of an Old Man's Feeling," a poem Frost's biographers called "a cruelly satiric poem" based on Frost's understanding that "the area in which Francis was the most vulnerable to attack was his preference for homosexual relationships."[49] Through this poem, Frost "struck out at the unwitting offender with a bitterness and cruelty Francis would probably not have imagined possible in his beloved and revered friend." Although the poem itself was not published during Frost's lifetime (and Frost's biographers quote only from "the poem's least virulent lines"), the biographers note that Frost wrote the poem in 1953 based on his awareness of Francis's sexual orientation.[50] Whether Francis reported accurately that he had never had a sexual experience before 1958, clearly Frost made judgments about Francis's sexuality prior to that. In a book about Francis, *The Man Who Is and Is Not There*, scholar Andrew Stambuk quotes from the rest of the poem, calling it "an ad hominem attack in which [Frost] condemns Francis's homosexuality and conveys his 'loathing' through epithets and derogatory stereotypes."[51] As Stambuk points out, if Francis's coming out in his 1971 autobiography "in an era when [homosexuality] was regarded as perverse, criminal, and a form of mental illness" had been "an extraordinary instance of courage," then the public revelations about Frost's attack-poem represented "a fear that was realized" that his openness had left him vulnerable.[52]

Francis's experience was only one among many cautionary tales—and a mild one compared to Arvin's and others—about the repercussions for a man of Still's generation if he were thought to be gay. Boggess's biography of Still touches on just such a danger for Still. In a passage where Boggess discusses Still's rift with longtime friend Albert Stewart (in the paragraph right before the detail that "at one time a vague rumor circulated that Stewart believed he had seen Still approaching some man in Morehead in a sexual or romantic way"), Boggess notes that "Still had implied to people in the community that Stewart tried to get him fired at Morehead."[53] Morehead State College, in Morehead, Kentucky, was where Still taught off and on from the mid-1950s through 1970, first on the faculty of the summer writers' workshop that was directed by Albert Stewart (and at which Robert Francis also taught), then later as a full-time member of the English Department's faculty. According to Boggess's biography, the reason for Still's falling out with Stewart might have centered on their time at Morehead: Boggess quotes a mutual friend as saying that "she was aware that Stewart had stumbled on something upsetting at Morehead that he would talk about only peripherally. Whatever it was made him mad."[54] In 1964–1965, very few misdeeds could have gotten someone of James Still's prominence dismissed from Morehead (a James Still Room had just been dedicated in the college library in 1961 to house his archives), although accusations of homosexuality had the potential to be damaging.[55] Still was not dismissed from Morehead: he remained on faculty until he resigned at the end of the 1969–1970 academic year. Regardless of the reason for the rift between these friends, by the end of the 1965 academic year, Albert Stewart had left Morehead State, after a career at Morehead lasting about a decade.[56]

Still's awareness of issues of gender and sexuality is evident in his work, although the subtlety of his treatment might allow these issues to be overlooked.[57] Still's critique of rigid gender roles and his portrayal of sexual undercurrents can go unnoticed by readers who aren't expecting to find those topics in a novel from 1940, or from an author who, later in his career, was perhaps better known for works for children or ones that appeal to regional nostalgia (*Rusties and Riddles and Gee-Haw Whimmy-Diddles*, *Appalachian Mother Goose*). Also, by the time that considerations of gender and sexuality were becoming more prominent in literary scholarship, Still was in the twilight of his career, and his earlier work was largely overlooked.[58]

In *River of Earth*, with Still's trademark subtlety and deft touch, we meet a narrator—a young, unnamed boy whose family (the Baldridges) moves back and forth between subsistence farming and life in the coal camps—who is alert to the gender expectations of his time and place and is pained that he doesn't meet them. At one point in the novel, he's ashamed of what he sees as cowardice after running away from the difficult birth of a colt. (The young boy's father, like Still's own father, is a "'horse doctor,' a veterinarian with no official training" in addition to being a farmer and a coal miner.[59]) The boy, "ashamed of my fear," not only must contend with his own "humiliation" and self-loathing over this incident, but also endures a beating and accusations of cowardice ("you Baldridges is spotted round the liver" and "yellow-dog coward Baldridge") from another boy who saw him run from the colt's birth.[60]

The narrator feels particularly inferior in comparison to his younger brother, Fletch, who is brash and bold, and who always runs forward when our narrator is hanging back. In one instance, a neighbor arrives at the family's cabin to get the father to treat a dying calf. The neighbor calls on the boy to help: "'Here, boy,' he called, 'help hold this critter.' I moved slowly, fumbling. 'Help hold!' Fletch sprang forward and caught the calf's hind legs, not flinching a mite." The father praises Fletch, "Here's a feller would make a good doctor," when he doesn't turn away from the gore.[61] Meanwhile, the narrator "handed the lamp to Mother so I could wipe away the shameful tears," his shame compounded by his desire to become a horse doctor like his father.[62] Late in the novel, Still shows the reader the consequences of Fletch's bold adventurousness: Fletch blows off two of the fingers of his right hand playing with a stick of dynamite. In contrast, while Fletch was under the house's porch smashing the dynamite between two rocks, the narrator is indoors, studying one of his family's only books, an almanac.[63]

A more complicated portrait of sexuality emerges from Still's posthumously published novel, *Chinaberry* (published in 2011, ten years after Still's death, compiled from manuscripts Still had left behind). The manuscript had profound personal significance for Still; Carol Boggess notes that it was "a story he had worked on for years, especially during the 1980s" and that "he had its pages with him in his hospital room the day he died."[64] The novel is the story of a thirteen-year-old boy who travels from Alabama to Texas with family friends to pick cotton for the summer. The boy is discovered and temporarily adopted by rancher Anson Winters and his wife, Lurie. Anson's relationship with the boy is unusual from the beginning: Anson explicitly selects the boy to replace his six-year-old son who had died—"I was looking for a boy to fit into the place of my son. . . . I've been looking for several years for you"—and treats this teenager (small for his age) as though he is six: " 'Let's say you're six,' he said. 'To me, you're six.' "[65] It is all curious, occasionally creepy. From the first, Anson will not call the boy by his name, referring to him as "the baby" or "the little man" and enrolling him in school as "Anson, Junior."[66] Only at the novel's end, when the boy is heading home to Alabama, does Anson address him by name: "Go home, Jim."[67]

Although it is unclear how much of the novel was autobiography and how much was fiction, there were tantalizing clues, including a note that was discovered with the "Texas manuscript," where Still wrote, "Could it have happened this way? It was long ago and I was thirteen, and since have indulged in fiction as a way of life."[68] Sometimes Still signed personal letters as "Anson," and he'd clearly discussed this story with friends for many years, some of whom were under the impression that he was recounting a story from his past. In a 1986 letter, Betty Jean Wells wrote to Still, "The afternoon in Hindman was one of the most pleasant and relaxing of the summer. I do hope you can finish the novel soon. I want to read it! The disease I was thinking of that the child might have had was cystic fibrosis, but I'm not sure children then lived as much as six years."[69]

The text's complexities relate both to the sexual awakening of the boy in relation to Lurie and the odd relationship with Anson. Anson encourages the boy to give him kisses, a practice the boy initially resists because it wasn't common in his own family. Anson persists, and the boy acquiesces, with sometimes unpredictable results: "I reached over and touched my lips to his chest three times. He said nothing for a moment, then said, 'There are other places.'"[70] Meanwhile, there are also glimpses of the boy's growing crush on Lurie, his gradual sexual awakening: "When she pressed me to her bosom, something stirred in my heart. It was that biologically unexplainable term—love."[71] And the boy recognizes his own jealousy of Anson, one afternoon when Anson arrives home from work and he and Lurie retreat to the bedroom (after Anson announces, "I can't wait"): "What did a thirteen-year-old in those days know? Not much. But I half-knew what they were about to do."[72] All of this while the boy is being treated as a six-year-old: stripped naked every night to be searched thoroughly for ticks, sleeping on a cot in Anson and Lurie's bedroom so Anson can listen for his breathing, and sometimes spoon-fed.

Scholars and reviewers of *Chinaberry* provide mixed accounts of this novel's relationships and their unclear boundaries. One reviewer worries that our modern reactions might be tainted by our "era of heightened awareness of child abuse and exploitation," causing "a jaded contemporary misprision of harmless, Depression-era family warmth," and insists that there is nothing "inappropriate or criminal" going on.[73] Another review notes these strange undercurrents not at all, calling it a "simple story of Americana, directly told" and a "classic story of adolescence."[74] Silas House's introduction to *Chinaberry* hints at the odd valences of the relationships: "What exactly are Anson and his wife up to, anyway? How does the narrator really feel about all of this?"[75] Carol Boggess offers the most sustained discussion of the text's complexities: "There is never a moment of overt sexuality on the page, but readers may get a sense of something beneath the surface. Is there an inkling of desire between the man and boy or a budding physical attraction between the boy and woman? Is this Still's exploration of puberty in general? Or does it reflect something of his own development?"[76] Certainly, there are no easy conclusions to draw from this complex story.

Before I began this project, a rumor had come to me that Still had had a relationship with Dr. Carlyle Cross, someone with whom he taught at Morehead State College; Cross taught there briefly, from 1964 to 1965. (Carlyle Cross's year at Morehead overlapped with Still's friend Albert Stewart's final year on faculty there.) To pursue this line of inquiry, I scoured James Still's papers in the University of Kentucky Library and in the archives at Berea College. I found no conclusive proof of a romantic relationship with Cross or any other person, male or female. Yet the evidence suggests that Cross and Still were close, becoming especially close during 1976 and 1977, with a major falling-out that began during their March 1978 trip to the Yucatan. They were out of touch completely from 1979 to 1985 (or, at least, Still saved none of this correspondence), then recommenced to exchange cards and letters, often newsy and referring to old times, until Cross's death in 1996.

I believe that Still and Cross met in 1964 when Cross joined the faculty of Morehead State College in Kentucky, where Still was a faculty member, and they kept in touch after Cross moved on to another school in 1965.[77] Cross left Morehead after only one year on the faculty, under circumstances that are not clear. Cross and Still corresponded after that; there are letters and postcards that Cross sent to Still from 1966 to 1969 (and that Still saved for decades) in the James Still archive at the University of Kentucky Library.

The secrecy that surrounds the relationship—the fact that Still almost never referred to Cross when writing about trips they took together, and the fact that Still's confidants were often so careful about these references as well—suggests that theirs was a *type* of relationship that, at that place and time, needed to be handled with discretion because a fuller understanding of it could have been damaging to Still. Certainly, it would have been damaging to Cross who, by the mid-1970s, worked at a Baptist college (Cumberland) and whose dismissal would have been assured if anyone had believed that Still was more than a longtime friend.

What seems most significant to me, in thinking through the nature of this relationship, the risks involved for Still, the reasons for Cross's quick departure from Morehead State, and the reason for Still's falling out with Albert Stewart, is the discretion demonstrated by mutual friend Betty Jean (B. J.) Wells, with whom both Still and Cross had taught at Morehead, in writing to Still about Cross. The most striking example of this is a postcard—so an item that could have been read by anyone in the postal service—that Wells sent to Still while he still taught (and lived, during the work week) at Morehead. In a note dated April 7, 1970, Wells writes, "Dear Jim, Here is the address you asked for: Room 446, Bon Air Hotel,

Augusta, Georgia 30904. If he's not there, I guess it will be forwarded. I'm going to write too. It was nice talking to you when I was in Morehead."[78] Although Wells doesn't refer to anyone by name, and makes no direct reference to the person about whose address Still had inquired, when I checked the 1970 Augusta City Directory, I found that Carlyle Cross was living at the Bon Air Hotel (2101 Walton Way) in Augusta, Georgia.[79]

So why would B. J. Wells not even include Cross's name in this note, when she did so by name in a later, sealed letter? It's impossible to know, but it seems significant to me that she exercised such discretion while writing to Still while he was continuing to teach at Morehead. Whatever the circumstances of Cross's departure from Morehead State, Wells's carefully crafted note meant that no one in the Morehead Post Office could know that James Still had inquired about Carlyle Cross's address. In this and other correspondence where she references Cross, she uses his name rarely. In contrast, she regularly mentions by name many other friends and acquaintances that she and Still share, including in a gossipy letter where she dishes about a mutual acquaintance who was arrested for shoplifting. In a January 4, 1972, letter, Wells does mention Cross by name: "I had a card from Carlyle Cross after not hearing of him for a long time. He graduated from Florida State with a degree in library science but was unemployed until December 1 when he took a job as librarian in Aiken, South Carolina. As usual he is unhappy and wishes he hadn't left teaching."[80]

Most of the early cards and letters from Cross to Still are conversational, reporting on Cross's travels and referring to occasions when they seem to have traveled together (or at least met up in New York City). Cross himself does send several postcards to Still at his Morehead address in 1968 (not displaying the same discretion as Wells), and then an April 1969 postcard suggests that they must have fallen out of touch: Cross tells Still that he's in the hospital after cancer surgery, and it appears that Still had been unaware of this illness.[81] If James Still wrote to Cross in 1970 after getting the Bon Air Hotel address, then Cross didn't write him back, or Still didn't save the correspondence: there's nothing more from Cross in the archive after that 1969 postcard until 1976.

Between July 1976 (when Cross was back living and working in Kentucky at Cumberland College, about a three-hour drive from Still's home) and March 1978, when they returned from an ill-fated trip to Mexico, there's a distinct shift in the archival record. The 1976–1978 correspondence from Cross to Still, as well as the photographs that Still saved, reveal a playful tone and many visits between these friends. In the first of those items, a brief note (not a postcard but very small, could have been included in a greeting card) dated July 28, 1976, with an evocative tone with a playful faux-formality, Cross writes, "Dear James Still, Please meet me one Saturday in Berea (or elsewhere) to discuss sealing wax, imaginary gardens, and unfound doors. Sincerely, Carlyle Cross."[82]

Only three weeks after that note, Still visited Cross at Cumberland College. We know about this visit thanks to an article in the *Whitley Republican* (the newspaper of Cumberland's home county), explaining that "when a noted writer takes time from his hectic schedule to visit a small college campus unannounced, a unique situation occurs." The article goes on to explain that "on his way to a family reunion in Alabama, Still stopped to visit long-time friend, Dr. Carlyle Cross, librarian and associate professor of English at the Baptist School." The article wraps up with the first mention I've found of what will be a momentous trip to the Yucatan planned for February 1977; Cross says, "Mr. Still invited me to accompany him on his next trip to Yucatan in February. I am presently contemplating whether I will make the journey with him."[83]

Further correspondence from 1976 and 1977 documents visits or intentions to visit: in November 1976, Cross apologizes to Still for not visiting him, noting, "I have been saving money for our Yucatan adventure" and ending with "I hope to see you soon."[84] In late 1976 or early 1977, Still again visits Cross at Cumberland, to present him with an autographed edition of *Pattern of a Man and Other Stories* for Cumberland College Library's collection. We know of this visit thanks to a clipping (including photo and brief description) found in the University of Kentucky's James Still Papers.[85] Although the date of the visit is unknown, it must have been after December 4, 1976, when Still received his first author's copy of the book.

In February and March 1977, the Yucatan adventure went awry in a big way when Still and Cross were caught in a revolution in El Salvador (February 28, 1977) and were on the streets when troops started firing on the crowds; they took refuge in a local building. They were sheltered by residents for twenty-four hours before they were able to safely make it back to their hotel (to retrieve luggage), then to the airport. In Still's descriptions of this incident—in accounts from that same week as well as years later—he elides Cross's presence: "I was either saved by women who shielded me, or by the arrival of the army," and "I went back to my hotel and asked them if they could get a taxi to take me to the airport."[86]

Although Still's accounts do not acknowledge that Cross was on the trip, we know he was there thanks to newspaper coverage from Whitley County and Cumberland College. An April 14, 1977, article, "Cumberland Professor Caught in Political Upheaual [sic] during Central American Tour," in the *Whitley Republican*, describes how "Still, through stories of his previous excursions, convinced friend and former colleague, Cross that a trip to the area would be both education [sic] and memorable," then goes on to describe the incidents, indicating that despite visa problems, "Cross and Still were permitted to enter Costa Rica" on March 1. A similar article in the newsletter of a Baptist organization assures the reader that "not even danger can dissuade the two adventurers, who plan a return trip to Central America."[87]

For two other occasions in 1977, in the late summer and early fall of 1977, the archives documented visits between Cross and Still or trips they made together. In August 1977, Cross accompanied a group of friends—Tom Frazier from Cumberland College, Danny Miller (who presented about "Homosexuality in Appalachian Literature" at the 1996 Appalachian Studies Conference) and his partner Darrell Hovious, and Ron Ball—to visit Still at his home on Dead Mare Branch. This visit is documented in letters and photographs at both the Berea College and University of Kentucky archives. Berea's collection includes twelve photographs from that day, which Thomas Frazier sent (with an accompanying letter about the visit) to Berea College for their James Still archive.[88] I found another photograph, taken that same day but not included in the Berea College collection, among James Still's papers at the University of Kentucky; the photo shows Still and Cross standing together outside Still's cabin.[89] In a letter to Carlyle Cross on September 18, 1977 (which Cross later enclosed in a letter to Still), Danny Miller thanks Cross "for your sincere hospitality when Darrell, Ron and I visited you for the now famous ["in" is whited-out before "famous"] James Still visit." Miller and Hovious thank Cross for the photos of the visit that he sent them, and they ask him to "convey to him [Still] the fact that we appreciated his warmth and interest extremely, and that the visit was just the highlight of the summer for me."[90] In a September letter to Still, Cross mentions the Miller-Hovious letter of thanks and also refers to a recent trip Cross and Still made to Shaker Town, calling it "a wonderful visit." This Shaker Town trip appears to have been meaningful, at least for Cross; he'll refer to it in a letter to Still ten years later. Cross ends by prompting Still to "surprise me by a visit in the near future."[91]

There are hints in the next few months that the relationship might be strained. Cross complains in an October 1977 letter that Still hasn't been to visit: "My ESP has been playing me false lately. I have delayed writing since I expected you at any time." Then, in a letter dated February 1978, Cross announces, "I have decided not to go on the spring tour with you," although he closes on a friendly note, asking Still, "Send me full details of your itinerary, and, above all, keep me informed of your adventures." However, there is reason to question whether by that time Still wanted Cross to accompany him: in a December 1977 Christmas card to another friend, Dean Cadle, Still invited Cadle to go on the trip, writing, "Fly with me to Mexico City in middle February." It is unclear whether Still intended for Cadle to go on the trip instead of Cross or as a buffer between Cross and Still; regardless, Cadle did not go.[92]

Ultimately, Cross accompanied Still on the March 1978 trip after all, and that's when the relationship disintegrates, a change that's discernible only from what Still's confidants write *to him*. In fact, it would be impossible to even know that Cross was on this trip if one read only Still's accounts. In a postcard dated March 6, 1978, postmarked Mexico City, Still writes to Al Perrin, a friend in Kentucky: "Flying South today to Villahermosa in the State of Tabasco, which should put me in reach of Palenque—this years [sic] target. Then on to the Yucatan."[93] Then, in a postcard sent to Perrin four days later on March 10th, we see the first signs that between March 6th and March 10th, something has happened to change Still's relationship with Cross profoundly: "To Palenque at last, after more 'adventure' in the State of Tabasco and Chiapas than I bargained for, or wanted."[94] Other postcards dated the same day, to people in whom Still did not confide—the Grover Farrs, Dean Cadle—do not hint at any trouble, only: "Salude desde Villahermosa, Tabasco, Mexico. Home when the snow melts."[95] A friend and colleague later noted of James Still that "he observes his own private holidays. 'March 10 is my own holiday,' he once told me. 'Because of something that happened to me on March 10.'"[96] Whether that momentous occasion was March 10, 1978, we cannot know.

What little we do know about March 6–10, 1978, comes from letters written *to* James Still by people in whom Still confided—Al Perrin and B. J. Wells—written after Still had spoken to them about the events; Still seems to have discussed the unwanted "adventure" only in face-to-face conversation. Perrin's initial letter responding to the vague March 10th postcard showed that he assumed these unwanted adventures to be sociopolitical, not interpersonal: "One of your earlier cards seemed to indicate that you and C.C. might have been on the edge of another street fight. I hope not. You both earned purple hearts last time."[97] Although Perrin's response mentions Cross and demonstrates that he knew Cross went on last year's and this year's trips, he uses only Cross's initials instead of his name.

In mid-April 1978, Still visited Perrin in Berea, Kentucky (on his way to or from a speaking engagement in Louisville), and confided in Perrin in person, for which Still apologizes in a letter a few days later: "Plumb feel sorry for you to have to listen to my long, tedious Tabasco (also Chiapas) tale but I was busting to tell it to somebody who might understand it better than I do. The good part, the part that mattered—Tula, Comancalco, Palenque—was barely mentioned."[98] The nature of the unwanted adventures becomes a little more clear in Perrin's follow-up letter to Still (as well as in a May 1978 letter to Still from Betty Jean Wells). Perrin writes to Still regarding invitations to an upcoming awards ceremony: "We are inviting your Morehead friends and not inviting Mr. Cross. Your story of his shredding himself with angry fits has troubled me ever since, but I haven't passed it on to anyone here."[99]

In Wells's letter dated a few weeks later, she recalls an evening recently spent with Still and carefully does not refer to Cross by name: "I'm sorry your trip to Mexico was marred by unpleasant experiences and that a decent sensitive human being who needs friends has reached a point where he can only alienate himself from them. I see no hope for him without professional help."[100] The closest that Still himself comes to writing about the event is a brief reference in a travel-diary entry from 1989, to "Dr. Cross the manic depressive of the Viahermosso [sic] episode."[101]

Later in 1978, there's documentation in the archives that Cross tries to maintain the friendship, but no indication that this was reciprocated: Cross extends an invitation for an upcoming performance at Cumberland College to Still, then sends a mid-December letter that he concludes with "Season's Greetings!"[102] This Christmas greeting is the last correspondence from Cross (at least, the last that Still saved) until July 1986, when Cross sends Still a birthday card.[103] After that, Cross sends Still birthday cards, plus occasional cards for holidays or of congratulations, almost every year until Cross's death in 1996. They feature messages such as "I often think of you" and "Ten years have certainly flown quickly since we were at Shakertown."[104]

It is clear that their later correspondence was *not* one-sided: Cross thanks Still for the card Still sent him from Mexico, thanks him "for your informative letter," and acknowledges receipt of an invitation to

Still's ninetieth birthday party at Hindman Settlement School.[105] Cross's name regularly shows up on Still's Christmas card list. And Still clearly reached out for information when he didn't hear from Cross for a while: a March 24, 1997, letter from Gerald J. Smith, in response to Still's recent letter of inquiry, informs Still about Cross's death the previous October.[106] Regardless of these traces in the archives, there's no definitive key to Still's relationship with Cross.

Despite Still's own statement of "I do not believe in that," a statement that might be misinterpreted as a blanket disapproval of queer sexualities, the archival evidence demonstrates that Still was comfortable around people of various sexual orientations, and suggests that Still was much more open-minded that his "I do not believe in that" would suggest.[107] Moreover, an analysis of Still's work, including *River of Earth* and *Chinaberry*, reveals that he was attuned to society's judgments about gender and sexuality, and to the undercurrents in relationships. For Appalachian writers of Still's generation (born in 1906, Still came of age in the 1920s and embarked on his literary career in the 1930s), being out was not an option. As he saw from the experiences of friends and acquaintances, laws and cultural practices made queerness too much of a limiting factor for one's career and community standing. But why is this a relevant issue, within the larger scope of this book, to an understanding of Appalachian literature as a whole, or to provide greater insight into the work and career of James Still? Silas House's careful strategies of coming out as a queer writer in Appalachia clearly demonstrated to us the high stakes, even for a very successful writer and even now in the twenty-first century, of being a member or writing about the concerns of an underrepresented and stigmatized group. Greater attention to the cultural concerns of earlier writers, in conjunction with careful rereadings of the portrayals of gender and sexuality in their work, will help us to understand how we arrived at our current moment in LGBTQ Appalachian literature, and why it took until 1976 for this movement to begin.

George Scarbrough: "Ah, Stonewall, how little you knew."

George Scarbrough, the Tennessee poet and Pulitzer Prize nominee (1990, for *Invitation to Kim*), was primarily known as a poet of nature, place, and family. Through collections such as *Tellico Blue* (1949), *The Course Is Upward* (1951), and *Summer So-Called* (1956), Scarbrough built a reputation based on lyric depictions of the natural world, elevated use of language, and consideration of the bonds and burdens of family. Some early reviewers compared Scarbrough's work to that of the Agrarians, although those reviews (such as one published in 1940) typically note that Scarbrough's appreciation for nature and farming had a far different origin than that of the Agrarians: as the child of a tenant farming family, Scarbrough grew up working the land with his parents and six siblings.[108] More recent scholars situate Scarbrough's celebration of the rural South as "a lonely representative of the generation between the Fugitive Poets and James Dickey."[109]

Scarbrough lived most of his long life (he died in 2008 at age ninety-three) in the closet, although he was certainly out with people with whom he was close: in 1994, Scarbrough wrote to biographer Randy Mackin, "Here is something, Randy, you should know. I am gay."[110] Although Mackin maintains that "everyone who knew George knew he was gay; the information was not a secret," Scarbrough was hesitant even through the late 1990s and early 2000s to be open about his sexuality. Yet Mackin recalls that although Scarbrough didn't want his sexuality written about while he was living, he asserted, "Wait until I'm dead and I don't care what is published."[111]

Although Scarbrough maintained (in a 1996 letter to Mackin), "I haven't written 'gay' poems. Not ostensibly," he also emphasized that his identity as a gay man infused everything he did: "All my poems are gay poems, all my religion has been gay religion, every breath I've ever drawn has been a gay breath. You see, I understand gayness as genetic in origin. I am that I am."[112] In that letter and in other writings and interviews, Scarbrough made clear that his identity carried a personal cost for him, writing, "I wear the 'coat' with pride, though mostly in hurt because of the world's way." These wounds were inflicted from an early age, by his father, who, Scarbrough said, "made fun of what he called my 'sissy' ways."[113] One of the most painful personal rejections for Scarbrough was the rejection by his younger brother, Kim, of whom Scarbrough said, "My brother, Kim, never forgave me for being gay," and who was so opposed to being touched by Scarbrough that when Scarbrough ran into him in their home town—when both were elderly men—and tried to hug his brother, Kim "shoved me so hard I nearly fell on the floor."[114]

Beyond rejections by Scarbrough's family members, Mackin reports that "on more than one occasion he had been physically threatened because of his homosexuality; he felt ostracized by society in general and by certain individuals who 'moved in darkness.'"[115] The discrimination that Scarbrough experienced occurred even in his time in college. In several interviews and letters, Scarbrough described an occasion during his time as a student at the University of the South at Sewanee when the university's chancellor summoned Scarbrough to a dinner at his home and said, "There is a bunch of you boys here who ought to put on dresses and enroll in a girls' school."[116] As Scarbrough observed in a 2000 interview, "I was always pursued by who I was, what I was, how I was."[117]

In the 1990s, Scarbrough began experimenting poetically by using the eighth-century Chinese poet Han-Shan as a "vehicle": Scarbrough "felt safe writing verse that utilized Han-Shan as the central character while, in actuality, dealt with matters that had been elusive in his own work: sexuality, loneliness, even isolation."[118] A number of Scarbrough's Han-Shan poems were published during his lifetime—including in nationally prominent journals such as *Poetry*—and were later collected in the posthumously published *Under the Lemon Tree* (2011). Many of these poems feature Han-Shan's male companion, Shi-Te, although scholars disagree about the nature of their relationship.[119] Mackin maintains that "one of the liberties that Scarbrough took with Han-Shan was assigning the Cold Mountain poet a sexual identity" and that "Scarbrough allowed Han-Shan to be gay so that he could examine his own sexuality."[120]

The Han-Shan poems—both those that remained unpublished until 2011's *Lemon Tree* and those that were published in regional and national journals in the early 2000s—unabashedly embrace same-sex desire and romantic love between men. In several poems, Scarbrough blames Han-Shan's exile (from the bustling capital to his present rural home) on punishment "for sins of love," often returning to Han-Shan's specific violation: "When I strolled with the young prince / In moonlight and kissed the smooth / Warm hand in the shadow of bamboo? / O that I had bitten my impassioned / Tongue instead of speaking / The offensive word!"[121] Many Han-Shan poems circle back to this image, of "the delicate ringed fingers," with the Han-Shan/George persona reminding himself, as he anticipates the day's visit from "the handsome postman," that "he is much like the young prince. / I must be careful, when he hands me a letter, / Not to caress those slim brown fingers."[122]

In the Han-Shan poems that focus on his relationship with Shi-Te, Scarbrough paints a picture of domestic partners, and many of these poems—including "In Memoriam for Shi-Te," "On the Third Anniversary of Shi-Te's Death," and "Revenant"—highlight the emptiness left behind in the wake of a partner's death. In "Revenant" (published in 2000 in *Poetry*), the nature of their relationship is clear as Shi-Te is called Han-Shan's "lover": "Han-Shan tries to confine his / Lover's absence to the bedroom" but encounters Shi-Te's ghost throughout their home and yard.[123] Other poems recall their domestic habits: Shi-Te's laughing at Han-Shan's practice of writing a new "last poem" every day ("Last Will and Testament"), their lunches together "on days when Shi-Te does not go / To work at the quarry" ("Grace"), as well as Han-Shan's loneliness on days when Shi-Te goes to market ("Absence").[124] In combination, these poems tell of a long-standing romantic partnership between two men. Scarbrough spoke openly to his biographer Mackin about how Han-Shan freed him poetically: "He is my alter ego and I'm finding that I can be, well perhaps, more truthful, hiding behind Han-Shan."[125]

In the final decade or so of his life, Scarbrough became more open about his sexuality in his poems, even without the poetic persona of Han-Shan. In a letter to Mackin in 1996, Scarbrough announced that a forthcoming poem ("Sunday Shopping," 1997) in *Poetry* would address his "sexual predilection," calling it "a poem that accepts my 'gay connection' in a way I've always understood it."[126] The poem's intimations of sexuality are discreet, so subtle that the poem could almost be interpreted as a portrait of enduring friendship rather than of romantic or sexual partnership. But the notes of flirtation ("A lurking smile in his hazel eyes"), of shared domestic habits ("Sunday became our day—great, soft music, / Bantering talk and laughter . . ."), and of longtime association (a coat that they picked out together is now "shabby with wear, / . . . long out of style") combine with an acknowledgment of deeper emotion: Sundays were their days "the more / Made so because we said love lasted."[127] Although there are no overtly sexual references in the poem (the closest we come is that the coat was left lying on a bed), it is a poem by a man, about a man, and dedicated to a man ("For Joe"). For someone of Scarbrough's generation who had suffered losses both professional and personal because of his sexuality, such a poem—in a prominent publication—was undoubtedly a bold act of coming out. Mackin asserts that "none of Scarbrough's hundreds of poems in print, up until 'Sunday Shopping,' published in the February 1997 issue of *Poetry*, could be labeled a 'gay' poem"[128] and calls this publication "an exercise in courage that Scarbrough had to face, and did, with clarity and purpose."[129]

Although I concur with Mackin in recognizing the courage Scarbrough displayed through this 1997 publication, in fact, Scarbrough had already published a "gay poem" in a national publication almost three decades earlier. In the 1970 anthology *In Homage to Priapus*, Scarbrough's poem "Love in the Afternoon" appeared alongside poetry and fiction by Walt Whitman, Allen Ginsberg, and other gay male writers. If the book's title—a reference to a minor Greek fertility god who was depicted with a constant and prominent erection—didn't make the volume's focus sufficiently clear, the book's cover left no doubt. (See fig. 1.1.) The poem itself, previously published in the literary journal *Hearse*, is so abstract, so steeped in the obliqueness and ambiguities of mid-twentieth-century American poetry that it would have been easy (for readers who first encountered it in *Hearse*) to miss the sexual content of the poem and instead to read it as a tale of boys killing a rooster. In light of the *Priapus* anthology's title and focus, as well as the poem's title of "Love in the Afternoon," the poem's phrases such as "the crying cock in his hand" and "cupping our hands under / the veined leather of our tender youth" instead evoke a sexual encounter in the woods.[130]

Although it may seem surprising that Scarbrough—living a closeted life in small-town east Tennessee—would have published a poem in an unabashedly gay-themed publication, it is also safe to assume that this would have carried little risk for Scarbrough. Who among his Tennessee acquaintances would have been likely to encounter the book, which was released in a small print run from Greenleaf Press, a publisher of erotic pulp fiction on the West Coast? Moreover, Scarbrough had a long-standing literary partnership with the book's editor, E. V. Griffith, who published Scarbrough's poetry in his literary magazines (*Hearse* and *Poetry Now*) both before and after the *Priapus* publication. In a December 1968 letter requesting to publish "Love in the Afternoon" in *Priapus*, Griffith also asks to publish "River Boys" in *Priapus II* as well as another of Scarbrough's poems in *A Beginner's Guide to Erotic Verse*, although neither book was ultimately published.[131] Clearly, in frank private correspondence between these two gay men, several of Scarbrough's earlier poems were understood to be "gay poems."

Scarbrough was able to write most frankly—about both his desire and his feelings of isolation and rejection—to Griffith, with whom Scarbrough corresponded from 1950 through (at least) the 1980s. Sometimes the letters are bawdy and jokey: "I should like to have sun-baked balls in California," Scarbrough writes in 1959.[132] At other times, Scarbrough complains about the difficulty of finding sexual partners in small-town

Figure 1.1 The front cover of the Greenleaf Classic anthology *In Homage to Priapus*, 1970. *Source*: From the collection of the author.

Tennessee. In a letter written in the early 1960s, Scarbrough describes cruising in a local park: "I must search out the red-headed one on this afternoon, in the park at the other end of town, and make spring at the water-line. Without him, this summer was a matter of self-violence and no respect."[133] More often, Scarbrough writes of his isolation and alienation from his family, in passages that make crystal clear—for those of us who may look back at these authors from our cultural climate of the 2020s and wonder why they were not out of the closet—the penalties for queer writers (and other queer folk) who didn't remain closeted. In writing of his family, especially his younger brother with whom he had been close, Scarbrough writes (in a 1983 letter to Griffith), "Being who, and what, I am, family ostracism is no stranger to me. But who can be other than the person he, through no devices, or vices, of his own came to be? . . . I love my brother, E.V. I want him to accept me as another human being only. Is that too much?"[134]

Although Scarbrough does seem to omit "Love in the Afternoon" (and *In Homage to Priapus*) when talking to Mackin about his publications, and although Mackin himself doesn't address this poem in his consideration of Scarbrough's poetic representations of sexuality, Scarbrough and Mackin did not try to hide this publication. Mackin lists it in the selected bibliography at the end of his book. Mackin wrote (in an email to the author), "George never mentioned 'Love in the Afternoon' to me, nor the anthology. In a resume he included in his journals, he listed the anthology, but offered no comment."[135] Scarbrough passed along his personal copy of *In Homage to Priapus* as part of his papers to the University of the South, as well as including the letters he received from E. V. Griffith, almost as though he was leaving a trail of breadcrumbs for future scholars. Scarbrough clearly hoped that his sexuality would receive greater critical attention after his death, writing in a 1996 letter to Mackin, "I'm only waiting for that biographer, gay himself, who will be able to see how, why, and where my young world was."[136] Although I am not the gay male biographer that Scarbrough hoped would one day revisit his life and work, and although I have barely scratched the surface of what the Scarbrough archives at the University of the South may contain, I hope to bring attention to the ways in which Scarbrough courageously made inroads for queer Appalachian writers many years before scholars have previously acknowledged, and I hope that other scholars will reexamine Scarbrough's body of work as a result.

Byron Herbert Reece:
"I am going to be absolutely truthful sometime before I die."

In 1959, E. V. Griffith wrote to Scarbrough about another Appalachian writer, "our poor lost friend Byron Reece."[137] Here Griffith refers to Georgia native Byron Herbert Reece, a nationally acclaimed poet and novelist, who shot himself through the chest while in his faculty apartment at Georgia's Young Harris College in spring 1958.[138] Born in 1917 to a farming family in Choestoe, Georgia, near the North Carolina line, Reece spent much of his too-short life within a few miles of that spot. Although he matriculated at Young Harris College (where he would later teach), Reece's education was delayed by financial worries and family responsibilities: maintaining the family farm and nursing his parents, both of whom were ill with tuberculosis.[139] Later, Reece was himself diagnosed with tuberculosis. Although he spent three months in 1954 recuperating in Georgia's free state tuberculosis hospital, he was plagued by illness until the end of his life.

By the time his career—and life—were ended by suicide, Reece had published four volumes of poetry and two novels and was twice awarded a Guggenheim Fellowship. Reece's work garnered respect both regionally and nationally. Kentucky writer Jesse Stuart championed Reece and arranged for his own publisher, E. P. Dutton & Company in New York, to publish Reece's first collection of poems, *The Ballad of the Bones and Other Poems* (1945).[140] Reece was sought after as a visiting speaker, writer, and teacher: he served as Poet in Residence at both UCLA (in the summer of 1950) and Emory University, as well as teaching at his alma mater, Young Harris College, all despite never having graduated from college.[141] In a memorial essay published in the *Georgia Review*, Jesse Stuart mourns Reece as "a genius among us . . . a true artist . . . whose own heart was his guide."[142]

In Griffith's letters to Scarbrough after Reece's suicide, he intimates that Reece had secrets and that Reece's family was actively trying to keep those hidden. In a letter written the year after Reece's death, Griffith writes, "I know much of his problems and his griefs . . . He suffered more ways and more deeply than most who read him will ever know."[143] Five years later, while preparing a memorial essay about Reece for a *Georgia Review* special issue, Griffith writes to Scarbrough about an ongoing dispute with Reece's family over quoting from Reece's letters to him (their correspondence lasted over a decade). This letter is significant enough to quote at length: "We are now haggling with Byron's sister over the right to quote from letters of his to me. . . . I know much of the secret heart of him and ached at the outcome of it. What his sister knows, and does not know, I know not—but I think some of her concern over what the quoted letters contain stems from fear. But I would do only <u>well</u> by him, for his mind and heart influenced my own, and I want to do what I can to keep alive an interest in the man and his works."[144] Griffith goes on to say that Reece's sister wants to review Griffith's essay before it is published.

Although it is impossible to know for certain why Reece's sister worried about these letters, evidence from Reece's biography and correspondence suggests that he was gay and was deeply closeted. (His literary works also touch on LGBTQ themes; more on that later.) Considering all that the Lavender Scare entailed, the prevailing attitudes toward and treatment of queer people in the US, and the constant refrain that queer people were un-American, abnormal, and dangerous, it is little wonder that Reece's sister, in the mid-1960s, might have wanted to protect her brother's literary reputation from the stigma that was associated with queerness at that time.

Within most biographies and scholarship about Byron Reece, scholars have carefully talked *around* his bachelorhood and his sexuality, with most sources suggesting that Reece would have married except for his illness, rural isolation, and responsibilities to his elderly parents and on the family farm. Reece's first biographer, Raymond A. Cook, cites Reece's illness and his devotion to writing as the reasons he never married, stating, "Reece concluded that his illness made marriage impossible, quite aside from the fact that his writing was so demanding that a wife would hardly put up with him."[145] Later biographer Bettie Sellers claims that "loneliness was the price that he was willing to pay," presumably for Reece's commitment to writing and family responsibilities, and assures the reader that Reece, "who was never married, understood the nature of romantic love between the sexes."[146] Both of these biographers (Cook writing in 1968, and Sellers in 1992) return to these claims a number of times.

E. V. Griffith, as Reece's friend and longtime correspondent, was more careful (in his 1968 memorial essay) in presenting the reasons for Reece's bachelor state: "Reece never married. His parents were, as he put it, 'old and ill,' and he devoted himself to their care and comfort."[147] Although Griffith's precision here allows a reader to infer causality, that Reece did not marry due to his devotion to his parents, Griffith doesn't state that directly. Correspondence between the two men, and between mutual friends Griffith and Scarbrough, suggest that Griffith knew there were other reasons why Reece never married. In a letter Byron Reece sent to

E. V. Griffith in 1950, Reece described his failed efforts to find a partner and proposed traveling to New York to find a companion: "I found no satisfactory companion with other people here, not in late years, that is; when I was a youngster I had no trouble in getting on common grounds with someone available . . . I'll probably try another city someday, probably New York, and if the search is fruitless there resign myself to solitude and try my own resources to the grave."[148] Here, Reece's careful use of "people" (rather than "women") and his suggestion of New York—at a time when New York's Greenwich Village was perceived as a place where gay people could be somewhat more open and safe—suggest that Reece's need for companionship was outside the norms of his North Georgia home. Even Reece's biographer Cook, in a statement in a 1968 essay that is not included in the later full-length biography, seems to hint at a mystery regarding Reece's romantic life: "The one enduring love of Byron Herbert Reece's life came in later years and was the source of much pain and bewilderment to him. . . . He was most reticent on the subject, and only a few persons . . . knew of the depth of his commitment."[149]

As Reece's 1950 letter to Griffith demonstrates, Reece was cautious even in personal letters—including to Griffith and longtime friend Edward Pratt Dickson, both of whom Reece knew to be gay men—and those correspondents were typically discreet as well. However, in a September 1957 letter, Dickson let slip a hint, while urging Reece (who was then staying at a writing retreat near Pacific Palisades, California[150]) to come visit him in Berkeley. In a section of the letter where Dickson notes that he might be traveling in the next few weeks, but urges Reece to come to Berkeley anyway and stay in his rented room, Dickson adds, "But I think it would be good for you to know my landlady, *who is one of us.*"[151] Such a reference seems as far as these men could safely go, even in personal letters sent through the US Postal Service.

By the phrase "one of us," Dickson was simply using the phrase common among queer people when referring to each other.[152] This phrase also invoked a highly controversial periodical in which Dickson later published (and of which both men would have been aware): *ONE: The Homosexual Magazine.* First published in 1953, *ONE* was initially affiliated with the Mattachine Foundation (a homophile organization founded in Los Angeles in 1951); a similar publication, the *Mattachine Review*, started publication in 1955.[153] These publications were well known within the gay and lesbian community, in part due to the decision of the US Postal Service to confiscate the October 1954 issue of *ONE*, "declaring it obscene, lewd, lascivious and filthy.'"[154] Pratt Dickson published essays and poetry in both publications under the pen name "Manfred Wise."

Reece was well acquainted with Dickson's work as Manfred Wise: as early as December 1953, Dickson was sending Reece drafts of Manfred Wise's works in progress, such as "Sex? Ignorance, Desire, Reverence and the Orgasm—A Letter to Dachine Ranier."[155] Dickson's side of this correspondence suggests that Reece provided him encouragement, feedback, and crucial connections in the publishing industry.[156] Regardless, Dickson's connection to these publications reminds us of the stakes for these two gay writers in the 1950s and demonstrates clearly that their caution was not misplaced, and their use of code—like "one of us"—was not the result of unfounded paranoia: by 1953, *ONE* and the Mattachine Society were under investigation by the FBI (including investigation of who had rented their Los Angeles PO box). The FBI's dossier on Mattachine reveals that the bureau began conducting investigations into writers who published in *ONE*, including uncovering the real-life identities behind the pen names.[157] That Byron Reece, conventionally thought of as a rustic balladeer from the North Georgia mountains, was in fact a literary mentor and friend to the notorious California-based poet Manfred Wise reminds us of the complexities of literary connections in the twentieth century, and reminds us that the conventional images of our Appalachian forebears, their images of respectability, may have been carefully constructed protective facades—or the masks of which Craig Loftin writes in *Masked Voices*—rather than the unvarnished truth.

Reece's published writing—his poetry as well as his two published novels—reveals complicated images of sexuality and is, overall, more queer-positive than a twenty-first-century reader might expect of Appalachian literature from the 1940s and 1950s. The most direct representations of queer sexuality in Reece's poetry appear in his 1950 collection of poetry, *Bow Down in Jericho*, in poems about the relationship between biblical figures David and Jonathan, while his 1955 novel, *The Hawk and the Sun*, portrays a homosexual relationship between two adolescent boys, Farley and Jonathan. Scholars take varying approaches to this material. Although Bettie Sellers, in *The Bitter Berry: The Life of Byron Herbert Reece*, acknowledges that "Reece considers homosexual love" in his David and Jonathan poems, she then implicitly undercuts Reece's portrayal of this as a queer relationship, writing that "whatever the truth about David and Jonathan, Reece has written singing words in his ballads about these ancient friends."[158]

However, other scholars have more fully engaged with the portrayals of queer sexuality in Reece's work. Hugh Ruppersburg, in his foreword to a 1994 reissue of Reece's *The Hawk and the Sun*, notes "the homoeroticism in both his novels" and the fact that Reece's David and Jonathan poems "treat homosexual love in an appreciative, positive manner."[159] Scholar and poet Jim Clark, in his 2002 introduction to *Fable in the Blood: The Selected Poems of Byron Herbert Reece*, describes what he sees as "Reece's ambivalent fascination with homosexuality."[160] Quoting from Reece's letters to Pratt Dickson—in which Reece says that Jonathan and David's love was "a homosexual attachment, which is a different matter from saying their relationship was that of perverts"—Clark argues, "Given Reece's situation and his complex and ambivalent attitudes toward love, relationships, and sexuality, he sought, consciously, I think, to sublimate his libidinal drives" in farming and writing.[161]

If part of my aim in discussing Byron Herbert Reece is to bring him to the attention of contemporary scholars and to those seeking a more complete history of LGBTQ Appalachians, I must call attention to Reece's poetic preoccupation with murder ballads, tales of inconstant love, and poems—in general—about the psychic and personal costs of illicit love. Known as a master of the ballad form, Reece published numerous ballads that feature unfaithful and/or murderous lovers, such as "Ballad of the Rider," a well-known poem from his first collection, 1945's *Ballad of the Bones*.[162] Reece's 1945 poem "If Only Lovers" suggests the costs of a relationship that must be conducted in secret and condemns community mores that prevent a couple from loving openly. The poem begins by describing lovers who "take of their love / In the shade of the wood," insisting that "It is not ugly / Nor is it unclean" and that "Never a sorrow / Was born of two / Couched in the shadow / The whole night through." Yet the poem—relatively brief at twenty-four lines—quickly establishes that although this love is neither unclean nor harmful, the couple is hounded by "people possessed / Of a very small mind // Who nod and whisper, / And poison the bread / Of innocent lovers / Until they are dead." Although other evidence from Reece's work leads me to interpret this poem as about same-sex relationships, many other romantic relationships—including interracial and interfaith relationships—were also taboo within mainstream US society in the 1940s. In the poem's defense of love that is seen as "ugly" or "unclean" by people with "small mind[s]," Reece offers an impassioned defense of relationships that must remain clandestine because they're outside the narrow parameters of what society finds acceptable.

Similar language—about the secrecy of relationships and the fear of prying eyes—can be found in Reece's early 1940s letters to Leon Radway, a classmate at Young Harris College to whom Reece dedicated thirty-two poems in a college anthology *The Lyric Poets*.[163] In a letter written to Radway in the spring of 1940, Reece notes, "I thought of dedicating a poem to you" in a recent column in the college magazine, "but for it to mean anything to you I would have to expose myself to these morons whose chief delight is prying into other people's affairs, and I don't intend to give them an opening."[164] In another letter written a couple of months later, Reece suggests both the depth and secrecy of his relationship with Radway. Reece describes to Radway the books he's planning to write, promising, "Another I am going so [sic] write will concern you and me, but it won't see print for years yet and there'll be time enough to explain it, if there'll be time enough. I am going to be absolutely truthful sometime before I die if I don't die too soon and unexpectedly, and the result will be worth looking at, though I'll make certain I'm safe and dead before it is seen."[165]

The fact that Reece feels he must be dead prior to the book's release, combined with his apparently unrealized wish to be "absolutely truthful sometime before I die," bespeaks a clandestine facet to his relationship with Radway, an aspect of their friendship that had to be concealed while they lived. Detractors may wish to claim that I am misinterpreting a perfectly innocent letter between close friends and could point out that Radway later married (to which Reece refers in a 1949 letter to a mutual friend).[166] However, it is perhaps too simple to note that people with same-sex desire sometimes married, not only in the 1940s but in the years before (Oscar Wilde, anyone?) and after. George Scarbrough discussed this phenomenon in a 1989 journal entry, in which he notes, "The gay men I know now are not gay in the usual sense: they are bisexuals, all married and with children of their own. . . . These men walk and talk and work like other men. And love vastly, more comprehensively, for their need of both sexes."[167]

It is not possible—and likewise not advisable—to discern the "true nature" of Byron Reece's relationship with Leon Radway, nor of his sexuality, from this distance of over sixty years after Reece's death. It is, however, important to recognize that the lives of our Appalachian forebears were often more complicated than could be seen on the surface. In addition, Reece's story reminds us of the dangers to LGBTQ Americans in earlier decades—not only of violence but of job loss, condemnation, and institutionalization during the Lavender Scare—and the undiscovered complexities in earlier Appalachian literature. Reece's work is long overdue for a reassessment by scholars so that it, as well as the work of other queer Appalachian authors who never saw a time when they could be "absolutely truthful" before they died, can be considered within a more nuanced and diverse vision of Appalachian identity and poetics.

2

The Conversation Begins

Landmark Texts and Trailblazing Authors

In the following chapter, I introduce readers to contemporary authors and texts who have been among the vanguard of LGBTQ Appalachian literature. These texts have in common that they were firsts in a variety of ways: the first texts whose Appalachian authors openly identified as LGBTQ, the first Appalachian writers to broach certain topics like rural Appalachians dealing with HIV infection or the dilemma faced by queer Appalachians—who may feel somewhat out of place in both of those communities. The order is chronological, specifically by the publication date of their first major work, and not by order of importance or level of impact. Equally important to remember is that no such list can be truly comprehensive: this is merely an attempt to provide an interested reader a broad introduction to the early greatest hits of LGBTQ Appalachian literature.

Lisa Alther: *Kinflicks* (1976)

Any consideration of contemporary LGBTQ Appalachian literature must begin with Kingsport, Tennessee, native Lisa Alther and her bestselling 1976 novel, *Kinflicks*. The novel was a sensation, favorably reviewed in national publications such as the *New Yorker*, *Village Voice*, *Esquire*, and the *New York Review of Books*. With an initial hardback print run of thirty thousand copies and "a $500,000 paperback deal tucked firmly into its bodice," *Kinflicks* had sold two million copies in paperback by 1987.¹ In the novel's laudatory national coverage, Alther was likened to the next Erica Jong or, greater yet, to novelist (and, later, Nobel laureate) Doris Lessing, a comparison reinforced by the fact that Lessing herself wrote a blurb for the dust jacket saying, "She had me laughing at four in the morning" and "No man could have written it, but it is very far from being 'a woman's book.'"² Other reviews favorably compared *Kinflicks* to canonical texts: "It is a fictional journey in the great tradition that includes 'Moll Flanders' and Voltaire's 'Candide.'"³

Kinflicks follows heroine Ginny Babcock Bliss as she comes of age, experiments sexually and intellectually, and grapples with mortality and with her own identity while caring for her dying mother. The scandalousness of *Kinflicks* arose from those sexual exploits (including Ginny's love affair with a woman), the novel's colorful language, the ridiculous predicaments that Ginny gets herself into, and the ruthless fun that the novel makes of Kingsport, Tennessee (featured in the novel as Ginny's hometown of Hullsport). As the editor of the Kingsport newspaper observed in the summer of the book's release, "Kingsport native Lisa Alther's runaway best-selling first novel has been secreted away in dresser drawers by a number of locals offended by its blunt language," although "others talk proudly of knowing Lisa when," concluding that the book is "taking the town by storm."⁴

Although this novel marks a key moment in the history of LGBTQ Appalachian literature, Ginny's sexual experiences are not exclusively with women, and relatively little of the novel's same-sex intercourse actually happens in Appalachia. (Ginny's sexual encounters with men receive a good deal of attention in the book, including with her high school boyfriend, Clem Cloyd; with Ginny's husband, insurance- and snowmobile-salesman Ira Bliss; and then with army-deserter Hawk in a never-consummated attempt at tantric intercourse.) In fact, her affair with Edna (Eddie) Holzer, her dorm-mate at Worthley, is Ginny's only lesbian relationship, although that was certainly enough to contribute to this novel's sensation in the mid-1970s. Ginny's relationship with Eddie begins when they are students at Worthley, continues while they live in a tenement apartment in Cambridge, then proceeds to its tragicomic end after they move to Stark's Bog, Vermont, to live in a rented log cabin and "leave behind the American capitalist-imperialist economy altogether."⁵ Only during Ginny and Eddie's brief visit to Hullsport, Tennessee—so that they can picket at the munitions factory that Ginny's father runs—does the novel attempt to locate LGBTQ intimacy within Appalachia. Ginny tries to make her relationship with Eddie into a political statement when she and Eddie arrive. After Ginny insists to her mother that she and Eddie will sleep in her room, thinking triumphantly, "There! I had done it! I had come out of the closet, and before my own mother!" Mrs. Babcock deflects this, saying, "Fine, dear. Fine. You girls have a slumber party if you want to."[6]

Lisa Alther has described her fiction as trying "to get at the human reality behind our society's stereotypes, particularly those regarding women and homosexuals. . . . I attempt to give my gay and lesbian characters full, complicated lives involving work, households, politics, children, friends, spiritual struggles, etc. And one important facet to their lives is that their partners are the same sex as themselves."[7] However, contemporary reviews of *Kinflicks* were mixed on the issue of whether it is a "lesbian novel." In *Ms.* magazine in 1976, a reviewer wrote that "the erotic scenes between these two women are sensitively drawn."[8] In stark contrast, in a 1979 article, "Lesbians in the Mainstream: Images of Lesbians in Recent Commercial Fiction," Maureen Brady and Judith McDaniel declared that "*Kinflicks* is a novel that will give lesbian readers nightmares," arguing that "*Kinflicks* did not establish, but rather continued, the time-honored tradition that lesbianism must be punished."[9] Yet another contemporary assessment of *Kinflicks* argued for the universality of *Kinflicks'* meditations on sex and death, maintaining that "this is no more a 'lesbian novel' than it is a 'woman's novel.'"[10]

Later feminist scholars writing about the novel have been similarly divided on whether Alther's portrayal of lesbianism is revolutionary or regressive. Lisa Maria Hogeland, in her study *Feminism and Its Fictions: The Consciousness-Raising Novel and the Women's Liberation Movement* (1998), criticizes "the literary-political limitations of Alther's novel," arguing that compared to *Kinflicks*, "Jong's *Fear of Flying* is hardly the most problematic novel of the decade."[11] Most troubling to Hogeland is the fact that Ginny's only lesbian relationship ends in death: "While Alther extends the woman's picaresque beyond the limits of heterosexuality and depicts her character in a lesbian relationship, which Jong does not do, Alther still preserves the marriage-or-death endings for both of the women in that relationship: Eddie dies and Ginny marries someone else."[12] A more recent scholarly assessment—in the entry on Alther in the encyclopedia *The Gay and Lesbian Literary Heritage* (2013)—has defended the novel and noted the groundbreaking nature of Alther's work, declaring that *Kinflicks* "is memorable for its depiction of lesbian feminism and separatist politics in the 1960s and for presenting lesbianism as a desirable way of relating to other women."[13] Regardless of whether one believes Alther's portrayal of lesbianism to be sufficiently feminist, this novel broke new ground in the topics that could be openly—and comically rather than tragically—addressed in a work of Appalachian fiction.

Maggie Anderson: *The Great Horned Owl* (1979) and *A Space Filled with Moving* (1992)

Maggie Anderson's poetry is as discreet as Lisa Alther's novel *Kinflicks* is bawdy. Yet these authors share an appreciation of what they see as Appalachia's gifts (the resilience of its people and its natural beauty), combined with sorrow at the exploitation of the region's resources and its residents. Anderson's first collection—a chapbook entitled *The Great Horned Owl*—appeared in 1979, and the following year Harper & Row published her first full-length collection of poems, *Years That Answer*. Since then, she has published four more collections of poetry: *Cold Comfort* (1986), *A Space Filled with Moving* (1992), and *Windfall: New and Selected Poems* (2000)—all from University of Pittsburgh Press—and 2017's *Dear All*, published by Four Way Books. Only later in her career did Anderson publicly identify as lesbian, and it was then that her work was discussed through the lens of sexuality studies. Reviews of *Windfall* appeared in both the *Lesbian Review of Books* and the *Lambda Book Report* (an early and important journal of LGBT literature); and, more recently, several of her poems have been anthologized in *LGBTQ Fiction and Poetry from Appalachia* (2019).

Throughout Anderson's body of work, her poetry employs a sexual tension and plays with ambiguities of gender, suggesting a flirtation with sexual orientation that leaves the reader uncertain. In Anderson's early poetry, references to sensuality figure the object of desire as ambiguously gendered, neither clearly male nor clearly female. In "Company" (a prose poem from *The Great Horned Owl*), for example, the speaker describes making love downstairs while a houseguest sleeps upstairs; the first-person plural pronoun of "We are making love underneath you. Our staggered breathing . . ." occludes the genders of both lovers.[14] Similar—or even coy?—phrasing marks Anderson's poetics throughout her career, although a few later poems edge closer, perhaps, to references to same-sex desire. In the multisection poem "In Singing Weather" (from the 1986 collection

Cold Comfort), the speaker—thinking through the connections among objects in memory—reflects on ". . . the warm brass / bracelets wrapping an arm I once caressed."[15] Only through that oblique reference to the object of desire does Anderson approach queer sexuality here, and even that is ambiguous: both men and women can wear bracelets, and one can certainly caress an arm—of a parent or a child or even a friend—in a nonsexual way. Who is even to say that the poem's speaker here is female? Nothing about this poem conclusively demonstrates LGBTQ Appalachian content.

Anderson's 1992 collection, *A Space Filled with Moving* (whose title is a reference to the work of American poet Gertrude Stein), includes a few sensual-relationship poems, but the interactions are described so fleetingly that it is difficult to discern much (let alone gender identification) about the object of affection, and these poems primarily focus on desire that wasn't acted upon. In "Celibate," the speaker recalls, "I understand I could have touched you / as we walked through the cemetery / . . . / . . . There were / moments then, close and warm enough, / . . . / I understand that I did not."[16] Again, the interaction in this poem is sufficiently ambiguous as to be difficult to identify as sexual, although the warmth and closeness, plus the potential for but refraining from touching, suggest sexual tension that was not acted upon. That tension is foregrounded in another poem in this collection, "Good Time," where the object of desire is similarly gender ambiguous. "Good Time" recounts an incident of flirtation; the speaker indulges in the interaction while knowing that nothing will ultimately happen, knowing that "You are not the one I love / but I'll give you a slow dance / to remember, this sweet hot tease / I trust you to resist, while my fingers / wander your spine to your neck." Only "your red scarf across my shoulder" hints at the gender of the partner—perhaps female—although men certainly can wear red scarves as well. Not all readers have interpreted these poems as intentionally and playfully oblique: an early reviewer of *A Space Filled with Moving* was highly critical of Anderson's circumspect and reserved approach, criticizing the poems' "vague metaphors" and the poet's "reluctance to share anything other than occasionally clever wordplay."[17]

Although Anderson's poetry became no more overtly sexual as her career evolved, by the time her collection *Windfall: New and Selected Poems* was released in 2000, the reception of her poetry was increasingly framed by her identity as a lesbian poet. In a review in the *Lesbian Review of Books*, the reviewer commends Anderson for her treatment of "the experience of separation—of internal and external divisions incurred by gender, by religion, by sexual orientation."[18] In the *Lambda Book Report*, the reviewer noted then defended the lack of LGBTQ content in Anderson's poetry: "Anderson . . . does not write of romantic and sexual relationships. Her volume does not identify her with a particular lifestyle orientation. Personally, I like this. Accuse me of heresy, but the older I get, the less I care about those kinds of categories. There is an exploration here of a topography of the heart that is rare, desperately needed in today's world, and universal to us all."[19]

There would have been many good reasons for Anderson to protect her privacy early in her career, including the cultural climate of the region and nation in the 1970s–1980s and the circumstances of her employment, including "working as a kind of 'circuit rider' poet in schools, community groups, prisons, and rehabilitation centers in West Virginia, Pennsylvania, and Ohio in the 1970s and 1980s."[20] In addition, Anderson's own preference for privacy has shaped her poetic aesthetic, as she asserted in response to an interviewer's question during the 2004 Emory & Henry Literary Festival. When the interviewer noted, "Some writers have a problem dealing with sensuality," and then asked, "How do you approach that subject?" Anderson acknowledged the importance of sensuality in her poems, discussing desire in gender-free terms and asserting her own preference for privacy: "I think there's a sensual element to all relationships. I've written, I think, some pretty sexy poems about trees. But, of course, what you're asking—and I don't mean to be coy about it—has to do with human sexuality, relationships among people. I haven't written a lot about that subject, a decision that's more a matter of temperament than anything else, but I do think that one of the great sources of joy we have available to us as human beings is our erotic selves."[21]

Maggie Anderson's poetry does not focus on sexuality; it does address many topics that have preoccupied other Appalachian writers: nature, food, family. A New York City–born daughter of Appalachians, she and her parents spent the school year in New York (where her parents worked as teachers) and returned to West Virginia each summer to visit family; Anderson and her father moved back to West Virginia (her mother had died a few years before) when Anderson was thirteen. Anderson has described how her in-between, neither/nor experiences—of community, of class, of language—shaped her perspective and her poetic vision: "In some ways, my perspective has been that of an outsider, and much of my work has been occupied with insider/outsider concerns," informed by her "struggle to unite my 'two-nesses.'"[22] In a 2019 interview, Anderson included her sexuality in a list of her marginal positions: "Living in the margins for much of my life (as a woman, as a lesbian, and as a poet with deep roots in Appalachia) I have come to (or have had to) understand the possibilities that can come from living on the edges, with little side trips to the mainstream from time to time. I resist binaries of any kind, so I like to move (write) in the interstices."[23] As Joyce Dyer has observed about Anderson's work, "To have both places, and neither, is often the better place to be, and Maggie knows this. This is where she lives, and where her poetry lives as well."[24]

Dorothy Allison: *Bastard Out of Carolina* (1992) and *Two or Three Things I Know for Sure* (1995)

Dorothy Allison's earliest published volumes were award winners: her short story collection *Trash* won the Lambda Literary Award for Lesbian Fiction in 1989, and her novel *Bastard Out of Carolina* (1992) was a finalist for the National Book Award. As a South Carolina–born writer whose hometown, Greenville, is on the southeastern edge of the Appalachian Regional Commission–defined Appalachian region,[25] Allison has often been categorized (like many other writers from that part of Appalachia) as "Southern." Regardless, Allison has claimed her Appalachian roots, saying in a 2017 interview that the work of "southern Appalachian writers" is where she goes to find "my people."[26] Those same writers have repeatedly claimed Allison as one of their own, signified through her inclusion in three important anthologies of the region's writing: *Listen Here: Women Writing in Appalachia* (2003), *Walk Till the Dogs Get Mean: Meditations on the Forbidden from Contemporary Appalachia* (2015), and *LGBTQ Fiction and Poetry from Appalachia* (2019).

Bastard Out of Carolina tells the story of Ruth Anne Boatright, nicknamed Bone, a child growing up in Greenville County, South Carolina, under the shadows of poverty, illegitimacy, and an abusive stepfather, Glen. Bone is sustained by relationships with the women in her family: her grandmother, mother, aunts, and sister. The novel ends with Bone, just out of the hospital and recovering from the latest injuries that Glen has inflicted, having been abandoned by a mother who couldn't bring herself to leave Glen despite having found him raping her daughter. Despite the harrowing events of the novel, it ends on a note of hope, with Bone remaining safe and loved with her Aunt Raylene: "I would be thirteen in a few weeks. I was already who I was going to be . . . When Raylene came to me, I let her touch my shoulder, let my head tilt to lean against her, trusting her arm and her love."[27]

Early reviews of *Bastard Out of Carolina* emphasized its Southernness; it was even criticized for being too Southern. One reviewer called it a "graceful, distinctly Southern first novel" and noted that its "depiction of snarled family ties is stunning."[28] In Randall Kenan's review of the novel, he compares Allison to other Southern writers such as Flannery O'Connor and William Faulkner and says of *Bastard Out of Carolina* that "few works are more entrenched" in the "eccentric archetypes" of Southern literature than Allison's novel. His review ends on a somewhat mixed note: "For this reason—pecan pie and gospel music, snuff-dipping grannies and kissing cousins notwithstanding—*Bastard Out of Carolina* is a singular and important act of art and courage."[29] Of course, Allison's characterization as a Southern writer isn't without merit. In a 1994 interview, Allison stated, in response to a question about her literary heritage, "I'm perverse. It's whatever they're denying me right now. I belong to the tradition of iconoclastic, queer, southern writer. I don't think there really is a lesbian tradition. We haven't worked toward that, but I'd like to steer where it goes." Moreover, Allison said about her literary forebears, "On good days I claim myself in the same tradition as Flannery O'Connor, James Baldwin, Tennessee Williams."[30]

The collection of essays *Two or Three Things I Know for Sure* is a memoir, its prose interwoven with photographs from Allison's personal collection. Reviewer Mary Ann Daly writes in the *Lambda Book Report* that although the book is "the text of [Allison's] tour performance in the wake of her searing, best-selling novel, *Bastard Out of Carolina*" that "it's not just a souvenir program"; the book "claims a life for itself apart from both her charisma and her novel."[31] The memoir's stories flesh out details of Allison's childhood, her coming of age, her journey to becoming a writer, and her efforts to come to terms with her past. In the text, Allison retells family stories—of charismatic uncles who can't seem to stay out of trouble, of long-departed aunts and cousins about whom no one wants to speak—and is inspired by her mother's box of photos, of which Allison writes that "the faces in Mama's box were full of stories—ongoing tragedies, great novels, secrets and mysteries and longings no one would ever know."[32] The book is a meditation on family and stories and memory, about the lies and half-truths that we tell ourselves and each other. The book's refrain, "Two or three things I know for sure," is woven intermittently throughout the text, in statements that range from universal—"Two or three things I know for sure, and one of them is that change when it comes cracks everything open"—to wrenching: "Two or three things I know for sure, but none of them is why a man would rape a child, why a man would beat a child."³³ Scholars praise *Two or Three Things*, calling it "an exceptional book, uncompromising, lyrical and inspirational," a text that explores "the nuances of confession and love, truth and body."³⁴ And of course, it is frequently compared to *Bastard Out of Carolina*: "Read this book, and you'll find out **Bastard** was *nicer* than the truth."³⁵

Despite Allison's roots in Appalachia and her persistent attention to issues affecting Appalachian families, her work has been discussed somewhat infrequently within scholarship on Appalachian literature. Although an early essay about Allison's work was published in *Appalachian Journal*, its aim was not to consider Allison's place within Appalachian literature but rather to consider her relationship to other "writers from poor-white backgrounds" and to compare her characters to "the white-trash character . . . in American literary consciousness."³⁶ The most sustained discussion of Dorothy Allison as an Appalachian writer (rather than a Southern writer) came in a 2004 dissertation, Karissa McCoy's "Re-Writing Region, Re-Constructing Whiteness: Appalachia and the 'Place' of Whiteness in American Culture, 1930–2003." In that study, McCoy considers Allison's work through the framing of race and class in Appalachian literature, arguing that Allison's work uses the concept of "trash" to undermine strictures of class identity.³⁷ In comparing Allison's work to other Appalachian writers such as Cormac McCarthy, McCoy situates Allison within an Appalachian literary tradition.

Notably, Allison's work was a focal point of an early, key work of scholarship on queer Appalachian literature: Danny Miller's 1996 presentation at the Appalachian Studies Association Conference on "Homosexuality in Appalachian Literature." In Miller's discussion of gay and lesbian characters in five works of Appalachian fiction, he analyzes the character of Raylene, protagonist Bone Boatwright's aunt in *Bastard Out of Carolina*. Calling Raylene the "true heroine of the novel," Miller argues that she is "the one caring loving person in Bone's terribly dysfunctional world."³⁸ The fact that Aunt Raylene has had a lesbian relationship—that the great love of her life was another woman, who left Raylene when forced to choose between her lover and her child—is not a focal point of the novel, although it finally explains (when the details are revealed) why her family has seemed protective of Raylene and eager to know if anyone has criticized her. As Miller explains, Raylene "is depicted in the novel as a likeable and admirable character. . . . All of her nieces and nephews come to her for friendship and care."[39] Miller contrasts Allison's positive portrayal of Raylene (as well as a positive portrayal of a queer couple in Denise Giardina's *The Unquiet Earth*) with several less positive depictions of LGBTQ characters in Appalachian fiction: a "tortured homosexual," a lesbian character who kisses one of her female students without consent, and then a novel filled with "a good deal of sexual ugliness" that includes attempted same-sex incest.

Although work remains to be done in considering Allison within the Appalachian literary tradition, her work does not suffer from the same overall critical neglect as some other queer Appalachian authors, such as Jeff Mann or doris davenport. Allison's work has been the subject of a Hollywood film (1996, dir. Anjelica Huston), has been recognized by national awards and accolades, and is commonly studied in literature classes, written about by scholars, and spoken about at conferences. Perhaps Dorothy Allison has inadvertently benefited from the same misclassifications as Alison Bechdel, who is the author of *Fun Home: A Family Tragicomic* and a native of Appalachian Pennsylvania: since scholars and critics do not see them as Appalachian—but rather as Southern in Allison's case and either midwestern or from New York City in Bechdel's—they are more likely to be written about and studied within the context of American literature or even queer literature, rather than relegated to studies of regional literature. Since people don't generally see Allison as a queer writer from Appalachia, she hasn't experienced the double erasure that has shaped the careers of so many other LGBTQ Appalachian writers discussed here.

Fenton Johnson: *Scissors, Paper, Rock* (1993)

Born in 1953, novelist Fenton Johnson grew up in New Haven, Kentucky, a place which is, by Johnson's own admission, "not in the heart of Appalachia but on its fringes, in the hill country of the Kentucky Knobs, some sixty miles south of Louisville."[40] His home county, Nelson, is one county's width away from the Appalachian Regional Commission's parameters for Appalachia. (Nelson's eastern borders are Washington and Marion Counties, and they border Appalachia.) This geographical distance perhaps accounts for the fact that at least three scholars of Appalachian studies have insisted to me that Johnson has no place in this book because "he is NOT Appalachian—he's from the Kentucky knobs."

However, Johnson has been widely categorized and has self-identified as an Appalachian writer. In a 1995 interview published in *Appalachian Journal*, Johnson claims his Appalachianness clearly: "And so when you ask the question, Do I believe myself to be among the first writers to claim openly the 'double identity' of being both gay and Appalachian, I think the answer has to be, surely, yes, just because 'the first' extends backwards for such a relatively short time into history."[41] In this response, Johnson's identities as an Appalachian and as a gay man appear to be a given; the question addressed here is the issue of whether he is among the "first." Moreover, scholars and other writers have categorized Johnson as Appalachian as recently as the 2019 anthology *LGBTQ Fiction and Poetry from Appalachia* (edited by Jeff Mann and Julia Watts) and at least as far back as 1995, when William J. Schafer declared, in his review of *Scissors, Paper, Rock* published in *Appalachian Journal*, that the novel is "a kind of 'You CAN Go Home Again' tale of Appalachian consciousness in and out of the wide world of modern America."[42] In including Johnson, I model my approach on the one that editors Bianca Lynne Spriggs and Jeremy Paden describe in their introduction to *Black Bone: 25 Years of the Affrilachian Poets*, where they reject the "temptation when thinking in regionalist, aesthetic, and even political terms to go narrow, to say that this but not that may be admitted into the canon."[43] Although some scholars may disagree, Fenton Johnson and his work are part of the landscape of Appalachian literature, and therefore his 1993 novel *Scissors, Paper, Rock* is included here.

Scissors, Paper, Rock is a novel composed of eleven interwoven short stories, featuring the Hardin family of Strang Knob, Kentucky. The protagonist Raphael Hardin, who like Johnson moved to California to attend college and then built a life there, is dying of AIDS and has returned home to be with his father, Tom Hardin, who is dying of cancer. The interwoven stories focus on various Hardins as well as on their next-door neighbor Miss Camilla: the novel's conscience, its most prominent narrative voice, and Raphael's friend (at whose home Raphael self-administers his daily infusions of medications). Told out of chronological order, the stories narrate events including Rose Ella and Tom Hardin's first date (in 1942) and the annual family party in 1988, the last one at which the remaining Hardins will be together. *Scissors, Paper, Rock* is a poignant story of loss, family ties, the inaccuracies of memory (and of storytelling itself), and our inability to speak the truth even to those closest to us.

When *Scissors, Paper, Rock* appeared in 1993, few texts—either literary or informational—had yet addressed the topic of AIDS in Appalachia.

Even in the next few years, scholars noted that people liked to think that AIDS was not an Appalachian problem, that it was instead "a big city problem . . . something that happened in other kinds of lives" and "a disease of urban life *outside* the region, a threat to the mountains."⁴⁴ A very few texts *did* do that work—of locating AIDS within Appalachia—during this time period.⁴⁵ In 1992, an Appalshop-produced documentary, *Belinda*, profiled Belinda Mason, a Kentucky native who—when she died in 1991 at the age of thirty-three—was the most famous AIDS patient in Appalachia. A writer and married mother of two who was infected with HIV through a tainted transfusion during childbirth, Mason became an AIDS activist who, in her role as the first person with AIDS (PWA) appointed to President George H. W. Bush's National Commission on AIDS, was a fierce critic of the Bush administration's AIDS policies. Mason advocated on behalf of all people with AIDS, refusing "to be used by the sanctimonious as a wedge between the 'innocent victims' and the rest of those with HIV," because she was "conscious of her relative privilege as a white, straight, insured and financially secure PWA."⁴⁶

Other than the 1992 documentary about Mason (and a 1989 article in the *Journal of Infectious Diseases*, "Urbs in Rure: Human Immunodeficiency Virus Infection in Rural Tennessee") most discussions of AIDS in Appalachia postdate *Scissors, Paper, Rock*.⁴⁷ A year after the publication of Johnson's novel, Abraham Verghese published his memoir, *My Own Country: A Doctor's Story of a Town and Its People in the Age of AIDS* (1994), chronicling his experiences as an infectious disease specialist in Johnson City, Tennessee, from 1985 (when a person with AIDS was first admitted to the hospital there) to 1989. At the 1995 meeting of the Appalachian Studies Association, a group of young people performed the AIDS-awareness drama *Gone Tomorrow*, and scholar Kate Black presented stories of the AIDS crisis in the region as part of a roundtable, "Rethinking Region: The Call of Stories."⁴⁸ In 1997, Mary Anglin wrote in the *Journal of Appalachian Studies* (in "AIDS in Appalachia: Medical Pathologies and the Problem of Identity") that the AIDS epidemic actually served to highlight Appalachia's diversity: "Rather than a disease of the world outside, AIDS thus makes evident the plurality of sociocultural forms which comprise life *within* the mountains and which connect people in contemporary Appalachia to other regions in the United States."⁴⁹ As these examples illustrate, the conversation about AIDS in Appalachia was just beginning in the 1990s, and Fenton Johnson's *Scissors, Paper, Rock* was a very early addition to the conversation.

A groundbreaking work in Appalachian literature, *Scissors, Paper, Rock* was innovative within AIDS literature as well, and it received more acclaim from outside the Appalachian region than from within. A 1993 profile of Johnson in the *San Francisco Examiner* noted that "unique among novels spawned by the [AIDS] epidemic, 'Scissors, Paper, Rock' is rural, not urban, and it is about the potency and complexity of family life, not its disintegration."[50] Early reviewers in national and international publications such as the *New York Times*, the *Boston Globe*, and the *Montreal Gazette* were enthusiastic about the novel, calling it "a story that teems with stubborn life" and a book filled "with deep, vivid imagery, rich characterizations and utterly right-on dialogue."[51] However, Johnson noted in a 1995 interview, "My writing has not been dealt with much at all in the South" other than a positive review of the novel in a Lexington newspaper.[52] The novel received a glowing review in the *Virginia Quarterly Review* (1994), where it was celebrated as "a brilliant novel that offers important commentary on our romantic ideals about the meaning of 'family' and the gritty reality that inevitably confronts us all."[53] With the exception of these few acknowledgments, Johnson's novel—although a groundbreaking portrait of an Appalachian family grappling with AIDS—received little attention in the region of his birth.

doris davenport: *Soque Street Poems* (1995) and *madness like morning glories* (2005)

doris davenport's LinkedIn page describes her vocation as a "Writer, College or University Professor or Performance Poet" and her origins as "lesbian-feminist working class Affrilachian from Northeast GA."[54] davenport has been on the forefront of many important intellectual and creative movements in the late twentieth and early twenty-first centuries—in her contribution to the groundbreaking anthology *This Bridge Called My Back: Writings by Radical Women of Color* (1983), in her work in performance poetry and intersectionality, and in her use of video to disseminate her work. Therefore, it is surprising how little critical attention she has received. Of her more than ten books of poetry, only one—*madness like morning glories* (2005)—was published by an academic or literary press. Others have been largely self-published or published through small community associations; for example, *Soque Street Poems* (1995) was published by the Sautee-Nacoochee Community Association in davenport's native Georgia. Published thus outside of established literary or academic circles, davenport's work has drawn only limited attention. My observation here is neither new nor unique: her 1993 entry in the encyclopedia of *Contemporary Lesbian Writers of the United States* notes, "Regrettably, davenport's three self-published works have not received any formal critical attention to date."[55] As James A. Miller observes in his 2002 essay "Coming Home to Affrilachia: The Poems of doris davenport," "The price for her unwillingness to claim convenient, tailor-made identities has often been critical neglect."[56]

Although the work that would lead to *Soque Street Poems* began years earlier, with the publication of a couple of Appalachia-themed poems in davenport's 1980 collection, *it's like this*, her primary contribution to LGBTQ Appalachian literature began with the 1995 publication of *Soque Street Poems*, a poetic portrait of her home community in Cornelia, Georgia. In introducing this collection, davenport calls these "love poems; praise poems of the unique African-American communities of Southern Appalachia."[57] As she wrote in a March 1995 journal entry, "Until two years ago and Frank X. [sic] Walker, I hadn't placed me or northeast Georgia in a context of Appalachia."[58] But by the time *Soque Street Poems* was published, davenport had come to see these poems as part of "a lifelong ongoing work in progress," designed "to recreate, preserve, and remind us" of the value of these African American communities.[59] In the next installment of this work in progress, davenport published a revised version of *Soque Street Poems* (SSP) in 2005 as *madness like morning glories (mlmg)*.

These two collections paint a portrait of a vibrant Affrilachian community and the people who inhabit it, including many of davenport's family members. In both collections, the predominant voices are female, keepers of the community's lore and the mouthpieces of the community's observation, conscience, and judgment. Many poems, written primarily in the distinctive voices of community members, are titled with the names of their speakers and often include their birth and death dates: "Lutecia Brown 1840–1986 [sic]," "Miz Amy," "Goatman Joe Harris," "Claude Davenport 1928(?)–1964" (titles from *Soque Street Poems*). Other poems are titled using street addresses or the names of businesses or community institutions—"103 Soque," "Cornelia Regional (Colored) High School," "Sally's Lunchroom," "Fred's Tavern"—thus fleshing out a complex portrait of a community that is comprised of both the people and the locations they inhabit. In other poems, the primary speaker appears to be a nameless, often omniscient figure who can, for example, recount davenport's own conception ("Parent-ogenesis") or describe events that occurred long before davenport was born ("attitude explained"). The result is a multifaceted portrait of an Appalachian community. In chapter 4, "Silences and Storytelling," I discuss *Soque Street Poems* and *madness like morning glories*, focusing on how these collections give a voice to an Appalachian population—the Affrilachian community—that has been underrepresented in Appalachian literature. In chapter 5, "HomePlaceBody," I examine davenport's emphasis on embodiedness—in her poetic imagery as well as in her work as a performance poet—and her celebration of pleasures of both the physical body and of Appalachia itself.

Among the gifts offered by davenport's work is an openness about sexuality, on an individual and a community level: her Affrilachia includes queer love and sensuality. The poem "Cleo Smith" from *Soque Street Poems* becomes "Miz Clio Savant" in *madness like morning glories*. In both poems, the Cleo/Clio character has a long-term relationship with a woman named Dina. Significantly, in both collections, that relationship is represented as having taken place elsewhere, outside the community, before Cleo/Clio moved to Cornelia. In *madness like morning glories*, Clio's relationship with Dina is represented as more long-lasting ("She stayed and / we stayed like that for a long, long / time until she died."), and the sensual intensity of their relationship is more overt: "I know her voice, her eyes, her thighs. She / dance the Spirits in too. Honey-sweet, her voice." In *Soque Street*, the relationship between Cleo and Dina is represented more subtly—"all the men wait & watch me walk— / some women watch, too, like my Dina"—and could almost be overlooked, even though Cleo calls her "my Dina" and asserts, "I dream of Dina in my blood."

In *madness*, it is impossible not to notice the sexuality of Miz Clio's relationship with Dina because Miz Clio's poem is immediately followed by a cacophony of community voices, all commenting on Miz Clio and her sexuality (and then devolving into arguments with each other). The comments range from condemnation ("I always knowed Miz Clio was a bull dyke" and "uh huh, knowed she was funny") to in-fighting among the community members ("y'all make me *tired*. just cause she didn't want nunna the sorry men y'all had") to the classic Appalachian dismissal of someone not born in the community: "she ain't even *from* Cornelia." This commentary continues for, apparently, ten more speakers. This poem's section of commentary is prefaced by a stage direction of sorts, a note to the reader: "*. . . and you are to hear these all speaking at once like somebody opened a tightly sealed jar of peach preserves gone bad or* *a jar of wasps*" (ellipses and italics in original). The synesthesia of these instructions—that we should *hear* these voices like a jar of rotten jam would *taste* or *smell*—hints at the complexity of davenport's poetic vision. And the portrayal of Cleo/Clio, the transplant to Cornelia who is still seen as a little bit of an outsider, hints at the potential role of a queer person in this community: once she's in Cornelia, Cleo/Clio's passion for Dina is in her blood and her memory but is distinctly in the past. In this extended poem-plus-response, davenport portrays a loving lesbian relationship as well as the ways an LGBTQ community member might have been received by her community.

Although davenport's work has received little attention within Appalachian studies and relatively little attention within academic circles as a whole, her work has been featured in a few important Appalachian anthologies, including *Bloodroot: Reflections on Place by Appalachian Women Writers* (1998), *Her Words: Diverse Voices in Contemporary Appalachian Women's Poetry* (2002), and *LGBTQ Fiction and Poetry from Appalachia* (2019). *madness like morning glories* was indeed reviewed in *Appalachian Heritage,* where Warren J. Carson declares the collection to be "a tremendously important contribution to Appalachian literature," noting both that davenport "captures beautifully the rhythms of black speech" and that she had "remedied that silence" that has surrounded the "minority voices" of Appalachia.[60] A few years later (2008), a number of davenport's poems were published in *Appalachian Heritage*. Other than these examples, however, davenport and her work remain largely absent within the context of Appalachian literature and Appalachian studies. Neither is she included among the Affrilachian Poets, either on the group's website or in the recent anthology *Black Bone: 25 Years of the Affrilachian Poets* even though, as Julie R. Enszer pointed out, davenport was "an Affrilachian poet working before Frank X. [sic] Walker coined the word, an early performance/spoken word poet before the spoken word movement became popular, an early lesbian and feminist."[61] Perhaps because davenport was an early adopter within so many aesthetic and literary movements, or because davenport's work embodies intersectionality—juggling identities as an Appalachian and an African American and a lesbian—or even because davenport is from an often-overlooked section of Appalachia (northern Georgia), regardless of the reason, davenport's work has been neglected by scholars of Appalachian literature and Affrilachian literature.

Julia Watts: *Wildwood Flowers* (1996) and *Finding H.F.* (2001)

Julia Watts was born (in 1969) and raised in Whitley County, Kentucky, a daughter of educators and potters June Queener Watts and Rayford Watts (who was also a longtime professor of English at Cumberland College). Watts's first novel was *Wildwood Flowers*, published in 1996 by Naiad Press, the groundbreaking lesbian/feminist press cofounded by Barbara Grier in 1973. Overall, attention to Watts's work has been limited, in part, by the fact that her work has been considered "popular fiction" rather than "literary fiction." For example, a 1999 blurb about Watts in the *Chicago Tribune* identifies her as a "popular lesbian romance writer."[62] Of course, both tags—"popular" and "romance writer"—signal the unlikelihood that Watts's work would be taken seriously by the literary establishment. Indeed, despite her having won the 2002 Lambda Literary Award for Children's/Young Adult Literature (making her one of only a handful of Appalachian writers, including Dorothy Allison and Jeff Mann, to hold the distinction of having won a Lambda Award up through 2014 when I began this study), Watts has received little attention from the Appalachian studies community. In recent years, Watts's work—especially her work as an essayist and an editor, including coediting *Unbroken Circle: Stories of Cultural Diversity in the South* (with Larry Smith, 2017) and *LGBTQ Fiction and Poetry from Appalachia* (with Jeff Mann, 2019)—has begun to receive more attention from the Appalachian literary community. In Watts's 2015 essay "Quare Theory: Some Thoughts on LGBT Appalachian Writing," she addresses the dilemma faced by a queer Appalachian writer, describing the chilly reception that her first queer Appalachian-themed short story received from publishers: "Half of the publications rejected it because they didn't like the Appalachian angle, the other half because they didn't like the 'gay thing.'"[63]

Wildwood Flowers follows a classic fish-out-of-water pattern, with lovers Bev and Andie moving from Boston to Morgan, Kentucky (a fictional town inspired by Watts's hometown of Corbin), so that Andie can take a new job as assistant professor of English at a Christian-affiliated college. Although Bev and Andie are a committed couple who have been together for years, they remain largely closeted in small-town Appalachia, claiming to be cousins, with Andie constantly afraid that she will lose her job at Randall College if the nature of their relationship is discovered. In this romantic comedy, the obstacle to the romance's success is the closet—specifically the fact that "Bev was irritated by the closet Andie was building around them"[64] and the pressures of trying to live closeted in Morgan, Kentucky.

Yet Watts also uses this novel to highlight the challenges and dangers facing queer Appalachians who have chosen to remain in Appalachia, especially rural or small-town Appalachia. In Morgan, Andie and Bev are befriended by Cricket Needham, Morgan's mortician who introduces himself to Bev as "not exactly the marryin' kind" and who later takes Bev to the nearest gay bar, The Hideaway, in Odessa, Tennessee: across the state line and three more counties over. There, Bev meets Doug, the club's owner and bartender, who is the community's dentist but runs The Hideaway as a sort of "community service project," to give the queer residents of the region a place to be with like-minded folks: "a lot of people around here would go nuts without it, myself included."[65] At The Hideaway, Bev also meets singer Rhonda Dudney and hears about Rhonda's love, Sam, a transgender man who was murdered by men who picked him up when his truck broke down on a country road.[66] Overall, *Wildwood Flowers* highlights the stresses that small-town Appalachian living can put on an LGBTQ couple, the paucity of public spaces where LGBTQ citizens can be open about their identities, and the dangers faced by LGBTQ Appalachians every day.

Watts's first novel for young adults, 2001's *Finding H.F.*, won the Lambda Literary Award for Children's/Young Adult Literature. A coming-of-age novel, *Finding H.F.* shows us the title character, Heavenly Faith Simms, and her best friend Bo, queer teens growing up in rural Morgan, Kentucky, trying not to get beaten up by the football team (in Bo's case) and dreaming of life after high school, preferably somewhere other than in Morgan. In this quest narrative, H.F. and Bo set off to find H.F.'s mother, who abandoned H.F. when she was born. In their travels, H.F. and Bo are surprised to encounter a more inclusive atmosphere in Atlanta, including queer couples holding hands in public, the Out Loud Bookshop and Café (where they find books by Adrienne Rich, Willa Cather, and Oscar Wilde, plus racier offerings such as "one big book that's got a picture of two women, naked and kissing, on it" and a "book with a picture of a muscle-bound guy with a policeman's helmet and no shirt on"[67]), and the Metropolitan Community Church.

In addition to its indictment of the homophobia in Appalachia, this novel celebrates Appalachia's natural beauty and the comforts of family. The beauty of the Appalachian landscape provides Bo and H.F. a refuge from the judgment and violence at their high school, where they endure bullying or, in Bo's case, beatings from classmates because they don't present as traditionally masculine or feminine: "The sissy boys always have it harder than the tomboys. If you're a boyish girl, other girls just snub you, but if you're a girlish boy, other boys beat the living hell out of you. Believe me, I've picked Bo up off the pavement more times than I can count."[68] The school's teachers are complicit in this homophobic violence—"most teachers pretend not to notice, because they're just older versions of the boys who are kicking the crap out of the 'faggot' "—and H.F. has to absorb taunts and name-calling, such as when the captain of the football team calls out, "Hey, H.F. . . . where's your girlfriend?" followed by "Fuckin' dyke."[69] Yet H.F.'s Memaw supports her by not forcing her to conform to gender norms: "she mends my ratty blue jeans instead of making me wear dresses."[70] Even so, H.F. fears that Memaw will never accept her sexuality because of what Memaw has been taught at church. *Finding H.F.* reminds readers that queer Appalachian teens walk a tightrope every day, negotiating family tensions and the bullying of high school.

Jeff Mann: *Bliss* (1998) and *Loving Mountains, Loving Men* (2005)

Jeff Mann was born in Clifton Forge, Virginia, in 1959 and grew up in Hinton, West Virginia. He graduated from West Virginia University with a dual degree that foreshadows the prominence of nature in his poetry—majoring in both English and Nature Interpretation (in the Forestry Department)—and later earned an MA in English as well. A prolific novelist as well as a poet and essayist, Mann teaches at Virginia Tech, offering classes in creative writing, Appalachian literature, and LGBTQ literature, and lives with his husband in Pulaski, Virginia.[71] Jeff Mann's poetry, most notably his 1998 poetry chapbook *Bliss*, is groundbreaking within Appalachian literature for introducing openly queer themes within Appalachian poetry. (As was discussed in the introductory chapter, he blazed similar trails with his 1999 essay "Stonewall and Matewan: Some Thoughts on Gay Life in Appalachia.") In his 2005 book *Loving Mountains, Loving Men*—a compilation of poetry and memoir—Mann addresses the conundrum highlighted by the book's title, the dilemma for queer Appalachians whose same-sex desires are matched by their love of Appalachia. The chapbook *Bliss* (winner of the 1997 Stonewall Chapbook Competition) sets the stage for Mann's dual foci in *Loving Mountains, Loving Men*, in that it toggles between poems about the natural world and poems about love and desire between men. A particularly notable theme in *Bliss* is the danger of homophobic violence and the vulnerability of the human body—and same-sex lovers—in the face of that violence. (I will discuss *Bliss* in greater depth in chapter 5, "HomePlaceBody.")

The 2005 publication of *Loving Mountains, Loving Men* as part of Ohio University Press's series on Ethnicity and Gender in Appalachia was a first within that series: while earlier books in the series had focused on race, class, and gender in Appalachia, Mann's was the first work to broach the topic of sexuality. In the book's preface, Mann identifies his aim: to more fully embrace and intermingle his identities as an Appalachian and a gay man. Although he acknowledges that "for gays and lesbians in Appalachia who want to live full lives, who want to embrace both their gay and their mountain identities, who refuse to dismember themselves in order to assimilate, it can be very difficult to find some compromise between love of the same sex and love of home," he pointedly tries to enact that balance in this mixed-genre book: "I have chosen to mix not only regional identity with sexual identity, but also poetry with prose."[72] Mann has summed up the book's approach as being "all about tension," noting that "so much of writing is about trying to make sense of your own contradictions."[73] Through this memoir in poetry and prose, Mann explores that tension and comes to terms with the seeming contradictions of being both proudly queer and determinedly Appalachian.

Reviews of *Loving Mountains, Loving Men* were overwhelmingly positive, in Appalachian regional publications as well as in national gay studies journals, with several reviewers explicitly situating Mann's work within the traditions of Appalachian and American literatures. John C. Inscoe, in a review essay that discusses Mann's book among a recent crop of Appalachian autobiographies (including Jeannette Walls's *The Glass Castle* and Jim Minick's *Finding a Clear Path*), praises *LMLM* as the "most introspective and self-analytical of all of the books under consideration here" and maintains that "no other author considered here captures both the pain and the joys of being Appalachian so adeptly, or even tries to."[74] Interviewers Dan Vera and Bo Young (in *White Crane*, a journal devoted to the connection between spirituality and queer sexualities) celebrate *Loving Mountains, Loving Men* as a "pioneering work," adding that it "is a very rich memoir, but it's as much a valentine to rural America as it is a memoir."[75] Frankie Finley, in *Appalachian Heritage*, argues that the book reveals "Mann's conscious subversion of the tradition in place since Mary Noailles Murfree: feminizing the Appalachian landscape."[76] Finley claims for Mann a central place in the history of LGBTQ Appalachian literature, calling *Loving Mountains, Loving Men* "the first book to show unhesitating pride in being both a hillbilly and a queer."[77] Both George Brosi (in *Appalachian Heritage*) and Marianne Worthington (in *Now and Then*) call the collection "ground-breaking," with Brosi going on to praise the book "because of its disarming candor, ingeniously revealing his [Mann's] innermost thoughts even about such delicate subjects as his lust and rage."[78]

Christopher B. Stewart, in the journal *West Virginia History*, also praises *Loving Mountains, Loving Men* for being "the first of its kind" and calls the book "a rich, multi-genre-autobiography" and "a needed and welcome addition to a small but growing body of regional queer literature."[79] In a critique that seems overly optimistic in hindsight, Stewart goes on to question Mann's portrayal of homophobia in Appalachia, suggesting that "the text's emphasis on intolerance as a feature of Appalachian culture" seems outdated and that "the tone of struggle may no longer be typical of the post-high school Appalachian queer experience." Although Stewart maintains that "the text is invaluable for any survey of sexuality or gender issues," he nonetheless suggests that the "broader national changes the region has participated in since the 1980s" have rendered Mann's account a relic of a past time. However, the experiences recounted by some contributors in *Electric Dirt: A Celebration of Queer Voices and Identities from Appalachia and the South* (2017), as well as the substantial list of hate crimes enumerated by House in his ASA keynote in 2014, would seem to suggest that homophobia is alive and well in Appalachia. Jeff Mann's insistence on claiming *both* his identities—as a gay man and as an Appalachian—seems as timely today as it did in 2005.

Karen Salyer McElmurray:
Strange Birds in the Tree of Heaven (1999)

Although Karen Salyer McElmurray was born in Kansas, her family's ties to eastern Kentucky were deep and strong, with her maternal grandparents in Floyd County and her paternal grandparents in Johnson County. McElmurray lived in eastern Kentucky, in Harlan County, from ages three through nine, then spent many weeks in the summer with her Granny

Salyer in Johnson County.[80] McElmurray very much identifies as an Appalachian, saying that she thinks of Appalachia as her "home-place" and that eastern Kentucky remains her "spiritual home."[81] McElmurray is active in the community of Appalachian writers: *Strange Birds* was awarded the Thomas and Lillie D. Chaffin Award for Appalachian Writing; she was the featured writer in the Spring 2011 issue of *Appalachian Heritage*; and she coedited (along with Adrian Blevins) the 2015 anthology *Walk Till the Dogs Get Mean: Meditations on the Forbidden from Contemporary Appalachia*.

McElmurray's first novel, *Strange Birds*, was first published in 1999, then republished in 2004 by the University of Georgia Press. Reviews were positive on both occasions. Three narrators tell McElmurray's story: Ruth Blue Wallen; her husband, Earl Wallen; and their son Andrew, a thirty-year-old gay man who lives with his parents in Mining Hollow, Kentucky. The novel begins *in medias res*, on August 16, 1983; subsequent achronological sections narrate events from 1926 through the present in order to reveal how the characters arrived at the opening moment. Although Ruth's voice dominates the narrative (there are nineteen Ruth sections, ten Earl sections, and only seven Andrew sections), it is Andrew whose story begins and then ends the novel. On this August night, Andrew faces a choice: whether to run away with his lover, Henry Ward, or to remain in Mining Hollow with his parents, in a house where he has been taught that his love for Henry Ward is an abomination. (As a complication of this choice, Ruth has placed a shotgun on Andrew's bed and suggested that he kill himself in order to escape his life of sin.) Reviewers and scholars have disagreed on whether this is ultimately Ruth's story, Andrew's story, or even the story of a family and its struggles.[82] Regardless, the novel is an insightful look at characters who are marked by loss and hamstrung in their attempts to love and to leave Mining Hollow. McElmurray deftly portrays the different ways that people become trapped: in relationships, in families, in geographic locations, in jobs.

Many reviewers have focused on the innovation of McElmurray's portrayal of a gay man in Appalachian fiction; when the novel was published in 1999, only a few texts—most notably Johnson's *Scissors, Paper, Rock*—had preceded it. In a review in the *Women's Review of Books*, Kathryn McKee notes that "locating a character who grapples with homosexuality in a landscape with little tolerance for individual difference is a courageous move on McElmurray's part."[83] Elizabeth Brownrigg suggests that the novel's focus is, in part, "about how Andrew, the gay son of tortured fundamentalists, can make sense of the lightness and darkness that is his inheritance."⁸⁴ In Danny Miller's review, published in 2000 in the *Journal of Appalachian Studies*, he calls the novel "relatively unique in Appalachian fiction" as the "portrayal of a gay man's life in Appalachia."⁸⁵ Miller praises McElmurray's portrayal of Andrew, stating that McElmurray "is intuitive and perceptive of the gay experience" and that she "gives a realistic picture of the isolation, loneliness, and fear that Andrew feels; the excitement and passion of first love; and the gay subculture that Henry and Andrew experience in the gay bars in Huntington, West Virginia."⁸⁶

The novel's lyrical prose seemingly inspired the most debate among critics. Miller declares that "one of the greatest strengths of the novel is McElmurray's beautiful language, which seems almost Biblical or mystical in its lyricism."⁸⁷ A brief review in the *Dictionary of Literary Biography Yearbook: 1999* calls her language "richly poetic and layered,"⁸⁸ while a reviewer in the *Lambda Book Report* notes the novel's "poetic language reminiscent of Thomas Wolfe."⁸⁹ Yet *Publisher's Weekly* calls this same prose "uneven—inspired in places and flat in others," while a reviewer in the *Chicago Tribune* seems to agree with this mixed assessment: "The novel's sensuousness . . . is its greatest strength. It works best, however, when it leaves the realm of overblown and arty emotional abstraction, which McElmurray's prose stumbles into."⁹⁰ In a 2011 interview, McElmurray noted that she began her writing life as a poet, and that this background marked her work in *Strange Birds*: "I always write in this sort of lyric, lush way, and I think sometimes I can get carried away with that and really in love with the sound of my own language."⁹¹

McElmurray has said that the fictional world of the novel has its origins in the "ghosts of real people and events," especially in the portrayal of Andrew: "Andrew is a combination of . . . my cousin Greg, and another Eastern Kentucky boy I once knew, one called 'an abomination in the eyes of God' because of his love for men."⁹² The novel's portrayal of Andrew is complex, thanks to the interior monologues of his seven sections. The reader sees through Andrew's eyes as he feels the first stirrings of an attraction to another man (a traveling preacher); as he enters and then flees a coal mine (trying to follow in his father's footsteps); as he searches for Henry in a Huntington nightclub; and as he escapes his parents' home and rides off into the night, a passenger in Henry's car, bound for Florida and a new life. Throughout the novel, the reader also has a close-up view of Andrew's self-contempt, the internalized messages of his mother ("abomination, abomination") and his father ("Act like a man, my father told me").⁹³

Alison Bechdel: *Fun Home: A Family Tragicomic* (2006)

When Bechdel's memoir-in-graphic-novel-form *Fun Home: A Family Tragicomic* was published in 2006, it made the *New York Times* bestseller list and received glowing reviews in the *New York Times Book Review*. In this graphic memoir, Bechdel describes her family, the family business (a funeral home), her sexual coming-of-age, the suspicious circumstances surrounding her father's death (maybe accidental but probably suicide), and the revelations about her father that followed after she came out to her parents. The musical theater version of *Fun Home* was a finalist for a Pulitzer Prize for Drama in 2014, and the 2015 Broadway production was nominated for twelve Tony Awards, winning five, including Best Musical. It has also become something of a sensation within academia. Scholar Hillary Chute's prediction, in a late-2006 piece in *Modern Fiction Studies*, that *Fun Home* "is sure to soon become an important reference point in academic discourse on graphic narrative" has undoubtedly come to pass.[94] Its allusion-laden text (with references to Proust, Joyce, Camus, and others) has led to its regular appearance on college syllabi and made it the subject of books, articles, conference presentations, and an academic conference (in France).

Discussions of the text and of its author frequently mention Bechdel's upbringing in a rural area: in "small-town Pennsylvania" or "a rural Pennsylvania town at the foot of the Appalachians" or "the tiny, rural town of Beech Creek, Pennsylvania," a town in Clinton County, solidly within the regional borders established by the ARC.[95] Although *Fun Home* is the story of a young woman growing up in a small Appalachian town, the book is rarely discussed in the context of Appalachian literature. Bechdel herself uses a form of the word "Appalachia" in the book only twice: once while describing a movie she saw with her father ("The movie was good. It was about how Loretta Lynn makes it out of Appalachia to become a big Country-Western star") and another while discussing the topographical isolation of her hometown: "The Appalachian ridges—many longer than Hadrian's Wall—historically discouraged cultural exchange."[96] More frequently, she describes Beech Creek's location as "right on the Allegheny Front," using "Allegheny" a number of times throughout the text. Most scholars note the Appalachian setting briefly, if at all. Scholar Fiorenzo Iuliano addresses the significance of Appalachia within the text in somewhat more depth when he suggests that Appalachia is almost un-reproduceable for Bechdel: "The impossibility of reproducing the open space of the region makes maps necessary, as abstract syntheses of an area that cannot be graphically and symbolically displayed otherwise."[97] None of these treatments of *Fun Home* appear in Appalachian studies journals, nor do they focus their arguments on issues of Appalachia. In fact, one scholar dismisses the significance of Bechdel's Appalachian upbringing as soon as he mentions it, noting that although "Alison Bechdel grew up in a rural Pennsylvanian town at the foot of the Appalachians, what is more important, however, is that she did so in an imposing Gothic Revival house, a downright mansion."[98]

The most sustained discussion of *Fun Home* as an Appalachian text is in Scott Herring's 2010 book, *Another Country: Queer Anti-Urbanism*, in which Herring argues that Bechdel's Appalachian origins (and her father's as well) are intertwined with the book's meditations on identity and loss. Herring frames *Fun Home* as a text in which Bechdel comes to terms not only with her father's death but also with her own metronormative impulse to reject Beech Creek, Pennsylvania. Herring recounts Bechdel's intentional stripping away of her accent, described in *Fun Home* as "my deracination" that was "kindly abetted by various friends at college."[99] (This ironic commentary appears above a panel showing a college friend mocking Bechdel's accent.) Although Herring characterizes this among the various ways that Bechdel separates herself—physically, linguistically—from her origins, he argues that we should read these as "testaments—rather than as disavowals—of deep loss."[100] Pointedly, the losses he enumerates include not only the loss of her father but also the loss of her roots in Appalachia: "the traumatic loss of Bechdel's 'bumpkinish' father, the loss of her Appalachian accent, the loss of her incorporated town, the loss of her rural central Pennsylvania habitus."[101] Ultimately, Herring argues, *Fun Home* simultaneously "mourns not just Bruce, but the urbane foreclosures that cast ruralized areas like Beech Creek as the outer darkness."[102]

Although Bechdel rarely uses the term "Appalachia" in *Fun Home*, details in the text will prove recognizable to those who are familiar with Appalachia and its history. Bechdel pointedly emphasizes how her hometown and the surrounding region have been marked by a culture of extraction—specifically of timber and of coal—and by the boom-and-bust cycles that accompany such an economy. Early in the book, when describing her family's home, Bechdel notes, "Our Gothic Revival house had been built during the small Pennsylvania town's one brief moment of wealth, from the lumber industry, in 1867. But local fortunes had declined steadily from that point."[103] Later in the book, we see that the extraction economy has shifted to coal, when Bechdel describes a 1970s childhood trip to the family's deer camp, "out in the forest of the Allegheny Plateau.... Now it was gouged with vast strip mines. My brothers and I were excited about seeing the monstrous shovels that tore off whole mountaintops."[104] A few pages later, Bechdel notes the toll that mining and industry have taken on the environment: "Our sun rose over Bald Eagle Mountain's hazy blue flank.... And it set behind the strip mine-pocked plateau ... Typically with some degree of pyrotechnic splendor, due to particulates from the pre-Clean Air Act paper mill ten miles away. With similar perversity, the sparkling creek that coursed down from the plateau and through our town was crystal clear precisely because it was polluted. Mine runoff had left the water too acidic to support life of any kind."[105] Bechdel's emphasis on these environmental costs helps to mark *Fun Home* as a text about an Appalachian childhood.

Bechdel also describes aspects of her family life—and of her father's seemingly deep ties to Beech Creek—that mark *Fun Home* as the story of an Appalachian family. As Loyal Jones reminds us in his landmark essay, later expanded into the book *Appalachian Values*, Appalachians are known for "Love of Place" and their reluctance to leave their homeplace: "Sense of place is one of the unifying values of mountain people, and it makes it hard for us to leave the mountains, and when we do, we long to return."[106] Alison Bechdel's memoir emphasizes the tendency—in her father and her father's family—to stick close to home, demonstrated by two maps on facing pages. In one, Bechdel illustrates that the landmarks of her father's life (his grave, the site where he died, the house where he raised his family, and the farm where he was born) were all located within a one-and-a-half-mile radius. In the other, with the notation that "many of his relatives displayed a similar reluctance to stray," Bechdel shows the proximity of the homes of her Bechdel relatives, with eight different close family members (her grandmother, three aunts, two uncles, and two cousins) all living within a few houses of her own childhood home.[107] In contrast to her own "deracination" (literally, the removal of her roots), Bechdel notes, "But my father was planted deep."[108]

Although Bechdel speculates about whether a life in an urban center might have saved her father by giving him a different (uncloseted) life, she concludes, "I can't really imagine him anywhere but Beech Creek."[109] In Herring's discussion of *Fun Home*, specifically a chapter entitled "Queer Infrastructure," he reads the narrative alongside the history of the US interstate highway system, especially I-80—which, as Bechdel notes in *Fun*

Home, "on its way from Christopher Street to the Castro, . . . passed only four miles from our house."[110] Herring argues that the nation's "'queer infrastructure'—the six-lane highways, the cloverleaves, the county roads, the suspension bridges, the no passing zones, the alleyways, the tollways, the stop signs, the exit ramps" have fostered metronormativity by furthering "the stereotype of the rural as a place of isolation, 'suspicion, persecution, and secrecy.'"[111] In a letter from her father that Bechdel reproduces in *Fun Home*, Bruce Bechdel defends the rural, noting that although he didn't go to New York City until he was twenty, "there was not much in the Village that I hadn't known in Beech Creek."[112] By the end of *Fun Home*, Bechdel seems to have made peace with the many uncertainties—epistemological and otherwise—explored in the text, just as Bruce Bechdel clearly came to his own peace with "the gravitational tug of Beech Creek."[113] As Herring observes of *Fun Home*, "What's remarkable, then, is how the book learns to tolerate the uncertainties of why people live where they do."[114]

Carter Sickels: Essays and Novel, *The Evening Hour* (2012)

Although the tradition of LGBTQ Appalachian literature has been building for decades, that conversation has only recently included work by and about transgender Appalachians. Writer Carter Sickels, a transgender man, has been a powerful voice in that conversation since 2012, when he began publishing essays and fiction. Sickels was not born in Appalachia, but his family ties to the region made him feel a connection: "My grandparents and most of my family lived in southeast Ohio, in the foothills of the Appalachian Mountains, and I spent a lot of time there as a kid. And as an adult, I visited whenever I could."[115] As an adult, his affiliations with Appalachia have deepened, inspired in part by the research he did in West Virginia for his debut novel, 2012's *The Evening Hour*, set in a small town in West Virginia where the twin scourges of mountain-top removal and opioid addiction stunt the lives and diminish the opportunities of the book's characters.[116] Sickels now makes his home in Kentucky, where he serves on the faculty at Eastern Kentucky University and teaches as part of the Bluegrass Writers Studio.

Through his essays and fiction, Sickels calls attention to the challenges facing queer Appalachians, especially those in the transgender community during the period of their gender transitions. For example, in his essay "Johnson City," Sickels describes accompanying a transgender friend on a trip home to visit family in East Tennessee, illuminating the pitfalls posed for a transgender person by family gatherings. In those circumstances, pronouns and family pictures carry the power to wound. In "Johnson City," Sickels also highlights the dangers of public spaces for non-gender-conforming individuals. About stopping at a rundown country gas station, Sickels writes, "Sometimes that's how it is when you walk into a straight space, especially in rural America—you know you don't belong, and they know it too."[117]

Sickels himself came out as a transgender man during the period surrounding his debut novel's publication. He has described this time as "complicated, but for the most part, positive. . . . I do think there is a lot of overlap—coming out with my first novel, and coming out as trans. You're sharing this vulnerable part of yourself with the public."[118] Although the protagonist of *The Evening Hour*, Cole, has had relationships with both men and women, Sickels resists a label for Cole's sexuality: "For me, the crucial question isn't so much about whether Cole is gay or not. With his upbringing and the environment he grew up in, it would have been impossible for him to identify as gay."[119] Like others of the writers whose works were profiled earlier, Sickels has emphasized that he wishes to call attention to queer lives lived in rural spaces: "You rarely see gay characters who are living in rural areas in contemporary fiction. Not all queers want to live in cities. People stay in small towns for different reasons, but sometimes they stay because this is home, because they love the land, they feel this deep connection."[120] In his 2020 novel *The Prettiest Star*, Sickels further explores that connection through the perspective of an expatriate Appalachian queer man who looks to return to his Appalachian hometown after watching his chosen family in New York City be decimated by AIDS. Sickels's work promises to continue to call attention to the challenges facing the queer Appalachian community.

Silas House: *This Is My Heart for You* (2012) and *Southernmost* (2018)

Surrounding the release of Silas House's 2018 novel *Southernmost*, it was frequently characterized as "his first explicitly gay Appalachian novel," as it was described in an article that compared the forthcoming novel with House's prior work.[121] In a June 2018 interview, House describes *Southernmost* as his first time writing about his sexuality, noting, "I had never written about being gay. It just seemed like the right time to do that."[122] *Southernmost* follows evangelical preacher Asher Sharp, whose defense of two gay men and impassioned sermon in favor of tolerance lead to the loss of both his pulpit and custody of his beloved son, Justin. Sharp must contend with all that his religion and his culture have taught him about homosexuality, and he embarks on a quest to find his older brother, whom Sharp had rejected a decade before when the brother came out as gay.

For an "explicitly gay" novel, *Southernmost* contains no explicit material and few gay characters. House has said that he "didn't want to write another 'coming out' story" and that he "thought it could resonate in a bigger way if I wrote about a person who is evolving and changing the way they think about an issue like this."[123] House has also noted that, although he "did want to write a book about gay issues," he found it both more challenging and, potentially, more impactful to *not* write from the perspective of a gay character: "I thought it was way more interesting to write from the point of view of a person who is struggling with the issue, a straight person who is evolving on this issue."[124] House's novel is not threatening, not explicit, and pointedly *not* written from the perspective of a queer character, making it more likely to be palatable to a straight audience than to give queer Appalachian teens a character with whom they could identify.

Certainly, *Southernmost* garnered accolades within Appalachia (the 2019 Weatherford Award for Fiction) and nationally, including being longlisted for the Carnegie Medal for Fiction. However, despite House's assertion that *Southernmost* was his first attempt to write about his sexuality, I would argue that House's 2012 play *This Is My Heart for You* is his first, and his most important, contribution to date to LGBTQ Appalachian literature. The play follows Jesse, a young gay Appalachian man who "doesn't love himself yet" (as the stage directions to scene 1 tell us). Jesse is the first of the play's characters to speak, and his soliloquy introduces us to the play's setting, frames the beauty of and challenges facing the region, and introduces issues and images that will recur throughout the play: kudzu, "words words words," and community. As audience members, we spend the most time with—and become deeply invested in—Jesse, as we watch his community in an uproar over an incident where two young men were ejected from a community pool for "exhibiting homosexual behavior."

When the play begins, the community remains unaware that Jesse was one of those young men. We watch Jesse endure rejection by his mother, Michelle, who cannot reconcile her faith with her son's sexuality. And we watch with trepidation as the community (including the online community, as the community's social media posts are projected on screen for the audience to see) condemns one young man (Jesse's boyfriend, Caleb) and tries to discover the identity of the *other* boy from the pool. Later in the play, the audience witnesses an attack on Caleb and Jesse, as a vigilante gang of community members (all wearing white hoodies, in a reference to Klan violence) restrains Caleb while they punch, kick, and spit on Jesse. The audience then watches Jesse heal (inside and out), watches Jesse and his father reconcile, and watches as Jesse and his chosen family resolve to move forward. By crafting a play in which the audience cares about and identifies with a young gay Appalachian man, Silas House has given us an Appalachian play with an openly gay main character, and he has crafted a work that marks his first contribution to LGBTQ Appalachian literature.

The reception of and reaction to this play are instructive in helping us think about the stakes, even now, for Appalachian authors and artists who choose to address this important topic. As House notes in the "From the Playwright" essay that accompanied the play's 2014 publication, "I received hate mail and death threats about 'my gay play'" once news of the play's content began to circulate. House acknowledges that he had been "afraid of the subject matter" because he expected that he would receive hate mail and "that people would get mad at me for writing it."[125] House's language is echoed by Octavia Biggs, director of a 2019 production of the play at Morehead State University, who wrote in her "Director's Note" that "I was afraid" when first approached about producing this play. Biggs worried about both the student-actors in her traveling company—"sending my college students into communities that may not be receptive to the themes and subject matter of this play"—and how this play would affect her own ability to do work in the community "with children and their families." Ultimately, reading the play caused Biggs to be "more attentive to the plethora of stories emerging from middle school aged children and older—stories filled with confusion, fear, sadness, and hatred," and she chose to produce the play in order to "potentially offer voices to those who have not found theirs" and "to **break down and dismantle barriers.**"[126]

In the performance that I attended (November 17, 2019, at Morehead State University), the play's power was apparent: numerous audience members were wiping away tears (myself included), and some scenes—especially of the beating and of Jesse's rejection by his mother—were excruciating to watch. It seemed clear to me that a number of audience members had endured similar violence and rejection, or at least loved someone who had. In *This Is My Heart for You*, Silas House has given us a work that has the power to move an audience, to provoke a powerful communal experience in real time, and to elicit an audience's identification with a queer Appalachian man whose experiences and beliefs might be very different than their own. This play is a powerful and much-needed addition to LGBTQ Appalachian literature.

3

Visibility and Seeing

Photography in LGBTQ Appalachian Literature

It is not surprising to find a preoccupation with visibility and seeing in any literature—Appalachian or not, gay or straight or none of the above—due to what one scholar has described as "a long-standing Western ideological bias toward vision. The empiricist belief whereby the ability to visualize almost becomes synonymous with understanding."[1] Even so, it is striking how prominently LGBTQ Appalachian literature emphasizes the importance of vision, including imagery of seeing and being seen, references to light, and the central role of photography and photographers. This pattern is apparent most notably in the work of novelists and essayists Dorothy Allison, Carter Sickels, Lisa Alther, Fenton Johnson, and Karen Salyer McElmurray; graphic memoirist Alison Bechdel; and poet Maggie Anderson. This pervasiveness surprised me, particularly the importance of photographs and home movies (or home video) to many of the texts. These texts represent issues of visibility and seeing (including through a camera's lens) as key to queer Appalachians, embodying their quest for recognition and their desire to forge their own identities rather than be defined by a censuring society. By making photography and photographers essential features of their literary works, Appalachian authors invoke questions of identity and challenge the way certain subjects are rendered invisible within Appalachian and American cultures.

This emphasis on vision and visibility is a predictable result of the overall invisibility of queer Appalachians. Queer theorist Jack Halberstam and others have noted that rural queer people tend to be absent from popular representations of homosexuality, a phenomenon that Halberstam called "metronormativity."[2] Appalachian writer and editor Jason Howard echoed this assessment when he commented, in a 2016 interview on Salon, that "by a lot of people's notions, gay people only live in cities—when we both know that there are plenty of gay people growing up in rural areas that have an experience that looks different."[3]

In another form of invisibility that compounds the metronormative erasure of queer Appalachians, Appalachians in general tend to be largely invisible within American popular culture and the national conversation. When visible, Appalachians most often figure as objects of ridicule (*Buckwild*, *Squidbillies*), as objects of pity and scorn (such as in images of the War on Poverty or other "poverty porn"), and more recently as objects of politico-touristic fascination (as wide-eyed visitors describe their sojourns into "Trump country").[4] Of course, Elizabeth Catte (in *What You Are Getting Wrong about Appalachia*) and the contributors to *Appalachian Reckoning* have pushed back against this scopophilic obsession with Appalachia and with its supposedly homogeneous politics.[5] Yet Appalachians so frequently become the object of viewers' gaze, as they did again recently with the release of Ron Howard's version of *Hillbilly Elegy*.

The prominence of photographs and photography in LGBTQ Appalachian literature can be attributed both to photography's key position within the heteronormative family and to the complicated relationship between Appalachians and photography, an art form that has been used as a means of objectification, colonization, and ridicule of Appalachians by sometimes well-meaning people, often (but not always) those from other regions.[6] Art historian Julia Ballerini notes in her essay "Photography as a Charitable Weapon: Poor Kids and Self-Representation" that photography chronicling poverty, including poverty within Appalachia, often bears a strong resemblance to the descriptions by "nineteenth-century explorers among 'primitive' peoples that are so much a part of Western colonialist ventures."[7] Ballerini reminds us that photography has served as a tool of objectification, noting (in 1997) that "until a little over a decade ago, photographs on display in major venues were *of* the poor and exclusively by adults, mostly professionals. Even outside the art world, the camera was rarely handed over to those who are usually deemed the appropriate objects of representation."[8] Appalachian photographers have worked to undermine this power structure, including West Virginia photographer Roger May who, through his Looking at Appalachia project founded in 2014, collects photographs of Appalachia made by Appalachians: "Drawing from a diverse population of photographers within the region, this new crowdsourced image archive will serve as a reference that is defined by its people as opposed to political legislation."[9]

The objectifying function of photography is compounded, for queer Appalachians, by photography's function of upholding the heteronormative family. In *Family Frames: Photography, Narrative, and Postmemory* (1997), scholar Marianne Hirsch notes "photography's connection to the family, its inscription in family life and its perpetuation of familial ideology."[10] Some of the texts discussed in this chapter—the work of Carter Sickels and Lisa Alther's *Kinflicks*, most notably—highlight photography's tendency to perpetuate heteronormative family ideologies, while other texts including Alison Bechdel's *Fun Home: A Family Tragicomic* and Dorothy Allison's *Two or Three Things I Know for Sure* reveal photography's capacity to rupture those seemingly monolithic family ideologies and narratives. In interrogating photography's role within the heteronormative family narrative, each of these texts employs the power that Hirsch attributes to "meta-photographic texts which place family photographs into narrative contexts, either by reproducing them or describing them: novels and short stories, fiction and documentary films, . . . autobiographies and memoirs"; Hirsch argues that those meta-photographic texts "both expose and resist the conventions of family photography and hegemonic family ideologies."[11] Therefore, the LGBTQ Appalachian literature discussed in this chapter undermines the hegemonic portrayal of Appalachians as well as the hegemonies of the heteronormative family narrative.

In contemporary visual culture, queer photographers from Appalachia and beyond have begun to reexamine the history of photography and its resonances of power and objectification; they've worked to reappropriate the photographic image and to undermine the erasure of the queer subject. For the Spring 2015 issue of *Aperture* photography magazine, the "Queer" issue, Stanford professor and photographer Richard Meyer was asked to respond to the prompt "Queer photography?" In his comments, Meyer makes clear that contemporary queer photographers have been engaged in excavating "the sexual and subcultural imagery" that has been occluded or erased by normative cultures.[12] Meyer describes queer photographers who have, among their projects, worked to reveal "what has been submerged that might yet be excavated or allowed to emerge."[13]

Photographs in the queer-themed work of contemporary Appalachian authors metaphorically represent that same erasure, that same occlusion, that has rendered queer Appalachians invisible within Appalachian culture and has rendered Appalachians invisible within American culture. Thus have queer Appalachians been doubly erased: rendered a ghost of a ghost, the other within the other, an outsider among outsiders, a spectral presence within an already marginalized group. In W. J. T. Mitchell's essay "Showing Seeing: A Critique of Visual Culture," he argues that "visual culture entails a meditation on blindness, the invisible, the unseen, the unseeable, and the overlooked."[14] In Appalachian literature with LGBTQ themes, the prominence of photographs, photographers, and films is meant to leverage the power of visual culture: its ability to draw our attention to the invisible and to compel us to look.

Photographs, Family, and Documentation in the Work of Carter Sickels

Photography assumes particular importance in the work of Carter Sickels, whose essays and short stories—specifically the essays "Photograph, 2007" and "Johnson City" and the short story "Wildlife"—use photographs to document the erasures and silences that mar relationships. In Sickels's work, photographs both cause and record ruptures within Appalachian families and between generations. By calling our attention to generational ruptures that can arise when a family member comes out, transitions, or otherwise steps outside of a heteronormative pattern, Sickels evokes issues of "queer time" discussed by Jack Halberstam in his 2005 study *In a Queer Time and Place: Transgender Bodies, Subcultural Lives*. In defining queer time, Halberstam notes that queer lives may follow a different pattern, both in the day-to-day and over a lifetime, from those of their heterosexual family members: "'Queer time' is a term for those specific models of temporality that emerge within postmodernism once one leaves the temporal frames of bourgeois reproduction and family, longevity, risk/safety, and inheritance."[15] Observing that lives structured according to queer time are often rendered invisible within heteronormative culture, Halberstam notes, "I try to use the concept of queer time to make clear how respectability, and notions of the normal on which it depends, may be upheld by a middle-class logic of reproductive temporality."[16] Just as rural queer lives are often obscured within both heteronormative and queer cultures because those lives don't fit an image of queerness centered in an urban landscape, Halberstam points out that this same elision happens for queer people whose lives might be outside that "middle-class logic of reproductive temporality." Queer people, both from Appalachia and beyond, therefore face heteronormative definitions of family that can leave little room for queer family members.

In Sickels's work, he makes visible those erased lives, revealing the insufficiencies of both photographs and language in recording lives that are lived in queer time and place. Photography's ability to reveal generational ruptures is most apparent in "Photograph, 2007," an essay in which Sickels describes a photograph he made of his father and grandfather on a day when they returned together to visit the family homeplace, the "Big Farm," in southeastern Ohio near the West Virginia border. As Sickels looks at the photograph and remembers that day, he keeps coming back to what the photograph doesn't and cannot show, all the things that family members don't say to each other, or the things we never know about each other. Sickels thinks about the fact that he lives "on the other side of the country, living a life that he [my father] doesn't know much about."[17] The essay inventories all the family issues that aren't addressed or acknowledged: the deep wounds caused by his grandfather's drinking ("No one ever talked about it"), his grandfather's recently diagnosed Alzheimer's ("He [Sickels's father] was the last to admit how sick his father was"), the love between fathers and sons ("in the photograph, he [Sickels's grandfather] holds his arm stiff at his side instead of around my father, his son"), and all the wisdom and family stories that his grandfather can no longer tell ("I didn't ask him until it was too late").

The essay is haunted by loss, by the contrast between a child's perception of time ("Time stretched out forever,"[18] Sickels writes about childhood summers spent at the Big Farm) and an adult's: "Today my father understood what I wanted. He knew how quickly time passes, how easily memories disappear. 'Ready to take some pictures?' he asked." The photograph in this essay is a *memento mori*, not only preserving the memory of what has been lost but also serving as a constant reminder of squandered opportunities, of conversations not had, of confidences that were not shared. At the end of the essay, Sickels remembers the photographic moment and remarks about the photograph: "I'm hiding behind the camera, and my father and grandfather look at me through matching tinted glasses. How can people know each other so well and yet not at all? They're standing in a shadow, same as me. But a single burst of sun slices across them. I see it now. If they would have taken just a few steps across the knee-high weeds, they would have found themselves exposed in a brilliant field of light." In this passage, Sickels pinpoints the limitations of photography, which are of course determined by the limitations of vision, the limitations of understanding, and the limitations of epistemology. This photograph fails to capture the truth (whatever that is) and instead preserves the failed potential that these family members could understand each other, a potential now rendered impossible by death. If they had taken a few steps through the weeds (and aren't all family relationships choked with weeds?), they would have been in a brilliant field of light; instead, they remain in shadow.

Photographs serve a similar function in Sickels's essay "Johnson City" and his short story "Wildlife." In both texts, photographs again fail to capture "the truth" and serve as painful reminders of family disjunctions. However, in both texts, this generational rift is specifically related to the gender identification of the young Appalachian narrators: the photographs—prominently displayed in the homes of parents and grandparents—show the characters before their gender transitions. Thus, these photos are emblematic of the characters' alienation from their families, especially from older generations, and memorialize an earlier time when these transgender men were uncomfortable in their own skins, reminders for a character that the version of himself in family memories is not the person he believes himself to be.

Using language pervaded by imagery of sight, Sickels's 2014 "Johnson City" describes a trip with a transgender classmate, Stephen, to Stephen's family's home in Johnson City, Tennessee. Stephen tells Sickels not to call him Stephen in front of his eighty-one-year-old grandmother: "They'd seen each other many times since Stephen started physically transitioning, and his grandmother never asked questions. As long as she didn't say anything, Stephen wasn't going to either. 'I guess people see what they want to see,' he said."[19] Sickels, who at the time of the essay's events hadn't yet changed his name "or started using male pronouns" and who writes, "I didn't call myself transgender, not yet," is very concerned with whether he was "seen" (understood) as a man or a woman by the people they encounter on the trip. When they stop at a gas station, Sickels feels uneasy, noting that "sometimes that's how it is when you walk into a straight space, especially in rural America—you know you don't belong, and they know it too." He asks his friend Stephen "what he thought—how did that guy see me?"; he feels certain that "to others, it must have been obvious how thirsty I was for recognition and validation."

Once they arrive at Stephen's family's home, the ruptures in the family relationships become clear, highlighted by photographs. After dinner on that first evening, they look at family pictures, with Stephen's mother consistently referring to Stephen by his deadname and as a "she." The photos show moments that are understandably precious to parents, treasured family memories, but ones that are painful for Stephen because they depict him as a girl: "In one of them, he wore a bunny costume for a dance class: a black leotard and silky pink bunny ears, long hair pulled in a ponytail."[20] In the language of this essay, vision is equated with understanding: "He [Stephen] wanted them to know who he was, he wanted to be seen." Later in the essay, Stephen describes another rupture within the family that he attributes to his gender transition: " 'I miss being able to go to family things,' he said. 'All my mom's side of the family lives in Virginia, and we used to have these big Thanksgivings. I can't do that now because everyone will know.' He paused. 'I miss seeing the old people in my family.' " In "Johnson City," the photographs mark the fissures between the generations, revealing the loss of family connections. The photographs remind Stephen that the older members of his family do not understand him and do not see him as he sees himself. Yet the dilemma for the parents is also clear: these are the only photographs that they have, or can possibly have, of their child's childhood, and hiding them would occlude part of Stephen's history. By focusing on photographs in "Johnson City," Sickels reminds us of the centrality of family relationships to Appalachians and the way that issues of gender and sexuality can complicate (and even sever) the relationships that our family photographs memorialize.

By marking the protagonist's alienation from his family, photographs play a similar role in Sickels's 2015 short story "Wildlife" (set in the Pacific Northwest but featuring a main character, Evan, who like Sickels moved there from North Carolina). Within this story, Sickels depicts both photographs and language—human technologies for recording and communicating information—as failures of representation. Evan, a thirty-something transgender man, remembers that "the last time he saw his parents, only old pictures of himself hung from the walls. Sister. Daughter."[21] These pictures memorialize Evan in identities that he no longer inhabits: he is now brother, son, but is visually suspended by those photographs in discarded roles. Just as the photographs are deceptive, so too is language unable to account for Evan's gender identification. Evan notes that "it was hard to find the right words, his body moving across borders, expanding beyond the limits of language." Here, the transgender body, in its changes over time and its refusal to occupy discrete categories, exceeds the representational capacities of the photographic lens and of spoken language.

In contrast with the failures of photos and language, throughout "Wildlife" seeing is synonymous with knowing, with knowing oneself as well as being accurately identified by others. Early in the story, Evan thinks about whether strangers can identify him as a transgender man, and notes that "he had reached a place in his life where people couldn't tell by looking at him, except for other trans guys—you know your own."[22] As Evan thinks back to the time before his transition, "back when he had changed his name but still not had top surgery or started T," his thoughts linger on how he was "seen" by others and how well that correlates with his own self-perception. Then, Evan "wanted to be seen by them [other men] the way he was beginning to see himself" and was "just aching to be recognized." Even now, especially when language's failure reveals that Evan is not being perceived as a native inhabitant of "this world of men," the story's diction equates seeing with knowing. Late in the story, when a would-be lover, Billy, misgenders Evan and says, "Well, I've never been with a woman before," Evan's despair is framed in the language of sight: "But the word was an arrow inside him. Billy didn't get him. He didn't see him." Here, in a narrative world where seeing is equated with understanding, both the inadequacies of language and the old photographs merely reinscribe old misunderstandings and misidentifications, imposing old (and abandoned) identities.

Photography plays a different role in Carter Sickels's 2020 novel, *The Prettiest Star*, a novel in which the main character, Brian Jackson, uses a camcorder to make a video diary chronicling the early days of the HIV/AIDS crisis from the inside. Brian is dying and has lost his partner Shawn and many of their friends in New York City to the disease. (The video camera itself was a gift from a dying friend who was giving away all his possessions.) Brian's early videos were more celebratory, as he recalls in one of the monologues of his video diary: "documentation of my friends just living their lives. Talking, kissing, dancing . . . Footage from clubs and bars. Drag queens sashaying down the street."[23] But before he died, Shawn had suggested a more serious purpose for Brian's filming: "Shawn told me to document everything, the good and bad. He was scared our lives would be forgotten."[24]

Although uncomfortable with this documenting at first, Brian begins to see its importance, its ability to make visible the people who were largely being ignored (or worse, shunned) by health authorities and the US government at that time: "The world is ignoring us. We've got to document, even if it's just me talking to the camera in my parents' basement. . . . The world wants to silence and disappear us. Well, here I am. Look at me."[25] In one videotape that Brian's father later finds and watches, the memorial use of Brian's diary is apparent: "He [Brian's father] pressed play. And there he was. His boy, talking, smiling, looking at him. Then, he wasn't smiling. He read the names of the dead. Don't forget. Say their names."[26] Brian's use of the video camera—to document the lives of queer people, to assertively insist on their existence despite the passive and active erasures of the Reagan-era's official silence about this global pandemic—turns photography into a tool to upend the heteronormative erasure of queer lives. As Brian explains to his little sister, Jess, the video camera allows Brian to document "how random things are, and you know, like, there's not one way of being. . . . The camera is my other set of eyes."[27]

Home Movies and the Heteronormative Family in Lisa Alther's *Kinflicks*

Like the photographs in Sickels's earlier short stories and essays, in Alther's 1976 comic novel *Kinflicks* (the earliest text included in this study), photography is closely associated with the heteronormative family. In *Kinflicks*, protagonist Ginny Babcock Bliss travels to her childhood home in Hullsport, Tennessee (a thinly veiled version of Alther's native Kingsport), to visit her dying mother, who is known only as "Mother" or "Mrs Babcock" throughout the novel.[28] The narrative alternates between chapters set in the present (Ginny's tending to her mother, encountering old acquaintances, and living in her now-vacant childhood home, as well as passages of interior monologue from Ginny's dying mother) and Ginny's past, as she recalls her teenage years and high school romances in Hullsport, her college years at Worthley, her life in Vermont as part of a lesbian cooperative farm, and her subsequent (and now crumbling) marriage to the inaptly named Ira Bliss. As Ginny tries to come to terms with her mother and with mortality (her mother's as well as her own), Ginny's thoughts dwell on her toddler daughter Wendy, wondering whether Ira will ever let her see Wendy again. Amid these meditations on family, sex, and death, Ginny looks through old family photographs and remembers her mother's obsession with making home movies, which Ginny and her brothers dubbed "Kinflicks."

In *Kinflicks*, photography connects Ginny to the heteronormative nuclear family, an association established both through Mrs Babcock's home movies and her devotion to family photographs. As Ginny recalls of her childhood, "Mother had many photographs, matted in eggshell white and framed in narrow black wood, on the fireplace mantel in her bedroom. As I was growing up, she would sit me on her lap and take down these yellowed cracked photos and tell me about the people in them."[29] It is these same photographs that Mrs Babcock misses deeply while she's in the hospital and that later prove so comforting when Ginny brings them to decorate her hospital room: "Mrs Babcock settled herself in bed and gazed with affection at the faces in the photographs."[30] Ginny herself continues this intergenerational connection through photographs when, worried about her maternal bond with her own daughter and concerned that "Ira was doing his best to make Wendy forget her," Ginny retrieves photos from one of Mrs Babcock's albums, "a shot of Ginny as a baby in a white dress being held by her own mother, and another of Wendy as a baby being held by Ginny," and mails them to Wendy.[31]

Mrs Babcock's "Kinflicks" further solidify the novel's connection between photography and the nuclear family, and they also evoke the significance of home movies within the history of the American family and within evolving patterns of American leisure and consumerism. As Patricia Zimmerman makes clear in *Reel Families: A Social History of Amateur Film* (1995), "by the early 1960s amateur film had become firmly ensconced within the patriarchal bourgeois nuclear family."[32] The popularity of home moviemaking in the US in the 1950s and '60s is a predictable result of the simultaneous post–WWII booms in babies and the economy, booms that resulted in consumers with both the disposable income to buy movie cameras and children to film with them: "Children constituted one of the most pervasive amateur-film subjects."[33] Mrs Babcock's use of her camera (identified by Ginny as a Kodak M24 Instamatic, one of the 8mm cameras whose popularity drove the spread of home moviemaking[34]), fits this familial, child-focused pattern perfectly. As Ginny recalls, "Her mother had always been addicted to home movie-making and had choreographed the upbringing of Ginny and her brothers through the eyepiece of a camera, eternally poised to capture on Celluloid those golden moments—the first smile, the first step, the first tooth in, the first tooth out, the first day of school, the first dance, year after tedious year."[35] Mrs Babcock's filming focuses on her children's developmental milestones like those just listed as well as on events that feature Ginny playing a socially endorsed feminine role, such as twirling a flag with the Hullsport High

School marching band or crowning her successor as Persimmon Plains Burly Tobacco Festival Queen. The Babcock family's Kinflicks, even the name of which yokes the concepts of family—*kin*—and movies—*flicks*, embody the ideological strictures of the heteronormative nuclear family and its clearly defined gender roles.

Yet photographs and home movies seem to disappear from the narrative entirely when Ginny—at the encouragement of her lover Eddie (Edna)—drops out of contact with her family, and later moves to a cabin in Vermont where she establishes a collective farm with Eddie and a few female friends. Alther's novel satirizes equally every region where Ginny lives and every facet of American life she inhabits. This satire is especially pointed at Ginny herself when she decides to "sever all ties with my reactionary family . . . thereby liberating myself with one deft hack from the net of capitalist hang-ups they had cast over me" although still living off the dividend checks from her trust fund.[36] Part of Ginny's new life, her relationship with Eddie, is explicitly framed as a resistance to the patriarchy: "Eddie took further comfort in the fact that we were boycotting one aspect of the corrupt death-dealing male power structure that was perpetrating all the misery in the world by seeking our sexual fulfillment elsewhere."[37] If, as scholars of photography have argued, portrait photography documents "the sitter's belief in a propitious future" and "belief in the continuity of familial generations,"[38] then Ginny's estrangement from her family of origin renders family photos beside the point.

The novel builds a powerful connection between photography, the heteronormative family, and time, particularly through the symbolism of Mrs Babcock's family photos. When she is hospitalized, before Ginny brings her the family photos and her treasured clock, Mrs Babcock's internal narration makes clear that the absence of her photographs has led to a sense of rupture with her past:

> She knew the date only by counting backward to some significant date in the recent past—a birthday or a holiday, some milepost on the calendar. . . . But here in the hospital there was nothing to look back on, to count forward from, with pleasure. There were no photos around to remind her of the children as babies, or of Wesley as a handsome young army officer, or of her wild white-haired father, or of any of the dozens of people that popped into her mind associatively at

home. At home she could spend hours doing nothing but strolling through the rooms recalling incidents from the past. Here in this gleaming hospital, here in this anonymous green room, she had no past.[39]

This passage situates photography within a traditional family structure and a familial vision of time, focused on procreation and on the family's replicating itself. The photos mentioned are of Mrs Babcock's children, of her husband (the father of her children), and of her own father, and are emblematic of the "ages of man" vision of human life: childhood, mature adulthood, old age. For Mrs Babcock, these family photographs help to orient her in time and document her ties to a family and thereby to a bloodline, to the generations of people whose work and perseverance and procreation gave rise to one's own generation.

Mrs Babcock's concept of time reveals a merging of calendar time and familial time, measured by birthdays and holidays and by special times spent with loved ones. As such, this is heteronormative time, clearly distinct from the "queer time" that Halberstam describes in *In a Queer Time and Place*. In Halberstam's account, "queer uses of time and space develop, at least in part, in opposition to the institutions of family, heterosexuality, and reproduction," and queer time "is also about the potentiality of a life unscripted by the conventions of family, inheritance, and child rearing."[40] Of course, one of the novel's ironies lies in Ginny's reliance upon her inheritance while living outside of heteronormative time.

The contrast between queer time and heteronormative time is emphasized through the structure of *Kinflicks*, in its alternating chapters of first-person narration (by Ginny, set in her teenage years through her recent breakup with Ira) and third-person narration (set in contemporary Hullsport with free indirect discourse filtered through Ginny and through her dying mother). The novel alternates between scenes of the present (Ginny at her mother's hospital bedside, Ginny at the family's cabin attempting to save some motherless birds) and scenes of the past in which Ginny transitions from a classically heteronormative role (high school cheerleader dating the captain of the football team, wearing his ring, and making out in his car) to a queer existence that steps outside of heteronormative time and space: an experimental lesbian relationship with Eddie Holzer in which they rent a cabin in Vermont, subsist on soybeans for months, and try to preach family planning and abortion rights to the local heterosexuals. Then, the novel traces Ginny's self-transformation into heteronormative cliché, as the stay-at-home wife of insurance agent and snowmobile salesman Ira Bliss (and, later, mother of Wendy Bliss) who attends Tupperware parties, makes casseroles, and keeps up the Bliss ancestral family mansion.

The segments of the novel that are situated in heteronormative time are suffused with photography, home movies, and meditations on time, change, and death. In contrast, when Ginny is Eddie's lover and part of the "Soybean People" (as the local Vermonters dub their group), there are no photographs or clocks and no way to mark time's passage other than through the natural cycles of days and seasons. Just as photos and home movies are absent from the novel when Ginny becomes estranged from her parents, so too does time disappear. As Ginny looks back on her relationship with Eddie (during which time she cuts off contact with her parents), she identifies this period as being "outside of time," arguing that "contrary to popular belief, there are *really* three kinds of people in the world: those who wear watches, those who don't wear watches, and those who sometimes do and sometimes don't. . . . I am in the third category, but that year I was decidedly watchless."[41] Thus, while Ginny is estranged from her family of origin and is decidedly not looking to produce the next generation of Babcocks, she is not only without photographs but also outside of (heteronormative) time.

Overall, *Kinflicks* is a novel obsessed with time: with historical time, with generational time, with philosophical theories of time (while a student at Worthley, Ginny is driven to near-madness by reading Heidegger's *Being and Time*), and with clocks. One of the novel's emblems of time—and one that clearly yokes time and family together into a potent symbol—is the Babcock family heirloom clock. Even the physical appearance of the clock likens it to a family home: "On the desk itself sat her mother's most treasured possession—a small walnut clock about a foot and a half high with a peaked top to its casing like a house roof. . . . Fluted pilasters ran up the sides of the casing."[42] Moreover, this clock has functioned—more than any other family heirloom—to unify generations, and it is Ginny's clearest tie to her Appalachian heritage: "The clock had belonged to Ginny's Grandmother Hull, and to her mother before her, and so on. . . . It had sat for decades collecting coal dust on shelves and tables in small crumbling company houses in southwest Virginia mining towns, until Grandma Hull had brought it, like the household gods in ancient Rome, to Hullsport."[43] This godlike clock is referred to as though it *were* a family member—"the ancestral clock"—and seems to become a substitute, a surrogate, for the family home when Mrs Babcock offers it to Ginny as a peace offering after she has sold the family home over Ginny's objections: "But I *would* like you to have my clock, to take with you wherever you decide to go."[44] At the novel's end, after Ginny's mother has died and Ginny has cleared out her mother's house for the new owners, the clock is indeed the only memento that Ginny takes with her: no photos, no Kinflicks. Instead, "she wrapped her mother's clock in her faded Sisterhood Is Powerful T-shirt and packed it in Hawk's knapsack with her other scant belongings."[45] Ginny cushions (or contains?) this symbol of heteronormative time within a powerful symbol of the second-wave feminism of the 1970s and leaves her family home with her destination and future uncertain.

Ultimately, Alther's 1976 novel raises some of the same questions about appearance and about photography that Sickels also addresses decades later: the conundrum of photography's gifts—it preserves memories and reminds us of loved ones who are long dead—and its pitfalls—it preserves versions of the self long after we feel that we've evolved into other selves. As Ginny thinks back about her mother's Kinflicks, she recalls the many versions of herself that were recorded on these films:

> A preview of the Kinflicks of Ginny's arrivals at and departures from this airport would have shown her descending or ascending the steps of neglected DC-7s in a dizzying succession of disguises—a black cardigan buttoned up the back and a too-tight straight skirt and Clem Cloyd's red silk Korean windbreaker when she left home for college in Boston; a smart tweed suit and horn-rim Ben Franklin glasses and a severe bun after a year at Worthley; wheat jeans and a black turtleneck and Goliath sandals after she became Eddie Holzer's lover and dropped out of Worthley; a red Stark's Bog Volunteer Fire Department Women's Auxiliary blazer after her marriage to Ira Bliss.[46]

The narrative makes clear that the Kinflicks recorded Ginny's many changes in wardrobe (and lovers) and frames those as markers for her mutable identity. Much later in the novel, as Ginny looks through some of her mother's family photos, she wonders which one of these identities—which image of herself—future generations will see: "Ginny wondered what one picture her descendants would seize on to remember her by. . . . Ginny had appeared in hundreds of photos by now, in various poses and moods and modes of dress, to say nothing of the thousands of feet of Kinflicks that featured her. How would her descendants be able to settle on one shot as representative?"[47] Here, Alther highlights the very reductive nature of photography: its preservation of one moment (or, if film, a sequence of moments) in time, thereby closing off possibilities for growth, evolution, and change.

By highlighting photography's capacity to freeze one moment in time, Alther simultaneously evokes and undermines photography's most potent (yet failed) promise: to stave off the effects of time, namely change and death. Both photography and film are art forms reliant upon time (exposing the film for just the right amount of time and projecting the film's images on a screen at a very precise rate), and scholars have noted photography's preservative effect and its function as a *memento mori*, reminding us of what is gone. In Marianne Hirsch's *Family Frames: Photography, Memory, and Postmemory*, she coins the term "postmemory" to describe one's vicarious, secondhand, usually second-generational memory of someone (or something): "postmemory characterizes the experience of those who grow up dominated by narratives that preceded their birth."[48] Calling photographs "ghostly revenants," Hirsch notes their connection to postmemory: "Photographs in their enduring 'umbilical' connection to life are precisely the medium connecting first- and second-generation remembrance, memory and postmemory. . . . They affirm the past's existence and, in their flat two dimensionality, they signal its unbridgeable distance."[49]

Ginny's childhood experiences sitting on her mother's lap and hearing all the family stories while looking at family photographs are perfect embodiments of what Hirsch describes as postmemory, an experience heightened by Mrs Babcock's precise descriptions of the manner of each family member's (slightly comic, slightly grotesque) death:

> Her grandmother, Dixie Lee Hull, in a blouse with a high lace neck, who had cut her finger on a recipe card for spoon bread and had died of septicemia at age twenty-nine. Great-uncle Lester, a druggist in Sow Gap, who became addicted to cough syrup and one night threw himself under the southbound train to Chattanooga. Cousin Louella, who drove into a nest of water moccasins in an abandoned stone quarry at a family reunion in 1932. Another cousin who stuck his head out of a car window to read a historical marker about the Battle of Lookout Mountain and was sideswiped by a Mason-Dixon transport truck.[50]

96 | Doubly Erased

In light of Mrs Babcock's habit of constantly drafting and revising her own obituary, the family vacations spent doing tombstone rubbings of "unvisited gravesites of remote relations," and Ginny's father's insistence that "death to him was a sneak and a cheat who was ever vigilant to ambush the unwary," it is no wonder that Ginny declares in the novel's famous first line, "My family has always been into death."[51] As Alther reveals, while photography and film may be key totems of the heteronormative family, their preservative function is limited: they preserve images, not people or relationships. When Ginny leaves Hullsport at the end of the novel, she leaves behind the Kinflicks and instead takes the clock, abandoning the "ghostly revenants" and embracing time itself.

Appalachian Epistemology:
Photography and Artifice in Alison Bechdel's *Fun Home*

In Alison Bechdel's 2006 graphic memoir, *Fun Home: A Family Tragicomic*, we find another account of a queer young woman growing up in small-town Appalachia, specifically in Beech Creek, Pennsylvania. In *Fun Home*, through Bechdel's use of photographs and her emphasis on artifice and appearances, she calls perception itself into question. In doing so, she evokes issues of epistemology, revealing the uncertainties of how we know the things that we think we know and thereby suggesting that memory is so marked by gaps and elisions that the very nature of truth is suspect.

Like the other LGBTQ Appalachian texts that have been discussed in this chapter, Bechdel's *Fun Home* is pervaded by photographs and focused on the nuclear family. However, unlike in *Kinflicks* where photographs and home movies are the emblems of the heteronormative family, photographs in *Fun Home* both reveal fissures in Bechdel's nuclear family and embody the narrative's preoccupation with epistemology. As Bechdel explained in a 2006 interview, "In many ways photographs really generated the book. In fact the whole story was spawned by a snapshot I found of our old babysitter lying on a hotel bed in his Jockey shorts."[52] That photograph, taken by Bechdel's father Bruce of the seventeen-year-old babysitter who accompanied Bruce and the children on a family vacation, was described by Bechdel as "literally the core of the book, the centerfold."[53] Surrounded by text that narrates Bechdel's discovery of the photo, the image itself is aesthetically centerfold-like, with Roy the babysitter stretched across a rumpled bed: "The blurriness of the photo gives it an ethereal, painterly quality. Roy is gilded with morning seaside light. His hair is an aureole."[54] It is the only two-page spread in *Fun Home*, a spread that also shows a hand—presumably Alison Bechdel's—holding the photo by the corner and thus revealing the photo's border, where Bruce has blotted out the year (which would have documented Roy's being underage). As Bechdel points out, "It's a curiously ineffectual attempt at censorship. Why cross out the year and not the month? Why, for that matter, leave the photo in the envelope at all? In an act of prestidigitation typical of the way my father juggled his public appearance and private reality, the evidence is simultaneously hidden and revealed."[55]

Bechdel's use of photography in *Fun Home* foregrounds photography's inability to capture "truth," its failure to capture the complexities of a scene or of the people pictured. In doing so, Bechdel's *Fun Home* does work similar to that performed by Sickels in "Photograph, 2007," in which he explores the family dynamics—all the unsaid hurts and unasked questions—that remained invisible when the camera captured the image of himself, his father, and his grandfather at the Big Farm. Through the course of the narrative, Bechdel points out numerous failures of photographs: to capture a subject's attractiveness, to define the context of a situation, or to illuminate the nature of the relationship between a photographer and the photographic subject.

Bechdel's attempt to discern the context of a photograph is central to her discovery of the photo of Roy, which has been stored in an envelope labeled "Family," written in her father's hand. As one scholar has noted, "Roy's level of awareness remains an unanswerable question—is he sleeping? Is he posing? Were they having an affair, or was Bruce merely sneaking a photo? . . . Despite its 'documentary' nature, the truth is incomprehensible from this lone photo that Bechdel uncovers."[56] K. W. Eveleth points out that the nature of the medium of photography—and the fact that the photos in *Fun Home* are Bechdel's carefully drawn reproductions of photographs—further distances us from the originary truth of the Roy photograph: "The photograph of Roy that she reproduces is already a mediation of reality, a way of 'seeing the world through someone else's eyes,' modified irrevocably by the photographic technology used to capture it."[57] Bechdel herself—in responding to an interviewer's question about the "much more tightly rendered, 'realistic' style" of the images of photographs in the book and how they relate to "the relationship between representation and interpretation (or 'objectivity' and 'subjectivity') in the way you drew the book"—acknowledges being very intentional in the look of these photographs, and makes clear that they're included to evoke the impression of realism: "I spent a lot of time thinking about the relative ontological status of these different kinds of drawings within the universe of 'Fun Home' . . . I wanted these drawings to be clearly legible as actual, extant photographs, so I could draw on the 'objective' property of photography to ground the story in real life."[58]

In that same interview, Bechdel reiterates that her discovery of the Roy photograph was the genesis of the book, commenting, "Finding that glimpse of the parallel life my father had been leading right under our noses was like finding the key to a cryptogram." However, as *Fun Home* itself makes clear, even with this key, Bechdel is unable to discern the real behind her father's carefully cultivated artifice. Immediately following the two-page centerfold of Roy in the narrative, Bechdel includes another image that sums up the dichotomies of Bruce's dual existence as respectable father-mortician-English teacher and lover of underage boys. Bechdel reproduces a four-image strip of negatives from the envelope of vacation photos in which she found the rumpled-bed photo of Roy. The first three images are typical family vacation photos of children (eight-year-old Bechdel and her younger brothers) playing on the beach; the fourth is the unreadable photo of Roy on the bed.

In another striking juxtaposition of images, Bechdel highlights an additional shortcoming of photography—its inability to accurately capture personality and attraction. Side by side, Bechdel contrasts her father's photograph from his high school annual with an image of Zelda Fitzgerald, noting that neither photo captures the appeal of its subject: "he was more attractive than the photographic record reveals. Zelda Fitzgerald also had a fluid charm, it was said, which eluded the still camera."[59] Bechdel's phrasing here, pinpointing the limitations of "the still camera," recalls the earlier discussion in this chapter about photography's relationship to time and to that casualty of time, loss. *Fun Home*'s central chapter, a chapter whose title—"In the Shadow of Young Girls in Flower"—is taken from the second novel in Marcel Proust's *In Search of Lost Time* (*À la recherche du temps perdu*), is an extended meditation on loss. Bechdel begins the chapter by revisiting the circumstances of her father's death, then outlines her father's most intense passions: his love of gardening and his relationships with young men. Bechdel narrates her discovery of the beefcake photograph of Roy, discusses another family trip with another young and muscular babysitter (Bill), and describes her own pubescent development (which happened concurrently with her father's affairs with these young men).

On the chapter's final page, Bechdel reproduces another set of photos, including one of her father as a young man dressed in a one-piece women's bathing suit. Bechdel tries but fails to discern her father's intention, the context of the photograph, its tone, its valence, and ultimately its meaning: "He's wearing a women's bathing suit. A fraternity prank? But the pose he strikes is not mincing or silly at all. He's lissome, elegant."[60] As Bechdel tries to read this photograph, she highlights her similar efforts to read her father, including the circumstances of his death. Here, Bechdel succinctly unites photography, unknowability, and loss: "What's lost in translation is the complexity of loss itself."[61]

The novel's preoccupation with epistemology, with knowing that which is hidden and with discerning whether to trust what we think we know, focuses also on Bruce Bechdel's death and the questions it invited: Did he commit suicide, or was it an accidental death? If suicide, why? Was he distraught over his impending divorce, or simply tired of living a lie as a closeted gay man in a small Appalachian town? Bechdel is even unsure whether to categorize him as a gay man: "I shouldn't pretend to know what my father's [erotic truth] was. Perhaps my eagerness to claim him as 'gay' in the way I am 'gay,' as opposed to bisexual or some other category, is just a way of keeping him to myself—a sort of inverted Oedipal complex."[62] As Alison Bechdel demonstrates throughout *Fun Home*, Bruce Bechdel spent his time cultivating appearances: that of the family's 1867 Gothic Revival house, those of the corpses that he attends to as the local mortician, and that of his perfect-seeming family. Bechdel notes, using language that emphasizes the artifice of her family as though they were staged figures in a diorama, "When things were going well, I think my father actually enjoyed having a family. Or at least, the air of authenticity we lent to his exhibit. A sort of still life with children."[63] In all aspects of his life, Bruce Bechdel "used his skillful artifice not to make things, but to make things appear to be what they were not";[64] this text appears above a panel showing Bruce Bechdel taking a photo of his perfect-seeming family, dressed up for church. In the book's first chapter, "Old Father, Old Artificer," Bechdel characterizes her father as preoccupied with appearances and focused on achieving the illusion of perfection. Calling her father "an alchemist of appearance, a savant of surface, a Daedalus of décor,"[65] Bechdel emphasizes that despite all of her efforts to know and discover, her father had spent his life trying to dissemble and conceal.

Within *Fun Home*'s thematic emphasis on knowing, on the dilemma of epistemology, Bechdel points out the same inadequacies of language—what she refers to as "that gaping rift between signifier and signified"[66]—as she did of photographs. This inadequacy is most apparent in Bechdel's early attempts to keep a journal (see fig. 3.1). As she describes (and depicts in the reproductions of her journal pages that are included in *Fun Home*), journaling brings about "a sort of epistemological crisis" because it makes apparent to her the inadequacies of language and the uncertainties of perception: "How did I know that the things I was writing were absolutely, objectively true? All I could speak for was my own perceptions, and perhaps not even those."[67] The journal entries that Bechdel reproduces in the book contain the most quotidian events, typical of a nine-year-old's journal, such seemingly incontrovertible facts as "Christian threw sand in John's face. He started to cry," or "We watched *The Brady Bunch*. I made popcorn."[68] Yet Bechdel begins to doubt both language and perception, commenting, "My simple, declarative sentences began to strike me as hubristic at best, utter lies at worst."[69] As a result, Bechdel begins to annotate her own journal entries, carefully writing "I think" beside each sentence.

Bechdel's inscription of doubt progresses when she adopts "a shorthand version of *I think*, a curvy circumflex," and eventually "I realized I could draw the symbol over an entire entry."[70] Calling *Fun Home* "an

Figure 3.1. A panel from Alison Bechdel's *Fun Home* in which "I think" begins to multiply in her journal (141).

Visibility and Seeing | 101

extended meditation on history, memory, identity, and trauma," scholar Jared Gardner likens Bechdel's curvy circumflex to "the caret used over a variable as an estimator (used in statistics to represent the unknown); or, more familiar to humanists, like the proofreading symbol indicating where additional text should be inserted."[71] Notable in Bechdel's progression (from "I think" to drawing the circumflex over entire pages) is the intermediate step that she adopts: Bechdel begins to reserve the circumflex, her symbol of epistemological doubt, for people: "Soon I began drawing it right over names and pronouns. It became a sort of amulet, warding off evil from my subjects."[72] (See fig. 3.2.) This moment highlights the central mystery of *Fun Home*: not merely an epistemological crisis, but rather an epistemological crisis of identity. Clearly, that mystery of identity includes other people—*Fun Home* devotes many panels to the mystery of who Bruce Bechdel really was. But the mystery of identity includes the mystery of the self. While she's trying to gain greater insight into her father—his life, his sexuality, his death—Bechdel tries to also better understand herself. Notably, one of the pronouns obscured by the curvy circumflex is "I."

The deep uncertainty about identity—represented by the circumflex-obscured names and pronouns—is emblematic of the uncertainties

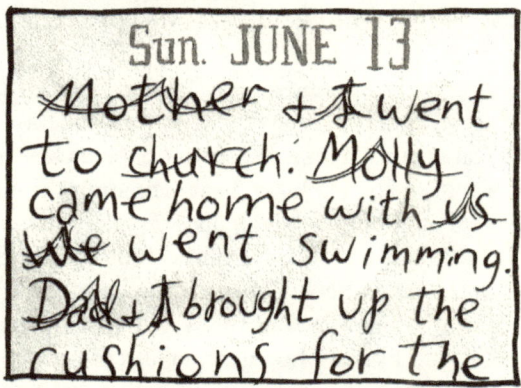

Figure 3.2. A panel from *Fun Home* showing the "curvy circumflex" written over names and pronouns in Bechdel's journal (142).

that plague Bechdel throughout *Fun Home*: the seeming impossibility of understanding other people or even oneself. In Robyn Warhol's essay "The Space Between: A Narrative Approach to Alison Bechdel's *Fun Home*," she argues that while graphic memoirs typically expand a memoirist's capability to represent the self—since the narrative includes both words and images—"this text operates through many more layers—on many more narrative levels—than two, because both the visual and the verbal subdivide into multiple separate and overlapping narrative tracks, creating narrative elements that 'work with' the space between image and words."[73] Even so, even with Bechdel's utilization of graphic memoir's affordances, identity is so difficult to capture that Bechdel can only approximate "the effect of a coherent subjectivity."[74] Bechdel's feedback loop of uncertainty is summed up in *Fun Home*'s final chapter. There, she narrates writing her parents to tell them she is a lesbian and then describes her reaction to her father's reply. In that letter, Bruce Bechdel appears to assume Alison knows about his affairs with men, and she attempts to decode his letter: "What, reduced to their simplest reciprocal form, were Dad's thoughts about my thoughts about him, and his thoughts about my thoughts about his thoughts about me? . . . He thought that I thought that he was a queer, whereas he knew that I knew that he knew that I was too."[75] Here, Bechdel's earlier assertions of "I think" have graduated into a more complicated emotional syntax of what we know, or do not know, about ourselves and our family members.

Photography in the Poetry of Maggie Anderson

In a 2004 interview, Maggie Anderson described herself as "fascinated with photography," with photography's "theoretical" quality—the fact that photographs "imitate reality."[76] In a sequence of poems in Anderson's 1986 collection *Cold Comfort*, she explores that fascination through ekphrastic poems inspired by photographs: a family photograph of her paternal grandmother as well as several of Walker Evans's photographs of Depression era–West Virginia. Much as Bechdel does in *Fun Home*, Anderson highlights the artifice of photography and the way that photographic subjects become tools employed by the photographer in the service of an artistic vision. Moreover, Anderson personalizes Evans's photographs—photographs that include scenes of West Virginia towns where Anderson's family has lived—reminding the reader that historical, documentary photographs are always already family photographs for someone. In so doing, Anderson raises key questions about the artist's appropriation of his or her subject and about the vagaries of interpretation: ultimately the reader (or viewer) can skew the artist's or poet's meaning, thus widening the gaps—of intention, interpretation, and ownership—between subject and artist and viewer.

Walker Evans, the American photographer who would later collaborate with the writer James Agee on *Let Us Now Praise Famous Men* (1941), was commissioned by the US government in the summer of 1935 "to photograph a government-built resettlement community of unemployed coal miners in West Virginia."[77] These photographs, as well as others Evans made while working for the Farm Security Administration, documented the effects of the Great Depression on people and small towns throughout the southern and midwestern US.[78] Anderson's ekphrastic poems talk back to Evans, interrogating the artifice in Evans's careful compositions, wondering whether her family members had interacted with the people in Evans's photographs, describing the present-day status of the sites in the images, and defending the people—both those pictured and those who are not—against the use that the photographer made of them.

In the most moving of these poems, such as "Among Elms and Maples, Morgantown, West Virginia, August, 1935" and "Street Scene, Morgantown, West Virginia, 1935," Anderson inserts her own absent family members into the narratives of Evans's images or explores the imagined interior lives of the photographed subjects. As poet Maxine Scates notes of "Among Elms and Maples" and "Street Scene" in a contemporary review, Anderson "suggests what the surfaces don't reveal, the lives that are blanketed by history—the lives beyond the careful compositions the photographs represent."[79] Anderson pays meticulous attention to detail, noting of "Street Scene"—a poem that describes African American women selling cakes on the street while white men "loiter" nearby and watch—that the women's faces betray their exhaustion and their careful negotiation of the racial divide: "They look away, / will not look a white man, / even with a camera, in the eyes." Similarly, in "Independence Day, Terra Alta, West Virginia, 1935," Anderson reads the expression of a young girl in the crowd to reveal the complicated dynamic between her, her mother standing beside her, and the townspeople who surround them: "She doesn't want her picture made beside her mother / . . . / She knows / what Evans doesn't: the talk behind the chance booth, / the way every gesture falls on her in a long shadow / of judgment and kin, . . ."

In other lines of these poems, it is Anderson's family members— who were living in these towns at the time but were not captured in these photographs—of whom she writes. In "Among Elms and Maples,

Morgantown, West Virginia, August, 1935," Anderson calls attention to Evans's composition and his careful placement of the camera: "Walker Evans liked standing on a hill, focusing / down so it seemed he was poised on a branch. / He liked the single telephone pole against / the flat sky, crossed off-center like a crucifix." She contrasts this precisely composed scene, with its attention to "the rough surfaces of clapboard / houses, their meshed roofs and slanted gables," to her family members' lives that were playing out—unphotographed and unacknowledged—beneath the canopy of trees: "He didn't want my mother peeling the thin skin / from tomatoes with a sharp knife, my clumsy / Aunt Grace chasing the ones she'd dropped / around the linoleum floor." Likewise, regarding the women selling cakes in "Street Scene," Anderson speculates, "My mother might have / bought from them." But, as Anderson remarks in "Among Elms and Maples," "That would be another / picture, not this one."

In an interview with Kate Long conducted at a 2004 literary festival dedicated to Anderson's work, Anderson alternately criticizes and praises Evans and these photographs, almost as though she is trying but failing to convince herself. Although she says, "I don't blame Walker Evans for those photographs. He was a wonderful photographer," she admits, "He got on my nerves a little bit. It's always awkward when we're looking at a perfectly composed picture. Evans was a fashion photographer, so even doing pictures of mining camp residents he arranges them the way he might have done in photos for *Vogue*. And when those mining camp residents are people in my family or people like those in my family, I get touchy."[80] In this statement, Anderson expresses a sentiment similar to others who have criticized the photographic tradition of objectifying Appalachians, yet she continues to waver: "But I don't blame him for the project. Also, what he did was a kind of propaganda that brought important attention to the problems of the Great Depression. It's complicated."

In two poems in *Cold Comfort*, "The Wash in My Grandmother's Arms" and "House and Graveyard, Rowlesburg, West Virginia, 1935," Anderson focuses on this discomfort of the photographic subject, compelling the reader to inhabit the position of the one being photographed and to think through the implications for those whose family members' lives have been documented and aestheticized by such photographs. In "The Wash in My Grandmother's Arms," Anderson describes a family photograph of her grandmother, a snapshot taken inside her own home. The photograph captures her grandmother's skepticism of and resistance to photography: her grandmother "squints at the camera / as if she finds photography too theoretical, / its attempt to capture history as it's made" and "resists / this fixing of the present in a beautiful nostalgia." As Anderson later said of the photograph upon which this poem was based, the photographer is clearly intruding on her grandmother's plans for the day: "She's not particularly interested in a photograph. She's got things to do. She's got washing to put on the line; she's got supper to put on the table."[81] As poet Maxine Scates has observed of this poem, in it Anderson "questions, just as her grandmother might have, had she the means, the capacity of art to fix any moment without considering the *lives* beyond the surfaces that art often comes to represent."[82] Anderson's grandmother embodies the skepticism and resistance of the photographic subject.

Anderson echoes this skepticism and resistance in "House and Graveyard," a poetic response to a Walker Evans photograph by (almost) the same title (see fig. 3.3).[83] Anderson highlights the difficulties that this

Figure 3.3. "Houses and Graveyard Rowlesburg, West Virginia," by Walker Evans. *Source*: [Houses and Graveyard, Rowlesburg, West Virginia], June 1935. Film negative, 8 × 10 in. Metropolitan Museum of Art, Walker Evans Archive, 1994 (1994.258.548).

photograph presents her—"I can't look long at this picture"—because it is the graves of her family members (and the homes of people she knows) that were so carefully framed and aestheticized in this image: "intimate for me because it focuses / on my private and familial dead." Although Anderson acknowledges the artistic merits of this image—"It's a good photograph" and is "interesting for the sharp light it throws / on poverty"—she resists it because of Evans's use of the landscape and people she loves for his aesthetic goals: "It warps my history into politics, makes art / of my biography through someone else's eyes." In the poem's final lines, Anderson gives voice to the estrangement felt by generations of Appalachians whose images have been co-opted by others for their own devices: "Walker Evans / didn't know my family, nor the distance / his careful composition makes me feel now / from my silent people in their graves." Yet Anderson's later commentary about this poem and this photograph, in the 2004 interview, emphasizes the same ethical obligations for the poet that she sees for the photographer: "the issue of appropriation, of what we have the right to take pictures of or make the subject of a poem, is always one that every artist faces to a certain extent."[84] In the poems of *Cold Comfort*, Anderson continually reminds us about the photographic aestheticization of Appalachian poverty, the beauties of the Appalachian landscape, and the deep pull of Appalachian families. Indeed, as she said of her reaction to Evans's photographs, "It's complicated."

Dorothy Allison, Photography, and Telling a (Queer) Appalachian Story

Another Appalachian writer who has much to say about objectification, photography, and the Appalachian family is Dorothy Allison. In Allison's work, particularly her novel *Bastard out of Carolina* (1992) and her memoir *Two or Three Things I Know for Sure* (1995), photographs play a central role, and Allison thereby employs the power that Marianne Hirsch attributes to "meta-photographic texts" to reveal and resist "hegemonic family ideologies." In its resistance, Allison's work resists not only the family ideologies that Hirsch describes but also other strictures—of class, gender, sexuality, and region—that would limit who has the power of self-representation, that would frame certain people as objects and others as subjects, certain people as the ones empowered to tell the story or take the picture. Scholar Katherine Henninger says that Allison's use of photographs "narrates the imbrications of gender, class, and sexuality in a visual field" and that *Two or Three Things* "speaks directly to the gendered, classed nature of southern cultured vision, in a narrative of access taken, and denied."[85] Like Carter Sickels, Lisa Alther, and Maggie Anderson, Allison explores how family photographs both reveal family fissures and tie us more closely to previous generations. And like Anderson, Allison explores and resists the photographic objectification that is the particular birthright of Appalachians.

Bastard Out of Carolina is filled with descriptions of photographs, both those taken by the novel's Boatwright family and those taken of them. *Two or Three Things* is filled with actual photographs: over thirty are included from Allison's personal collection, of her family and herself. (Although the photos are uncaptioned, there's a key to them—identifying the subject, location, and year taken—at the end of the book.) In both of these texts and other works, Allison has made clear that photographs are central for her concept of storytelling, and that understanding the difference between appearance and the truth is key to understanding her work and her life.

In her essay "This Is Our World," Allison discusses the power of photographs for her, writing, "I love black-and-white photographs, and I always have. I have cut photographs out of magazines to paste in books of my own, bought albums at yard sales, and kept collections that had one or two images I wanted near me always. Those pictures tell me stories—my own and others, scary stories sometimes, but more often simply everyday stories, what happened in that place at that time to those people."[86] Of the "constant images of happy families" that she sees in magazine ads, Allison expresses her distrust of those photos ("I do not believe those families. . . . I believe in hard-pressed families, the child huddled in fear with his face hidden") and her preference for photographs and stories that reveal a truth, even if a painful one, and especially if these make visible lives that too often have been hidden, or misrepresented: "For everyone who will tell us our work is mean or fearful or unreal, there is another who will embrace us and say with tears in their eyes how wonderful it is to finally feel as if someone else has seen their truth and shown it in some part as it should be known."[87] In a 1994 interview, Allison described how writing functions for her in a similar way: "It became the way I figured things out. When I couldn't find my story, I wrote it. . . . And so I made my own story, writing it down so that it would be real, and I could see it and step outside of it."[88]

Moreover, Allison's work has consistently demonstrated her desire to control the story that's told about her, for disenfranchised people to take back the power to represent themselves, whether that's through storytelling, photography, sexual power, government documents, or other forms of representation. As Katherine Henninger describes this effort, Allison does this "by directly engaging, critiquing, and revising the representations, especially the photographs, that have constructed her own and her characters' identities."[89] In *Bastard Out of Carolina*, Allison depicts photography's initial function as a societal weapon against the Boatwright family, including against the protagonist, twelve-year-old Bone. Bone observes that photos in the newspaper—whether candid news photos, wedding announcements, or obituaries—never flatter the Boatwrights: "We look worse than other people ever seem to look."[90] Bone's aunt attributes that issue to their class, their poverty: "The difference is money. It takes a lot of money to make someone look alive on newsprint . . . to keep some piece of the soul behind the eyes." Those newspaper photos typically show the aftermath, of wrecks, arrests, or scandals: "We're always turning up in the news," observes Bone's aunt.[91] That is later true of Bone herself: after Bone is sexually assaulted and beaten by her stepfather Glen, a news photographer lurks outside the hospital where Bone is being treated and takes a photo of Bone that then appears on the front page of the local newspaper. However, Bone's Aunt Alma repurposes the newspaper images of the Boatwright family, including this one of Bone, into a family album, embodying what Henninger calls "the power of the private self-representations, especially as embodied in family photographs and albums," that Allison explores in her work.[92]

Allison herself compiles just such an album in *Two or Three Things I Know for Sure*, weaving in photographs of her mother, her aunts and uncles, and herself, meditating on the connections between photography, memory, and story. In both this text and *Bastard Out of Carolina*, Allison self-consciously inverts the dynamic of the photographic subject and the powerful photographer. Like Maggie Anderson, Allison engages with issues surrounding the public consumption of photographic images that are a little too close to home. In Anderson's case, these images were art photographs, aestheticized images that largely documented the absence of her family—Anderson's family graveyard, "my private and familial dead"— or the public spaces, such as in "Among Elms and Maples, Morgantown, West Virginia, August, 1935," near where her family members were living private lives. In Allison's case, as she describes in *Two or Three Things I*

Know for Sure, her family was part of the tradition of the photographed, objectified Appalachian: "My family? The women of my family? We are the ones in all those photos taken at mining disasters, floods, fires."[93] Yet Allison insists on using photographs on her own terms to tell her own story: "*Two or three things I know for sure, and one of them is what it means to have no loved version of your life but the one you make.*"[94] Through the photographs included in *Two or Three Things I Know for Sure*, Allison resists not only the invisibility of queer Appalachians but also the visual stereotyping and visual exploitation of Appalachians, in which their images are co-opted and used to tell stories about, not by, them.

In one especially memorable passage of *Two or Three Things*, Allison achieves this effect through the strategic juxtaposition of powerful words and seemingly everyday images from a family album. Right before a double-page spread containing several photos of Allison and her younger sisters—including a snapshot of eight-year-old Dorothy Allison in her Easter finery, a photo of the three girls standing in front of the family's Christmas tree, and a vacation photo of two of them on a beach—Allison writes of her stepfather, "The man raped me. It's the truth. It's a fact. I was five, and he was eight months married to my mother. That's how I always began to talk about it—when I finally did begin to talk about it."[95] The layout of the book amplifies the impact of these words. These are the last words on the right-hand (recto) page; readers turn the page and finds themselves looking at photographs of the child to whom this crime happened, including two photos of five-year-old Dorothy. As Timothy Dow Adams explains, Allison has made clear that although the "apparently normal childhood pictures" of that two-page spread appeared to illustrate happy childhood moments, even those were more complicated than they appear, and Adams notes Allison's "conflicting needs both to conceal and reveal . . . the images belying the confession."[96] Scholar Katherine Henninger calls *Two or Three Things* "a feminist photo-text" whose photos "stand on the border of public and private, and they function as potent symbols of the paradoxical power of facades (representations, stories) simultaneously to permit and deny access to the 'truth.'"[97] In this section of *Two or Three Things*, Allison takes charge of the storytelling and of the images, using them to craft a truth of which she is in control.

Two or Three Things I Know for Sure ends with Allison's description of a dream that includes photographs and a home movie, happening inside a structure built of bricks that turn into words and words that turn into bricks. The dream's imagery, Allison implies, was inspired by a fan's suggestion that she should publish in hypertext: "We could put you in hypertext. . . . All the way through, people can reach in and touch a word. . . . Every time you touch a word, a window opens. Behind that word is another story. . . . All the stories you've ever told. All the pictures you've ever seen."[98] In Allison's dream, the story of her life is pictured on the wall of a museum, and the words/bricks shift and open to other images and other stories when they're touched. When she touches a scene of her mother sorting through family photographs, "the window opened onto a movie," in which she's a child again and in her mother's arms. When touched, this scene shifts to Allison's mother—as a young child—holding on to her own mother, and then to Allison's young son climbing into her arms and saying the word that had been repeated in earlier brick/window/stories: "Mama." The memoir and the dream end on this note: "I was whispering the word over and over, and it was holding me up like a loved hand. *I can tell you anything. All you have to believe is the truth.*"[99] Although Allison's work firmly rejects patriarchal family structures and ideologies that would justify the subjugation of identities on the basis of gender, sexuality, class, or other qualities, she nonetheless maintains the sustaining value of family, especially mothers, aunts, and sisters. Here, the photographs of Allison's dream operate as the "ghostly revenants" that Marianne Hirsch described as characteristic of postmemory: photographs both "affirm the past's existence and . . . signal its unbridgeable distance."[100] The photographs of Allison's dream, like the photographs in her texts, are reminders of the past but serve as building blocks providing the raw material to make new truths, tell new stories.

The Pictureman in Appalachian LGBTQ Fiction

The year after Evans made this photograph in West Virginia, he and James Agee set off for Appalachian Alabama to do the work that would later become the book *Let Us Now Praise Famous Men* (1941), a study of the effects of sharecropping on three families. The book's photographs—by Evans—emphasize the families' poverty, while the prose—by Agee—chronicles the deprivations of the families' lives and features himself as a character in the narrative, presumably as a surrogate for the reader, reacting to the food, people, and accommodations. Agee's description of how the photographs were taken would seem to confirm Appalachians' suspicions of photographers from outside the region. Agee describes Evans taking photographs secretly, without the knowledge or consent of his subjects, before they had readied themselves or their children to be photographed: "you washed the faces of your children swiftly and violently with rainwater . . . but Walker made a picture of this; you didn't know; you thought he was still testing around."[101] Agee notices the discomfort and powerlessness of the mother, yet he and Evans proceed with the photographs regardless: "to you it was as if you and your children and your husband and these others were stood there naked in front of the cold absorption of the camera in all your shame and pitiableness."[102] Agee even critiques the poor quality of the "Sunday best" clothing that one of the daughters quickly slips on: "one could only tell it from a really good party-dress by the intense sleaziness and fragility of the cloth, through which your body was visible, and the safety pinned floursack you wore for a clout."[103] Later, despite Agee and Evans's objectification of these families, Agee manages to convince himself that he was as powerless as the people being photographed: "It occurs to me now as I write that I was as helpless as she."[104]

The work of Evans and other photographers has been central in establishing the myth of Appalachia that persists in American popular culture: through the photographs included in *Our Southern Highlanders* (Kephart, 1913), through Bayard Wootten's photographs of costumed Appalachians in staged scenes in *Cabins in the Laurel* (Sheppard, 1935), through Doris Ulmann's photographs (in *Handicrafts of the Southern Highlands* and elsewhere), up through the "poverty porn" photos from the War on Poverty.[105] The people, landscape, and homes of Appalachia have often been photographic objects, framed by outsiders eager to capture an "authentic" picture of Appalachia. As in the case of Agee and Evans, photographers of Appalachia were often outsiders who "had their own agendas: principally to depict mountain people as living survivors of the pioneer age."[106] Moreover, as Agee's text demonstrates, the unequal power relationships between photographers and their subjects meant that the photographs were not intended to be keepsakes or to represent photographic subjects as they saw themselves. Instead, these staged scenes, with the photographic subject often costumed or photographed in the midst of a task, are "anti-portraits" or "nonfiction novels."[107]

However, Appalachia's own "rudimentarily trained, indigenous 'picturemen'" served their neighbors and the region as traveling photographers, weaving a circuit through the mountains and making portraits, then returning a few weeks later to deliver the developed images.[108] These were often very low-cost affairs: W. R. Trivett (who photographed in and around Watauga County, North Carolina, from 1907 through the late 1940s) charged as little as five cents for a portrait, and Paul Buchanan (who photographed in Mitchell, Avery, Yancey, and McDowell counties in North Carolina from the 1920s through early 1950s) reported similar rates, even bartering photographs in exchange for rabbits, chickens, and old peanut butter jars.[109] Most importantly, these indigenous picturemen "did not try to explain or interpret" their subjects or tell them "what to wear or hold,"[110] unlike Bayard Wootten, whom Charles Alan Watkins argues "functioned entirely from a position of power; she denied her sitters even a shred of control."[111] As scholars describe these picturemen and their work, the diction reflects the same equation—that being accurately seen equals being understood—discussed earlier. As Ann Hawthorne notes of Paul Buchanan's work, "When he did his job well you could clearly see who the subject was. . . . While Paul would 'pick out the place' or 'find a bunch of flowers,' it was the people themselves who directed their presentation and its record. *They are here as they chose to be seen.*"[112] As Ralph E. Lentz II explains, "The picturemen's work was perhaps no less contrived than that of outside photographers who came to the mountains, but with the picturemen it was the mountain people who were in control of the contriving."[113]

Just as photography (and imagery of sight and light) is often linked with truth in LGBTQ Appalachian literature, so too is the figure of the pictureman/traveling photographer, specifically in Fenton Johnson's novel *Scissors, Paper, Rock* (1993) and Karen Salyer McElmurray's novel *Strange Birds in the Tree of Heaven* (1999). As they appear in these novels, picturemen are sexualized (or at least sensualized) figures but are, crucially, outsiders who come to objectify and extract the value of Appalachia and use it to their own ends.[114] In Johnson's novel, the traveling photographer is described by the characters as "the young pictureman" although he appears to be from outside the region,[115] while the photographer in *Strange Birds* is, like Wootten and Ulmann, there for the sake of art. However, *Strange Birds*' photographer, Jules Cameron, takes candid photographs of the residents of Inez, Kentucky, not posing or costuming anyone. The "picturemen" characters in these novels are not the LGBTQ characters in the novels, but the portrayal of their work—of photography—in both texts continues the LGBTQ Appalachian literary pattern of tying photography to truth. In both novels, the work of the pictureman promises (or threatens) to reveal the truth that some characters may prefer remain hidden.

Pictureman in *Scissors, Paper, Rock*

The pictureman in Johnson's *Scissors, Paper, Rock* (1993) is, like the photographers for *Cabins in the Laurel* and *Handicrafts of the Southern Highlands*, an outsider to Appalachia. In Johnson's novel, this pictureman is a near-mythical figure, mentioned throughout the novel by characters in its interlocking short stories, yet one who never appears in the novel and whom most of the characters have never met. He is also the father of one of the novel's main characters, Miss Camilla, who serves as the conscience and primary narrative voice of the novel. The interlocking short stories of *Scissors, Paper, Rock* focus on the Hardin family and their neighbors in Strang Knob, Kentucky. Much of the novel centers on Raphael, the Hardins' youngest son who had moved to San Francisco to live openly as a gay man but who is now ill with AIDS and has returned home to Kentucky, where he's supported by his friend and the Hardins' neighbor, Miss Camilla.

The photographs of the novel are seen only by Miss Camilla and Raphael, ironic considering that neither of these two characters is "seen" accurately by friends, neighbors, or family. The photographs were made by Miss Camilla's father, a pictureman from Chicago, whose visit to Strang Knob two generations prior led to the seduction of Miss Camilla's mother, Miss Camilla's conception, and the fleecing of the residents of Strang Knob, who gave this pictureman money in exchange for photos that he never delivered. As Miss Camilla explains of picturemen, "Sitting for one of them, placing money in his hands was like teaching or farming, making art or having children, a gesture of faith in the continuity of things—in this case, that the pictureman would return the following spring with the developed prints."[116] But this pictureman never returned; instead, as we learn through Miss Camilla's internal monologue in the novel's final chapter, "he took the train west with his equipment and his negatives and his customers' money, leaving my mother with a stack of receipts and me in her belly. A few months later she took herself to Chicago, his hometown, where she hoped, I can suppose, to find him."[117] Miss Camilla grew up without this father, and after her mother's death discovers a strongbox filled with all the photographs taken in Strang Knob, never knowing how her mother came to have them. Miss Camilla moves back to her mother's hometown, then conceals the photographs for forty years. All the while, her neighbors talk incessantly about these photos, yearning for the mementos that were paid for but never delivered. Through these photographs and all the Strang Knob stories about them, photography is linked to truth, yet it is a truth that most characters would prefer not to see. As Miss Camilla says to Raphael Hardin, "None of us wants to see the world as it really is unless we're shocked into it."[118]

Just as Raphael's truth is never spoken within his family—he never talks to his father, Tom Hardin, about AIDS, while Tom Hardin never talks to Raphael about the cancer that's slowly killing him—the truths contained in these photographs are never revealed. The townspeople never realize that the photographs have survived and that they are right there in the town among them, in Miss Camilla's possession. The reader has heard of these photos throughout the novel—about the photo of Leola's mother, the glamorous photos taken of Rose Ella Hardin's parents' wedding, the photo marking Tice Flaherty's family's renunciation of alcohol at the beginning of Prohibition—but we discover only in the novel's last thirty pages that these photos have been in Strang Knob for years, in the locked strongbox in Miss Camilla's house, where she is able to look through them and see the uncomfortable truths that are revealed, their stories that differ so dramatically from those told by her neighbors.

Chief among the lies revealed in the box of photographs is the one of Miss Camilla's parents' nonexistent marriage. Instead, the strongbox holds a photo of Camilla's mother in her nightgown: "huddled on a rough cot, rumpled bedclothes at her feet. . . . Her eyes are bold with desire."[119] The official story is told by a silver-framed photo of Camilla's mother in a wedding dress, supposedly documenting the marriage that followed her hasty departure from Strang Knob, reuniting her with Camilla's pictureman father. Instead, a close study of the wedding photo would have revealed a dress that wouldn't have come into style until well after she and Camilla's father were supposedly wed. As Miss Camilla ponders the slippage between narrative and truth, between belief and reality, she wonders, "Which is more *true*: The strongbox photograph of my mother in a nightgown on a disheveled bed? Or my end table photograph of her in her rented wedding dress?"[120] Ultimately, when Camilla dumps the strongbox full of photographs into a river, the only one she saves is the one that she knows to be a lie: the silver-framed photo documenting her parents' nonexistent wedding. As Camilla thinks to herself, "I exaggerate only a little when I write that the photographs in the box constitute, for some several hundred people under Strang Knob, the difference between the world that they have created and need to believe in—a world in which they can have faith—and the world as it is, or was. As for me, I have heard their stories so often repeated and embellished that they have taken on the authority of truth, until it is the photographs that I begin to doubt."[121]

Of these stories, Camilla maintains that "the truth lies not in the facts of the stories but in the longings that set them in motion."[122] As I explore in further depth in chapter 4, LGBTQ Appalachian literature explores those longings—the ones that cannot be spoken as well as the stories that are born from them—through a focus on silences and storytelling.

Pictureman in *Strange Birds in the Tree of Heaven*

Jules Cameron, the pictureman of *Strange Birds in the Tree of Heaven* (1999), like the pictureman in *Scissors, Paper, Rock*, is a figure of sensuality, a bringer of knowledge, and an emissary from a world outside of Appalachia. Having come to Inez, Kentucky, to do a "photographic essay of Inez,"[123] he performs the key functions of the colonial intruder: he extracts the value (sexual or photographic) from Appalachia and takes it with him when he leaves. While in Inez, Jules Cameron meets Ruth Blue—one of the novel's three narrators—who will serve as his native informant of sorts, guiding him around Inez and helping him locate photographic subjects. Through the figure of Jules Cameron and through Ruth Blue's brief relationship with him, Karen Salyer McElmurray links light (via the symbol of photography) with truth and knowledge, including the knowledge of self. By situating the sensual (and mildly exploitative) Jules Cameron as the voice of truth and light, McElmurray links the visual and the sexual: that which is seen and open is sexual and lifegiving and sustaining. On the other hand, as we will see from Ruth Blue's narration and the repeated references to closets, that which is dark or hidden is deadly and life-depriving, even though it might feel safe.

Ruth Blue (who later becomes Ruth Blue Wallen, mother of Andrew Wallen, the young gay man who is another of the novel's narrators) meets Cameron in 1941 when she is fifteen. He tells her about photography, the world outside of Inez, and "what he knew about light."[124] Through her interactions with Cameron, Ruth explores forbidden desires: not only sexual desires but also the desire for knowledge and experiences beyond those allowed her by her fanatical preacher-father. Ruth's attraction to Cameron is evident in the sensory imagery that pervades the narrative when she is with him. Ruth's first encounter with Cameron—when she stares into the storefront window of his downtown Inez photography studio and then ventures inside—is marked by the overwhelming senses of scent and sight: "But I went on into that world of scents, some of them I knew, the soapy odor of ginseng, a musky smell of furs drying. Beyond that was a light scent, whiskey light and sharp. Room spinning, I saw Jules Cameron."[125] Later, Ruth gets as physically close to Cameron as is possible in the absence of a sexual relationship when she rubs his sweat on herself ("Sweat shone on Jules Cameron's forehead and I touched that, held my damp palm against my cheek"[126]) and when she lies down beside him in a rowboat. Ruth's description of the latter moment focuses on the senses of sound and sight, substitutes for the touch she longs for but cannot have: "After awhile I moved back to where he was, laid myself near him. We didn't speak, had never touched, but I was as close to him as I could get, imagined the sound of his heart, watched the shadows between leaves and the shapes of branches."[127]

Ruth's careful, close watching of Jules Cameron highlights the importance of the visual in this very sensual relationship. In one passage, Ruth's emphasis on visuality is so dominant that even language itself becomes visual: "I watched his red lips and his beautiful, short fingered hands as he drew words in the air."[128] Cameron's overall role in the novel is to draw Ruth's attention to the visual, to focus her attention on photography and its capacity—through light—to reveal and to communicate truths. Cameron tells Ruth about photography that "the camera . . . does not lie" and that "the camera reveals a truth the subject does not always understand."[129] In some cases, Cameron's photographs seem to distract Ruth from painful truths, although the narrative (with Ruth insisting that the photographs help take her mind off painful events) clearly undermines her characterization of the photographs as distracting. Instead, the war photographs that Cameron shows her—products of his time documenting World War II in Europe—evoke the truths that Ruth cannot speak, of her father's violence and the nightmarish quality of her home life: "With the pictures he took, I didn't think of how, nights sometimes, I'd pull free of my daddy and he'd be after me, setting me spinning with the back of his hand, like I was no more than play animals on top of a wind-up music box. I never told Jules Cameron of these things. I told no one these truths."[130] Ruth's home life is not only nightmarish and violent but also one that Ruth describes as largely untouched by natural light, lit only by weak artificial light: "Outside there was still good, late light of an afternoon, but our house never took it in much. The hall past the bedrooms and to the kitchen was already like dusk. . . . At the kitchen table, a flame was turned too high on a lantern spewing smoke and kerosene fumes, casting light over my daddy, slumped there."[131] For Ruth, her home in Mining Hollow contains neither truth nor light.

After Jules Cameron departs and Ruth thinks back on her relationship with him, she realizes that she misses the light and truth that he brought more than she misses Cameron himself: "I wished for Jules Cameron. Or not for him, his too-short leg and his thick-soled shoe, but for the light I'd seen when I'd looked through my hand at the sun."[132] Although Ruth's father purports to talk to Ruth about the light of religion ("Nights like that, I held him as his body shook and while he said, God's the resurrection and the light"[133]), this proselytizing is undermined by his violence, his drunkenness, and his perverted desire for her: "Then he was beside me, pulling my face next to his, those whiskery cheeks, saying, go on, kiss on me like she done on him."[134] In contrast, the light that Ruth found through Jules Cameron and his photography is the light of the wider world: the possibilities beyond Inez, Kentucky, and the restrictive world that her father allows her (no makeup, no magazines, no worldly goods).

In the first weeks after Jules Cameron left, Ruth clings to these insights—"I would not repent of my wish for shadows to have light, for all the world I knew to become all the world I might have had, true as a photograph"[135]—despite resistance from Ruth's father, who senses a change in her. So her father locks her away for months, leaving her to starve, freeze, and eat paint chips (since he only occasionally brings her food). Ruth's sensual memories of Jules Cameron begin to fade—"In the eighth week I no longer remembered Jules Cameron's full, red mouth"[136]—and she begins to lose the sense of light and truth that she had gained through Jules Cameron's introduction to photography: "A negative, Jules Cameron once told me, though I never completely understood how the world was better seen through a small square of light, an instant in time. The world now had no shape to me at all, or only the shape of air passing through an open window, how the screen rippled and smoothed."[137] In this passage, it is no longer light that comes through an open window for Ruth but, instead, air. When Ruth loses her newfound understanding of light and truth, it is replaced by her father's version of religion, through which she'll later urge her son, Andrew Wallen, to kill himself rather than live as a gay man.

In a contrast that is central to the LGBTQ themes of *Strange Birds* and that links the topic of this chapter—visuality and seeing—with the topic of the next—silences and storytelling, Ruth portrays the light and truth of photography as antithetical to darkness and death, embodied in a key image in the novel: the closet. Although not framed explicitly as the closet of homophobia (or the closet of concealing one's sexuality), the closet Ruth refers to is one in which someone hides or in which treasured things—such as knowledge—are hidden away. In an extended passage, Ruth explicitly contrasts the light and truth of Cameron's photographs with death and with the darkness of a closet, in which she wants to hide:

> I saw right away what was wrong with all of his pictures. It wasn't their lack of light. . . . Light flooded these pictures, white, straight at the sun light. I wanted to hide from these lit pictures, imagined instead the first blackness after a candle is blown out, a closet, the door shut, darkness behind the clothes.
>
> If Jules Cameron had wanted to show me the valley of the shadow of death, it wasn't anywhere in these pictures of light, no shadows in them. It was what I heard when I stood and left the table, walked back toward Mining Hollow, just thinking. A voice I knew followed me saying, *remember, you will always remember what has been left behind, the last moment of breath.*[138]

Even though these photographs include Cameron's images from a war-torn Europe—photos of bombed-out buildings and dead civilians—their truth carries a light that is absent from the "valley of the shadow of death" that she finds back in her home at Mining Hollow. A few pages later in the novel, Ruth finds concealed in a closet "news that had been kept from me": a box that Cameron had sent containing a letter and photographs, including ones of her that document their relationship.[139] That box—containing light and truth—becomes Ruth's refuge and touchstone; she continually takes the box out of the closet, examines its contents, then rewraps it to conceal her knowledge from her father, "until one day I reached back and found no box at all."[140] Silence—like the silencing that constitutes being in the closet—is a potent trope in the work of LGBTQ Appalachian writers, writers whose truth and light persist despite attempts to silence them.

4

Silences and Storytelling in LGBTQ Appalachian Literature

Another characteristic of LGBTQ Appalachian literature is its focus on silences: those enforced by a punitive culture and those chosen for self-protection. These silences are coupled with a practice common to Appalachian literature and Appalachian culture: storytelling. These twin poles—silences and storytelling—evoke key questions for queer Appalachians: When do they have a voice, who gets to tell their stories, and who defines the "truth"?

Silence, Speech, and the Closet

Even though we often speak of "silencing" as a form of rhetorical violence, silence itself is a neutral concept, rendered positive or negative (empowering or disenabling) by the issues of choice and power: who has the power to speak or to remain silent if they wish (and with what consequences). As Michel Foucault points out in *The History of Sexuality*, volume 1 (1985), "there is not one but many silences," and one's relation to silence—who chooses to remain silent versus who is silenced versus who is compelled to speak—reveals power differentials: "we must try to determine the different ways of not saying such things, how those who can and those who cannot speak of them are distributed, which type of discourse is authorized, or which form of discretion is required in either case."[1] In contrast to the rhetoric that equates speech—or, in the common parlance of liberation, *having a voice*—with having power, Foucault makes clear that the regulation of sexuality (in western Europe since the late seventeenth century) operated through "incitements to speak of sex" (to religious, medical, and civil officials), thus marking sexuality with a central paradox: "What is peculiar to modern societies, in fact, is not that they consigned sex to a shadow existence, but that they dedicated themselves to speaking of it *ad infinitum*, while exploiting it as *the* secret."[2] Foucault thus calls us to be attentive to the differing circumstances and power relations that mark discourse: compelled speech is no more empowering than forced silence.

The issue of silence is one that is especially relevant to queer people in the United States, and certainly no less so for queer Appalachians. Far too often, queer people have had to keep silent about their sexuality, while in other cases they have been forced to speak. Silence and silencing have been and remain fraught issues for queer people: from "the love that dare not speak its name" to the strictures of Don't Ask Don't Tell, to the more general question of whose voices are heard, issues of silence and speech are potent ones within gay life in America. According to communication studies scholars Gust A. Yep and Susan B. Shimanoff, "LGBTQ individuals have experienced silence as oppressing, repressing, undermining, erasing, and annihilating. Given this history, it is not surprising that the rhetoric of the US LGBTQ movement has celebrated voice and speech. . . . In this sense, silence has been equated with sexual oppression and speech with sexual liberation."[3]

An especially potent feature of that oppression has been the closet, which Eve Kosofsky Sedgwick labels in her 1990 book *Epistemology of the Closet* as "the defining structure for gay oppression in this century,"[4] and which is imbricated with strictures of silence: "'Closetedness' itself is a performance initiated as such by the speech act of a silence."[5] However, Craig M. Loftin, in his introduction to *Letters to ONE: Gay and Lesbian Voices from the 1950s and 1960s*, argues that "the modern closet metaphor did not exist in the 1950s and early 1960s because there was no expectation that gay people would reveal their homosexuality to anyone except to other gay people. 'Coming out' to heterosexuals was a political strategy introduced by gay activists in the late 1960s and early 1970s."[6] Loftin bases his conclusion, in part, on an examination of thousands of letters written to *ONE: The Homosexual Magazine*, the first American magazine for gay and lesbian readers.[7] Of the many thousands of letters (available in the archives of *ONE* National Gay and Lesbian Archives in Los Angeles) that Loftin read, "the word 'closet' appeared only once," seemingly in reference to society's treatment of sex in general, not just same-sex relationships.[8] Instead of "closet," Loftin argues that earlier generations of queer people "thought of themselves as wearing masks," a metaphor that "restores agency because gay people controlled when to put on or remove their masks."[9] Regardless of the metaphor, Loftin makes clear that communication within and among gay communities was essential to queer activism and organizing.

In Steven Seidman's *Beyond the Closet: The Transformation of Gay and Lesbian Life* (2002), he claims that thanks to late-twentieth-century shifts in American culture, gay and lesbian people can be more open about their sexuality, making their "speech act of a silence" as a situational, strategic choice rather than an overarching approach to life: "Almost all of the individuals I interviewed spoke of concealing their homosexuality in specific situations or with particular individuals. . . . There is a huge difference between concealing from an uncle or a client and marrying or avoiding certain occupations in order to pretend to be straight."[10] Although he acknowledges that, "sadly, the closet remains a reality for too many lesbians and gay men," he notes that his "research suggests that many gay Americans today live outside the social framework of the closet."[11] Of course, Seidman based his conclusions on interviews with thirty individuals who had answered his ads placed "in local and regional gay newspapers and newsletters."[12] Individuals who lived where such publications could not be purchased, or who couldn't take the risk to have a publication delivered to their homes that might "out" them to their families or to the mailman, are unlikely to have been included in Seidman's study.[13]

In Mary L. Gray's 2009 book *Out in the Country: Youth, Media, and Queer Visibility in Rural America* (based on interviews with queer young people in Kentucky), she contradicts Seidman's "beyond the closet" thesis, maintaining that Seidman and others who privilege "gay visibility" ignore the lived experiences—especially the ties of kinship—of queer young people in rural areas.[14] Gray explains that queer youth in rural areas might not live an "out" life in the same way as would a queer young person in an urban area; however, that doesn't mean these young people do not see themselves as queer, even if their lives aren't marked by the gay visibility that shapes popular notions of urban queer lives. Gray argues that "the rural United States . . . operates as America's perennial, tacitly taken-for-granted closet," thereby resulting in "the privileging of some queer identities over others."[15] Gray describes the myriad strategies that these young people employ "to create belonging and visibility in communities where they are not only a distinct minority but also popularly represented as out of place."[16] I would argue that queer youth throughout Appalachia—not only in the eastern Kentucky counties where Gray did her ethnographic work—engage in the same mediations that Gray describes, as they decide precisely how out they will be, or with whom, as they negotiate their lives as queer Appalachians.

Many LGBTQ Appalachian authors—including those represented in this book—have described their process of coming out of the closet, and of the personal (and sometimes professional) risks they took to break this silence. Dorothy Allison, in her foreword to *Crooked Letter i: Coming Out in the South* (2015), recalls her own struggles in coming out and notes the dangers involved in doing so at that place and time (early 1970s, Florida): "I could be cast out—literally expelled from college or sent off to a mental institution," as she had seen happen to a non-gender-conforming classmate, whose family "appeared in the middle of the night to arrange to have her taken away by force to a facility where, it was expected, she would be fixed."[17] Fenton Johnson observed about that same time period, the early 1970s, that "in 1971, the gays and lesbians of Appalachia had little choice but silence or flight"; Johnson himself emigrated from his native Kentucky to California when he graduated from high school.[18] Dorothy Allison's explanation of her present-day (2015) moment—"this new wondrous age with Supreme Court decisions affirming gay and lesbian marriages, and gender being redefined as nowhere near as rigid as it has previously been defined"—is that these steps were achieved through a refusal to be silent: "the simple act of declaring our truth and refusing to back down or lie no matter how virulent the response."[19]

Other Appalachian LGBTQ writers have chronicled their own coming out experiences and have described the aftermath when that silence was broken. For Elizabeth Craven, a Tennessee-born writer who exchanged letters with her girlfriend Julia, that moment came when her mother found one of the letters: "I was disowned. The closet door was blown off forever."[20] Jeff Mann's coming out conversation with his mother was likewise prompted by a discovery, of "a few queer newspapers I'd picked up at a gay bar in Columbus, Ohio,"[21] but his story had a happier ending. She cried; they talked; they moved on. In "Dancing in the Dirt," O. James Napier's essay in the 2017 collection *Electric Dirt: A Celebration of Queer Voices and Identities from Appalachia and the South,* Napier explains, "When it came to coming out to my family . . . I didn't just come out; I was outed" through anonymous phone calls to his grandmother, aunt, and mother.[22] Other writers describe coming out on their own terms and in their own time. After Julia Watts figured out that she "was queer (or 'quare,' as Appalachians pronounce it)" while in college, she was comforted by the knowledge that her parents "would ultimately be fine with it" although "my grandparents could never know."[23] In *Fun Home*, Alison Bechdel describes having come out to her parents via a letter sent home from college. Overall, the moment of coming out, especially of coming out to family, has been foregrounded in many texts by LGBTQ Appalachian writers.

This dilemma—to whom should one speak of these issues? and when?—was foregrounded by Silas House in his 2014 keynote address at the Appalachian Studies Conference. House related that some professors in Appalachia recently told him "that they rarely broached the topic of sexuality in Appalachian studies classes because so many of their students are so terribly divided on the issue," and went on to describe being disappointed, after surveying fifty colleagues about what books they teach in Appalachian studies classes, that "only two teachers of Appalachian studies reported using books that focused on gay issues."[24] House maintains that "the scholarly community must lead the way on talking more about these issues."[25]

Responses to House's address (published in the Fall 2014 issue of the *Journal of Appalachian Studies* alongside a transcript of the speech) followed suit in exploring these issues using diction that foregrounds silence and speech. Pam McMichael (then executive director of the Highlander Research and Education Center and a founder of Southerners on New Ground), in an essay entitled "The Power of Conversation," maintains that "Silas House knows this power of words, that words lead to action and that words are action, and he is spot-on in calling for a broad and inclusive dialogue to break this code of silence and help build a new Appalachia."[26] In bell hooks's response to House, she notes that those who have already been speaking out against injustice may fear that their words have had no impact: "there are those who have answered [the call], but whose voices grow weary from burnout, from encroaching fear and despair that there will be no change coming. All too often, when freedom fighters are telling our stories again and again, speaking truth to power with no response that brings about progressive change, we grow weary."[27] hooks calls on her reader to keep working toward justice, even as we honor those who have worked for progressive change in the past. In their individual essays, both McMichael and bell hooks invoke Audre Lorde's poem "Litany for Survival," quoting the lines that read, "when we are silent / we are still afraid / So it is better to speak."

This charge, that we must speak up on these issues, recalls the importance of the oral tradition—including folklore and storytelling—to Appalachian literature and to the writers highlighted in this book. In a 1995 interview, Fenton Johnson stated that his novel *Scissors, Paper, Rock* was shaped by his region's storytelling tradition: "I had grown up in a storytelling culture, and I knew how to tell a story in a way that virtually no one that I encountered out here [California] knew how to do."[28] Lisa Alther credits her grandmother's *lived* stories—faced "with a reality too grim or too complicated to endure, she simply decided that she was a Tidewater lady and then turned herself into one"—with teaching her "almost everything I know about creating fiction."[29] Likewise, doris davenport notes that her Affrilachian community in Cornelia, Georgia, determined her "worldview, behavior, and value system." davenport continues, "I still prefer a live(ly) conversation or a good story to anything on the electronic highway."[30] Silas House traces his origins as a writer to this important part of his Appalachian heritage, claiming, "I am a writer because I grew up in a family of storytellers, of working people."[31]

Many Appalachian writers—both those who address LGBTQ themes and those who do not—have described Appalachian storytelling as key to both their lives and their work; this has been especially true for LGBTQ Appalachian authors in particular. The influence of the oral tradition on Appalachian literature has been well documented by scholars.[32] Weatherford and Dykeman, in their overview of Appalachian literature since 1900, argue that "the accumulated wisdom of many ancestors, the colorful words and phrases and similes of folk language, are part of the heritage of this century's mountain literature," and that "modern novelists and poets of the mountains have drawn on this rich source of inspiration in both story and style."[33] Jim Wayne Miller agrees, noting, "There has always been and continues to be a reciprocal relationship between oral and written literature. And so oral literature is a legitimate concern of Appalachian literary scholarship."[34] Deborah Thompson and Irene Moser, in their discussion of Appalachian folklife in *A Handbook to Appalachia* (2006), note that "a rich repertoire of storytelling forms is an especially important inheritance for the region's talented writers."[35] Tina L. Hanlon notes that "scholars now recognize that the Appalachian oral tradition is one of the richest in America,"[36] and Hanlon has documented the impact of that inheritance in texts by several talented writers, from Lee Smith's *Fair and Tender Ladies* to Sharyn McCrumb's ballad novels and James Still's *River of Earth*.[37] Carter Sickels in fact has an MA in folklore in addition to his MFA in creative writing; he notes that "fiction ensures that stories don't go untold."[38]

An important feature of the discourse around rural queer people and Appalachian queer people is the prominence of oral histories.[39] Many of the earliest groundbreaking texts (some of which were covered in more detail in the introduction) within LGBTQ Appalachian studies have been based on oral histories. Black and Rhorer's 1995 essay "Out in the Mountains: Exploring Lesbian and Gay Lives" was based on interviews with queer Appalachians. The documentary *Through Their Eyes: Stories of Gays and Lesbians in the Mountains*, a 1999 short film produced through Appalshop's youth media training project, is composed of interviews with several young queer residents of Appalachia. Carrie Kline's reader's theater production "Revelations: Appalachian Resiliency in Lesbian, Gay, Bisexual, and Transgender People," first performed at Marshall University in March 2001, was based on Kline's interviews with twelve residents of West Virginia (eleven of them native to the state) who identified as queer.[40]

Important oral history work continues to shape LGBTQ Appalachian studies today, especially through communication channels that include the internet and social media. In 2013, Rae Garringer founded Country Queers, which began as a multimedia oral history project focusing on rural queer Appalachians. Since then, the project's scope has broadened: it now includes "a collection of over 70 oral history interviews across wide geographical distance, a traveling gallery exhibit featuring images and oral histories gathered through the project, and a podcast."[41] Garringer has said that the project arose out of their "intense feeling of frustration with the lack of rural queer visibility, and the extreme sense of isolation I felt as a queer person living back home in Southeastern West Virginia."[42] The project now has a vibrant presence through its website (where podcast episodes are available, including interviews with Dorothy Allison and Silas House), Twitter, Facebook, and Instagram. Garringer seems to echo Mary Gray's thesis in *Out in the Country*, about rural queer youth utilizing media to make connections, when describing this project's inspiration: "Country Queers was also born out of an intense personal need to connect to LGBTQI folks living outside of major cities. . . . I really needed community, not just rural community or queer community, but country queer community."[43] Garringer is another in a long line of scholars and historians who have empowered queer Appalachians by providing them a forum for speaking out, thus highlighting their experiences and fighting the cultural erasure of LGBTQ Appalachians.

Speaking Up and Keeping Secrets in LGBTQ Appalachian Literature

Dorothy Allison, in her memoir *Two or Three Things I Know for Sure* and her essay "Deciding to Live," emphasizes the value of stories and the way that telling stories—stories that expressed her truth—helped to save her life. In the 2015 essay, Allison describes a time in her life: "The desire to live was desperate in my belly, and the stories I had hidden all those years were the blood and bone of it. To get it down, to tell it again, to make something—by God, just once to be real in the world, without lies or evasions or sweet-talking nonsense."[44] In her memoir published twenty years earlier, she expresses this even more succinctly: "The story becomes the thing needed."[45] For Allison, it is not that the story must be 100 percent true, because she knows "the use of fiction in a world of hard truth, the way fiction can be a harder piece of truth."[46] Indeed, Allison frames this truth-telling as an embrace of life and a rejection of silence: "my own shout of life against death, of shape and substance against silence and confusion."[47] This dichotomy—of speech/life versus silence/death—pervades the literature that will be examined throughout the remainder of this chapter.

In Carter Sickels's 2015 essay "Early in My Transition, Two Teenagers Helped Me Embrace My Identity," he highlights one way that speech can be powerful for and signify recognition of LGBTQ Appalachians: through naming and the appropriate use of pronouns. In this essay, he describes attending a gay pride festival in North Carolina, when he "was just beginning to take the first steps toward transitioning,"[48] and the power in that day's events for him stemmed from words of recognition from others. Sickels describes being followed by two boys, a teenaged couple, who first compliment his jeans and share fashion tips, then begin asking about his sexual orientation and gender identification. Sickels faces a dilemma when they ask his name: "Do I hesitate, just for a moment? I'm still nervous saying my name aloud, worried people will ask, *No, what's your* real *name?*" Saying his name aloud and getting a positive response from the teens—"That sounds good. That's a good name"—gives Sickels key affirmation: "I'd been thinking about this name for years, held it close. Now I hear it the way it sounds to them—the same way, in the quietest of moments, I also hear it: a single, clear, enduring note. He is right; it sounds good. My name sounds like me."[49]

An even more important moment of recognition comes after the boys ask Sickels, "like, what's your sex?" After he tells them "I've been going more by 'he,'" they enthusiastically approve: "Yeah, 'he.' You should go with that," Tommy says. 'You're definitely a 'he.'" Sickels describes "the joy, the sudden adrenalin of that sweet and unexpected encounter," making clear that the boys' affirmation of his name and pronouns was central to this encounter's significance.[50] For Sickels, giving voice to his identity in the form of a name and a pronoun—and having these heard and reaffirmed by these young people—becomes a key step in his transition.

In contrast to Sickels's openness, a number of characters in early LGBTQ Appalachian literature remain in the closet, either to ensure their own safety or to help a community or their family maintain its status quo, at least superficially. In Julia Watts's young adult novel *Finding H.F.* (2001), Morgan, Kentucky, high schooler Heavenly Faith (H.F.) Simms and her best friend, Bo, both keep quiet about their sexuality, rarely even giving voice to this between themselves. Early in the novel, H.F. explains to the reader why she stays in the closet: "to keep from making trouble for me and other people, I keep my mouth shut and try to feel good that at least I won't break Memaw's heart by getting pregnant before I finish high school, which is what my momma did."[51] Although H.F. can be open with Bo, Bo himself—until after he and H.F. have traveled to Atlanta and met other queer teens and seen that there is a life after high school—will not openly discuss his sexuality with his best friend: "Bo has never come right out and told me he likes boys. He'll say things like, 'bein' the way I am' or 'not bein' a real masculine type of person.'"[52] Even by the end of the novel, when both H.F. and Bo have met uncloseted queer people, have earned college scholarships, and have a clear path out of Morgan, Kentucky, H.F. is careful to hide her sexuality from her grandmother: "Memaw don't suspect a thing, and right now I want to protect her from what she can't understand."[53]

Similar reasons are given in Johnson's *Scissors, Paper, Rock* (1993) for the closeted life led by Nick Handley, a gay tobacco farmer who—unlike his high school classmate Raphael Hardin—remained in their native Strang Knob, Kentucky, rather than moving off to the West Coast.[54] As the narrative makes clear, although remaining in the closet has proven immensely damaging to Nick (because his unspoken sense of himself eats away at him), this arrangement has suited his community just fine, allowing his neighbors to pretend that they all live in a homogeneous, un-diverse bubble. Raphael notices the physical manifestations of Nick's repressions, the fact that "Nick carried himself with the distance and gracelessness of a man who could not allow himself to be touched, who from his earliest self-knowledge had placed himself beyond touching."[55] This self-imposed isolation results in a brittle tension in Nick's demeanor: he "had been hardened . . . by years of turning in on himself."[56] As Johnson's narration reveals, Nick's closetedness has not fooled anyone; his movements are "singing with desire so urgent it announced itself . . . and all the while Nick himself clearly so certain of what he needed to believe: that nobody saw his wanting, not his sister, not his neighbors, not the townspeople whose eyes he avoided on the street. As for them, they were relieved to aid and abet."[57] Johnson's diction here characterizes this secrecy as criminal. The reader sees the damage it inflicts on Nick, and we can further understand the damage done to Appalachia when LGBTQ community members are either exiled or compelled to live a closeted life.[58]

Another clear example within LGBTQ Appalachian literature of the destructive power of secrets is in Alison Bechdel's *Fun Home: A Family Tragicomic* (2006). In this graphic novel-memoir, she chronicles growing up in a small town, Beech Creek, in Appalachian Pennsylvania and describes the momentous events of her first years in college: coming out to her parents, the revelations about her father that soon followed, and her father's death (perhaps by suicide). Early reviews of *Fun Home* emphasized it as a text marked by secrets, with the review in the *Lambda Book Report* describing the Bechdels as "a family shaded by terrible secrets,"[59] while the review in *Publisher's Weekly* describes the story as "tied to a family secret—her father was a closeted homosexual who led a double life and may have committed suicide."[60] Bechdel herself has commented on the way the power of her father's secret affected her own writing, noting, "I wanted to write this story since shortly after my dad died . . . but it was about this intense family secret that I couldn't tell. No one knew that he was gay or that he possibly killed himself."[61]

As *Fun Home*'s narrative makes clear, the damages wrought by Bruce Bechdel's secret included an arrest (during the summer when Alison Bechdel was thirteen) that could have cost him his job, his distance from (and occasional neglect of) his children, and of course effects on the underaged young men with whom Bruce apparently had affairs. Bruce's arrest was ostensibly for providing beer to a minor, but Bechdel observes (in language evocative of the Oscar Wilde case) that "the real accusation dared not speak its name."[62] The police had carefully crafted the police report to mention only the beer and the fact that the witness "was seventeen years old and that he told Mr. Bechdel his age."[63] But as Bechdel points out, "a whiff of the sexual aroma of the true offense could be detected in the sentence," six months of counseling, although the thirteen-year-old Alison Bechdel didn't perceive that at the time.[64]

Much of *Fun Home*'s narrative contrasts Bechdel's ability to speak her truth—albeit after she went away to college—with Bruce Bechdel's inability to speak his, as a married, closeted resident of small-town Appalachia. In a letter to Alison written not long before he died, Bruce Bechdel contrasts Beech Creek and New York primarily in terms of what could be spoken: "There was not much in the Village that I hadn't known in Beech Creek. In New York you could see and mention it but elsewhere it was not seen or mentioned."[65] At Bruce's funeral in Beech Creek, his daughter wonders, "What would happen if we spoke the truth?" then imagines saying to a fellow mourner, "He **killed himself** because he was a manic-depressive closeted **fag** and he couldn't face living in this small-minded small town one more **second**."[66] As she contrasts her father's closeted life and her own coming out, she observes, "The end of his lie coincided with the beginning of my truth."[67] Bruce Bechdel's closet, like that of Nick Handley and of H.F. and Bo and of other LGBTQ Appalachians, was a place of secrets and voicelessness yet was primarily a question of safety.

Silence = Death in Appalachia

Another, more deadly version of the silence that is foregrounded in LGBTQ Appalachian literature is the silence surrounding the AIDS epidemic. As the iconic poster of the early years of the AIDS epidemic declared, "SILENCE = DEATH," a tagline that the poster's original creators hoped would inspire political action and that they used to call attention to the costs of silence: "the deadly effects of passivity in crises, communal silence and the nature of political silencing, silence as complicity, and scenarios where bystanders became participants without intending to be."[68] As this poster—later associated with the New York–based group ACT UP (AIDS Coalition to Unleash Power)—made clear, the silence surrounding AIDS was a problem throughout the US, not simply in Appalachia. Mary K. Anglin argues in her chapter in *Back Talk from Appalachia: Confronting Stereotypes* that although some AIDS patients in Appalachia were indeed met with ignorance and exclusion (as they were in other regions as well), other Appalachians with AIDS were supported by caregivers who were "willing to confront racism, elitism, homophobia, sexism, and fear of infection in order to provide care for people with AIDS," and "equally important have been the local people who quietly contended with prejudice in order to care for their own kin."[69] As Anglin and others have made clear, responses to AIDS in Appalachia were as varied—ranging from compassion to shunning—as they were in other regions in the US.[70]

The dilemma of the queer Appalachian who is infected with HIV is embodied in a figure I've come to think of as "the hummingbird," inspired by a poem of the same title by Frank X Walker: this "hummingbird" character is a gay man from Appalachia who has moved off to a city (usually on the East or West Coasts), become infected with HIV, then moved home to die. The most extended (and earliest) depiction of this figure in LGBTQ Appalachian literature is Raphael Hardin from Johnson's 1993 novel, *Scissors, Paper, Rock*; Brian Jackson in Carter Sickels's 2020 novel, *The Prettiest Star*, is the most recent. Walker's "Hummingbird" (published in the 2000 collection *Affrilachia*) differs from these other portrayals in that the hummingbird figure in Walker's poem is unable—and clearly not welcome—to return home to be with his family in his final days.[71] Instead, the hummingbird of Walker's poem—a man "dead / from AIDS / at thirty-seven"—will be buried in California, his death acknowledged by his family in the same way that they marked his life: silence. Walker writes, "they're not even flying / him home / gonna plant him in Cali / . . . / and come back to Kentucky / believing nobody ever knew / the truth." In this poem, the family has responded to hate speech with silence—they ". . . didn't defend him / when others called him / punk, faggot or sissy"—and treat the news of his death in the same way. Like Nick Handley's neighbors who cheerfully "aid and abet" his closeted life, this hummingbird's family perpetuates the silence.

This figure—that of the gay man with AIDS who moves home to die—is evoked in West Virginia–born writer Jeff Mann's essay "Fried Chicken and Spoon Bread," from his 2005 book *Loving Mountains, Loving Men*. In this essay, Jeff recounts a phone conversation he had with his mother on the evening in 1985 when she watched *An Early Frost*, the first television movie about AIDS. Jeff's mother calls him, in tears, and she invokes the specter of the families—like that of Walker's hummingbird—who had turned their backs on their loved ones: " 'Please be careful,' she begged. 'And you know, don't you, that if you ever got sick, we wouldn't turn our backs on you. We'd want you to come home.' "[72] That gift given to Mann by his mother—that promise of a home whose doors will be open to him regardless—is one that too many queer Appalachians have been denied. In the essay, Mann revels in that sense of security, with the pleasures of home interspersed with his love of the landscape of Appalachia: "Home. Where I would have dwindled quietly, reading many books and thinking about the many handsome men unmet. Where she would have baked me spoon bread and lemon cake, where we would have rocked on the porch together, watching the sunset over the New River, and eventually, fireflies floating in the park."[73] In Mann's essay, his imaginings of coming home to die have a more peaceful resolution than that available to Walker's hummingbird.

In Carter Sickels's novel *The Prettiest Star*, set in 1986 in the early years of the HIV epidemic, protagonist Brian Jackson—unlike Walker's hummingbird—is able to move home to live with family in the last few months of his life. However, he doesn't receive the loving welcome that Jeff Mann's mother promised nor find the serenity that Mann anticipated. Although Brian has been homesick for the landscape and places of his hometown in Appalachia—"He was thinking of green hills and the clean smell of baseball fields and the light-filled woods on a summer day"[74]—Brian's return home is far from tranquil. At first, the indignities are isolated: his parents insist on his using separate dishes from the rest of the family, and they insist on silence, first about his homecoming and later about Brian's being a person with AIDS: "If others find out, they'll run him out of town."[75] Later, when word does get out, and then when Brian attempts to swim in the community swimming pool (he's thrown out, the police are called, and the pool is drained and closed for a week), most community members (and even extended family) turn against the Jacksons: Brian's family receives harassing phone calls and wakes up to graffiti on their garage door and a gunshot through their windshield.

Brian knows that this intolerance isn't isolated to his hometown: "I get why my parents don't want anyone to know. In Chester [Brian's hometown], people think we don't deserve to live, but it's not just Chester that thinks this way—it's most of America. Even in New York you feel the disgust grinding you into the dirt. *God is taking care of the homosexuals.*"[76] In Brian's video diaries, he refers to the hummingbird phenomenon: "I've known guys who were sick and went back to small towns all over the country—upstate New York, Kansas, Florida, Kentucky—and never said a word about what was wrong. They went back to their hometowns and died from a mysterious illness."[77] Yet Brian also remembers the hummingbirds who weren't so fortunate: "Guys try to go back home and their parents turn them away. Hospital beds hold skeletons of men who the nurses and doctors do not want to touch. Even after we die they don't want us. Bodies in morgues that parents will not claim."[78] In contrast, Brian's final days, although certainly not calm or carefree, are spent in his grandmother's home, family and friends by his side, dreaming of the places and people he has loved.

Scissors, Paper, Rock provides a quite different version of the hummingbird's story from that seen in Walker's poem, a version closer to that imagined by Jeff Mann and his mother: a story in which a person with AIDS can come home and be with family and where the silence surrounding this illness is finally ruptured.[79] Certainly, Johnson's novel is strongly marked by silences, by things that the characters cannot or will not say to each other. (Johnson also writes evocatively of "the ability to speak aloud the unspeakable" in his 1996 memoir *Geography of the Heart*, in which he recounts his relationship with partner Larry Rose and Rose's 1990 death from AIDS-related complications.[80]) An early reviewer of *Scissors*, writing in the *Virginia Quarterly Review* in 1994, notes "the awkward silences that mark Tom Hardin's interactions with his prodigal son, Raphael," observing that "neither can find the words to bridge the lacuna that threatens to yawn eternally between them."[81] Most of the novel's silences are like the ones mentioned by this reviewer: not the enforced, public silences of oppression but rather the uncomfortable private silences that descend on families.

The most marked of these family silences, however, and the silences that mirrored the cultural silences of the book's milieu, the early 1990s, are silences about HIV and AIDS. As Johnson explained in an interview shortly after the novel's publication, Raphael's situation in the novel—and that of his family—is representative of a larger cultural phenomenon Johnson observed at the time: of men in small-town Appalachia dying of AIDS but whose families "have had to suffer in silence" because of the "stigma attached to the disease which has made it practically impossible for the community to grieve with them in the way that a community should."[82] Johnson's observation (in this 1995 interview) foreshadows the 2012 conclusions of researchers who studied "disenfranchised grief"—the grief of people in stigmatized groups or whose loved ones died in a stigmatized manner—within Appalachia. These researchers concluded that "people from Appalachia who grieve the loss of a loved one to an AIDS-related death or suicide are often neglected and forgotten" because "AIDS-related mourning is more pronounced, but less supported than with other terminal illnesses like cancer," a dilemma that "exacerbates the impact of the loss, and diminishes social support."[83]

Within the novel, Raphael's disenfranchised grief—and the larger silence surrounding the AIDS crisis—is foregrounded each time the topic of AIDS comes up, as Johnson reminds the reader what Raphael, a gay man living in San Francisco in the 1980s and 1990s, would have known of loss. The most notable reminders take place in the novel's pivotal chapter (also entitled "Scissors, Paper, Rock"), when all the living members of the Hardin family, plus their friends and neighbors, gather in the backyard for the Hardins' annual summer party. Earlier that evening while going over the guest list, Raphael's mother, Rose Ella, had been telling Raphael about all the friends and neighbors who have died, then announced chirpily of herself and Tom Hardin, "'Su'vivors,' she said gaily, 'we're just su'vivors,'" to which Raphael replied, "'You could say that about us all.'"[84] This—Raphael's status, for now, as a survivor of the AIDS crisis—is the last thing that Rose Ella wants to discuss. She has noticed that "for the first time in [her] memory . . . Raphael came home from San Francisco without a friend" and with "blackness hovering over his head. . . . But over the years she'd been careful not to ask questions of Raphael or his California friends and everyone, including Raphael, seemed to like it that way."[85] However, after Raphael's comment about being a survivor, a silence engulfs them, making manifest all of the things that Rose Ella wants—but is afraid—to ask: "The silence that followed grew into something she could touch, the size and shape of themselves. Raphael said nothing more, and as for the questions that crowded Rose Ella's tongue, each looked like a door closed on things she knew but didn't want to know and in any case couldn't bring herself to speak the words she'd have to say to learn more."[86] Here, the reader sees Rose Ella's sense of the power of language, her feeling that something will become more real if she puts her fear into words. Later that evening, she finally will begin to ask these questions, and Raphael will tell her about his diagnosis. (This conversation between mother and son is discussed in detail in chapter 6, within the context of the scene's feast imagery.)

That same silence descends again during the party, when a guest pontificates about family responsibilities and declares what carefree lives the childless adults (Raphael and another guest) must be leading. Again,

Raphael alludes to the AIDS crisis, responding, "Instead I'm taking care of friends who are dying, . . . A lot of them a thousand miles from parents or brothers or sisters who could care less."[87] Johnson sets apart the crowd's reaction in a paragraph by itself, for emphasis: "Silence." Rose Ella fills this silence with a deflection—"There's a time and place for this conversation and it's someplace else and later on"—followed by a well-meaning lie, declaring, "Right now we're all in good health and happy to be here."[88] This is a difficult fiction to maintain when Tom Hardin is there, unable to eat and dying of cancer, although Rose Ella's own illness (she'll die suddenly within a year) and Raphael's are as yet unnoticeable.

In several notable moments that evening, either Raphael or one of his family members will break this silence: in all cases, these are productive, empowering, enriching moments. First, Raphael's sister Catherine acknowledges what no one else has even mentioned, when she consoles Raphael on the death of his partner: "Raphael. I'm sorry about your friend. . . . You don't have to say anything. I just wanted to say I know what he meant to you, and I'm sorry I didn't say that when he died."[89] It is significant that even in this key moment of acknowledgment, Catherine can only call this lost love a "friend." When Raphael asks how she knew that the man was his "boyfriend" (Raphael's term), Catherine describes her habit of reading the significance of silence: "How does anybody ever figure out what's going on in the world? You open your ears and listen to what people aren't talking about."[90]

Then Raphael himself breaks the silence with his nephews, speaking to them about his diagnosis more directly and forthrightly than he has spoken at any point in the novel: "I'm filled with anger and rage that no one will acknowledge that my friends are dying, and that they're dying of AIDS. . . . And I have the virus. I've had it for years."[91] Although the nephews' initial reaction is more silence—"The silence that followed now was too large to comprehend or speak into"—the young people clearly are grateful for Raphael's frankness, and they then inundate him with questions. The ignorance of their questions and the eagerness with which they ask them make Raphael sorry that he has delayed this conversation for so long: "Any number of times he might have chosen to speak; instead, he had held his tongue and contributed another brick to the great wall of silence. Tonight he released to the clouds the breath of his stories."[92] As Johnson's novel makes clear, truth and stories have power, especially when the speaker has previously been denied a voice.

Silences, Radio, and Hearing Voices in *Strange Birds in the Tree of Heaven*

As in *Scissors, Paper, Rock*, issues of truth and silence pervade Karen Salyer McElmurray's novel *Strange Birds in the Tree of Heaven*. Imagery of light and darkness predominate, and the closet serves as a metaphor for the dark concealment of truth. For a novel that is so pervaded by silence—by all the things that its characters cannot or will not say to each other—it is also a novel filled with voices, one whose characters are often overwhelmed by those voices. The silences are usually a source of pain: Tobias Blue, Ruth Blue Wallen's hyper-religious father, brings ominous silence and violence to his family; Ruth Blue Wallen cannot bring herself to speak to anyone about the violence in her home or about her deep unmet needs; her son, Andrew Wallen, cannot tell his mother about his love for another man. Maurice Manning has described the effect of the novel's multiplicity of voices, internal and external, noting that "each of the novel's three narrators hears voices, a voice inside themselves, strangely familiar and prophetic at once. Each episodic chapter, therefore, feels listened to, the sound of a voice listening over and over to itself."[93] The voices have a shifting valence within the narrative and are not always positive; when these voices are Ruth's internalization of her father's religiosity or Andrew's hearing his parents' words of criticism, they lure the characters toward death. In contrast, popular radio and the voices of love and light help to empower Andrew Wallen and compel him to choose love and life.

Through the novel's three narrators—Ruth Blue Wallen, her husband Earl Wallen, and their son Andrew—and their first-person accounts (largely internal monologues), the reader is privy to the characters' innermost thoughts and hears the characters' deepest secrets, even though, as Ruth notes in one of her chapters, "I told no one these truths."[94] From this internal perspective, near the end of the novel, the reader witnesses both Ruth and Andrew deciding whether to end their lives. For Ruth, who sinks to the bottom of her family's pond, she must decide whether to drown herself or to float up toward light and breath. Likewise, we read Andrew's internal debates about whether to commit suicide after his mother gives him a shotgun and locks him in his room, providing him with the means to kill himself. In keeping with the novel's pervasive silence, Ruth doesn't give voice to this suggestion, but her implication is clear, and she thinks,

"You want to save him from all this dark world where love has failed, want to send him up and up and up."[95]

Throughout the novel, radio—especially the radio in Ruth Blue Wallen's childhood home—is employed by McElmurray as a symbol to highlight the contrast between stifling silence and invigorating sounds. In the Blue family home, the radio was alternately tuned to religious programming (by Tobias, Ruth's father) or to popular music and radio shows. In fact, *popular* radio was a central feature of one of Ruth's earliest memories (and one of the first stories she narrates to the reader), a moment of playfulness with her mother, Stella (who will run away within a year, to escape Tobias's physical and mental abuse). Ruth and Stella were together one afternoon after school, listening to music and "the stories, Amos and Andy or Charlie McCarthy"[96] on the radio, and they dance together,

> right there in the kitchen with all that supper going on and the potato water boiling away and the radio still on. For a long time I wanted to cry about it when I thought how she took my hands. She had big, warm hands that could hold on to a body so tight you thought they'd never let you go. She whirled me around and around. I was dizzy from it, that and how beautiful she was. . . . We were the radio our own selves, and forgetting all about Tobias.[97]

This dyadic moment of mother-child intimacy is interrupted by the fiercely religious Tobias, who approves of neither worldly things nor dancing. The togetherness and beauty and radio listening are all abruptly halted: Ruth's mother's face looks "like all the light of the world went out of it. . . . We shut the radio off, quick, and we ate in the quiet, that night."[98] Although Tobias vehemently endorses religious programming, he is framed more frequently as a source of deathly silence. On that evening, Tobias doesn't say anything to make his displeasure known, but instead just stares, as Ruth tells us in a passage that hints at Tobias's abuse: "It wasn't like he did anything or said anything like sometimes, when his fist would slam hard against the wall and he'd say, no. . . . He didn't even have to say a word or do a thing."[99] Tobias had had this silencing effect even before Ruth was born: after Stella's marriage to Tobias, "All the music she had ever wished for became a ghost of itself, lost in grayness and long afternoons so quiet she could hear her own breath."[100]

In contrast to the silence (or occasional religious programming) that Tobias endorses, his grandson Andrew uses music from the radio to combat those judgmental voices. Throughout the novel, music serves as a buffer between Andrew and a voice whispering "abomination." On the evening that the novel opens, Andrew slips away to meet his boyfriend, Henry Ward, and Andrew is "glad not to hear anything but steel guitar sound."[101] A few pages later, Andrew explicitly associates radio rock and roll music with escape: "Saturday nights, hand on the radio dial, music promised to take me. Take us anywhere."[102] For other characters—specifically Andrew's father and mother—popular music had offered an escape, but that escape promised by the music never unfolded because it was drowned out by silence. Earl had dreams of a career in music—"I wanted music any way I could get it," wanted to be "a rock-n-roll star, showing some little town what was what."[103] By the end of the novel, when Earl calls out for his wife and son (one of whom is rising from the family's pond, the other headed for a new life in Florida, having escaped from the shotgun and the locked room), the only response Earl hears is the "never-written song of my own life. The ghost of love waiting in my song-empty mouth."[104] Whereas music offers Andrew an escape and a solace, it is for Earl yet another reminder of the life he'd wanted but never built for himself.

For Andrew, the little voice that he hears in his head alternately expresses his self-loathing (the internalized version of his parents' judgment) and deepest desires, especially his hope for a future outside of Mining Hollow, with Henry Ward. Henry encourages Andrew to move with him to Florida, where they'll live together in a beachside condo. Andrew's having a voice himself would mean making a choice, actively taking a stand to move away from "the rooms of my boyhood"[105] toward "roads beyond all I have known, . . . the endless ocean and the power of forever,"[106] answering Henry's question: "When will you know if it's me or them?"[107] The "them" of this question is Andrew's parents: Earl, who regularly "recites to me a litany of ineptitude, the ways I have failed my manhood's tests,"[108] and Ruth's religiosity, whispering, "You are an abomination in the eyes of. Abomination, abomination."[109] Early in the novel, this voice tries to prevent Andrew from going out with Henry on a Saturday night:

> A voice hurried after us, caught at the bumper of Henry's car as we careened around the easy highway curves. This voice knew me, like it had for time immemorial. . . . Which voice?

My mother's? grandfather's? Voice of this night, of God himself, riding like an angel made of coal dust and sin on the bumper of Henry's car. You, the voice said. You who looketh not into your own sinful heart. Why, you are no man at all. Words settling across my chest so I could hardly breathe.[110]

By the novel's end, which occurs later that same evening when Andrew chooses life over death, chooses love with Henry rather than the dark and oppressive home of his mother and father, the voice has changed its message. Rather than judgment and hate, the voice now encourages and promises: "And then a voice said, surely, surely the light of God is sweet, and it's right to behold the sun."[111] The changing voice that Andrew hears demonstrates his emerging acceptance of his sexuality and his rejection of the judgments of his family.

doris davenport: Giving Voice to an Affrilachian Community in *Soque Street Poems* (1995) and *madness like morning glories* (2005)

A consideration of doris davenport's poetry collections *Soque Street Poems* (1995) and *madness like morning glories* (2005) reveals another layer of silencing that affects residents of Appalachia who have ancestral origins in Africa. Queer Affrilachians have been triply erased and silenced: through the invisibility of Appalachians in American culture, the invisibility of queer people within Appalachia, and the invisibility of being an African American native of Appalachia. davenport has stated that she hadn't thought of herself as *Appalachian* until Frank X Walker coined the term "Affrilachian" in 1991 because, as davenport wrote in a 1995 entry in her journal, "I hadn't placed me or northeast Georgia in a context of Appalachia."[112] By the publication of her 1998 essay in *Bloodroot: Reflections on Place by Appalachian Women Writers*, davenport writes about her "Affrilachian experiences" and meditates on all the ways that she and her community were Appalachian, although earlier cultural definitions of Appalachia denied them that identification.[113]

In *Soque Street Poems*, davenport gave us the voices and the stories of her family, her hometown, her community, her origins: a vibrant Affrilachian community in Cornelia, Georgia. A decade later, davenport published a revised version of this collection as *madness like morning glories* (2005). These texts are apt means for reasserting the voices of Affrilachians (and davenport's own queer Affrilachian voice), as the individual poems are written in the voices of community members. The poems of both collections give voice to this community, largely allowing the community members to tell their own stories. Through this approach, davenport carries on the important Appalachian and African traditions of storytelling. (davenport relies even more heavily on an oral storytelling tradition for her performance poetry, discussed in more detail in chapter 5.) Many of the poems' voices speak from beyond the grave, almost as though davenport has become one of the "conjure women" of the poems (and thus highlighting davenport's debts to mysticism and voodoo). In these texts, davenport tells the stories of her Georgia home.

Many scholars have observed the importance of poetic voice to davenport's work and have described these poems—both *Soque Street Poems* and their later iteration in *madness like morning glories*—as stories, and davenport as a storyteller. In a 2005 review of *madness*, Warren J. Carson says that davenport "has resurrected the people who gave life to Soque Street and invites them to tell their stories. And do they ever tell stories!" He proceeds to note the poems with "the more compelling voices."[114] In another contemporary review, Janet St. John calls davenport "a storyteller" who "understands true spoken language," suggesting (as have other scholars) that davenport's "poems may work best when read aloud."[115] St. John notes the voices in the poems, calling *madness like morning glories* a "unique collection highlighting the voices of Afrilacians [*sic*], that is, African Americans in Appalachia" in which davenport "re-creates the voices of a Georgia community in a narrative of personal histories told from different perspectives." In a 2002 essay, "Coming Home to Affrilachia: The Poems of doris davenport," James A. Miller argues that in bringing "the voices and personalities that inhabit Soque Street" to life, davenport has essentially stepped aside and let those voices alter her poetic style, "most notably davenport's adoption of long, prose-like lines and stanzas—in sharp contrast to the short sentences and sometimes staccato phrasing of her earlier work."[116]

The voices of these poems, in both *Soque Street* and *madness*, are feisty, forthright, and even combative, challenging the reader, contradicting other speakers, and asking pointed questions to an implied poetic interlocutor. For example, in both collections, the second poem, entitled "Now, I know you remember . . . so and so,"[117] establishes the tone of the volume, demonstrating the poems' reliance on storytelling and on multiple poetic voices. The story told by the poem actually begins in its title; the first line is the primary speaker's commentary: "meaning somebody who rode through town once, ten years / ago or someone who lived and died before your birth." The speaker then contrasts tale-tellers like this one (who say "Now I know you remember so and so") with Fannie Mae:

> Not like Fannie Mae. She will get all into a story and catch
> herself: "But that was before you were born." Fannie Mae
> will pause, grin for emphasis and say, "And I *wish* you
> coulda seen it!"

The speaker then establishes her own differences from Fannie Mae and sets the tone for the collection of poetry to follow:

> not me.
> when i get through
> when i'm done
> won't be no wishing
> you could see.
> you gone see.

That tone—forthright and boasting—characterizes the poetic voice throughout this collection. In addition, this poem sets the stage for the ones that will follow, signaling that these voices will often tell of events long past or of the goings-on of departed neighbors and family.

In this and other spots in the collection, an individual speaker seems to talk back to the collection's implied author, challenging the collection being compiled. This phenomenon is most apparent in "while we on the subject; / Let's tell the rest of it. / (Tell it like it i-s is.)," a poem in *Soque Street* that does not appear in *madness*. In this poem, the speaker undermines the positive, nostalgic portrait that the collection has thus far painted of this Affrilachian community and its contented residents, insisting that some of the residents were "Scared to go, and hating it the whole time. / Hating everything about these hills and valleys." These lines carry a starkly different tone from many of the other poems, poems that sometimes reveal neighborly conflicts or romantic entanglements but do not characterize Cornelia's inhabitants as being unhappy there. This poem concludes with the speaker's parting challenge to *Soque Street*'s implied author: "Tell about / that, / while you on the subject." Through this poem, located about a quarter of the way into this collection, davenport establishes that not all was perfect in Cornelia; she develops this theme further in poems later in the collection. Despite the fact that davenport maintains (in the introduction to *Soque Street Poems*) that "*my* Northeast Georgia" is marked by "a passionate love that binds us to each other and to these hills,"[118] she demonstrates that not everyone loved living in Cornelia, Georgia. Even while chronicling Appalachia's racial diversity through this poetic portrait of a vibrant Affrilachian community, she makes room for diversity of thought within that community.

What differing stories do the voices of these two poetry collections tell? Although there are poems in common between *Soque Street Poems* and its successor *madness like morning glories*, many poems have been revised in the intervening decade, while others have been added or excised in the building of *madness*. Overall, although the revisions that shaped *madness like morning glories* result in the addition of some voices, these revisions also seem to sanitize the community, making Cornelia seem a bit more conventionally wholesome in *madness* than it appeared in *Soque Street Poems* and focusing the reader's attention on the community's racial diversity rather than its robust pleasures. By removing "Fred's Tavern" (a poem in *Soque* that's absent from *madness*), by turning Sally's from a "Lunchroom" (in *Soque*) into a "Cafe" (in *madness*), and by adding a "Church" segment to *madness*, davenport depicts, in *madness like morning glories*, a community that is less ribald and raucous, more marked by respectability than the community represented in *Soque Street*. Another distinction between the two collections, overall, is that *madness* removes many of davenport's family narratives, the community tales (the "vampire" at the local movie theater), and the celebrations of food that pervade *Soque Street Poems*. Both collections are undoubtedly groundbreaking; davenport's depiction of an Affrilachian community was a definite rarity when *Soque* was published in 1995, only four years after Frank X Walker had coined the term "Affrilachian." Yet *Soque Street Poems* feels more like an honest portrayal of a human community, rife with the passion and longing that propel human endeavors, than its revised, tamer twin collection.

Another key element in *Soque Street* that is absent from *madness* (and ties *Soque Street* back to the discussions of visuality and photography in chapter 3) is davenport's family photographs. Many of the "characters," the voices who enliven Soque Street, are visible to the reader in the pages of *Soque Street*, including three photographs of Fannie Mae Gibson Shuebergh (davenport's great-aunt); a photo of doris and her siblings; and a photo of her mother, Ethel Mae Gibson, as a young woman. In *Soque Street*, these photographs allow the reader to make a human connection with the subjects of the poems, to see these folks and families as not unlike one's own. That effect is blunted in *madness* by the photographs' absence.

In these two collections as well as her other poetry, davenport gives voice to people who are rarely heard from in poetry or in academia, including Affrilachians and queer people. Scholars have suggested for many years that this—davenport's speaking out against oppression and her giving voice to underrepresented groups—may account for the general lack of scholarly attention to her work. Denise R. Shaw's 2007 entry on davenport in the *Encyclopedia of African American Women Writers* credits davenport with "giving voice to those silenced (especially oppressed voices in her hometown region of south [sic] Georgia)," and Helena Louise Montgomery (in a 1993 entry on davenport in *Contemporary Lesbian Writers of the United States*) blames "publishers who refuse voice to those whose views and realities do not fit into the scheme of things" for davenport's difficulty finding a publisher for her work.[119] Melinda Cardozo's entry on davenport in the *Encyclopedia of Contemporary LGBTQ Literature of the United States* (2009) makes especially clear how davenport has actively resisted the status quo: "She is an emphatic voice for black lesbians, insisting upon whole scale social change and exposure of the difficultly gendered truths of American racism and homophobia."[120] In addition to acknowledging the power of voice in davenport's poetry and the rarity of queer Affrilachian poetic voices (especially in 1995 when *Soque Street Poems* was published), it is important that we acknowledge what this may have cost davenport in terms of her career and critical success.[121]

davenport's commentary about her work highlights not only the importance of voice in her poetry but also the role played by her hometown of Cornelia—and her family's homeplace on Soque Street—in shaping her poetic voice. In a 1990 essay, "Music in Poetry: if you can't feel it / you can't fake it," davenport locates the origins of her poetry in the sounds of her home community. Situating herself within a tradition of black poets and writers including Paul Laurence Dunbar, Langston Hughes, and Zora Neale Hurston, davenport observes, "My poetry . . . is 'controlled' or created via the richness of the music I heard in a small, rural, working class, Black community in the hills of Northeast Georgia," and that "the specific intonations of the people's voices—including a certain kind of mountain twang—also affect my work."[122] For davenport, the people and locations of her homeplace in Cornelia were key to establishing her poetic sensibility and poetic voice: "Some aspect of the people or the place appears in everything, prose and poetry."[123] In chapter 5, "HomePlaceBody," I explore how davenport and other LGBTQ Appalachian writers and filmmakers grapple with the pleasures and perils of their Appalachian homeplaces and Appalachian bodies.

5

HomePlaceBody

The Pleasures and Perils of the Physical World

In Loyal Jones's 1994 book *Appalachian Values* (expanded from his landmark 1973 essay), he describes "Love of Place"—especially of the "homeplace"—as one of nine quintessentially Appalachian values and an essential part of an Appalachian's worldview. Jones's description and the photographs included in the "Love of Place" chapter of the 1994 book primarily emphasize *place* as nature and landscape. Jones mentions rivers and creeks, isolated areas, and a home "so far back in the mountains, the sun set between [the] house and the road."[1] The photos and their captions focus almost exclusively on the natural world and the isolated small structures (houses, general stores) within that landscape, including a swinging bridge, a "farmstead," and haystacks. The chapter's only exceptions emphasize either the isolation of the rural scene (through the caption, "A girl walks a lonely road on Long Branch, Estill County, Kentucky") or the quaintness of the location ("Mr. and Mrs. Oscar Carter sit in their general store in Pulaski County, Kentucky, among life's necessities and niceties, including folk art").[2] Up to that point (two-thirds of the way through the book), these two photographs are the only ones to include a visible human figure; the focus is on the landscape of Appalachia. Overall, Jones's essay and book do not account for the Appalachia that lies outside the mountains, away from the farmstead, haystacks, and "lonely road" of the coffee-table book's photographs. Jones emphasizes Appalachians' attachment to that landscape and to the homeplace, noting, "We remember our homeplace and many of us go back as often as possible."[3]

For queer Appalachians, "home" itself can be a complicated construct. On one hand, it is likely to be the place where one's family resides, where one's earliest memories were fashioned, and where one returns in times of celebration or trouble. Also, for Appalachians and non-Appalachians alike, home is likely to be associated with one's development of identity, through the pivotal processes of coming of age. On the other hand, "home" might not be the space where one feels the most free to be oneself, and especially not where openness about sexuality feels possible or safe. This dilemma offers a central challenge to the self-definitions of many Appalachians who identify as LGBTQ. Neema Avashia writes in her 2022 memoir, *Another Appalachia: Coming Up Queer and Indian in a Mountain Place*, that she has a deep attachment to West Virginia, the state where she was born and raised, yet she grew up fielding racist epithets at elementary school and felt especially out of place due to her sexuality: "Growing up, I never knew anyone—neither Indian nor West Virginian—who was openly gay. . . . I found it difficult not to imagine the worst: that it hadn't been discussed because it wasn't condoned."[4] In the book's concluding section, she writes, "I do not know what it means to possess a love of place so strong you remain rootbound even when the soil sometimes rejects your very existence."[5] As writer Zach Shultz, a native of rural Kentucky and longtime resident of New York City, writes in his review of Carter Sickels's *The Prettiest Star*, "Growing up queer in Appalachia, home has never been a simple matter. . . . I never felt I belonged, never felt at home there—or anywhere, really. Though I've learned to hide it well, the acute sting of otherness follows me wherever I go."[6]

This dilemma plays out in Appalachian LGBTQ literature as authors explore both the notion of home or homeplace and their own relationship to that home: the hills and hollers and cities and towns that form the Appalachian landscape. Writers' portrayals of the Appalachian homeplace are, inevitably, as complicated and multiple as Appalachians' real-world relationship with the region and its natural landscape. The work of Sickels, Watts, Johnson, and McElmurray figures the natural world of Appalachia as a peaceful refuge, while acknowledging the culture of extraction that has long commodified the landscape. Some writers, especially Julia Watts and Jeff Mann, have explored the specific dilemma that queer Appalachians face: remain in Appalachia and risk rejection (or worse) for one's sexuality, or migrate to an area—usually urban—with a large gay population and risk rejection for being Appalachian. Finally, Mann, Elizabeth Stephens, and doris davenport have explored the sensuality of the Appalachian landscape and the ways that the physical body both enables the pleasures of Appalachia as well as renders one vulnerable.

Nature as Refuge

The natural world itself has a complicated resonance within Appalachian literature, just as it does in the lives of Appalachians, intensified by the people's historically close relationship to the land: for many years, much of the region's population made its living off the land, either through subsistence farming or extraction of resources (lumber, coal, natural gas). Consequently, in *A Handbook to Appalachia: An Introduction to the Region* (2006), a chapter entitled "Natural Resources and Environment of Appalachia" replicates a crucial (and typical) conflation of Appalachia's natural world and natural *resources*. Both this history of extraction and Appalachians' attachment to place have indelibly marked its literature. In Danny Miller et al.'s essay "Appalachian Literature" in *A Handbook to Appalachia* (2006), the authors note that there are "many novels about the coal-mining industry in Appalachia," explaining that "coal mining is arguably the single most influential force in the lives and culture of late-nineteenth-century and early-twentieth-century central Appalachians."[7] In Maggie Anderson's essay "The Mountains Dark and Close around Me" (in the 1998 collection *Bloodroot: Reflections on Place by Appalachian Women Writers*), she takes stock of the *confluences* (she prefers this word to "influences") on her writing, consisting of both other writers and the "landscapes I have known," especially those of her native West Virginia: "I love the West Virginia landscape and grieve for its maimed reconfiguration and destruction in the name of money and progress."[8]

Other Appalachian writers, from a variety of religious traditions, imbue the Appalachian landscape with a deep sense of spirituality, emphasizing the sacredness of the land yet decrying the way this land has been exploited. Marilou Awiakta, a "Cherokee/Appalachian poet" whose family has lived in the mountains for more than seven generations, has described her book *Abiding Appalachia: Where Mountain and Atom Meet* (1978) as an exploration of "the sacred law of taking and giving back with respect," a law that governs "the interconnection of all that lives and the need for reverence for all."[9] As Awiakta warns in one of the poems of *Selu: Seeking the Corn-Mother's Wisdom*, "When the people call Earth 'it,' / they use her / consume her strength. / Then the people die."[10] Similarly, one scholar notes of Silas House's work that he "often links a devotion to the land with a spiritual element that transcends conventional religious experience," while "House's characters often fight to save the land from the destructive and dishonest maneuvers of businessmen and coal companies."[11] In bell hooks's work on Appalachia, she emphasizes "all the ways agrarian black folks hold the earth sacred" as well as her personal desire to protect "a landscape violated and plundered, taken over by greed and ruthless capitalism."[12] As those writers and many others have expressed, while many may regard the land as sacred, Appalachians are accustomed—if not resigned—to seeing the natural world parsed as if a commodity.

That natural world—whether sacred or commodified—has been central to Appalachian literature; overviews of the region's literature frequently emphasize its rootedness in the place of Appalachia. In their landmark 1962 essay, "Literature since 1900," W. D. Weatherford and Wilma Dykeman note the complicated relationship of Appalachians (and Appalachian authors) to the land. They describe early literary portrayals of Appalachia (in the late nineteenth century) marked by "the overwhelming impact on authors of the natural world," arguing that in later portrayals, "nature has assumed both a larger and a lesser role . . . as native writers revealed the larger influences of the mountains, of the natural world, on the people who live therein."[13] In the 2006 essay "Appalachian Literature," Danny Miller et al. observe that in early literary depictions of Appalachia (by local colorists Mary Noailles Murfree and John Fox Jr.), "the focus . . . was often on their setting, the sublime natural beauty of the Appalachian mountains," and note that, as a whole, Appalachian literature is "sometimes distinguished from other literatures by its strong emphasis on setting, or 'place,' as an influence upon the values and motivations of characters."[14] Similarly, in the introduction to the "Contemporary Appalachia" volume of *The Southern Poetry Anthology* (2011), editor Jesse Graves notes a thread running through contemporary Appalachian poetry: "Perhaps no single concern emerges so strongly from these poems as the importance of landscape in preserving a way of life from the past, in the present, and for the future."[15] Graves maintains that even though Appalachian culture is changing, it is "still deeply in touch with its natural environment" and that "landscape . . . is central to Appalachian writing."[16]

In the work of Carter Sickels, the place of Appalachia includes both the natural environment—so central to Appalachian literature—as well as the "homeplace." Sickels's nostalgic description of his family's homeplace, the "Big Farm," in the essay "Photograph, 2007" evokes Loyal Jones's point about Appalachians' attachment to "the homeplace." Yet it is Sickels's treatment of the natural world, rather than the homeplace, that so clearly characterizes place as a refuge for queer Appalachians. In Sickels's essay "Johnson City," the natural world is figured as a means of escape, not from other people but rather from naturalizing discourses, an escape from the constant pressure to define or explain oneself. In "Johnson City," Sickels recounts a trip with his friend Stephen to visit Stephen's family in Johnson City, Tennessee. As Stephen and Sickels are driving back home after the visit (a visit filled with awkward moments and exposed generational rifts), they pull off the road at a scenic overlook and admire a river and a waterfall. In the passage that follows, Sickels describes nature as a refuge, making clear that nature allows a queer Appalachian to escape the constant pull toward a seemingly impossible self-definition: "We felt more at home here [in the mountains] than we ever would be at a gay bar or around our families. Here, there was nothing to explain. . . . We stood next to each other as ourselves, surrounded by forest that was millions of years old and feeling content with all its mystery. Here, now, the two of us, we could just be."[17] In this description, the natural world provides these young Appalachians a moment of respite, away from naturalizing discourses or from the pull of self-definition or self-justification.

Significantly, in an essay pervaded by concerns about pronouns and gendered proper names, in these last sentences of the essay, here in the natural world, the pronouns shift to a gender-free unified first-person plural: *we, our, ourselves,* and *us.* These lines in Sickels's essay—through their description of the freedom, unity, and anonymity imparted by nature—evoke Ralph Waldo Emerson's 1836 text *Nature.* In that book's first chapter, Emerson describes his famous—and famously perplexing—trope of a human as a transparent eyeball. Emerson writes:

> In the woods, we return to reason and faith. There I feel that nothing can befal [sic] me in life,—no disgrace, no calamity, (leaving me my eyes,) which nature cannot repair. Standing on the bare ground,—my head bathed by the blithe air, and uplifted into infinite space,—all mean egotism vanishes. I become a transparent eye-ball. I am nothing. I see all. The currents of the Universal Being circulate through me; I am part or particle of God. The name of the nearest friend sounds then foreign and accidental. To be brothers, to be acquaintances,—master or servant, is then a trifle and a disturbance.[18]

Here, Emerson describes a simplification imparted by nature, similar to the freedom that Sickels describes when he says that he and Stephen "could just be": for the individual, freedom from names, ego, hierarchies, and, of course, threats of physical violence.

In Julia Watts's coming-of-age novel *Finding H.F.* (2001), the natural world serves as a refuge for the title character and her best friend Bo, queer teens who explore their sexuality while trapped in the ecosystem of a high school in Morgan, Kentucky, where difference is punished: "the cheerleaders and jocks and popular kids know I'm different. Different on the inside. Like lions on nature shows that sniff out which gazelle is ripest for the picking, those people can sniff out difference—and it's a smell they hate."[19] H.F. and Bo find relief from that threatening atmosphere in a waterfall that they discover while walking in the woods. Not only is the waterfall beautiful and remote, but Watts also links it to another power of nature for some Appalachians: it is a "sign." H.F. observes, thinking of their discovery of this isolated waterfall where they can be free from judgment and bullying, that "sometimes nature puts a sign in front of you, and when it does, you'd better do what it tells you. 'Findin' this place *is* a sign . . . a good sign.'"[20] On the day they find it, the waterfall serves a restorative function for H.F. and Bo. H.F. feels "awake and alive," crediting the water with "washing all my fears downstream."[21] The baptismal imagery of this scene is evoked again at the end of the novel, when H.F. and Bo have traveled to Florida to find H.F.'s mother (who abandoned her as an infant). They go skinny dipping in the Gulf of Mexico. H.F. and Bo frolic in the water "like a pair of toddlers in the world's biggest wading pool," their affection for each other framed as a reconceived Biblical Fall, one in which

> we're a new kind of Adam and Eve. We already ate the fruit from the Tree of Knowledge, and instead of being punished for it, we learned that the world is big and full of opportunities, and that love is always good: Girls can love girls if they want to, boys can love boys if they want to, and a girl and a boy can love each other as dear friends and nothing more or less. We are naked, and we are not ashamed.[22]

The natural world not only shields Bo and H.F. from the prying eyes of Morgan, Kentucky, and the violent beatings that Bo endures at the hands of his homophobic classmates, but it restores and rejuvenates Bo and H.F., giving them hope that their futures will transcend the violence and small minds of their hometown.

Nature serves a similar purpose in the work of another Kentucky-born writer, Fenton Johnson, whose *Geography of the Heart: A Memoir* (1996) interweaves an account of his Kentucky childhood with the story of his relationship with his love Larry Rose, who died in 1990 of complications from AIDS. In a passage near the end of *Geography of the Heart*, Johnson describes a daydream-vision of him, Larry, and a collection of men: "men who have loved me and whom I've loved, and men whom I've wanted to love."[23] The landscape of this vision is distinctly that of a dreamworld, as it combines "the landscape of my childhood" (in Kentucky) with the redwoods of Northern California. Although Johnson acknowledges that many of these men "are surely ill or dead," all the inhabitants of this dream are "alive and full of joy on the grassy bank of my heart."[24] The landscape of the dream encompasses both life and death—the dream's inhabitants being "young enough still to be beautiful, old enough to know the meaning of the coolness beneath the sun's warmth"—and makes a space for safety and togetherness, where "we give ourselves over to making memory and remembering."[25]

Karen Salyer McElmurray has described how her own Kentucky homeplace is central to her sense of identity, stating, "There's some land near that [Hagerhill, Kentucky] in a place called Bear Hollow, and that is the land that is like my bones and blood."[26] In McElmurray's novel *Strange Birds in the Tree of Heaven* (1999), the natural world functions in ways similar to "Johnson City" as portrayed by Sickels and Julia Watts's representation in *Finding H.F.*: the natural world provides a refuge for the characters, often featuring baptismal imagery to suggest that the characters are renewed and refreshed through their encounters with the natural world. However, encounters with the natural world are complicated in *Strange Birds*: the baptismal moments, even though sensual in nature, can be ominous or threatening as well. Often, the natural world of *Strange Birds* is not beautiful or placid but is instead the ravaged dumping ground of a culture that values nature only for what can be commodified or extracted.

In one of the novel's earliest scenes, nature figures as a refuge for Andrew when he and Henry Ward go to nearby Frazier Lake to skinny dip. Andrew's swim in the lake provides sensual indulgence and comfort: "I dove, clean and shallow, into floating strands of moss, amongst slick bodies of minnows nipping, so gently, at my legs as I glided forward toward water that was deeper, seemed farther than I had ever gone before."[27] This swim ends with Andrew and Henry lying on the lake's shore, making love, the water imagery used to characterize the body and soul of the two lovers: "We were heat entering that dark place, pushing into that unknown ocean, ourselves. . . . *Surely the light of God is sweet*, I whispered, *and it's right to behold the sun*. Like all the times before, I drank him in, the salt sea taste of him."[28] The swim and the sexual encounter are explicitly characterized as a baptism: "My skin was still wet and cool from the waters of the lake. . . . Stolen moments of loving, nothing but a precarious transformation, *baptism* leaving my mouth tender, body forever new and strange with the memory of touch."[29] In this characterization of the natural world, the Appalachian landscape provides a space for sexual intimacy that is more secure and homelike than the protagonist's home.

Somewhat ironically, this scene is followed a few chapters later by a parallel scene of Andrew's mother—Ruth Blue—as a young girl, swimming in a pond behind her house and meeting her future husband (Andrew's father) for the first time. This scene also has a baptismal quality, compounded by the fact that Ruth Blue recites prayers as she swims. Yet the narrative's strongest emphasis is on Ruth's sensual experience of the swim, on the renewal and sense of freedom she experiences in the pond. Ruth is naked except for her cotton slip and is swimming in the morning (rather than in the dark of night, as she usually does), thinking, "So seldom by the light of good day did I feel my own bare self, skin and sun and wind no longer bound to the earth, held up only by light and cool and water."[30] Ruth's sense of solitude and suspension is interrupted by her future husband, Earl Wallen, who has come looking for her father and instead encounters Ruth. Earl Wallen's memory of the encounter focuses on the lush sensuality of the natural world surrounding the pond, in a description reminiscent of the description of Calypso's cave in the *Odyssey*: "The only path behind the house was overgrown with wild roses and honeysuckle vine and I took it. May, and already that sweet odor. . . . Then what I saw was a girl, floating on her back at the edge of the clear water of a pond."[31] Earl's memory as he recalls his first sight of Ruth focuses on her body—"A little thing, jet black hair and pale skin, a girl so slight she was like a skeleton of a leaf, her cotton slip transparent with water. Small breasts showing through, full lips whispering"[32]—and Ruth's memory focuses on his body—hair, eyes, skin—and lingers on his hands, with a suggestion of sexual threat or promise: "the hand gripping the brim of his gray hat was not pale at all. I thought of hands that knew how to do things, though I had no idea what those things were."³³ Like the swimming scene for Andrew that would happen many years later, his parents' encounter evokes the sensuality and promise of the natural world.

Although many of the descriptions of the natural world in *Strange Birds in the Tree of Heaven* contain similarly lush and sensual imagery, other passages make clear that the natural world is a dumping ground for the human inhabitants and frame the natural world as a resource to be plundered. Ruth recalls an occasion from her childhood when she and her family walked the six miles to town to do some shopping and other business. On the way, they passed the Big Paint River, whose primary functions appear to be waste disposal and commercial transportation: "Into the waters of that river, people cast off what they no longer had any use for—ashes from burning off spring soil, scraps of food, cans and bottles and bones, dead tires and dogs. In times past, the river had carried flatboats of coal and timber to foreign cities far and beyond, north and south."³⁴ This river is not picturesque, lush, or lifegiving; Ruth calls it "slow-moving, stagnant," its banks covered by "rusted tin and cattails" and its water staining her clothes a "brownish red."³⁵

In other passages, the natural world serves not to transport resources (the Big Paint River carrying barges of coal or timber) but rather as the resource, especially coal. Andrew Wallen and his family live in the small community of Mining Hollow, Kentucky, and both Andrew's father and grandfather worked as coal miners. Andrew tried to go down in the mines himself when he was sixteen, at the insistence of his father. But after only a moment in the darkness, Andrew turns and runs, toward "the light of sun and air" and away from "this world below the earth, world of soot and hours."³⁶ For Andrew, "the mine is the no-light of death."³⁷ For his father Earl, on the other hand, mining is a livelihood and the path to prosperity: "Earl believed it would be himself, strip mine rich, on the striped bare road to fame and glory."³⁸ Andrew also briefly worked with his father in a strip-mining operation, where he "drove a fork lift and scooped out the rich, black insides of hills."³⁹ Earl Wallen "for his twenty years of service [to the mining company], had been given a quilt pieced with black and white and rose and appliques of miners with head lamps and picks and a cross stitch saying, Well Done, Earl Wallen."⁴⁰ Andrew realizes, "That could be my own life,"⁴¹ but it is not the life he chooses. Instead, he slips out of his parents' house, "left the house and the whole coal black world," and heads to Florida with Henry Ward, where he can forge a life unavailable to him in Mining Hollow or Appalachia, thinking to himself, "And so you chose what you could scarcely believe. Love."[42] Like many other queer Appalachians, Andrew Wallen flees Appalachia in search of safety, openness, and the freedom to love whomever he loves.

There's No Place Like Home:
The Pull of the Homeplace and the Queer Appalachian Diaspora

> Growing up in a little town in West Virginia in the seventies where I was at home and not, very much *not* at home, you understand.
>
> —Jeff Mann, inaugural event of Voices from the Hills: A Celebration of Appalachian Writers, in Honor of Danny Miller (1949–2008)

Although nature is indeed figured as a refuge in some LGBTQ Appalachian texts, many authors have acknowledged the complexities of Appalachia—both its rural landscape and its cities—for queer Appalachians. Appalachia is of course not always safe or welcoming for its queer inhabitants. Consequently, many queer Appalachians choose to emigrate, whether for the same reasons that other Appalachians have moved—including job and educational opportunities—or for safety or Andrew Wallen's motivation: the chance to live and love openly among a larger queer community. In a passage from Loyal Jones's original 1973 "Appalachian Values" essay, a passage later omitted from his 1994 coffee-table book *Appalachian Values*, Jones argues that "Love of Place" can be a disadvantage to Appalachians. He observes that "our love of place sometimes keeps us in places where there is no hope of maintaining decent lives"[43] and that this attachment to place foils the efforts of some reformers: "it is a great problem to those who urge mountaineers to find their destiny outside the mountains."[44] Yet Jones notes the homesickness felt by many Appalachians who have migrated to other regions: "Sense of place . . . makes it hard for us to leave the mountains, and when we do, we long to return."[45] Both in their literary works and their essays, Appalachian LGBTQ authors have frankly addressed the identity crisis faced by queer Appalachians whether they choose to stay in their rural hometowns or to migrate to the "big city."

The tendency to overlook urban Appalachia is noted by Danny Miller et al. in their essay "Appalachian Literature," in which they observe that Thomas Wolfe's *Look Homeward, Angel* is not typically identified as an Appalachian novel, "perhaps because it does not deal with the typical Appalachian backwoods people and is set in the more urban area of Asheville, North Carolina," going on to observe that typical misconceptions of Appalachia result in "the rural stereotyped as the norm."[46] Similarly, Ted Olson, in his essay "Literature" in the edited collection *High Mountains Rising: Appalachia in Time and Place* (2004), argues that earlier scholarly overviews of Appalachian literature "had focused largely on the literature of the highland areas and coalfields of Appalachia and had devoted far less attention to literature from the region's valley and urban areas"; Olson notes a turn in contemporary Appalachian fiction to "increasingly emphasizing urban and suburban life."[47] In Miller's earlier (1996) essay "The Appalachian Migratory Experience in Literature," he argues that "the experience of Appalachian migrants in the city—is a distinctive fictional genre . . . so well established that it is replete with recurring themes."[48]

A number of scholars, including Jack Halberstam, have examined the ways in which rural queerness—and for the purposes of this study, I would argue especially Appalachian queerness—is rendered invisible or seemingly impossible by the dominant narrative of contemporary US queer lives, a narrative in which one can flourish (or even exist) only in an urban, urbane landscape.[49] Among the sources that Halberstam cites in *In a Queer Time and Place* is "Get Thee to a Big City: Sexual Imaginary and the Great Gay Migration," Kath Weston's 1995 article in which she demonstrates the central role of the urban/rural divide in the self-concept of gay Americans during the 1970s and 1980s. Based on interviews (conducted in 1985–1986) with lesbians and gay men who had moved to the San Francisco Bay Area, Weston concluded that the contrast between urban and rural shaped the self-definition of many lesbians and gay men. Many interviewees' coming-out narratives began with descriptions of isolation, of feeling like "the only one in the world," followed by a push—from "books, television, movies, and personal contacts"—to migrate to urban areas.[50] Weston describes a culture in which gayness cannot be imagined outside an urban setting: "The result is a sexual geography in which the city represents a beacon of tolerance and gay community, the country a locus of persecution and gay absence," a "space of dead-end lives, oppression, and surveillance, [and] a landscape emptied of gay people."[51] However, many of Weston's interviews undermined these stereotypes—of urban as free and filled with sexual opportunity versus rural as isolating and dangerous for queer people—revealing that "homosexual contacts and desire could occur in the countryside" and "isolation could also characterize life in the city."[52] Ultimately, Weston chronicles the ways that "the gay imaginary is not just a dream of a freedom to 'be gay' that requires an urban location, but a symbolic space that configures gayness itself by elaborating an opposition between rural and urban life."[53]

Similarly, Mary L. Gray in *Out in the Country* examines the way that popular images of queerness obscure the lives of rural queer people, and Gray contradicts representations of visibility as inherently liberatory or empowering for queer youth in rural areas. As Gray points out, "For rural youth . . . the politics of LGBT visibility do not provide greater access to unequivocal pleasures of acceptance and identification and put at risk the necessities of familiarity."[54] Gray's study—an ethnography based on interviews with queer-identifying youth "in rural Kentucky and the small towns scattered along its Illinois, Indiana, West Virginia, and Tennessee borders"[55]—counters the stereotype of rural areas as being devoid of queer people by amply demonstrating the presence of queer youth in Kentucky. Most importantly, she documents the ways these rural queer youth carve out identities for themselves in a place where, according to the prevailing narrative, they don't exist: "LGBT-identifying youth and their allies use their status as 'familiar locals' as well as tenuous access to each other, public spaces, and media-circulated representations of LGBT identities to rework the boundaries of public recognition and local belonging."[56] The strategies employed by these rural young people, as they leverage their dual statuses as both insiders and outsiders, parallel the strategies of Appalachian LGBTQ writers who carve out places for themselves. As Gray says of the youth of her study, they "work every day, through strategies of familiarity, pushing public boundaries of recognition and renarrativizing the meaning of queer realness to reconcile identifying as queerly different from their local communities while still intimately a part of them."[57]

Although Gayatri Gopinath, in her 2005 monograph *Impossible Desires: Queer Diasporas and South Asian Public Cultures*, was discussing a far different landscape and origin story from that of Appalachian queer youth, her description of queer youth who may choose to remain in their home communities can illuminate queer Appalachians' sometimes conflicted relationships to the homeplace. Gopinath describes much of the same insider-outside dynamic as that outlined by Gray in *Out in the Country*, a dynamic in which queer subjects leverage their roles as community natives. In many of the texts that Gopinath examines, the "queer diasporic subjects transform the meanings of 'home' from within its very confines. Given that leaving, escaping, and traveling to a presumably freer 'elsewhere' is not an option or even necessarily desirable for many subaltern subjects, we must take seriously the myriad strategies through which those who remain (out of choice or necessity) conspire to rework the oppressive structures in which they find themselves."[58] As Gopinath argues, these queer diasporic subjects remake the very concept of home by their insistent, persistent presence: "Rather, 'home' is a space that is ruptured and imaginatively transformed by queer diasporic subjects even as they remain within its confines. This queer transformation . . . may very well escape intelligibility within a logic of visibility and 'coming out.'"[59] Perhaps queer Appalachian youth are similarly transforming their homeplaces—their communities and their region—as their very presence there challenges the dominant ideologies and narratives of those spaces.

Much of what Weston describes in "Get Thee to a Big City"—the sense among LGBTQ young people that one must go to the city to find one's "people," only to discover that one may not fit in with the dreamed-of gay community because that community "has been gendered, racialized, and classed"[60]—is recounted in an Appalachian context by West Virginia–born writer Jeff Mann in his 2003 essay "Appalachian Subculture." In this piece, Mann grapples with some of the same topics he first broached in the 1999 essay "Stonewall and Matewan," as he describes the dilemma for someone who identifies as both queer and Appalachian since the "gay imaginary" (described by Weston) does not allow for the possibility of being both. Mann observes that "making a life as a gay man or lesbian in the countryside or in a small town can be tough; not surprisingly, many young Appalachian gays and lesbians hightail it to the nearest city as soon as possible."[61] Mann explains that queer Appalachians are torn between their two subcultures, although both groups—queer people and Appalachians—"are frequent objects of satire, hostility, and contempt" within US culture. Mann notes that "those who remain in the mountains often feel compelled to hide or minimize their gayness, while those who leave for the cities try to erase their accents and assimilate into urban culture."[62] Although Mann's essay enumerates the challenges of being a queer Appalachian, he concludes that successfully straddling two subcultures leaves one richer: "the world shimmers with twice the meaning, twice the beauty."[63]

Julia Watts's 2015 essay "Quare Theory: Some Thoughts on LGBT Appalachian Writing" similarly reveals the complications of "Love of Place" for queer Appalachians. Watts highlights the complexities of rural Appalachia as she tries to account for the seeming contradictions of a queer writer remaining in Appalachia: "I try to show the gay lives that are not often depicted in contemporary literature, to show that not all small-town Southern gays flee to New York or San Francisco or Chicago. Some of them, like me, flee a relatively short distance, to the nearest decent-sized city in their region. . . . Others stay in their small towns of origin, some of them closeted, some of them . . . flamboyantly obvious."[64] Yet Watts also points to the aspects of Appalachia that make the decision to stay—and the decision about whether to remain closeted—so charged for queer Appalachians. In a passage where Watts describes experiencing culture shock during a summer spent back home from college, she explores what makes her "you can't go home again" experience different from Thomas Wolfe's:

> The first was the nature of my family's home—a cabin in a holler off a gravel road, the nearest neighbor a clapboard Pentecostal church. . . . I would breathe in the clean air and let my eyes follow the feminine curves of the mountains. Breaking the silence were sounds from farther down the holler: singing and shouting from a tent revival and the crowing of one of the roosters that a neighbor raised to fight to the death in the ring. These are the sights and sounds of rural Appalachia to me: the light of natural beauty and tranquility with the shadows of dogmatic religion and violence.[65]

Watts makes clear in the essay, "The real answer to why I live in and write about Appalachia is love," and she argues, "somehow this queer feeling of simultaneously being an outsider and an insider feeds my creativity."[66] Watts's description here—of being an outsider and an insider—recalls Mann's account of the difficult balance in straddling the subcultures of queerness and Appalachia. Like the youth that Gray described in *Out in the Country* who self-consciously leverage their status as "familiar locals" to enact change from within, and like the subaltern subjects whom Gopinath described as redefining their communities by their very presence, LGBTQ writers in Appalachia are helping to rewrite the narrative of Appalachia. In the future, young queer Appalachians will be able to find portrayals of themselves in literature and will know they are not "the only one in the world."

For writers like Mann and Watts who have remained in Appalachia, and likewise for writers like Lisa Alther and others who have migrated to other regions, the pertinent issue has been how the mindscape of these Appalachian writers is situated in the region's literal landscape. Alther has made her home in Vermont for most of her adult life, although she divides her time between there, New York City, and Tennessee.[67] Yet she has written eloquently about the pull of Appalachia for her, and has defined herself clearly (and been defined in the scholarship) as an Appalachian: she wrote in "Border States" that "it often takes leaving a place behind to recognize how it has shaped you."[68] Certainly, Alther's status as a fixture in Appalachian literature was well established by the year 2000, when the annual Emory & Henry Literary Festival—designed to honor "a living writer with strong ties to the Appalachian region"[69]—was devoted to her work. (Other honorees have included writers such as James Still, Lee Smith, Ron Rash, Crystal Wilkinson, and Silas House.) Alther has frequently spoken of the impact of her Tennessee upbringing upon her and her work, noting, "Wherever you grow up leaves an indelible stain that defines who you are right through your life. I spent my first 18 years in Kingsport, and I take those experiences with me—I have them inside me—even though I'm living in Vermont," and her brother (noted sociologist John Shelton Reed) has said that she is "a local girl, a child of the Appalachians, determined and strong willed."[70]

Critics have sometimes seemed uncertain how to reconcile Alther's claiming her Appalachian heritage and yet aiming sharp satire at features of her Appalachian home. In *Kinflicks*, for example, Alther skewers everything from the East Tennessee accents (the cheerleaders chant, "Sparky! Sparky! He's our may-un! If he cain't do hit, Dole cay-un!"[71]) to Kingsport itself ("From eight thousand feet Ginny's home town looked like a case of terminal acne"[72]). Harriette C. Buchanan argues that Alther's novels that are most "rooted in her Appalachian culture" feature characters who are deeply ambivalent about "the changes brought by the late twentieth century to the southern Appalachian region of eastern Tennessee and Kentucky where factories and mines bring economic advantage at the expense of the landscape and traditional ways of life."[73] Frederick G. Waage, in "Alther and Dillard: The Appalachian Universe," argues that in *Kinflicks* Alther exploits contemporary Appalachia's contradictions in order to explore the mysteries and contradictions of modern life; she demonstrates that "the effectual pilgrimage must be a *return* to native origins—in time and space—to the small and primal elements of individual and collective existence."[74] Clearly, Alther and the other writers examined in this chapter engage with the many contradictions of Appalachia—particularly those that make it even more challenging, though no less home—for those who embrace both their queer and Appalachian identities, regardless of where they currently live.

The Queer Appalachian Body and the Natural World

Jeff Mann's poetry, Beth Stephens and Annie Sprinkle's film *Goodbye Gauley Mountain*, and the poetry and performances by doris davenport all exemplify another key feature of LGBTQ Appalachian literature: the consistent link between the beauty of the natural world and the beauty of the sexual body. In Mann's work, the natural world is not a refuge from sexuality but, rather, is often linked to sexuality, a metaphor for sexuality. In *Goodbye Gauley Mountain*, a film codirected and produced by West Virginia–born Beth Stephens and her wife Annie Sprinkle, the natural world is not a metaphor *for* the sexual object: it *is* the sexual object. In her work, poet and essayist doris davenport employs a similar dynamic, celebrating the sexual body and her Appalachian community in similarly impassioned detail. In fact, davenport's role as a performance poet makes her work particularly challenging to analyze on the page: the presence of davenport's physical body and the delivery of the poetry in her voice are crucial, she has argued, for the appropriate "reading" of her work. These writers and artists celebrate the body while embracing the richness of the Appalachian landscape.

Nature and the Body in *Bliss*

It is not surprising that nature plays such a key role in the work of Jeff Mann. After all, his father "encouraged non-conformity by having young Jeff read Emerson and Thoreau,"[75] and Mann's undergraduate degree (from West Virginia University) is a double major in English and forestry (technically "Recreation/Nature Interpretation").[76] The importance of the natural world is apparent throughout Mann's work, especially in the essays and poems of *Loving Mountains, Loving Men* (2005), a text that blends memoir, essays, and poetry. As the title suggests, there is a key and consistent link in Mann's work between the beauty of the natural world and the beauty of the sexual body. In the essay "Appalachian Beard Stubble," Mann sums up that connection, observing about his work that "the poems have always shifted back and forth between the beauty of nature and the beauty of men."⁷⁷

For Mann, the natural world is not a refuge from sexuality but, rather, is often linked to sexuality: the natural world becomes his key metaphor for sexuality. In his essay "Bodies We Have Loved," Mann describes nature almost as though it is a substitute lover, providing solace for the brokenhearted: "Without the body of a beloved to touch, one learns to love the body of nature, to reach the past, make sense of it, through the present."⁷⁸ Later in that same paragraph, Mann writes that "in other words, and obviously, one's emotional history shapes the way one views the world, makes the details of landscape into metaphor," a sentiment expressed concisely in "Rotting Crab Apples" when he writes, "In bleak moods, I love bleak landscapes."⁷⁹ In these passages, as in other moments of Mann's work, he echoes Emerson's depiction of nature; Emerson insisted that "nature is not always tricked in holiday attire. . . . Nature always wears the colors of the spirit. To a man laboring under calamity, the heat of his own fire hath sadness in it."⁸⁰

In Mann's poems, the sexual body of a lover is often conveyed via metaphors from the natural world, from plants to insects to the landscape; this pattern is especially apparent in his 1998 chapbook *Bliss*. In some of the book's poems, this imagery likens the body to the lushness and promise of nature. For example, in "Scotch and Valentines," the speaker remembers a former love, thinking of a moment when ". . . We still believe / gentle germinations are possible between us, / pure phototropism is urging us together."⁸¹ Similar plant imagery is found in "Risk," when the speaker compares the "ripeness" of himself and his lover to the landscape: "Driving as wildly into ripeness as we, / these cornfields, the distant horizon / of Brush Mountain . . ."⁸² Similarly, in "Pupae," a dark poem pervaded by threats of homophobic violence, Mann specifically tackles the concept of the closet, likening it to the dark, intermediate stage of insect development: the pupa. Just as love between same-sex partners can be safely expressed only within enclosures—in a gay bar in DC (lines 30–38), in a car going sixty-five miles per hour on the interstate (lines 10–16), "in air-conditioned privacy, behind a series / of locks, the opaque permission of plaster walls"—the developing creature is safe but constrained by its pupal case.⁸³ Yet Mann clearly imagines a safer, more open, more visible future for same-sex love, just as the growing insect will emerge, transformed, from its encasement: "Look around: we are too many, too strong,

/ too fine for holes. See how brave the young become. / Breathe deeply: the air and the light are ours."[84] In all of these examples from Mann's poetry, the LGBTQ body and nature are equated: in their ripeness, their promise, and their potential.

In other poems from *Bliss*, "Three Lovers at Walden Pond" and "Peepers," Mann compares the sexual body more directly to features of the landscape. In "Three Lovers at Walden Pond," this link—the impassioned love for the body likened to a passionate love for the natural world—is seen through the lens of transcendentalism. Mann makes the link explicit early in the poem, stating that "one can love a man as Thoreau loved this land."[85] Later, Mann paraphrases Thoreau's famous line from *Walden*: "I went to the woods to live deliberately." Then, in the lines that immediately follow, the speaker recalls his past with his lover, thinking, "I entered the hills of your muscles, the thorn-thickets / of your neuroses, your history, to live deep." Here, Mann likens the landscape of the lover's body and mind (muscles and neuroses) to the woods around Walden Pond (where he's currently visiting with his lover and the lover's partner). Similarly, in "Peepers," the speaker metaphorically frames the lover's body as the natural world, noting, "Your body was no destination, only // a landscape I travelled through: / the cleavage of low, oak-hairy hills, // the cheek-cupping curves of mossy sandstones, / rock still warm long after sunset."[86] In these lines, the sexual body is the landscape, suggesting that the pleasures and beauty inherent in the body can likewise be found in nature.

Mann's poetic imagery of body-as-nature relies not only upon the lushness and potential and physicality of the body but also on its similarities to the natural world, including its mutability and vulnerability to death. Most often, this imagery is celebratory, likening the way a decomposing body intermingles with the soil to the way the bodies of two lovers intermingle during sex. In "New Market Battlefield," the poem's speaker—after visiting the site of a Civil War battle—looks forward to a reunion with his lover, "When after long absence my body slips ecstatic / into yours . . ."[87] Only two lines later, the speaker describes their eventual mingling with the earth after death, like the soldiers whose Civil War gravesite he is visiting: "the blessed diffusions of muscle into earth, / the dead we will become, the budding our bodies / know together, the orchards that outlive us." Through the diction of "budding," the human body is again likened to plant life in its generative, sexual potential, as the speaker also characterizes the natural world as more persistent and more lasting than the human form.

In Mann's poems and essays in *Loving Mountains, Loving Men*, he likewise focuses on the human body's vulnerability to death and loss, connecting this vulnerability to the evanescence of good food (a connection to be explored more fully in chapter 6, "Flight and Food: Transcending Life and Death in LGBTQ Appalachian Literature"). One poem of *Bliss*, "Biscuits and Honey," foreshadows those preoccupations in *Loving Mountains, Loving Men*. In "Biscuits and Honey," Mann continues his consideration of the natural vulnerabilities of the physical body and its sexual potentials, here linking all those qualities through the image of honey, alternately used as a sex toy and a food. The enjoyment of both is pervaded by the sense of the evanescence of the physical world and its pleasures: "We lap / frantic, knowing how soon all honey / dwindles, all sweet and heat / evaporate, how soon the breath— / mist leaves the mirror."[88] In his reference to the old-fashioned way to see whether someone is still breathing—holding a hand-mirror up to the face to see if the mirror mists over—Mann evokes the old ways and reminds his reader of the vulnerabilities that unite us all. In these lines, the perils and the pleasures of the physical world intermingle and feed each other; the joys of sex and of food are all the sweeter given the knowledge that they'll be consumed all too soon.

Marrying the Earth in *Goodbye Gauley Mountain: An Ecosexual Love Story*

Perhaps the most literal example of the sexualization of nature to be found in this study is the film *Goodbye Gauley Mountain: An Ecosexual Love Story* (2013), codirected and produced by West Virginia native Beth Stephens and her wife Annie Sprinkle. Stephens was inspired to make this film in 2007 when, flying into West Virginia on a visit to her family (Stephens is an artist and professor at UC Santa Cruz), she got an aerial view of the mountaintop-removal-caused damage to her beloved West Virginia mountains.[89] The film is a documentary about mountaintop removal (MTR), but also an exploration by Stephens of her West Virginia home, her family's deep connections to the mining industry, and the conflicts within Appalachia over environmental issues. In addition, *Goodbye Gauley Mountain* documents Stephens and Sprinkle's wedding to the Appalachian Mountains (one of several weddings in which Stephens and Sprinkle have married different parts of the Earth) and explores their ecosexuality.[90]

As Stephens and Sprinkle explain in their "Ecosex Manifesto" (previously published on their website and now available in their 2021 book, *Assuming the Ecosexual Position: The Earth as Lover*), ecosexuality is an identity, coexisting with other sexual identities, for people who are devoted to being "polymorphous and pollen-amorous."[91] The sexual relationship with the Earth that is described here is quite literal; in item ii of the manifesto, "We Make Love with the Earth," they declare, "We caress rocks, are pleasured by waterfalls, and admire the Earth's curves often. We make love with the Earth through our senses."[92] Stephens and Sprinkle maintain that ecosexuality should involve activism, filtered "through love, joy and our powers of seduction."[93] For these filmmakers, the creation of art is one of the most potent forms of ecosex activism: "We embrace the revolutionary tactics of art, music, poetry, humor, and sex."[94]

The treatment of the Earth in this film—and in Stephens and Sprinkle's work more generally—blurs the boundaries between self and other, between human and nonhuman, and thus lends itself to analysis through feminist ecocriticism and posthumanism. Ecofeminist scholar Theresa L. Burriss describes blurring of the human/nature binary as a thread within Appalachian literature: "the natural environment figures prominently, often assuming character status equal, if not superior, to humans."[95] In her analysis of queer Appalachian novelist Ann Pancake's *Strange As This Weather Has Been* (in which a family deals with the impact of local MTR mining), Burriss recounts a main character who "recognizes the interconnectedness of all living things and refuses to place humans at the top of some socially constructed hierarchy."[96] A similar reconsideration of human boundaries and hierarchies characterizes posthumanism. According to posthuman theory, "the posthuman subject travels 'across and among' the borders of self and other, the 'other' including people, communities, regimes, and technologies."[97] Like the permeable subject of posthumanism, the subject in the literature examined in this chapter—especially in the work of Jeff Mann and the film *Goodbye Gauley Mountain*—supplements itself by merging with entities outside itself, especially with the natural world of Appalachia (as well as with the sexual bodies of others). In Stephens's critical essay about her film, "PAR: *Goodbye Gauley Mountain: An Ecosexual Love Story*," she draws on the work of posthuman theorist Donna Haraway and on the work of Eve Kosofsky Sedgwick in explaining "the relationship that I have with the mountains."[98] For Stephens, this relationship (depicted in *Goodbye Gauley Mountain* and discussed in other texts such as the "Ecosex Manifesto") destabilizes the binary logic that characterizes modernism, specifically "the human/nature binary that delegate[s] nature as less valuable than human" and that "enables human exploitation of nature as well as humans that are deemed closer to nature as in the case of women or people of color."[99]

In *Goodbye Gauley Mountain*, Stephens depicts an expansive vision of the Appalachian subject, especially the LGBTQ subject (to which she would like to add "E," for ecosexual[100]), whose permeable boundaries yield a more sensual body that takes pleasure from (and attempts to give pleasure to) the natural world of Appalachia and elsewhere. In this film, Stephens and Sprinkle employ the body as a tool of activism and performance art, preventing it from being co-opted by corporations for the sake of progress and profit. Stephens and Sprinkle's use of the body, and of the natural world, is one that yields no material goods or commodities but, rather, one that yields pleasure and preservation.

In *Goodbye Gauley Mountain*, Stephens and Sprinkle undermine other definitional boundaries beyond that of self and nature. In particular, filmically, they play with the boundaries of genre. The film is explicitly styled as a documentary (with documentary footage of MTR sites and blasts, as well as many first-person POV video interviews with subjects), and it is understood by viewers to be a documentary, as is evidenced by the press quotes that Stephens and Sprinkle include on the film's webpage.[101] However, I argue here that the film can productively be read within the genre of romantic comedy. Just as the LGBTQ Appalachian authors of this study are remaking the LGBTQ Appalachian subject, Stephens and Sprinkle have crafted a new style of romantic comedy for a new subject in the age of posthumanism. This is a romantic comedy that follows the classical "marriage plot," yet one in which our heroines marry the Appalachian Mountains at the story's end.[102] It is a film in which the boundaries of self and other are explicitly questioned and a posthuman worldview is embraced. Here, the Appalachian Mountains are afforded the same status as a person: legally (in the weddings chronicled in the film), ethically (in our mutual responsibility to love and care for one another), and narratively (as one partner in the back-and-forth story structure of a classical romantic comedy).

In the book *An Introduction to Film Genres*, Friedman et al. explain that the conventional marriage plot of romantic comedy consists of three stages: "1) meet, 2) separate, 3) unite."[103] In *Goodbye Gauley Mountain*, the meeting—between West Virginia native Stephens and Gauley Mountain—is implicit, since it is the mountain "whose shadow I had grown up in."[104] The separation—in the sense of a situation or barrier that separates the two lovers and must be overcome for the union to take place—is both one of geography (because Stephens now lives and works in California, although she visits her West Virginia family regularly) *and* also one caused by harmful, external forces: coal corporations are blowing Gauley Mountain apart, piece by piece, in order to extract the coal that lies beneath the surface. Much of *Goodbye Gauley Mountain* focuses, like most romantic comedies, on the separation, with Stephens and Sprinkle investigating and documenting the ravages of MTR on their beloved—Gauley Mountain.

GGM embodies many traits of the romantic comedy genre beyond its meet-separate-unite plot. Friedman et al. maintain that romantic comedies incorporate and respond to changes in society, especially changes to concepts of love and marriage.[105] Certainly, *GGM*'s advocacy for ecosexuality, its exploration of growing up queer in Appalachia, and its culmination in the wedding of two women to the Appalachian Mountains all reflect our era's reconsideration of subjectivity, romance, and marriage.

In another nod to romantic comedies, and perhaps one that most clearly indicates the film's posthumanism, *GGM* also adheres to an editing technique that is typical of romantic comedies: the "dual focus" structure in which the film toggles back and forth between the adventures of one lover, then the adventures of the other.[106] In *GGM*, this dual focus is manifest as we—the viewers—first follow Stephens and then follow Gauley Mountain itself. Scenes focusing on Stephens's childhood in West Virginia (visiting her elementary school, for example) are followed by scenes focusing on Gauley Mountain (or the Appalachian Mountains more generally), in which the viewer is educated about mountaintop removal or encouraged to consider the beauty of the mountains. Such scenes include (as described in the "Film Structure" document on the director's website),

> 10. Beth at Mink Shoals Elementary School
> . . .
> 11. Annie and Beth propose to the mountains
> Kiss the earth
> 12. Paige WV hills song>good bridge
> . . .
> 13. Joe Hampshire
> Clean water act
> 14. Nature Montage
> Poison river
> Smoke stacks + night shot of factory
> Learn to make due
> Montage factory w/machinery[107]

As this outline reveals, there are moments within the dual-focus structure of *Goodbye Gauley Mountain*, in classic romantic comedy fashion, when the narratives—and the lovers—converge, although here those moments of convergence include Stephens and Sprinkle sensuously rubbing themselves with mud in a mountain stream (thereby tactilely appreciating the Earth) and admiring the pulchritude of a ripe homegrown tomato. In keeping with romantic comedy tradition, the film culminates with the lovers coming together permanently, united through a wedding that has been described by Stephens as "our magnificent Purple Wedding atop a lush green mountain, where . . . all come together, vowing to love, honor, and cherish the Appalachian Mountains until death brings us closer together forever."[108]

An unexpected but unmistakable quality that *Goodbye Gauley Mountain* shares with romantic comedies is the prevalence of dogs in the film. In *Introduction to Film Genres*, Friedman et al. note that "dogs play a pivotal role in romantic comedies because they straddle the realms of the wild and the domesticated."[109] This is a particularly important concept in understanding the posthuman aesthetics of *Goodbye Gauley Mountain*: dogs in romantic comedies blur the boundaries between the civilized and uncivilized worlds, just as *GGM* blurs the boundaries between human and nonhuman and between the seemingly distinct film genres of environmental documentary and romantic comedy. Viewers can even notice the prominence of dogs in the film's trailer (available on Vimeo or through the film's website, www.goodbyegauleymountain.org): three dogs are featured within the trailer's first thirty seconds. The presence of dogs is so noticeable in the film that Donna Haraway, posthumanist theorist and author of "The Cyborg Manifesto" and *When Species Meet*, made note of them in her commentary on the film, writing, "*Goodbye Gauley Mountain* is deep, full of feeling, effective, beautifully made and powerful! Especially dear to my heart are all the fine ecosexual West Virginia dogs."[110] These dogs matter because they demonstrate how much this film straddles realms (just as do dogs in romantic comedies), thus linking the genre of romantic comedy with the posthumanism that underlies *GGM* and its eroticization of the Appalachia earth.

Poetry of Place and of the Body:
The (Performance) Poetry of doris davenport

doris davenport's poetry, much like *Goodbye Gauley Mountain* and the poetry of Jeff Mann, is characterized by an emphasis on embodiedness and a celebration of the pleasures both of the body and of place, especially davenport's Appalachian community of origin in Cornelia, Georgia, described as "my sanctuary, my sacred place of mental, physical, spiritual, and psychic renewal."[111] The davenport collection most solidly rooted in Appalachia is 1995's *Soque Street Poems*, named for the street where she grew up and written from the perspectives of the neighbors and family members (and ghosts) who constituted her community. For davenport, the *place* of Cornelia includes both Cornelia's geography and its people. Her description of Cornelia in the essay "All This, and Honeysuckles Too," emphasizes that duality: "This is an area of exquisite beauty with people living off in the woods along tricky, circuitous highways."[112] davenport maintains that her identity was formed from the place and people of her Appalachian roots: "even as a girl I already 'had an I,' defined by people, experiences, and landscapes of northeast Georgia."[113]

In *Soque Street Poems*, that place—the natural landscape as well as the town of Cornelia—is celebrated alongside its inhabitants. The poems emphasize the sensory details of the landscape—the "red dirt" ("103 Soque"), the "dusty red / dogwood trees, a big flower garden" ("1002 Desota Drive"), "the summer field of / tall golden grass" ("Parent-ogenesis")—as well as the buildings and businesses of a small town. davenport's poems focus not only on private homes (with street addresses as the titles of the poems) but also on the public spaces of Cornelia, with the names of the establishments as titles: "Cornelia Regional (Colored) High School," "Sally's Lunchroom," "Fred's Tavern." The poems capture the lived experience of the community members and are intended to "recreate, preserve, and remind us that we had (and have) viable, culturally rich communities."[114] Even poetic images that seem focused on landscape in fact emphasize the interactions of people with that landscape. The "red dirt" of "103 Soque" is, in another poem, the coating of a street sign (in ". . . Because once you turned the corner"); the summer field of tall golden grass (in "Parent-ogenesis") is the location of davenport's own conception; and the dogwood trees and flower garden are part of the description of a family member's home. In davenport's poetic recollections of her Affrilachian community, the landscape is given definition by the lives that are lived there.

However, the collection acknowledges the social circumstances—segregation—that brought the community together, calling it "a beautiful hill of apartheid" ("Ceremony for 103 Soque Street"). In *Soque Street Poems*, several of the poetic voices discuss the landscape and community not in celebratory tones but rather emphasizing the extent to which they are, in the repeated language of these poems, "bound." Several of the poems in the collection are not articulated in the voice of a specific community member and not named for (and about) a home or business in the community. Rather, these poems' speaker seems to be a chorus of sorts, a communal voice that often interjects a previously unheard perspective. One of these poems, "while we on the subject;/ Let's tell the rest of it./ (Tell it like it i-s is.)," speaks for members of the community who felt stuck there, or remained because there were no other good options. The speaker says, "We were bound, some of us, like being in jail, or on the / chain-gang" (1-2) and characterizes this entrapment as internal rather than external: "Something / fixed it so you couldn't *think* of nowhere else to be." This language, of being bound or on a chain gang, evokes images of the entrapments of slavery: the bondage that would have marked the family histories of many in this Affrilachian community. In fact, the speaker of the poem that follows ("Mr. Arthur Wright / 1873-1961") refers to slavery, emphasizing its impact on the community, noting, "I wasn't born / in slavery, but / close enough / to it to see / what it did to / the little ones."

At other points in the text, binding (or being bound) is linked to voodoo and the work of the community's conjure-woman, Cleo Smith, who says that she "spoke on them all: got them all dreaming the same dream" and that "The power of the word binds them," thus providing one explanation for the force that may have bound Cornelia's unwilling residents to its hills and valleys. The word "bound" also appears in the poem "Connect these bones/ these dry bones . . ." as a description of the family connections forged by blood and marriage: "Connected, these bones, / by blood, mixed and remixed / by kin close and kissing bound / and connected." This diction appears most prominently in the poem "Bound Georgia," in which davenport plays with various meanings of the word bound. In the lines of this poem, bound is used alternately to mean "bordered by" (children instructed to "Bound Georgia!" must name all the surrounding states), "yoked to" ("Bound to and in that hill, in / Cornelia"), or "going to" ("people bound somewhere / else"). In its final appearance in the volume, bound signifies the bonds of memory (and is linked to photography, harking back to the issues discussed in chapter 3), as the speaker—presumably davenport, home for a visit—tries to get twenty young people (from the ages of eighteen months to eighteen years) to gather for a group photograph. At the poem's end, the speaker says to the young people, "This you will / remember / & in that memory / be bound" ("'Take my picture' Aug. 25, 9991 [sic]"). Here, binding is enacted through the community: its physical togetherness and its shared memories.

It is impossible to discuss images of the body and embodiedness *in* davenport's poetry without examining the embodiedness *of* that poetry: davenport's poetry is meant to be heard and experienced as delivered by the poet. davenport describes herself as specifically a "Performance Poet" in her LinkedIn profile, and scholars have stressed the importance of davenport's physical presence to the delivery of her poetry. Becky Birtha, in an 1985 review of *eat thunder and drink rain* (davenport's second collection of poetry), wonders whether davenport's poetry could "stand on its own, being quietly read from a page in a book, without Davenport's electric presence" and notes that "hers is a poetry meant to be read aloud—or performed—by the poet herself."[115] Katharine Newman (one of the founders of MELUS, the Society for the Study of the Multi-Ethnic Literature of the United States) wrote, in her 1991 introduction to davenport's collection *voodoo chile: slight return*, "I never heard of a 'performance poet' until doris found me. I don't forget the thrill of being one of the audience crowded into the Sisterhood Bookstore in L.A. to hear doris read. I did not get all the words that afternoon, but I certainly got the beat, the crescendos, the laughter shared by the poet and the audience together."[116] This performative essence of davenport's poetry even creeps into the titles of her collections, most notably 2016's *performance pieces*.

Readers can get a glimpse of davenport's performance poetry through a number of videos available on YouTube. These range from informal settings (the fifteen-minute video of davenport reading at the Sweetwater Coffeehouse in Sautee, Georgia, complete with traffic noise) to selfie-videos to more formal addresses (such as the video of "A reading and conversation with doris davenport at the Black Women Writers Symposium at Berea College on Friday, October 21st, 2016"). Although URLs are transitory (and YouTube videos even more fleeting), I have included a list of these videos (with URLs and brief descriptions) in the appendix of this book.

davenport's later work, especially the poetry she has published in the last five years or so, often focuses on the physicality of the poetry's composition or, at least, of its inspiration. In the introduction to her 2014 collection *65 poems* (written in celebration of her sixty-fifth year of life), davenport notes, "Most of these poems were composed on a smartphone, in the mornings, as i [sic] daily exercised on a treadmill or walked down by the river."[117] The titles of many poems situate them precisely in time or space. The titles "*at CLA (the College Language Association) in New*

Orleans . . . ," "outside in 94 degree heat," and "Alternate ROOTS Annual Meeting (2013)" (all from davenport's 2016 collection *performance pieces*) exemplify this pattern.[118] Other poems in these later collections emphasize the sensuality of the body (not a new theme for davenport) in conjunction with the vulnerability yet tenacity of that body, especially the female body, the black body, and the aging body. In these poems, davenport celebrates the sensual body—"when you sit / naked facing me all / glorious dark coffee / golden brown (knee to knee)" (from " 'Flash' love story" in *65 poems*)—and laments the frailties of the aging body—"everyday a push each / new ache negotiated / [. . .] / this Senior Citizen brigade" (from "everyday a push each"). davenport's work—centered in the body through not only her themes but also her physical performance of that poetry—continually reminds the reader of all the pleasures and the vulnerabilities that the body brings with it.

6

Flight and Food

Transcending Life and Death in LGBTQ Appalachian Literature

Just as LGBTQ Appalachian literature explores the pleasures and vulnerabilities of the material world (nature and the body), so too does it celebrate the transcendence of those limitations. In the literature examined in this book, the vehicles of this transcendence are most frequently birds and food. While these may appear, at first glance, to be too mundane to be agents of transcendence, a closer look reveals their rich tradition of symbolism and cultural significance. Regarding birds, numerous cultures have represented birds as intermediaries between the human world and the world beyond, whether that *beyond* is a realm of divine being(s) or animistic spirits. Of food, Russian scholar Mikhail Bakhtin reminds us that it—in the context of a feast or other communal meals—simultaneously symbolizes life and serves as a reminder of death. Moreover, feasts open a space for truth-telling, even in the face of authority or against cultural norms. In addition, both birds and food are, like human life, evanescent, transitory, subject to the vulnerabilities and decay that plague all matter. Thus, items that represent our transcendence of the human world also constantly remind us that we are tethered to the vulnerability and loss that mark us as human.

Throughout the literature examined in this study, these means of transcendence—birds and food—often feature references to religion, spirituality, and divinity. These authors—such as Alther in *Kinflicks*—explore the consolations offered by religion even as they lament the way religion has been wielded as a tool, used to condemn and exile queer Appalachians. The topic of religion figured into the earliest discussions of LGBTQ issues within Appalachian studies: in 1995, Black and Rhorer noted of their interviewees that "organized religion played an important part in most of the interviewees' lives—socially, morally, and spiritually. . . . Many had deep inner struggles over their homosexuality, rooted in religious notions of sin and guilt."[1] In the 1999 documentary film *Through Their Eyes*, two interviewees recount occasions when church members tried to "pray the demons of gayness out of me," while another interviewee describes the way that the religiosity of the region intensifies the exclusion of queer Appalachians, noting, "There are churches everywhere that you go in this county. . . . Basically, churches rule everything, and if you're against the church, then the community is against you."[2]

In a literary portrait of this dilemma faced by young queer Appalachians, the protagonist of *Finding H.F.* experiences culture shock when she attends a service at the queer-friendly Metropolitan Community Church in Atlanta. H.F.'s observations reflect the messages that queer Appalachian teens receive from their churches and communities: "All my life I've heard gay people preached against as perverts, and now finding out that there's such a thing as a church for gay people . . . well, it's awful to say, but it feels like I just found out that the Ku Klux Klan started accepting black members and working for racial equality."[3] However, H.F. fears that her Memaw can never accept her sexuality, because "the only person Memaw loves more than me is God, and since she don't go to the Metropolitan Community Church, the God she worships says all gay people are going to hell."[4]

An accepting church congregation is one among many discoveries for H.F. on her travels. Others include new foods—discussed in more detail later in this chapter—as well as the symbolism of the rainbow flag that H.F. encountered in a number of the queer-friendly spaces that she and Bo visited, including the Out Loud Bookshop and later behind the cross at the Metropolitan Community Church. The novel's epigraph—"God gave Noah the rainbow sign, don't you see?"—is from a traditional hymn.[5] (The conclusion of House's 2014 keynote address at the Appalachian Studies Conference—in which a number of singers and musicians joined House onstage to sing "God Gave Noah the Rainbow Sign"—was surely inspired by *Finding H.F.*, the cover of which had been projected on the screen behind him only minutes earlier.) In the novel's epilogue, H.F. explains the story of Noah in a way that reconciles her sexuality with her spirituality and gives voice to the hope that is a lifeline for so many queer young people: "to me, the rainbow sign God put up in the sky for Noah said pretty much the same thing as the sign I saw at the gay bookstore, at the church, and in the faces and hearts of the rainbow of people who are my gay family: 'Here you were, thinking it was the end of the world, when it turns out it was only the beginning.'"6

Birds in LGBTQ Appalachian Literature

In tracing the religious significance that has been attributed to birds, scholars of art and literature have noted that birds live part of their lives in the air—in the realm of the spirits. Perhaps this explains why birds have been interpreted variously as manifestations of the human soul, as spiritual intermediaries between human and divine, or as supernatural beings themselves.7 Other scholars have observed that some writers anthropomorphize birds, for good or ill. For seventeenth-century poet John Milton, birds "serve to illustrate human vices," while nineteenth- and twentieth-century British and American authors frame birds as human analogues due to the "resemblance of their activities to common patterns of human family behavior."8 In literature as well as in religious traditions of various cultures, birds commonly carry a significance far beyond the features of their daily existence.

Within LGBTQ Appalachian literature, birds are notable for their vulnerability or their absence, marked by the traces that they leave behind. Reading the figure of the bird in LGBTQ Appalachian literature, I was inspired by Thomas C. Gannon's discussion of bird symbolism in *Skylark Meets Meadowlark: Reimagining the Bird in British Romantic and Contemporary Native American Literature* (2009). Through the lenses of ecocriticism and posthumanism, Gannon describes the role that birds have often played in literature—as "these oh-so-*other* species"—and argues that we must "consider them as the Other of *species*, victimized by anthropocentric colonization, both physically and ideologically."9 In Gannon's description, birds serve as rhetorical others, their differences magnified and exploited in service to a larger colonialist/ideological project. By serving as the other, birds play a role similar to that of Appalachians within American culture and of queer Appalachians within Appalachia. In casting Appalachians as radically different—their dialect laughable or incomprehensible, their living conditions or voting habits out of step with mainstream America—contemporary culture continues to perform the othering that is necessary to foster the Appalachian colonialist project, wherein Appalachia's resources (including our young people) can rightfully be extracted, relocated to a place where they can be of more use. Queer Appalachians have likewise been doubly othered within Appalachian culture. Like Appalachians and Appalachia itself, birds have been subject "to severe economic exploitation," and imagery of trapped or caged birds has been "readily used in metaphors comparing the plight of trapped animals to human beings caught in some sort of desperate situation."[10]

"Ornithology Lesson," a poem by Affrilachian poet Bianca Spriggs, embodies this exploitation in the figure of a bird-woman, the poem's speaker. In "Ornithology Lesson," the speaker is held captive by or in servitude to some kind of a circus or freak show. In this poem, Spriggs highlights the scopophilia—the pleasure from looking—that men derive from looking at women's bodies (and that is similarly derived from the spectacle of Appalachia as it is depicted in American popular culture). Using the second-person "you," the bird-woman addresses someone who is both reader of the poem and participant in its narrative. The bird-woman comments in the poem's first stanza, "You find me pirouetting slow / in a tent before an exaltation of men," thus casting the reader in an uncomfortable role as the one who looks, the one who inspects, and, later, the one who interrogates the bird-woman. (The crowd of men is also figured as birdlike through the use of the collective noun "exaltation," typically used to describe a group of larks.) In the second stanza, the poem's "you" asks the bird-woman a sequence of increasingly intrusive questions, so that by the third stanza, she is "Weary of your eyes," and introduces "you" to another exhibit, Python Woman. In the fourth stanza, the reader's intrusions move beyond questions and looks; the bird-woman narrates the occasions when you have touched her. By the poem's end, you have been ejected by the ringmaster, with the bird-woman explaining why she herself does not leave: "Why I no longer fly: / From here, it is the same view." In a flat tone of resignation, the bird-woman describes herself, her fellow exhibits, and perhaps all beings as simultaneously entrapped and angelic: "Here, we are all seraphs caught / in a mist net, and left / abandoned by the sky." Through these lines and in the bird-woman's voice, Spriggs encapsulates the lack of recourse and opportunity experienced by many Appalachians, who choose not to leave but who clearly recognize the exploitation that shapes their experience and their landscape, as well as the viewing pleasure that this exploitation provides for the rest of the nation.

Winged Things in *Strange Birds*

The traditional connections between birds and the human soul may be most apparent in Karen Salyer McElmurray's *Strange Birds in the Tree of Heaven*, where most winged things are of the spirit, while actual birds are found only in the traces they leave behind. On the first page of the novel, Andrew Wallen listens from outside the house as his mother Ruth casts out demons while she cleans her kitchen, and he feels the rejected spirit speed past him: "Whatever blessless thing she had cast out winged past, touched the top of my head with a kiss and flew at the sky just as the sun went down."[11] Throughout this novel, the force of the spirit—whether demon or angel or Holy Ghost—has wings, and these winged things often appear at turning points for the characters. In a scene midway through the novel, Andrew describes the summer when he was nine years old and first felt an attraction to another man—in this case, a traveling preacher. Holy Spirit becomes bird becomes spirit as Andrew watches Preacher Martin at work: "I stared too, waited for the Holy Ghost to settle on the preacher's shoulders, or on mine. The mid-afternoon sun danced, became a bird darting from behind the World War II soldier's monument beside the courthouse door. It flew in quick, flashing circles, became a motion of wings just the shape of Preacher Martin's fist. He held his Bible high and the pages fluttered in the warm July air, made wing sounds."[12] In this scene, the winged spirit embodies Andrew's awakening sexuality. He remembers that summer as one in which love—like a moth—was fragile and elusive: "That whole revival summer I tried to store up love like the hungry store up food. At night, love flew against the glass of my painted-shut window. It was like moth's wings, saying let me in, in. I lay still, my hands open and uncupped, ready to catch hold of that love at its most unsuspecting minute. But love escaped me."[13]

Although flying things are often a force of love or life for Andrew (these same moths seemingly save his life at the end of the novel), for his mother, Ruth, winged things more often provide a direct connection to God, offering a route out of the loveless and unfulfilled life that she knows. When she's a young girl, Ruth yearns for "a fierce-winged angel" who could take her "above the storms of dust and departure and wishing that would be my life."[14] Later, her visions figure Ruth herself as the winged thing, as McElmurray plays with the similar sounds of "falling" women and "fallen" women, and Ruth wishes that her life had involved more love and less wanting: "You dream of lovers, of love as it might have been. You dream of falling women, and how you have been one. . . . You dream other women. At first they have the faces of angels, then they become moths, and then candle flames. Before you wake up, they are nothing but ash."[15] Throughout the novel, Ruth increasingly hopes for a future that will allow her to ascend into the sky: pulled up to the heavens or, at least, away from life in Mining Hollow. Near the end of the novel, when Ruth contemplates killing Andrew and herself, she thinks, "You imagine rising like morning light over house and trees, over how all of Inez sleeps. . . . Soon both of you will know the morning, its light, its heavenly wonders. . . . *Rising to God, ash and air and forever, better than love.*"[16] For Ruth, flight—whether she is carried by an angel or rises into the sky as a plume of ash—will allow her to transcend her disappointments and losses.

Elsewhere in the novel, birds themselves are present only as traces—their songs, their feathers, their shapes—perhaps serving as a reminder of the transcendence that the characters long for but cannot find. The "strange birds" of the book's title never appear. Their songs (or the absence of their songs) are mentioned only twice in the novel: once in Andrew's memory of his sixteenth birthday, drinking apple brandy with his father ("The night sang with sounds I'd never heard, strange birds in the tree of heaven out back by the well"), and another in Ruth's sensory perception of the night of the novel's climax, as she listens for Andrew to return from his date with Henry Ward: "Nothing, not a sound, car, no birds in the tree of heaven out back by the well."[17] In other moments, birds embody the power of voice and prophecy, as when Ruth calls out Andrew's name and thinks "feel the name, *Andrew, Andrew,* come alive. Hear it rush out of your hand, a night bird with raggedy wings darting fast and gone."[18] Elsewhere in the novel, Ruth hears a "night bird calling" in Mining Hollow and interprets its song to mean that "it's come. The longest, darkest hour."[19] In her attention to the night birds, Ruth is like her mother, who "was a woman who believed in signs, the way a stray hair'd lay on a pillow or the way a whippoorwill would call out, just so."[20]

The most common physical traces of birds in the novel are their feathers. Sometimes, those are floating in stagnant ponds; Ruth sees them as she sinks through the water: "layer upon layer of silt and green, fish and the feathers of birds."[21] Elsewhere, feathers are decorative, features of hats and dresses that are too worldly, forbidden by Ruth's father Tobias, and that are part of the world Ruth yearns for but cannot have. Early in the novel, Ruth's mother had tried on a hat in a department store, "a maroon silk hat with peacock feathers," only to be surprised by Tobias, who slapped the hat off her head, saying, "Vain objects."²² Elsewhere, feathers are again associated with Ruth's mother, who ran away when Ruth was young. When Ruth was a child and swimming in the family's pond, she has a vision in which she sees her mother, who "wore her tap dance best, a waterlogged feather boa, silver stockings."²³ Then, at the end of the novel, while sinking in that same pond and trying to decide whether to end her life, Ruth has a similar vision of her mother, "all of her alight, hair, feather boa, her strong hands that once held love."²⁴ The novel's feathers are often remnants of other worlds, reminders of lives that Ruth wishes she had lived, or residue of a mother who escaped Mining Hollow and left Ruth behind.

In a key scene, McElmurray unites the novel's winged things in a parodic vision of imitation angels and fake birds, when Andrew goes looking for Henry Ward in a gay nightclub, Johnny Angel's, in "a want-to-be West Virginia city." There, Andrew doesn't find Henry, and he doesn't find love. Instead, he finds "swarms of balloons in the shapes of angels, set loose from somewhere overhead."²⁵ Rather than rising, these angels fall and then burst, releasing showers of heart-shaped confetti. Meanwhile, the bar gives everyone "a light-weight paper umbrella, which opened into the shape of a flamingo."²⁶ Later, dancing, Andrew and the club's other patrons all open their umbrellas and dance, holding their flamingos aloft. However, without Henry, without love, and without affirmation from his parents ("Act like a man, I had once been told. How should a man act?"), Andrew falls instead of rises: "I felt myself falling, deeper than the sky, the sea, the mines of the earth, into a hollow mouth dark and unfathomably deep."²⁷ Although these fragile balloon angels and paper flamingos offer no substance or transcendence, they foreshadow the life that Andrew will later build in Florida after he escapes Mining Hollow with Henry.

Chimney Swifts in *Kinflicks*

Kinflicks addresses the consolations of organized religion as surely as it tackles the questions of life and death. Ginny's mother contemplates these issues in her last days, when she announces to Ginny, "My conclusion from nine years of encyclopedia reading . . . is that all the great world religions have been training systems to instruct adherents in how to die."²⁸ Through the course of the novel, Ginny had experimented with a number of philosophical approaches and religions; Ginny thinks to herself that "she was an easy lay, spiritually speaking."²⁹ However, these were of little comfort to her in the face of the death of her mother and her estrangement from Wendy.[30]

Within a novel preoccupied with issues of life, death, and the intense relationships between parents and their children, Lisa Alther concentrates these issues in a symbol of birds, specifically a nest of abandoned baby birds that the protagonist, Ginny Babcock, attempts to save. Ginny finds the nest—full of tiny, flightless chimney swift chicks—where it fell, at the base of the chimney in her family's cabin. This cabin itself is a powerful symbol of Ginny's Appalachian roots and of New Appalachia: purchased and rebuilt by Ginny's grandfather, Mr. Zed, a former coal miner who had founded Hullsport (Kingsport), Tennessee, and who persuaded a chemical company to open a factory in his soon-to-be town. Ginny was born in this cabin, which was surrounded by the kudzu that Mr. Zed had planted all over town, late in his life when he regretted bringing the chemical industry and suburban sprawl to the East Tennessee hills; he was trying to make sure it all "would be returned to Nature" by the voracious kudzu.[31]

Ginny begins trying, and failing, to save these baby birds from the moment she finds them clinging to the bricks at the base of the chimney. Within a few hours of rescuing them, Ginny accidentally kills two of them. She'd placed them in a bowl on the cabin's roof, hoping the swifts' parents would come back to fetch them. Instead, the chicks all flop out of the bowl, and two of them "fried to a crisp on the hot tin roof."[32] As Ginny struggles to keep the remaining three birds alive—feeding them, teaching them to fly—the birds evoke alternately the parent-child relationship and the fragility of life, with Alther drawing a parallel between the dilemma of these chicks and the fate of Ginny's mother (who is in the hospital in Hullsport, gravely ill with a bleeding disorder).

The baby birds, and Ginny's attempts to care for them, quickly become surrogates for Ginny's absent two-year-old daughter Wendy, who is back in Vermont with Ginny's husband Ira, who kicked Ginny out after finding her seemingly in flagrante beside the family swimming pool. Ginny agonizes over the separation from her daughter and channels this energy into her care of the swifts. The comparison of Ginny's mothering the swifts to Ginny's mothering Wendy is apparent when Ginny likens a bird guide that she consults to a well-known parenting manual: "she got down Birdsall's book and searched through it as frantically as she had searched through Dr. Spock when Wendy had been an infant, for some clue as to what she should be doing."[33] Ginny articulates this surrogacy late in the novel, acknowledging that she "had needed something to fret over and fuss with, something to stand in for Wendy."[34]

Scholars and critics have mixed reactions to this surrogate mothering, with most coming down on the side of Anne Larsen, who declared in a contemporary review of the novel in the *Village Voice* that the novel's birds, "literal and symbolic," offered up "tedious hammer blows of 'message.'"[35] Ginny's interactions with the birds are treated more sympathetically by some later scholars, one of whom sees in these chimney swifts Alther's allegorical "question of which is dominant, early parental conditioning or genetic programming."[36] Ginny is preoccupied with exactly such questions throughout this tragicomic bildungsroman, as she tries to determine her identity as a woman, as a mother, and as a person. Her rescue of the swifts is one of Ginny's many experiments in the novel, like her experiment with the communal farm and her relationship with Eddie Holzer, and it is not the only experiment that ends in a fatality: Eddie accidentally decapitates herself—as she rides off on a snowmobile in a huff—with the barbed wire that she herself had placed around the communal farm to deter trespassers.

Ginny's interaction with these birds becomes a conduit for communications with her mother and, later, an allegory of her mother's fate. On a visit to the hospital, Ginny—whose relationship with her mother (whom she's seen only twice in the past nine years) has been strained—asks her mother's advice about the birds: "Mrs Babcock was startled to be asked for an opinion."[37] Ginny keeps her mother updated on the progress of the swifts throughout the novel, as Ginny increasingly realizes her need for her absent daughter ("Maternal behavior couldn't be turned on and off at will. . . . What was she to do with these infernal instincts of hers when the bird had gone?") and her need for her own soon-to-be absent mother: "Christ, her mother was abandoning her! She'd die, and Ginny would be left behind all alone."[38] The final chick dies only two days before Mrs Babcock does. Ginny's telling her mother about it is the last conversation they have, and Ginny's narration of the bird's death—plus Mrs Babcock's reaction—makes unmistakable the connection of bird death and human death. Ginny tells her mother that "the bird beat itself to death on a closed window. But the door next to it was *wide open*."[39] Mrs Babcock, largely uncommunicative in her last days, "said with amused detachment at Ginny's earnest metaphorical efforts, 'Maybe.'"[40] The day after this conversation, Mrs Babcock herself dies, and Ginny's reaction—while perhaps too obvious for some readers—makes clear their common mortality: "Ginny went back to the cabin and lay down on the bed in which she had been born and wept—because the people she had loved had all grown up and moved away and changed; because mountains corroded and rivers carved new courses and nothing stayed the same forever; because every living creature, herself included, had to die, and die alone."[41] For Alther, the deaths of the baby birds and Ginny's mother are manifestations of the evanescence of the material world and all living things; their vulnerabilities serve to remind us of our own.

Food in LGBTQ Appalachian Literature

In literature by LGBTQ Appalachian authors, food serves a few primary functions: it brings people together, often transcending generational and ideological differences; it provides pleasure, often representing sublimated sexual pleasures; and it serves as a marker of loss, reminding us of family members who once prepared these foods or warning us of the impending loss of Appalachian foodways. These functions are especially apparent in the poetry and essays of Jeff Mann, the novels of Julia Watts, and Fenton Johnson's *Scissors, Paper, Rock*. In other texts, such as Carter Sickels's essay "Johnson City" and Karen Salyer McElmurray's *Strange Birds in the Tree of Heaven*, food carries a darker significance—it is a marker of the family rupture associated with a queer Appalachian's coming out, or it is a symbol of the toxicity of the family relationship. Although Appalachian authors generally celebrate food and family, this literature makes clear that neither food nor family is always healthy.

The various significances of food in LGBTQ Appalachian literature might, at first glance, seem contradictory: uniting people and offering sensual pleasure while simultaneously carrying a reminder of impending loss and even death. However, Russian scholar Mikhail Bakhtin's work on banquet imagery suggests that these meanings aren't contradictory at all: Bakhtin maintains that food—especially in the abundance that one finds at a banquet or feast—is simultaneously evocative of achievement and of death. For Bakhtin, the eating at collective feasts is a symbol of triumph: "In the oldest system of images food was related to work. It concluded work and struggle and was their crown of glory. Work triumphed in food."[42] Yet Bakhtin also notes "the special relation of food to death and to the underworld" and elaborates, in another essay collected in the same volume, that "where death is, there also is birth, change, renewal."[43] The seeming paradox here is easily solved: If the subtext of a feast is "Whew, we've made it another year, and we've dodged famine thanks to an abundant harvest," then the specter hovering over every feast is death, like the witch who wasn't invited to Sleeping Beauty's christening but showed up anyway.

Other writers and scholars, in writing about Appalachian culture, have made similar arguments about the connection between food and death. Kentucky writer Wendell Berry, in his essay "The Pleasures of Eating," observes that food is part of an annual cycle and that the action of eating—whether of animal or plant—is a final step in the process: "Eating ends the annual drama of the food economy that begins with planting and birth."[44] Later in the essay, Berry bemoans the suffering of livestock in industrial farms and the alienation of most people from that experience: "It would not do for the consumer to know that the hamburger she is eating came from a steer who spent much of his life standing deep in his own excrement in a feedlot."[45] Indeed, Berry insists that an awareness of the animal's death—and of the circumstances of the life that preceded that death—is essential to truly enjoying one's food: "The thought of the good pasture and of the calf contentedly grazing flavors the steak. . . . It means that you eat with understanding and with gratitude."[46] Similarly, in a 2016 ethnographic account of fieldwork at a small Appalachian goat farm, scholars Michael Broderick and Sean Gleason frame this dilemma—the connection between food and death—more simply when they write, "This transformation-through-consumption, however, requires loss; some die so that others may live."[47] However, as Bakhtin reminds us, the abundant food of the banquet temporarily marks "the triumph of life over death."[48]

Literary scholars have examined the portrayal of food in literature *about* Appalachia and in literature *by* Appalachians, arguing that in both cases, authors employ food to communicate their attitudes about Appalachia and its people. In "A Matter of Taste: Reading Food and Class in Appalachian Literature" (2014), Erica Abrams Locklear notes that in late nineteenth- and early twentieth-century depictions of Appalachia, "food became another means by which Appalachians were socially marginalized," such as instances where they are mocked for eating cornbread rather than biscuits made with higher-status white flour.[49] Locklear observes that as Appalachians began to tell their own stories in the twentieth century, portrayals of Appalachian food became more positive, "often celebrating the distinctiveness of mountain food." However, Locklear traces a cultural transition from mocking Appalachians for their reliance on Appalachian cuisine (cornbread) to mocking Appalachians for their reliance on fast food and processed food ("Mountain Dew Mouth"), noting "that those bent on criticizing Appalachian people have long relied on a rotating menu of Appalachian foods to do so." Among the Appalachian authors who offer up "instances of culinary resistance and pride" in the face of such contempt, Locklear discusses the work of Harriette Arnow, Denise Giardina, and Jeff Mann. Mann's embrace of Appalachian foods in *Loving Mountains, Loving Men* can be read, Locklear writes, "as an antidote for the detached relationship many Americans have with the food that they eat," and she notes that food appears to help Mann "bridge such identity gaps" as those between his identities as an Appalachian and a gay man.

Food as Connection, Pleasure, and Loss in the Work of Jeff Mann

This function of food—as a bridge between people or between facets of one's identity—is prevalent in Mann's work, where food often helps people transcend differences, whether those are differences of generations or ideologies. This effect is most apparent in Mann's poem "Yellow-Eye Beans." The poem is addressed to his grandmother, Nanny, who has, according to the poem, been dead for twenty years, and the poem links even Mann's motions while preparing the food to his family heritage and his Appalachian roots:

> Some more objective
> observer might see in
> my kitchen gestures—sorting
> these yellow-eye beans, or
> stringing half-runners, or
> rolling out pie crust or biscuits—
> my father's, and, behind those,
> his mother's, yours . . .

He imagines a dinnertime reunion between himself and Nanny, wondering what she would think of

> my lust for chest hair
> the man I live with?

and concludes that

after a short lecture
on the Bible, a book I never
much cared about to begin with,
. . .
you'd be proud
of how well the beans
and cornbread came out
. . .
   But
before we ate, I'd invite
you to say what grace
you wanted in this queer
and pagan home, and so you
would, words brief and deep,
Pass the chowchow
following closely on Amen.

In this poem, the generations share a meal as though they are taking communion, and the food truly is eaten in remembrance of a deceased loved one. The benediction of saying grace is yoked to the benedictions of eating (note here the connection of Amen to chowchow, a quintessentially Appalachian food). Despite the many differences here, of religion, sexuality, and generation, food bridges those divides.

Although Mann's work highlights the family connections evoked by food, he also calls attention to the common bond that food can forge between queer Appalachians and straight friends and neighbors. In Mann's essay "Southern (LGBT) Living," anthologized in the collection *Crooked Letter i: Coming Out in the South*, his discussion of being Southern and queer focuses on food—or occasions of sharing food—as a means of bridging differences and establishing connections with folks who might otherwise disapprove of a queer neighbor. Mann describes food as a key element of commonality, one with the potential to overcome differences when a queer Southerner comes out to a possibly resistant interlocutor. In the essay's first description of a coming-out moment, Mann emphasizes the country background he shares with two coworkers, noting that he and they all "grew up on the same food."[50] (The moment of his coming out to them happened at a K&W Cafeteria in Roanoke, over a meal of "down-home Southern food."[51]) When he describes his move to a small town in Virginia and his worries about whether the neighborhood would "take to an openly gay writer," he focuses on food as a peace offering, a way to make a connection with these strangers who will be his neighbors: "So I wasn't too worried about my female neighbors. Plus I'm a good cook, and I thought my pies and nut breads might serve nicely as caloric buffers against homophobia."[52] The essay describes several occasions when food functions precisely as Mann hopes, including with his elderly neighbor "Mizz Mayberry": he takes her fresh-picked blueberries, baked goods, and chocolates, and she serves cookies and lemonade when she hosts a reading of his poetry on her front porch, after he has been written up in the *Roanoke Times* as "The Brokeback Professor."[53] Time and time again, food serves as a balm, a common language that helps to bridge the differences between people.

Much of the food imagery in *Loving Mountains, Loving Men* consists of descriptions of gardening or canning, thus linking family, Appalachian traits of resiliency and self-reliance, and, of course, loss: anyone who has done any food preservation—canning or drying or pickling—knows that this is just a desperate attempt to slow down the natural process of decay and stave off loss. Mann explicitly and repeatedly likens his art—his writing—to food, and attributes to both of them a preservative function, writing in "Saving What We Can" that "art is a form of preservative," and noting, "In poetry, I try to preserve what I am able of loveliness and longing. . . . I try to commemorate home."[54] For Mann, that preservative function of art mirrors his family's traditions of preserving food: "These poems and essays are my attempt to do what my father does every summer when he fills the pantry with home-canned garden produce, those rows of pickled beets, corn relish, tomatoes, and green beans: capturing the generosity of the earth, saving summer's gifts for hard times, preserving the past to feed the future."[55] Elsewhere, Mann describes food as "more substantial than a poem," asserting that preparing dishes that his grandmother taught him to cook will allow him to reconnect with her: "Biscuits, sausage gravy, pecan pie: something that tastes like home."[56]

Although Mann celebrates both abundance and the self-reliance offered by food preservation—self-reliance that he calls "Ball jar autonomy" in the poem "Dilly Beans"—he often pairs those celebrations with a sentiment whose fatalism seems quintessentially Appalachian to me: "Abundance is, in the long run, always brief."[57] That brevity—of abundance, of life, of love—is something that Mann addresses in a 2003 interview, where he describes himself as "haunted—constantly, constantly—by evanescence. The brevity of beauty."[58] Mann suggests that acknowledging the evanescence of mortal pleasures, recognizing that "beauty cannot be kept," in fact heightens pleasure, "stokes intensity."[59] In a sentiment that recurs in *Loving Mountains, Loving Men*, Mann says, "Let's contradict John Keats: a thing of beauty is not a joy forever, unless it is a work of art."[60] Mann repeatedly connects art and death, framing mortality as a driving force in his work, when he notes of Keats that "Keats, dying of tuberculosis, knew about mortality better than anybody, and the rest of his work is obsessed with the transitory nature of pleasure, beauty, youth, and human life. My work is too."[61] Not surprisingly, food in Mann's work tends to be a slippery symbol, alternately the pleasures that one must seize while one can ("fresh tomatoes with mayonnaise on my father's hot buttermilk biscuits," in "Saving What We Can") and the impending end to those joys, like green tomatoes that must be harvested before the first frost (in "Gathering Green Tomatoes in the Rain").[62]

In his essay "Fried Chicken and Spoon Bread," Mann links food and family with the specter of loss. In this text, Mann grapples with the death of his mother, thinks through her disappointments with him and with her own life, and chronicles her reactions to his sexuality: from the painful conversation in 1978 when she confronted him about "a few queer newspapers" she found hidden in his bedroom, to her opinions of his lovers, to her love for John, Mann's then-partner (now husband) whom Mann had met only a few months before his mother's death.[63] And all of this—quite heavy-duty stuff—is bookended by passages about food: Mann and his sister cook their mother's favorite meal—fried chicken, spoon bread, and lemon cake—on her birthday each year, and the essay begins and ends with descriptions of the siblings together, eating the food their mother loved and remembering her. In "Fried Chicken and Spoon Bread," as in "Yellow-Eye Beans," Appalachian food is eaten in remembrance and brings family together.

Beyond images of human mortality, Mann's writing about food dwells on another type of loss, the worry that mainstream culture—often embodied by fast-food chains—will overwhelm and homogenize Appalachian culture (including its food). Mann writes, "Despite the frequent depictions of Appalachia as a charming, static archaism, mainstream culture has swamped the mountains, and I wonder how long the native folk culture—that rich self-reliance that has taken centuries to develop—will last in the face of such onslaught."[64] In "Regional Oddities," Mann celebrates Appalachian items like sassafras tea and chowchow (and other cabbage-related delicacies), contrasting this appreciation with a tale his student told him, of a family member from another region who turned up his nose at a home-cooked breakfast—"fried apples, grits, scrambled eggs, and sausage gravy with biscuits"—declaring, "This is a hillbilly breakfast! I want to go to McDonald's."[65]

Mann's contempt for that particular food chain is especially clear in his sarcastically titled poem "Civilization Comes to Summers County," in which he chronicles the opening of "The first McDonald's in Summers County." Throughout the poem, Mann contrasts the nourishing Appalachian food that fed his ancestors—and the skills needed to produce those foods—with the instant, unhealthy gratification available at McDonald's. Using the first-person plural "our" that implicitly draws in the poem's reader, Mann writes of Appalachian fare, "Our grandparents used to gather ramps / and creecy greens, boil down sorghum, // can tomatoes, peppers, chowchow, beans. / Who needs all that now?"

In contrast to this delicious abundance, the poem emphasizes that the restaurant's structure mars the landscape, its play area framed as "intestines in neon red and orange" and its sign's "monstrous / yellow *M* humps, visible for miles." Even more damning is Mann's description of the restaurant's refuse and the unhealthy nature of its food, when he notes that "Every morning, out back, // the garbage heaps: cups, wraps, / the little Styrofoam coffins // whose fatty innards were gobbled yesterday." Mann's description of the fast-food containers as "coffins" evokes the harm that this franchise brings with it: harm to people (from unhealthy foods), harm to local restaurants (from this restaurant chain Juggernaut), and harm to Appalachian foodways. Moreover, Mann's careful excision of humans from those lines, in the passive-voice construction of "whose fatty innards were gobbled yesterday," makes the McDonald's seem even more sterile, less nurturing. The poem offers a contrast, Mann's stark imagery of local abundance going to waste in favor of the bounty to be found at McDonald's: "Down the road, amidst eager yellow jackets, // crab apples ripen, / drop to the sidewalk, rot." What could our grandparents have made from those crab apples, Mann implies. And what does such waste suggest about the future of our culture?

Food as Pleasure or Poison in LGBTQ Appalachian Literature

One of the bodily pleasures often celebrated by Appalachian writers is the pleasure of eating favorite Appalachian foods. Cookbook author and scholar

Ronni Lundy argues that Appalachian foodways provide a counternarrative to the common stereotypes of Appalachians as lazy, insular, ignorant, and purely Anglo-Saxon. Instead, Lundy explains, a study of Appalachian food and foodways reveals a people and culture that are hard-working, resourceful, and diverse.[66] Similarly, Julia Watts, in response to an interviewer's question about the role of food in Appalachian culture and literature, noted the resourcefulness of Appalachian cooks, commenting, "There's something about the way that many Appalachian dishes seem to make something out of nothing that seems key to the Appalachian experience to me. . . . I think that historically, Appalachians have displayed a great resourcefulness . . . they make use of what they've got and transform their hardships into something nourishing."[67] In trying to define Appalachian foods in *Appalachian Home Cooking: History, Culture, and Recipes*, Mark Sohn includes pleasure as part of his definition. Sohn provides a list of one hundred foods that "are of Appalachia not only because the region embraces them, but, more importantly, because Appalachians prepare them and recall them with joy."[68]

In Julia Watts's novels, in addition to bringing generations together or marking a character as in or out of her element (as I have written elsewhere), food is often one of the first ways that characters experience a new culture.[69] Moreover, these cultural encounters are chronicled with an intense, almost sexual level of sensory detail. This connection—of food and sexuality—is a natural one in Watts's work, since her characters' encounters with non-Appalachian food are almost always simultaneous with her characters' sexual awakenings. Although many—like Jeff Mann in "Civilization Comes to Summers County"—have bemoaned the loss of Appalachian foodways, the pleasures of unfamiliar foods (or foods from outside the region) can be particularly intense for those accustomed to a diet, even a nutritious one, with limited variety.

Watts depicts that pleasure, and the sensual exoticism of new foods, repeatedly in *The Kind of Girl I Am*, her 2007 novel about Vestal Jenkins, a character who grew up in a Kentucky coal camp but went on to be one of Knoxville's most notorious madams. As Vestal leaves the coal camp and ventures into the county seat, Morgan, Kentucky, and then into the big city of Knoxville, her encounters with new foods—and her descriptions of others' encounters with new foods—are always suffused with pleasure: At the soda fountain of City Drug in Morgan, Vestal watches a miner's family solemnly eat hot fudge sundaes, thinking, "I knew by looking at them that those hot fudge sundaes were the best things they'd put in their mouths all week, but they weren't going to let the town people see their pleasure. Too much visible joy over the ice cream would tell the town people what a rare treat it was and serve as evidence of the family's poverty."[70]

Vestal feels that intense pleasure herself a few pages later, when Morgan County's wealthiest bachelor offers to buy her anything on City Drug's menu, and she chooses a banana split (her first), the menu's most expensive item: "I wish I could say I was as subtle as that miner's family in enjoying my treat, but oh, when the first bite of banana and vanilla ice cream drenched in chocolate syrup touched my tongue, it was so good I closed my eyes so I could shut out the world and do nothing but taste."[71] The sensuality of the sundae is reinforced when the bachelor "seemed to be so busy watching the ice cream spoon disappear between my lips that he forgot to strike up a conversation."

Characters in other Watts novels express unrivaled joy when first experiencing foods that might seem to many people to be run-of-the-mill fast food or diner food. In *Phases of the Moon*, Glenda Mooney—an aspiring singer-songwriter who has just been hired to perform on a Grand Ole Opry–like program, *The Shady Grove Barn Dance*—has the following experience on her first night away from the coal camp, eating supper at the Dixie Diner: "It was the first time I had eaten in a restaurant. There weren't any restaurants in Argon, and besides, Daddy always said eating out was a waste of money. . . . I had two chili dogs, a bag of potato chips, and a fried apple pie. It was the best food I had ever eaten."[72]

Later in the novel, Glenda's soon-to-be-girlfriend, Susan, is shocked by the limited variety of foods that Glenda has tried, or even heard of, especially by her unfamiliarity with spaghetti: "Like I told Susan after she was through pitching her little fit, I could just about count on two hands the kinds of food I ate on a regular basis back in Argon: pinto beans, corn bread, fried potatoes, biscuits, gravy, eggs, ham or bacon when we could get it, squirrel when Daddy could shoot it, chicken on Sunday, and greens and corn and tomatoes in the summertime."[73] So Susan makes Vestal a meal of spaghetti, a meal whose exotic features are described in sensuous detail: "The sharp tomato, the pungent garlic, the zesty oregano, the sweet basil—there were so many tastes going on at once that I almost wanted to hold it in my mouth forever."[74] This meal immediately precedes the conversation when Susan and Glenda tell each other about their previous relationships with women or, as Susan puts it, "Do you mean to tell me that out there in the ass-end of nowhere, you were getting naked with the preacher's daughter?"[75] Then Glenda learns a new word: Susan says, " 'Here's your second vocabulary lesson for the day. A *lesbian*'—she squeezed my hand—'a *lesbian* is someone like us.' So there's a word for it, I thought."

Of course, food in LGBTQ Appalachian literature is not always unifying or sensual, not always nourishing or sustaining. Food does not always bring peace and reconciliation, and family dinners at which food is shared can be fraught occasions for queer Appalachians, especially when those dinners compel difficult conversations or highlight unspoken (or unspeakable) transitions. Carter Sickels, in his essay "Johnson City," describes one such occasion when family meals reveal family disagreements or alienations. In that essay, an account of his trip with his friend Stephen (who is transitioning) back to Stephen's family home in Johnson City, Sickels notes the disjunctions that are laid bare when they gather for family meals. The meal itself starts on an up note, with Stephen, "smiling like a little kid," exclaiming, "Oh good. Mama made cupcakes."[76] But after the meal, Stephen's mother pulls out a box of old family pictures, including ones of Stephen before he transitioned, when he still identified as female and took dance lessons. Stephen's mother and father continually call him "she" and refer to him by his dead name, and Stephen's "jaw clenched like he was biting down on all the pain he'd been carrying around for so long." More painful than the awkward moments and misgendered pronouns of family meals are the family meals that Stephen misses out on due to his transition: " 'I miss being able to go to family things,' he said. 'All my mom's side of the family lives in Virginia, and we used to have these big Thanksgivings. I can't do that now because everyone will know.' He paused. 'I miss seeing the old people in my family.' " For some families, like Stephen's, the ruptures that already exist are brought to the fore by big family events, events that so often center on food.

Food and Life and Death in *Scissors, Paper, Rock*

Bakhtin explains that banquets—large communal gatherings of people for festive eating and drinking—not only symbolize "the triumph of life over death" but also serve as "the occasion for wise discourse, for the gay truth. There is an ancient tie between the feast and the spoken word."[77] The significance of the food itself, for Bakhtin, hinges upon that food's abundance, its excess. In Bakhtin's description, banquet imagery—of food and drink in abundance—not only represents the triumph of the body "over the world, over its enemy" as the body "grows at the world's expense" but also signifies the "open unfinished nature" of the grotesque body.[78] Food transgresses the boundaries of the body; and eating is merely one of that body's many interactions with the world: sexual, gustatory, excretory, and so on. In other words, banquets are all about excess: an excess of food, of bodies, and of words. "Bread and wine have their own truth," Bakhtin writes.[79]

Johnson's *Scissors, Paper, Rock* comprises eleven interwoven short stories that span fifty years of the Hardin family's history. In the midpoint of the book sits the longest chapter, also titled "Scissors, Paper, Rock," telling the story of one of the family's annual summer parties, where they invite all their friends and neighbors and fry catfish and serve deviled eggs and then feast. Although the family doesn't realize it, this summer party will be their last: Rose Ella will die suddenly the following year, Tom will succumb to cancer the year after, and unbeknownst to the family, the youngest son Raphael—who has come home to Kentucky for a visit from his home in San Francisco—is infected with HIV and will die (of AIDS-related complications) in the same year as his father.

At the Hardins' family feast, all the banquet elements that Bakhtin highlighted appear; joy, the truth of the spoken word, and reminders of (or harbingers of) death all intermingle. As always, death is in attendance at the feast, waiting for Tom and Rose Ella and, although this remains unspoken before the feast begins, also waiting for Raphael. This feast is—in true Bakhtinian fashion—a celebration of the culmination of work: before the fish fry begins, Rose Ella kills and guts the fifteen-pound catfish she caught that morning, and much of the food on the table is a product of the family's garden, or at least Rose Ella's hard work:

> Next to the fish were bowls of dark green kale cooked since morning with a side of fatback, with cider vinegar at hand in Rose Ella's great-grandmother's silver-and-crystal cruets. A gilt-edged platter carried a small mountain of thin fried potatoes, encircled by a moat of Rose Ella's green tomato ketchup. Quartered watermelons showed speckled crescents next to pyramids of homegrown tomatoes, yellow and red. Deviled eggs peered up at the sky, their scrambled yolks bloodshot with paprika. A pile of corn on the cob filled a silver platter. At the center of the table three jam cakes iced with caramel ringed a cut-glass punch bowl filled with layers of fruit cocktail, cubes of electric-green Jell-O, Cool Whip, and miniature marshmallows,

topped with a sprinkling of toasted coconut and luminescent maraschino cherries.[80]

The Hardins' feast is marked by abundance, and this buffet contains numerous items that can be found on Sohn's (and others') lists of Appalachian foods.

The most significant overlap between the Hardins' feast and Bakhtin's argument about feast imagery is the way this scene is filled with what Bakhtin called "wise discourse and the gay truth." Many truths are spoken at this feast (and in the conversations that follow), sometimes inadvertently. One Hardin grandchild greets a guest using a racial slur, which he then makes clear he had learned from his grandfather: "Grandfather told me," he explains.[81] Rose Ella tries to deflect this awkwardness with a seemingly superficial comment about the food arrangement that inadvertently "outs" Nick, one of the neighbors at the feast, a local farmer who is gay but closeted: "'Let's every one of us here take a last look at that platter of fish, . . . it takes a woman to make it look pretty.' 'Nick arranged the fish,' Raphael said."[82] One character's question about another character's wife—"So where's Crystal?"—leads to an awkward exchange about whether Crystal and her husband are getting divorced.

During other occasions throughout the evening, characters speak the truth intentionally and deliberately, although that typically happens only when Raphael is part of the conversation. Raphael tells Nick (the gay, closeted farmer) about life in San Francisco. Raphael tells his teenaged nephews that he's infected with HIV and also about how infection occurs (and how to prevent it). In the most poignant example of truth-telling associated with this feast, after the party has broken up and the food has been put away, Raphael and his mother, Rose Ella, have a frank talk about his illness, his sexuality, and her refusal or inability to broach this subject with him until he is thirty-four years old. It begins, ironically enough, with Rose Ella encouraging her son to practice safe sex (although she doesn't use those words): "Promise me you're being careful, out there in San Francisco."[83] This leads to a testy exchange:

"Why in the hell didn't you tell me that twenty years ago?"
"Because I didn't know the words," Rose Ella snapped.
"You couldn't *say* the words. A different thing entirely."
"So you're young, you live in California. You tell me the words," Rose Ella said quietly. "I'm no fool, even if I do watch

TV. I know what's going on out there. What are the words for all that? What words do you use?"[84]

After a pause in the conversation, Rose Ella asks, "Are you sick already? . . . Is that what you're trying to tell me?" and Raphael tells her: about his prognosis, the progress of the disease, possible treatments.

In the discussion that follows, they absolve each other and discuss the inadequacies of language, especially for queer kids (and their parents) from rural areas who don't have words to express their desires or their worries.[85] When Rose Ella asks if it would "have made a difference if you could have told somebody, talked to somebody, back then?" Raphael voices their mutual frustration with language (and with the limits of his knowledge as a teen): "What words could I have used? I'd never heard them. *You'd* never heard them. And even if I'd had the words—who would I have talked to?" After a long pause, Rose Ella asks, "What if I had asked, when you got old enough? What if I had sat you down and made up words, if it had come to that? What if I had said, 'Rafe, how can I help?' Could I have helped?"[86] Although Rose Ella's questions are coming years too late, one can imagine many queer teens—Appalachian and otherwise—who would love to hear such offers of help from adults in their lives. In making the Hardins' feast the centerpiece of the novel, Johnson has staged a Bakhtinian occasion of truth-telling and wise discourse, helping Rose Ella and Raphael transcend both their generational differences and the limitations of language. The truth and wisdom that Rose Ella and Raphael share in this scene enable this Appalachian family to break many silences, like the writers discussed in this book who have broken the silence in Appalachian literature about queer Appalachian sexuality.

Conclusion

As I noted in the introduction, the genesis of this book was the 2014 Appalachian Studies Conference, when I discovered a gap in the scholarship about LGBTQ Appalachian literature and when I heard the call to action in Silas House's keynote address. While seated there in the auditorium at Marshall University, I took these words to heart: "As members of the scholarly community, it is our responsibility. . . . We must make The Other visible."[1] Earlier in the talk, he'd made a clear demand of literature teachers like me: "There are plenty of books out there that specifically handle issues of gay Appalachia. . . . Let's stop being reticent about this issue just because it's difficult to talk about. Instead, let's foster that discussion for that very reason."[2] That's me, I thought. I'm an educator; I can help.

I also realized that the circumstances of my life provided a buffer from the possible repercussions of such a scholarly choice. As an associate professor (not yet tenured, but on the way) at a public university, I had protections that an early-career researcher or a grad student wouldn't yet have. My veneer of conventional respectability, my white privilege, and my cisgender privilege all afforded me protections that are, I know, not available to all. I am less likely to be attacked by those who would say that I'm only teaching or writing about this literature because I'm "one of them." If "them" is Appalachians, then yes—I *am* one of them. If "them" is humankind, then yes, I'm one of them too. If "them" is people who would like Appalachia to be more accepting than our region is today, as a person who would also like for my LGBTQ-identified friends and students and neighbors to feel safe and comfortable in our home of Appalachia, then yes—I'm one of them.

In addition, I wanted to write about this literature because I find these to be moving, powerful texts and was startled at the critical neglect they have suffered from literary scholars and from scholars of Appalachian studies alike. These earlier writers—including Lisa Alther, Maggie Anderson, doris davenport, Fenton Johnson, Jeff Mann, Julia Watts, and Karen Salyer McElmurray—received less critical attention because at the time when their work was published, they and their work didn't fit into the comfortable, popular narratives of Appalachia and Appalachian studies. Likewise, their work garnered little attention within scholarship of contemporary American literature because of their Appalachian setting and themes. (Exceptions include Lisa Alther, whose *Kinflicks* was a national bestseller in the feminist *Fear of Flying* mold, and Fenton Johnson, whose *Scissors, Paper, Rock* was praised nationally—but not within his home region—within the context of early novels of the AIDS crisis.) I wanted to explore LGBTQ Appalachian literature because I found that too little had been said about this important tradition within Appalachian literature.

In the years since I began this project, significant shifts have occurred not only in Appalachian literature but also in US culture as a whole. After the 2013 Supreme Court decision *United States v. Windsor* (in which section 3 of the Defense of Marriage Act was declared unconstitutional) and 2015's *Obergefell v. Hodges* (requiring that jurisdictions in all fifty states must perform and recognize same-sex unions), LGBTQ Appalachians—and LGBTQ Americans as a whole—have come closer to enjoying the protections and privileges that are ostensibly guaranteed to all Americans under the law. However, the backlash against these rulings (and against changing attitudes toward gender and sexuality) has been fierce. Legally, the famous 2018 *Masterpiece Cakeshop* case was just one of many challenges, and this struggle continues to play out each time a state legislature (or county commission) passes a "bathroom bill" or a ban of transgender athletes. Anti-LGBTQ hate crimes—such as the Pulse shooting in June 2016, when forty-nine patrons of an Orlando gay nightclub were murdered—have continued to increase.[3] Although the landscape for LGBTQ Appalachians has improved in tangible ways over the past few years (for example, when spouses of my LGBTQ coworkers could be covered under our employer's health insurance), it is still legal in many places to fire someone or deny them public accommodations for being queer, and many hate crime laws still do not include provisions for sexual orientation and gender identification.[4] And now, in the wake of the *Dobbs v. Jackson* case, it is likely that many rights will be called into question, signaled by one justice's concurring opinion that recommends this ruling as precedent for overruling earlier decisions: "in future cases, we should reconsider all of this Court's substantive due process precedents, including *Griswold, Lawrence,* and *Obergefell*."[5] Take one step forward, and someone pushes back.

Despite—and also in reaction to—this pushback, the voices of people from marginalized groups are gaining new prominence: through social justice movements; in mass media (film, television, publishing), politics, and the workplace; as well as in Appalachian literature and the Appalachian scholarly community. In the past few years, several anthologies were released that began to include the diverse voices of this region: *Walk Till the Dogs Get Mean: Meditations on the Forbidden from Contemporary Appalachia* (2015), *Unbroken Circle: Stories of Cultural Diversity in the South* (2017), *Electric Dirt: A Celebration of Queer Voices and Identities from Appalachia and the South* (2017), *LGBTQ Fiction and Poetry from Appalachia* (2019), and *Storytelling in Queer Appalachia: Imagining and Writing the Unspeakable Other* (2020). Now, the forums for diverse voices in Appalachia include not only anthologies but entire book series: Fireside Industries, an imprint of the University Press of Kentucky in partnership with the Hindman Settlement School, is dedicated to publishing "creative work by authors with unique perspectives, diverse backgrounds, and compelling voices."[6] In 2021, the University Press of Kentucky announced a new book series, Appalachian Futures: Black, Native, and Queer Voices, seeking to give "voice to Black, Native, Latinx, Asian, Queer, and other nonwhite or ignored identities within the Appalachian region."[7] The attention to—and the respect afforded to—diverse voices within Appalachia appears to grow daily.

Consequently, in the past eight years, we've seen a rich flowering of new voices in LGBTQ Appalachian literature. Some of our most talented writers—including Mesha Maren (*Sugar Run*, 2018; *Perpetual West*, 2022), Savannah Sipple (*WWJD and Other Poems*, 2019), Jonathan Corcoran (*The Rope Swing*, 2016)—have published their first book-length work within the last few years, and these writers and others are addressing LGBTQ themes. Perhaps even more exciting are the emerging writers who are beginning to publish in journals (like *Still: The Journal, Appalachian Review, Scalawag*) or who are using new media, including blogs, Facebook pages, Instagram accounts, to speak and spread their truth. In addition, the contemporary writers discussed in the "Landmarks" chapter in this volume continue to publish, and their newest works build on the themes and traditions discussed in those earlier chapters. For example, Fenton Johnson's novel *The Man Who Loved Birds* (2016) explores the solace and peril found in organized religion and in the natural world. In Julia Watts's YA novel *Quiver* (2018), the culture wars play out through an unlikely friendship between a gender fluid teenager and a young woman from a strict, evangelical family. (Yet a 2019 incident in which Watts was uninvited as a presenter at a teen literary festival—sponsored by a public library system—after complaints about the sexual content of some of Watts's novels for adults reminds us of how far we have yet to go.[8]) Soon, additional studies will be written tracing the work of these emerging writers who will carry on these traditions—and forge new ones—while giving voice to the diversity of Appalachia.

As *Doubly Erased* has demonstrated, this recent work builds upon a rich foundation of contemporary Appalachian writers who addressed LGBTQ themes and framed common concerns within traditional literary imagery such as photography, silence, the homeplace, birds, and food. These contemporary texts—from Alther's *Kinflicks* to Sickels's *The Prettiest Star*—continue the work of older generations, many of whom did not feel free to come out during their lifetimes. Byron Herbert Reece's 1940 declaration, "I am going to be absolutely truthful sometime before I die"—a wish that was never realized in Reece's lifetime—reminds us of the intense pressures to conform felt by earlier generations of queer Appalachian writers. Moreover, the bravery of poet George Scarbrough's coming out in the late 1990s—and the rejection by family that he suffered even as an elderly man—recalls the high stakes that such openness carried for these early writers. I hope that other scholars will take up this work and will further explore the complex treatments of sexuality within contemporary Appalachian literature, acknowledging the innovations of these writers as well as honoring the bravery of our literary elders in ways not possible while they lived.

Appendix

doris davenport Videos

Title: "PoetsIntroVideo30Apr2021," https://www.youtube.com/watch?v=ra-S5O13khDo (published on April 30, 2021, by doris davenport; captioned: "This 8.52 minute video is an excerpted piece from an article meant to accompany the art exhibit #notastereotype, commissioned by Director La Ruchala Murphy"; 8m52s).

Title: "'Ceremony for Soque Street' for ROOTS Grant," https://www.youtube.com/watch?v=7ZbqV3yUJ-w (published on September 11, 2018, by doris davenport; captioned: "This is a reading of one key poem, that hopefully demonstrates the community, the theatricality and originality of the community"; 4m50s).

Title: "Black Women Writers Symposium: doris davenport," https://www.youtube.com/watch?v=W1OQa4cQDG4 (published on November 4, 2016, by Howdylzzy; captioned: "A reading and conversation with doris davenport at the Black Women Writers Symposium at Berea College on Friday, October 21st, 2016"; 44m48s).

Title: "100kPoetsIntrodd" (a fifteen-minute video from Sweetwater Coffeehouse in Sautee, GA), https://www.youtube.com/watch?v=U0HAohESkoI (published on October 4, 2016, by doris davenport; captioned: "At the 100 Thousand Poets & Other Artists, 2016, at Sweetwater Coffeehouse in Sautee, GA. As coordinator and participant i am introducing and providing background. This is the 6th global event, organized and created by Michael Rothenberg"; 15m26s; davenport begins talking about her own poetry at about 7m30s).

Title: "ddAug2014ALTRTsAM" (short seventeen-second segment from a longer feature performance), https://www.youtube.com/watch?v=6yXcV1STlAs (published on September 15, 2016, by doris davenport; captioned: "very, very short (18 seconds) excerpt from longer featured performance at AlternateRoots 2014 Annual Meeting from new book, "65 / poems"; 17s).

Title: "ddAR2016," https://www.youtube.com/watch?v=JiKmMRb3Zkc (published on September 15, 2016, by doris davenport; captioned: "doris davenport in performance at Alternate ROOT's 40th Annual Meeting, Café Bizzozo (#1)"; 3m23s).

Title: "ddavenportCantrell interview 2015SD," https://www.youtube.com/watch?v=QvlUrr79JBg (published on September 15, 2016, by doris davenport; captioned: "An interview conducted by Dr. Jaime Cantrell (via Skype) in Feb. 2015 as part of her essay 'Put a Taste of the South in your Mouth . . .' published Sept. 2015 in http://southernstudies.olemiss.edu/pu . . . [sic]"; 27m27s; Skype interview of davenport by Dr. Jamie Cantrell, focusing on food in davenport's work).

Title: "aesthetics of being 65," https://www.youtube.com/watch?v=qA46PxrZfOE (published on April 25, 2014, by doris davenport; captioned: "A 3 min video (selfie, Samsung tablet) for an application to ROOTs 2014 Annual Meeting Performance Showcase. Me in the backyard around 6 pm, performing from my new book, "65/poems" (book cover photos by Ariston). 25 april 2014"; 3m10s).

Title: "davenportPoetry 2011-05-27 at 14.33.mov," https://www.youtube.com/watch?v=s7PcP2sbgYw (published on May 31, 2011, by doris davenport; captioned: "This very short, very rough homemade video is my first. It was done with photobooth on my iMac; specifically created to submit with an Artistic Assistance grant, since i think the panelists need visuals of what i do. Unfortunately, there is or may be a problem with the audio—out of sync. This 'rough draft' at least demonstrates that i need some *real* video equipment. Constructive criticism / feedback welcomed"; 1m48s; davenport appears to be reading from her poem "Sometimes I wonder" during part of the video).

Notes

Introduction

1. Silas House, "Our Secret Places in the Waiting World: Or, A Conscious Heart, Continued," *Journal of Appalachian Studies* 20, no. 2 (Fall 2014): 121. House's keynote was also filmed and is available on YouTube at https://www.youtube.com/watch?v=ZR7A69yOL-k.

2. At the time, in 2014, there were no book-length studies of any LGBTQ writers who are typically classified as Appalachian. However, in 2021, *Silas House: Exploring an Appalachian Writer's Work* (edited by Sylvia Bailey Shurbutt) was published by the University Press of Kentucky.

3. Silas House, "The Other in an Othered Culture: LGBTQ Writers in Appalachia," panel at Appalachian Studies Association Conference, Cincinnati, Ohio, April 2018.

4. Of course, many of these writers work in multiple genres. For instance, Mann is also a prolific novelist, while Allison's memoir, *Two or Three Things I Know for Sure*, will be discussed later in the book.

5. Jack Halberstam, *In a Queer Time and Place: Transgender Bodies, Subcultural Lives* (New York: New York University Press, 2005), 36–42.

6. Halberstam, 15.

7. Halberstam, 41.

8. Richard Meyer, preface to *Art and Queer Culture*, by Catherine Lord and Richard Meyer (New York: Phaidon Press, 2013), 9–10. See also House, "Conscious Heart, Continued," 108.

9. Kate Black and Marc A. Rhorer, "Out in the Mountains: Exploring Lesbian and Gay Lives," *Journal of the Appalachian Studies Association* 7 (1995): 18.

10. Black and Rhorer, 18.

11. Black and Rhorer, 21.

12. My thanks go to Jeff Mann, who alerted me to this paper's existence and found a copy for me through the still-vibrant network of Danny Miller's friends,

and to Steve Mooney, who provided that copy. At a 2009 roundtable discussion held as part of a celebration of Danny Miller (not long after his death in 2008), Mann spoke about the impact that Miller's essay had on him—years before Mann published *Loving Mountains, Loving Men* (2005)—and about urging Miller to publish the essay, which he never did.

13. Danny L. Miller, "Homosexuality in Appalachian Literature," paper presented at the Appalachian Studies Association Conference, March 30, 1996, 1.

14. Miller, 22, underline in original.

15. Jeff Mann, "Stonewall and Matewan: Some Thoughts on Gay Life in Appalachia," *Journal of Appalachian Studies* 5, no. 2 (Fall 1999): 208, 209.

16. Mann, 213.

17. Danielle Burke, April Caudill, Charles Cupp, and Brittany Rowlette, *Through Their Eyes: Stories of Gays and Lesbians in the Mountains*, Appalachian Media Institute/Appalshop, 1999, https://scholarworks.moreheadstate.edu/appalachian_kentucky_video_archives/50/; Kate Black, "Review of *Through Their Eyes: Stories of Gays and Lesbians in the Mountains*, by Burke, Caudill, Cupp, and Rowlette," *Journal of Appalachian Studies* 6, nos. 1–2 (2000): 251.

18. Black, "Review of *Through Their Eyes*," 251.

19. Craig M. Loftin, *Masked Voices: Gay Men and Lesbians in Cold War America*, Queer Politics and Cultures (Albany: State University of New York Press, 2012), 6.

20. Loftin, 11, emphasis in original.

21. "Fiction Book Review: *Clay's Quilt* by Silas House," *Publishers Weekly*, March 1, 2001, https://www.pubishersweekly.com/9781565123076; Kim Kobersmith, "Clay's Legacy," *Kentucky Monthly*, September 30, 2021, http://www.kentuckymonthly.com/api/content/21188b28-21e5-11ec-a885-12f1225286c6/; Erik Lundegaard, "Books in Brief: Fiction and Poetry," *New York Times*, July 15, 2001, sec. Books, https://www.nytimes.com/2001/07/15/books/books-in-brief-fiction-poetry.html.

22. Emily Satterwhite, *Dear Appalachia: Readers, Identity, and Popular Fiction since 1878* (Lexington: University Press of Kentucky, 2011), 184.

23. Ashlie Stevens, "Kentucky Writer Silas House on *Southernmost*, Sexuality and His Faith Journey," WFPL, June 4, 2018, https://wfpl.org/kentucky-writer-silas-house-on-southernmost-sexuality-and-his-faith-journey/.

24. House, "Conscious Heart, Continued," 112.

25. Jennifer Harlan, "Theater: Play Examines Homosexuality and Harassment in Appalachia: Author Silas House Takes on Homosexuality and Harassment in Appalachia," *LEO Weekly*, January 8, 2014, sec. Arts and Culture, https://www.leoweekly.com/2014/01/theater-play-examines-homosexuality-and-harassment-in-appalachia/.

26. House, "Conscious Heart, Continued" 121.

27. Jason Kyle Howard, "Creative Process Blog Tour," *Jason Kyle Howard* (blog), August 19, 2014, http://www.jason-howard.com/blog.html.

28. Silas House, "Kentucky County Gets Media Attention Over Clerk's Stand on Marriage," interview by Steve Inskeep, NPR, September 3, 2015, https://www.npr.org/2015/09/03/437132849/kentucky-county-gets-media-attention-over-clerks-stand-on-marriage; Kim Davis was a county clerk in eastern Kentucky who refused to issue marriage licenses to same-sex couples in 2015 right after the *Obergefell v. Hodges* decision, even when ordered to do so by a US District Court. Davis was jailed (briefly) for contempt of court and celebrated by various politicians (including presidential candidates Ted Cruz and Mike Huckabee, and candidate and later governor of Kentucky Matt Bevin) for what was described as Davis's being persecuted for her faith.

29. Silas House, "The Masterpiece Decision Isn't Harmless," *New York Times*, June 5, 2018, sec. Opinion, https://www.nytimes.com/2018/06/05/opinion/masterpiece-cakeshop-decision-kentucky.html.

30. Josh Inocencio, "Identity, Family, Belief: Novelist Silas House Chats Writing about Appalachia," *Spectrum South: The Voice of the Queer South* (blog), July 31, 2017, https://www.spectrumsouth.com/novelist-silas-house/.

31. Silas House, "Looking in the Mirror," BookBrowse.com, June 1, 2018, https://www.bookbrowse.com/author_interviews/full/index.cfm/author_number/3103/silas-house; Stevens, "Kentucky Writer Silas House"; Carter Sickels, "Silas House: On Capturing the Rural South and Loving in a Fraught . . . ," *Lambda Literary* (blog), June 14, 2018, https://www.lambdaliterary.org/interviews/06/14/silas-house/.

32. House, "The Masterpiece Decision Isn't Harmless."

33. Silas House, "From the Playwright," in *This Is My Heart for You*, by Silas House (Berea, KY: Loyal Jones Appalachian Center, 2014), 9.

34. In June 2022, House was awarded a Duggins Prize for Outstanding Mid-Career Novelist by Lambda Literary.

35. Doris Davenport, "Music in Poetry: If You Can't Feel It / You Can't Fake It," *Mid-American Review* 10, no. 2 (1990): 59–61.

Chapter 1. The Elders of LGBTQ Appalachian Literature

Page 00: "Ah, Stonewall, how little you knew." George Scarbrough, "Something of a Bio and an Itinerary: September 13, 1992," in *George Scarbrough, Appalachian Poet*, by Randy Mackin, Contributions to Southern Appalachian Studies 29 (Jefferson, NC: McFarland, 2011), 185.

1. See Loftin, *Masked Voices*, 10, for a discussion of the "closet" metaphor for earlier generations. Loftin argues that "gay people in the 1950s did not 'come out of the closet.' Instead, they 'came out to gay life.'"

2. Alison Bechdel, *Fun Home: A Family Tragicomic* (New York: Houghton Mifflin, 2006), 107.

3. "Arresting Dress: A Timeline of Anti-Cross-Dressing Laws in the United States," *PBS NewsHour*, May 31, 2015, https://www.pbs.org/newshour/nation/arresting-dress-timeline-anti-cross-dressing-laws-u-s.

4. For more on "archives as a discursive system" or as metaphor, see Alana Kumbier, *Ephemeral Material: Queering the Archive*, Series on Gender and Sexuality in Information Studies 5 (Sacramento: Litwin Books, 2014), 12; Marlene Manoff, "Theories of the Archive from Across the Disciplines," *Portal: Libraries and the Academy* 4, no. 1 (January 2004): 9–25, https://doi.org/10.1353/pla.2004.0015.

5. Ann Cvetkovich, *An Archive of Feelings: Trauma, Sexuality, and Lesbian Public Cultures* (Durham, NC: Duke University Press, 2003), 242.

6. Valerie Rohy, "In the Queer Archive," *GLQ: A Journal of Lesbian and Gay Studies* 16, no. 3 (June 1, 2010): 343, https://doi.org/10.1215/10642684-2009-034.

7. Kumbier, *Ephemeral Material*, 13, 14.

8. Cvetkovich, *An Archive of Feelings*, 242.

9. David K. Johnson, *The Lavender Scare: The Cold War Persecution of Gays and Lesbians in the Federal Government* (Chicago: University of Chicago Press, 2004), 4–10; Douglas M. Charles, *Hoover's War on Gays: Exposing the FBI's "Sex Deviates" Program* (Lawrence: University Press of Kansas, 2015), 71–72.

10. Johnson, *The Lavender Scare*, 123; "Executive Orders," National Archives, August 15, 2016, https://www.archives.gov/federal-register/codification/executive-order/10450.html.

11. Johnson, *The Lavender Scare*, 4, 209–12.

12. Craig M. Loftin, introduction to *Letters to ONE: Gay and Lesbian Voices from the 1950s and 1960s*, ed. Craig M. Loftin, Queer Politics and Cultures (Albany: State University of New York Press, 2012), 8.

13. Loftin, 9; for more on the postal service's crusade against *ONE*, see Loftin, *Masked Voices*, 38–39.

14. Barry Werth, *The Scarlet Professor—Newton Arvin: A Literary Life Shattered by Scandal* (New York: Anchor Books, 2002), loc. 151 of 5733 (p. 5 of 302), Kindle.

15. Werth, loc. 3503 of 5733 (p. 195 of 302), Kindle.

16. Werth, loc. 3535 of 5733 (p. 196 of 302), Kindle.

17. Werth, loc. 3937 of 5733 (p. 219 of 302), Kindle.

18. "2 Smith Teachers Held in Vice Case," *New York Times*, September 4, 1960.

19. Werth, loc. 3669 of 5733 (pp. 203–04 of 302), loc. 4101 of 5733 (p. 229 of 302), Kindle.

20. Werth, loc. 4491 of 5733 (p. 250 of 302), loc. 4949 of 5733 (p. 275 of 302), Kindle.

21. Werth, loc. 5376 of 5733 (p. 299 of 302), Kindle.

22. Werth, loc. 5190 of 5733 (p. 289 of 302), Kindle.

23. Werth, loc. 5171 of 5733 (p. 288 of 302), Kindle.

24. Johnson, *The Lavender Scare*, 206.
25. Loftin, *Masked Voices*, 4.
26. Loftin, 4.
27. Carol Boggess, *James Still: A Life* (Lexington: University Press of Kentucky, 2017), 383.
28. Boggess, 131–33, 139–42.
29. George Brosi, review of *James Still: A Life*, by Carol Boggess, *Appalachian Journal* 45, no. 3/4 (2018): 788, https://doi.org/10.2307/j.ctt1tg5p23.
30. Boggess, *James Still: A Life*, 161. See Boggess, 157–61, for more on the reception of *River of Earth*.
31. Boggess, 42–43, 166–67; Jim Wayne Miller, "Jim Dandy: James Still at Eighty," in *James Still: Critical Essays on the Dean of Appalachian Literature*, ed. Ted Olson and Kathy H. Olson, Contributions to Southern Appalachian Studies 17 (Jefferson, NC: McFarland, 2007), 220.
32. Qtd. in Boggess, *James Still: A Life*, 389.
33. Teresa Perry Reynolds, "James Still: Alabamian, Transplanted Knott Countian," *Appalachian Heritage* 38, no. 4 (Fall 2010): 50, https://doi.org/10.1353/aph.2010.0036.
34. James Still, "Mountain Heritage," *New Republic* 85, no. 1098 (December 18, 1935): 170.
35. Boggess, *James Still: A Life*, 167.
36. Boggess, 318.
37. Boggess, 488.
38. Brosi, review of *James Still: A Life*, 790.
39. George Brosi, "Draft Book Review of *James Still: A Life*," October 10, 2018.
40. George Brosi, interview by author, November 9, 2018.
41. Werth, loc. 1669 of 5733 (p. 92 of 302), Kindle.
42. Boggess, *James Still: A Life*, 133–34; Robert Francis, *The Trouble with Francis: An Autobiography* (Amherst: University of Massachusetts Press, 1971), 19–20.
43. Letter from October 2, 1959, Box 25, Folder 5, James Still Papers, Special Collections Research Center, Margaret I. King Library, University of Kentucky Libraries. An audio recording of Robert Frost's speech from that day is available at https://digitalamherst.org/items/show/1922, Frost, Robert, 1874–1963, "Robert Frost Speaks at the Dedication of the Robert Frost Room at the Jones Library in Amherst, Massachusetts," Digital Amherst, accessed July 4, 2022.
44. Postcard dated "20 Nov 59," Box 25, Folder 5, James Still Papers, Special Collections Research Center, Margaret I. King Library, University of Kentucky Libraries.
45. Francis, *The Trouble with Francis*, 211.
46. Francis, 213.

47. Correspondence from James Still to Robert Francis, Box 6, Folder 90, Robert Francis Papers (MS 403), Special Collections and University Archives, UMass Amherst Libraries.

48. Correspondence from Robert Francis to James Still, dated January 1, 1982, Box 30, Folder 1, James Still Papers, Special Collections Research Center, Margaret I. King Library, University of Kentucky Libraries.

49. Lawrance Thompson and R. H. Winnick, *Robert Frost: The Later Years, 1938–1963*, 1st ed. (New York: Holt, Rinehart and Winston, 1976), 205.

50. Thompson and Winnick, 204.

51. Andrew Stambuk, *The Man Who Is and Is Not There: The Poetry and Prose of Robert Francis*, 1st ed. (Amherst: University of Massachusetts Press, 2011), 162.

52. Stambuk, 119.

53. Boggess, *James Still: A Life*, 318, 317.

54. Boggess, 317.

55. Boggess, 282.

56. Boggess, 487.

57. A hallmark of Still's work was its subtlety. See Silas House, introduction to *Chinaberry*, by James Still, ed. Silas House (Lexington: University Press of Kentucky, 2011), xvi. See also Boggess, 159, about critiques of *River of Earth* because its exposure of social injustice was too restrained.

58. Jessica Christensen, "'There's Been Blood Shed a-Plenty': Female Vengeance in *River of Earth*," *KPA Bulletin* 30 (2015): 75–86; Michelle Justus, "Patriarchal Trauma in Appalachian Literature" (text, 2016), OpenDissertations, https://search.ebscohost.com/login.aspx?direct=true&db=ddu&AN=D1F86287F95E5712&site=ehost-live, are among the few exceptions.

59. Boggess, *James Still: A Life*, 3.

60. James Still, *River of Earth* (Lexington: University Press of Kentucky, 1978), 27, 30, 31.

61. Still, 61.

62. Still, 65, 123, 200.

63. Still, 217–22.

64. Boggess, *James Still: A Life*, 431; Carol Boggess, afterword to *Chinaberry*, by James Still, ed. Silas House (Lexington: University Press of Kentucky, 2011), 143.

65. James Still, *Chinaberry*, ed. Silas House (Lexington: University Press of Kentucky, 2011), 6, 27.

66. Still, 67, 81.

67. Still, 141.

68. Boggess, *James Still: A Life*, 433–34; see also Silas House's introduction to *Chinaberry*, xiii–xiv.

69. Letter from Betty Jean Wells to James Still, dated Tuesday, September 16, 1986, 87M12, Box 34, Folder 16, James Still Papers, Special Collections Research Center, Margaret I. King Library, University of Kentucky Libraries.

70. Still, *Chinaberry*, 74.

71. Still, 66.
72. Still, 66.
73. John Sledge, "Posthumous Novel *Chinaberry* Adds to James Still's Legacy," *Press-Register*, April 3, 2011, https://www.al.com/entertainment-press-register/2011/04/posthumous_novel_chinaberry_ad.html.
74. Unsigned review of *Chinaberry*, by James Still, *Publishers Weekly* 258, no. 7 (February 14, 2011): 38–39.
75. House, introduction to *Chinaberry*, xv.
76. Boggess, *James Still: A Life*, 433.
77. According to Carol Boggess in *James Still: A Life* (283), Still began teaching part-time at Morehead in 1961 and joined the faculty full-time in fall of 1963. Dr. Carlyle Cross joined the faculty in 1964, according to a September 15, 1964, article in the school newspaper, the *Trail Blazer*.
78. Correspondence from B.J. [Betty Jean Wells] to James Still, dated April 7, 1970, 87M12, Box 26, Folder 8, James Still Papers, Special Collections Research Center, Margaret I. King Library, University of Kentucky Libraries.
79. *Polk's Augusta (Richmond County, GA.) City Directory 1970* (Richmond, VA: R. L. Polk & Co., 1970).
80. Correspondence from Betty Jean [Wells] to James Still, dated January 4, 1972, 87M12, Box 27, Folder 1, James Still Papers, Special Collections Research Center, Margaret I. King Library, University of Kentucky Libraries.
81. Correspondence from Carlyle Cross to James Still, dated July 12, 1966 (Box 26, Folder 1); undated but postmarked July 12, 1967 (Box 26, Folder 3); postcard from Greece dated July 29, 1968 (Box 26, Folder 5); postcard dated August 28, 1968 (Box 26, Folder 5); postcard dated September 15, 1968 (Box 26, Folder 5); postcard dated April 10, 1969 (Box 26, Folder 6), 87M12, James Still Papers, Special Collections Research Center, Margaret I. King Library, University of Kentucky Libraries.
82. Correspondence from Carlyle Cross to James Still, dated July 28, 1976, 87M12, Box 27, Folder 12, James Still Papers, Special Collections Research Center, Margaret I. King Library, University of Kentucky Libraries. (The finding aid for Still's correspondence, https://stillbib.omeka.net/items/show/64623, indicates no return address/origin for this item.)
83. "James Still Comes to Cumberland," *Whitley Republican*, August 19, 1976, 87M12, Box 2, Folder 10, the James Still Papers, Special Collections Research Center, Margaret I. King Library, University of Kentucky Libraries.
84. Correspondence from Carlyle Cross to James Still, undated (but marked "[c. November 1976]" by archivist, based on context clues), 87M12, Box 27, Folder 13, James Still Papers, Special Collections Research Center, Margaret I. King Library, University of Kentucky Libraries.
85. Clipping is undated, with no notes about the source, 87M12, Box 2, Folder 10, James Still Papers, Special Collections Research Center, Margaret I. King Library, University of Kentucky Libraries.

86. Letter from James Still to Alfred Perrin, dated March 2, 1977, Series 1, Box 1, Folder 11, James Still Papers, Berea College Special Collections and Archives, Berea, KY; Jim Wayne Miller, "'Daring to Look in the Well': A Conversation," in *James Still in Interviews, Oral Histories and Memoirs*, ed. Ted Olson, Contributions to Southern Appalachian Studies 23 (Jefferson, NC: McFarland, 2009), 53. In *James Still: A Life*, Carol Boggess argues that "when recounting his adventures, Still rarely referred to travel companions, though he was usually accompanied" (339).

87. "Cumberland Professor Caught in Upheaval during Central American Tour," *Whitley Republican*, April 14, 1977, sec. B; Thomas B. Frazier, "Vacation Became 'Run-for-Your-Life' Situation," *BP [Baptist Press]—Features*, April 19, 1977; both clippings in 87M12, Box 2, Folder 10, James Still Papers, Special Collections Research Center, Margaret I. King Library, University of Kentucky Libraries.

88. Series 2, Box 3, Folder 13, James Still Papers, Berea College Special Collections and Archives, Berea, KY.

89. Labeled on back [by archivist] "Still and unidentified man—by Thomas B. Frazier Sept. 1977," PA87M12, Item #743, Box 4, Folder 17, James Still Papers, Special Collections Research Center, Margaret I. King Library, University of Kentucky Libraries.

90. Enclosed with letter from Cross to Still dated October 20, 1977, 87M12, Box 27, Folder 18, James Still Papers, Special Collections Research Center, Margaret I. King Library, University of Kentucky Libraries.

91. Correspondence from Carlyle Cross to James Still, 87M12, Box 27, Folder 18, James Still Papers, Special Collections Research Center, Margaret I. King Library, University of Kentucky Libraries.

92. Letters from Cross to Still dated October 20, 1977 (Box 27, Folder 18), February 16, 1978 (Box 28, Folder 1), 87M12, James Still Papers, Special Collections Research Center, Margaret I. King Library, University of Kentucky Libraries; Christmas card from Still to Cadle, undated but marked "[Dec. 17, 1977]" by archivist, 87M12, Box 27, Folder 13, James Still Papers, Special Collections Research Center, Margaret I. King Library, University of Kentucky Libraries.

93. Postcard from James Still to Alfred Perrin, Series 1, Box 1, Folder 12, James Still Papers, Berea College Special Collections and Archives, Berea, KY.

94. Postcard from James Still to Alfred Perrin, Series 1, Box 1, Folder 12, James Still Papers, Berea College Special Collections and Archives, Berea, KY.

95. Postcard from James Still to the Grover Farrs, Series 1, Box 1, Folder 12, James Still Papers, Berea College Special Collections and Archives, Berea, KY.

96. Miller, "Jim Dandy," 220.

97. Letter from Alfred Perrin to James Still, dated April 8, 1978, Series 1, Box 1, Folder 12, James Still Papers, Berea College Special Collections and Archives, Berea, KY.

98. Letter from James Still to Alfred Perrin, dated April 19, 1978, Series 1, Box 1, Folder 12, James Still Papers, Berea College Special Collections and Archives, Berea, KY.

99. Letter from Alfred Perrin to James Still, dated April 22, 1978, Series 1, Box 1, Folder 12, James Still Papers, Berea College Special Collections and Archives, Berea, KY.

100. Letter from Betty Jean [Wells] to James Still, dated May 12, 1978, 87M12, Box 28, Folder 2, James Still Papers, Special Collections Research Center, Margaret I. King Library, University of Kentucky Libraries.

101. Item headed "Havana, Cuba," and dated "March 11, 1989"; entry dated "March 12 Saturday," 87M12, Box 83, Folder 7, James Still Papers, Special Collections Research Center, Margaret I. King Library, University of Kentucky Libraries.

102. Correspondence from Carlyle Cross to James Still, 87M12: postcard dated 11/11/78, Box 28, Folder 8; letter dated 12/16/78, Box 28, Folder 9, James Still Papers, Special Collections Research Center, Margaret I. King Library, University of Kentucky Libraries.

103. Cross's name and his Augusta, GA, address appear on a typed list in Still's papers at Berea, headed "Christmas Cards received: 1985," but the card isn't among Still's other correspondence at the University of Kentucky Library.

104. Correspondence from Carlyle Cross to James Still, 87M12: greeting card postmarked 11/24/86, Box 35, Folder 2; postcard dated 8/18/87, Box 35, Folder 11, James Still Papers, Special Collections Research Center, Margaret I. King Library, University of Kentucky Libraries.

105. Correspondence from Carlyle Cross to James Still, 87M12: greeting card dated 4/16/87 in Box 35, Folder 7; letter dated 6/24/91 in Box 39, Folder 7; greeting card dated 7/1/96 in Box 45, Folder 7, James Still Papers, Special Collections Research Center, Margaret I. King Library, University of Kentucky Libraries.

106. Letter from Gerald Smith to James Still, 87M12, Box 46, Folder 3, James Still Papers, Special Collections Research Center, Margaret I. King Library, University of Kentucky Libraries.

107. Another longtime friendship for Still was with Wade Hall, professor of English at Bellarmine University and like Still a native of Alabama. The James Still Papers at the University of Kentucky contain over sixty letters and cards that Hall sent to Still (and that Still saved) between 1971 and 2000. Through the course of this correspondence, a reader can see the deepening friendship; and beginning in 1984, Still becomes a frequent houseguest at the Louisville home of Hall and Hall's life partner (since 1971), Gregg Swem. Still clearly knows of Swem's existence: Hall's letters refer to him, and later a few letters include notes to Still from Swem. It is unlikely that a perceptive student of the human condition like James Still could have repeatedly stayed in the Hall-Swem home—and even traveled with them—and not intuited that they were romantic partners.

Still's friendship with Eliot Wiggington (of the *Foxfire* books), a friendship that letters in the James Still Papers suggest continued after Wiggington pled guilty to child molestation (and spent a year in prison), is a more complicated demonstration of Still's acceptance of others. (The only letter from Still that survives was written about six weeks before Wiggington pled guilty. The letters from Wigginton in the Still Papers indicate that Still wrote to him while he was in prison, and after.) See Wiggington correspondence to Still, November 25, 1992, and December 10, 1993.

108. Gilbert E. Govan, "When Writers Live Close to Earth," *Chattanooga Daily Times*, November 17, 1940, sec. 3; Robert B. Cumming, "Resonance Across Time and Cultures: An Introduction to George Scarbrough's Han-Shan Poems," in *Under the Lemon Tree*, by George Scarbrough, ed. Rebecca Passmore Mobbs and Robert B. Cumming (Oak Ridge, TN: Iris Press, 2011), 16.

109. Rodney Jones, "Entering *Tellico Blue*," in *Tellico Blue*, 2nd ed. (Oak Ridge, TN: Iris Press, 1999), vii–viii.

110. Qtd. in Randy Mackin, *George Scarbrough, Appalachian Poet: A Biographical and Literary Study with Unpublished Writings*, Contributions to Southern Appalachian Studies 29 (Jefferson, NC: McFarland, 2011), 4.

111. Mackin, 3–5.

112. Qtd. in Mackin, 4.

113. Jerry Williamson and George Scarbrough, "The County and Beyond: A Conversation," *Iron Mountain Review* 16 (Spring 2000): 31.

114. Mackin, *George Scarbrough, Appalachian Poet*, 199; Williamson and Scarbrough, "The County and Beyond," 35.

115. Mackin, *George Scarbrough, Appalachian Poet*, 4.

116. Williamson and Scarbrough, "The County and Beyond," 33. See also Mackin, 190.

117. Mackin, *George Scarbrough, Appalachian Poet*, 190.

118. Mackin, 100. Beat Generation poet Gary Snyder translated the poetry of Han-Shan in the 1950s; his translations were later published as the *Cold Mountain Poems*.

119. Sources disagree on whether the works of Han-Shan were in fact authored by an individual person, as well as about whether the historical Han-Shan, if he existed, had such a companion as Shi-Te. See Cumming, "Resonance Across Time and Cultures," 19–20; Robert G. Henricks, introduction to *The Poetry of Han-Shan: A Complete, Annotated Translation of Cold Mountain* (Albany: State University of New York Press, 1990), 7–11.

120. Mackin, *George Scarbrough, Appalachian Poet*, 105.

121. From "News from the Capital" and "Poetry Festival," in George Scarbrough, *Under the Lemon Tree*, ed. Robert B. Cumming and Rebecca Passmore Mobbs (Oak Ridge, TN: Iris Press, 2011).

122. From "News from the Capital" and "Acknowledgment," in Scarbrough.

123. George Scarbrough, "Revenant," *Poetry* (July 2000): 207.

124. From "Last Will and Testament," "Grace," and "Absence," from Scarbrough, *Under the Lemon Tree*.

125. Interview excerpted in Mackin, 100.

126. Qtd. in Mackin, 4.

127. George Scarbrough, "Sunday Shopping," *Poetry* (February 1997): 283.
128. Mackin, *George Scarbrough, Appalachian Poet*, 105.
129. Mackin, 109.
130. George Scarbrough, "Love in the Afternoon," in *In Homage to Priapus*, ed. E. V. Griffith, Greenleaf Classic GL152 (San Diego, CA: Greenleaf Classics, 1970), 31–32.
131. Correspondence from E. V. Griffith to George Scarbrough, December 17, 1968, George Scarbrough Collection-P100, William R. Laurie University Archives and Special Collections, the University of the South, courtesy of William R. Laurie University Archives and Special Collections, University of the South.
132. Correspondence from George Scarbrough to E. V. Griffith, July 31, 1959, M1136, E. V. Griffith Papers, Box 2, courtesy of the Department of Special Collections, Stanford University Libraries.
133. Correspondence from George Scarbrough to E. V. Griffith, Undated, M1136, E. V. Griffith Papers, Box 2. Context clues suggest this letter was written in the summer of 1960.
134. Correspondence from George Scarbrough to E. V. Griffith, September 18, 1983, M1136, E. V. Griffith Papers, Box 2.
135. Randy Mackin, email message to author, November 8, 2019.
136. Qtd. in Mackin, *George Scarbrough, Appalachian Poet*, 4.
137. Correspondence from E. V. Griffith to George Scarbrough, May 23, 1959, George Scarbrough Collection-P100, William R. Laurie University Archives and Special Collections, University of the South, courtesy of William R. Laurie University Archives and Special Collections, University of the South.
138. Bettie Sellers, *The Bitter Berry: The Life of Byron Herbert Reece*, Southern Literature Series (Atlanta: Georgia Humanities Council, 1992).
139. Although some attribute Reece's failure to graduate on his home responsibilities, others blame his refusal to complete requirements in mathematics and French.
140. Raymond A. Cook, *Mountain Singer: The Life and the Legacy of Byron Herbert Reece*, rpt. ed. (Atlanta: Cherokee, 1980), 35–37.
141. Sellers, *The Bitter Berry*, 19, 25.
142. Jesse Stuart, "Byron Herbert Reece: In Memoriam, I," *Georgia Review* 12 (1958): 361–62.
143. Correspondence from E. V. Griffith to George Scarbrough, May 23, 1959, George Scarbrough Collection-P100, William R. Laurie University Archives and Special Collections, the University of the South, courtesy of William R. Laurie University Archives and Special Collections, University of the South.
144. Correspondence from E. V. Griffith to George Scarbrough, December 28, 1964, George Scarbrough Collection-P100, William R. Laurie University Archives and Special Collections, the University of the South, courtesy of William R. Laurie University Archives and Special Collections, University of the South. Underlining in original.

145. Cook, *Mountain Singer*, 120.

146. Sellers, *The Bitter Berry*, 16, 14.

147. E. V. Griffith, "Byron Herbert Reece: A Personal Memoir with Letters," *Georgia Review* 19, no. 2 (1965): 133.

148. Griffith, 149.

149. Raymond A. Cook, "Byron Herbert Reece: Ten Years After," *Georgia Review* 22, no. 1 (1968): 78.

150. Cook, 87.

151. Correspondence from Edward Pratt Dickson to Byron Herbert Reece, September 10, 1957, UGA Archives Byron Herbert Reece family papers, ms3055, Hargrett Rare Book and Manuscript Library, University of Georgia Libraries, Box 11, Folder 4, emphasis added.

152. Dan Luckenbill, "ONE, Inc., Is Founded," in *LGBTQ Events*, ed. Robert C. Evans, Great Events from History (Salem Press/Grey House, 2018), 103, Gale eBooks, https://link.gale.com/apps/doc/CX7241200054/GVRL?u=hunt91316&sid=GVRL&xid=e9de1d02.

153. Charles, *Hoover's War on Gays*, 157–61, 188. For a history of the Mattachine Society's chapter in Washington, DC, see Johnson, *The Lavender Scare*, 169–211. Among the damning evidence found in the raid on Newton Arvin's apartment in 1960 were "copies of *One*, the 'common denominator' in many of [the state policeman's] arrests," Werth, *Scarlet Professor* loc. 3515 of 5733 (p. 196 of 302), Kindle.

154. Martin Meeker, "One," in *Encyclopedia of Lesbian, Gay, Bisexual and Transgender History in America*, ed. Marc Stein (New York: Charles Scribner's Sons, 2004), 359, https://link.gale.com/apps/doc/CX3403600373/GVRL?u=hunt91316&sid=GVRL&xid=57758e06.

155. Typed manuscript, marked "Manfred Wise," enclosed with a letter from Edward Pratt Dickson to Byron Herbert Reece, December 1953, Byron Herbert Reece family papers, ms3055, Hargrett Rare Book and Manuscript Library, University of Georgia Libraries, Box 11, Folder 4.

156. I've been unable to confirm from the archival record when Dickson first published in *ONE* or the *Mattachine Review*, although I've found reference (in letters to the editor in the May 1958 *Mattachine Review*) to a March 1958 essay by Wise as well as a poem by Wise ("How Thin Your Nose Is") in the September 1958 issue of *ONE*. For examples of references to Reece's encouragement of the Manfred Wise poems, see letters from Dickson to Reece, May 1, 1955, and June 21, 1955, Byron Herbert Reece family papers, ms3055, Hargrett Rare Book and Manuscript Library, University of Georgia Libraries, Box 11, Folder 4.

157. Federal Bureau of Investigation, *Freedom of Information/Privacy Acts Release, Subject: Mattachine Society*, https://vault.fbi.gov/mattachine-society-part-01-of-03, accessed November 11, 2019.

158. Sellers, *The Bitter Berry*, 15.

159. Hugh Ruppersburg, foreword to *The Hawk and the Sun*, by Byron Herbert Reece (Athens, GA: Brown Thrasher Books, 1994), xvi–xvii.

160. Jim Clark, introduction to *Fable in the Blood: The Selected Poems of Byron Herbert Reece*, by Byron Herbert Reece, ed. Jim Clark (Athens: University of Georgia Press, 2002), xxx–xxxi.

161. Clark, xxxi.

162. Reprinted in Byron Herbert Reece, *Fable in the Blood: The Selected Poems of Byron Herbert Reece*, ed. Jim Clark (Athens: University of Georgia Press, 2002), 25.

163. Raymond A. Cook and Alan Jackson, "Glossary: Who's Who Among Recipients," in *Faithfully Yours: The Letters of Byron Herbert Reece*, by Byron Herbert Reece (Atlanta, GA: Cherokee, 2007), 125.

164. Byron Herbert Reece, *Faithfully Yours: The Letters of Byron Herbert Reece*, ed. Raymond A. Cook and Alan Jackson (Atlanta, GA: Cherokee, 2007), 5.

165. Reece, 8.

166. Reece, 66.

167. Reproduction from a page of Scarbrough's journals, labeled 217, copy mailed to author by Randy Mackin, November 2019. Scarbrough's unpublished journal entries are available for review at William R. Laurie University Archives and Special Collections, University of the South, courtesy of William R. Laurie University Archives and Special Collections, University of the South.

Chapter 2. The Conversation Begins

1. John Lang, "The Editor's Page," *Iron Mountain Review* 17 (Spring 2001): 2; Anne Larsen, "Reeling through a Daughter's Decade," review of *Kinflicks*, by Lisa Alther, *Village Voice*, March 8, 1976, 39.

2. Lessing quoted in Patricia Beer, "Sickbed Humor," *The Listener*, August 26, 1976, 253, and in Richard Todd, "Two Good Old-Fashioned Young Novelists," *Atlantic Monthly* 237, no. 5 (May 1976): 107. See also Larsen, "Reeling through a Daughter's Decade"; John Leonard, "Pop Goes the Novel," review of *Kinflicks*, by Lisa Alther, *New York Times Book Review*, March 14, 1976.

3. Ann Switzer, "Kingsport Skin Shows through in *Kinflicks*," *Kingsport Times-News*, March 14, 1976, newspapers.com.

4. Vince Staten, "Who'd Want to Read a Novel about Growing up in Kingsport?," *Kingsport Times-News*, June 5, 1976, newspapers.com.

5. Lisa Alther, *Kinflicks* (London: Virago, 1999), 318.

6. Alther, 307.

7. Quoted in Jan Hokenson, "Alther, Lisa," in *Gay and Lesbian Literature*, ed. Tom Pendergast and Sara Pendergast (Detroit: St. James Press, 1994), 5.

8. Lore Dickstein, "An Easy Lay, Spiritually Speaking," *Ms.* 4, no. 12 (June 1976): 90.

9. Maureen Brady and Judith McDaniel, "Lesbians in the Mainstream: Images of Lesbians in Recent Commercial Fiction," *Conditions* 6 (1979): 84, 85.

10. Alice Adams, "Endjokes," review of *Kinflicks*, by Lisa Alther, *Harper's Magazine*, May 1976, 98.

11. Lisa Maria Hogeland, *Feminism and Its Fictions: The Consciousness-Raising Novel and the Women's Liberation Movement* (Philadelphia: University of Pennsylvania Press, 1998), 73.

12. Hogeland, 73.

13. Sherrie A. Inness, "Alther, Lisa (b. 1944)," in *The Gay and Lesbian Literary Heritage: A Reader's Companion to the Writers and Their Works, from Antiquity to the Present*, ed. Claude J. Summers (New York: Routledge, 2013), 21, http://web.b.ebscohost.com.marshall.idm.oclc.org/ehost/ebookviewer/ebook/bmxlYmtfXzcwNzg1Ml9fQU41?sid=5511af65-1578-4ea0-acdd-851abbdb9ba2@sessionmgr102&vid=0&format=EB&rid=1.

14. Maggie Anderson, *The Great Horned Owl* (Riderwood, MD: Icarus Press, 1979).

15. Maggie Anderson, *Cold Comfort*, Pitt Poetry Series (Pittsburgh: University of Pittsburgh Press, 1986).

16. Maggie Anderson, *A Space Filled with Moving* (Pittsburgh: University of Pittsburgh Press, 1992).

17. Unsigned review of *A Space Filled with Moving*, by Maggie Anderson, *Publisher's Weekly* 239, no. 17 (April 6, 1992): 58.

18. Sheela Ardrian, "Bright and Dark," *Lesbian Review of Books* 7, no. 1 (Fall 2000): 14.

19. Patricia Roth Schwartz, "Profound Pitt Poets," *Lambda Book Report* 9, no. 2 (September 2000): 21.

20. John Hoppenthaler, "Maggie Anderson Interview with John Hoppenthaler," ConnotationPress—An Online Artifact, March 2019, https://www.connotationpress.com/hoppenthaler-s-congeries/2017/november-2017/3128-maggie-anderson-poetry.

21. Kate Long and Maggie Anderson, "The Spaces Between: A Conversation," *Iron Mountain Review* 21 (2005): 40.

22. Maggie Anderson, "Two Rivers," in *Liberating Memory: Our Work and Our Working-Class Consciousness* (New Brunswick, NJ: Rutgers University Press, 1995), 149, 150.

23. Hoppenthaler, "Maggie Anderson Interview with John Hoppenthaler."

24. Joyce Dyer, "Confluences: Fluidity in the Art and Vision of Maggie Anderson," *Iron Mountain Review* 21 (2005): 28.

25. "About the Appalachian Region," Appalachian Regional Commission, https://www.arc.gov/about-the-appalachian-region/, accessed June 9, 2022,

26. Dorothy Allison, "A Conversation with Dorothy Allison," interview by Mary Flinn and Randy Marshall, *Blackbird: An Online Journal of Literature and the Arts* 16, no. 2 (Fall 2017), https://blackbird.vcu.edu/v16n2/features/allison-d/conversation_page.shtml.

27. Dorothy Allison, *Bastard Out of Carolina* (New York: Dutton, 1992), 309.

28. Mark Annichiarico and Barbara Hoffert, "Best Books of 1992," *Library Journal*, January 1, 1993.

29. Randall Kenan, "Sorrow's Child," *Nation*, December 28, 1992.

30. Carolyn A. Megan, "Moving Toward Truth: An Interview with Dorothy Allison," *Kenyon Review* 16, no. 4 (Fall 1994): 81.

31. Mary Ann Daly, "Roses Grown for Their Thorns," review of *Two or Three Things I Know for Sure*, by Dorothy Allison, *Lambda Book Report* 4, no. 12 (October 1995): 25.

32. Dorothy Allison, *Two or Three Things I Know for Sure* (New York: Penguin, 1995), 17.

33. Allison, 48, 43.

34. Joy MacKenzie, "Harrowing Tales from a Hard Life," review of *Two or Three Things I Know for Sure*, by Dorothy Allison, *Sunday Star-Times*, April 28, 1996, A edition, sec. Features—Books, Newspaper Source Plus; Daly, "Roses Grown for Their Thorns," 26.

35. Daly, "Roses Grown for Their Thorns," 26, emphasis in original.

36. David Reynolds, "White Trash in Your Face: The Literary Descent of Dorothy Allison," *Appalachian Journal* 20, no. 4 (Summer 1993): 357, 359.

37. Karissa McCoy, "Re-Writing Region, Re-Constructing Whiteness: Appalachia and the 'Place' of Whiteness in American Culture, 1930–2003," PhD dissertation, Vanderbilt University, 2004, Nashville, TN.

38. Miller, "Homosexuality in Appalachian Literature," 12.

39. Miller, 10.

40. "Claiming a Place on Earth: The Conscious Heart of Silas House," *Journal of Appalachian Studies* 20, no. 2 (Fall 2014): 152, https://doi.org/10.5406/jappastud.20.2.0151.

41. Anna Creadick, "Interview: Fenton Johnson," *Appalachian Journal* 22, no. 2 (Winter 1995): 167.

42. William J. Schafer, "The Bridges of Fenton Johnson," *Appalachian Journal* 22, no. 2 (1995): 154.

43. Bianca Lynne Spriggs and Jeremy Paden, introduction to *Black Bone: 25 Years of the Affrilachian Poets*, ed. Bianca Lynne Spriggs and Jeremy Paden (Lexington, KY: *pluck! The Journal of Affrilachian Arts and Culture*, reprinted by University Press of Kentucky, 2018), 17.

44. Abraham Verghese, *My Own Country: A Doctor's Story of a Town and Its People in the Age of AIDS* (New York: Simon & Schuster, 1994), 15; Mary K.

Anglin, "AIDS in Appalachia: Medical Pathologies and the Problem of Identity," *Journal of Appalachian Studies* 3, no. 2 (1997): 172–73.

45. See Anglin, "Stories of AIDS in Appalachia," for an analysis of 1990s portrayals of AIDS in Appalachia.

46. Kate Black, "Kentucky Woman," POZ, September 1, 2000, https://www.poz.com/article/Kentucky-Woman-10169-4008.

47. Abraham Verghese, Steven L. Berk, and Felix Sarubbi, "Urbs in Rure: Human Immunodeficiency Virus Infection in Rural Tennessee," *Journal of Infectious Diseases* 160, no. 6 (December 1, 1989): 1051–55, https://doi.org/10.1093/infdis/160.6.1051.

48. "Program of the 1995 Appalachian Studies Association Conference" (Morgantown, WV: WVU, 1995). Note that *Gone Tomorrow* has been performed by high school groups all over the US and is not specific to Appalachia.

49. Anglin, "AIDS in Appalachia: Medical Pathologies and the Problem of Identity," 183, italics in original.

50. Joan Smith, "AIDS and the American Heartland: Local Writer's Newest Work Echoes Kentucky Memories of Love, Family Life," *San Francisco Examiner*, July 11, 1993.

51. Julie Bruck, "Novel of Rare Compassion from AIDS Era," *The Gazette*, September 4, 1993; Charles E. Cohen, "Painful Homecomings," review of *Scissors, Paper, Rock*, by Fenton Johnson, *San Francisco Examiner*, July 25, 1993.

52. Creadick, "Interview: Fenton Johnson," 166. Another positive review appeared in the Louisville *Courier-Journal* in 1993, the year of the novel's release.

53. Unsigned review of *Scissors, Paper, Rock*, by Fenton Johnson, *Virginia Quarterly Review* 71, no. 1 (Winter 1994): 22.

54. "Doris Davenport, Ph.D.," LinkedIn, https://www.linkedin.com/in/davenportpoetprofessor/, accessed October 31, 2018. Note that davenport's name—on her own publications and on publications about her—is sometimes written with or without capital letters, and sometimes written with or without the middle name "diosa." I've generally followed the lead of the text about which I'm writing or from which I'm quoting in how I represent davenport's name.

55. Helena Louise Montgomery, "Doris Davenport (1949–)," in *Contemporary Lesbian Writers of the United States* (London: Greenwood Press, 1993), 158.

56. James A. Miller, "Coming Home to Affrilachia: The Poems of Doris Davenport," in *Her Words: Diverse Voices in Contemporary Appalachian Women's Poetry* (Knoxville: University of Tennessee Press, 2002), 96.

57. doris davenport, introduction to *Soque Street Poems* (Sautee-Nacoochee, GA: Sautee-Nacoochee Community Association [SNCA], 1995), iv.

58. doris diosa davenport, "All This, and Honeysuckles Too," in *Bloodroot: Reflections on Place by Appalachian Women Writers*, ed. Joyce Dyer (Lexington: University Press of Kentucky, 1998), 93. (March 1995 journal entry was quoted in "All This.") Frank X Walker is a Kentucky poet and professor at the University

of Kentucky who coined the term "Affrilachia" in the 1990s to describe African Americans who live in Appalachia. See https://www.frankxwalker.com/about.html.

59. davenport, introduction, v, iv.

60. Warren J. Carson, review of *madness like morning glories*, by Doris Davenport, *Appalachian Heritage* 33, no. 2 (2005): 78, https://doi.org/10.1353/aph.2005.0102.

61. Julie R. Enszer, "doris davenport's *it's like this*," *Huffington Post* (blog), September 25, 2013, https://www.huffingtonpost.com/julie-r-enszer/doris-davenport-its-like-this_b_3972323.html.

62. "Literary Events," *Chicago Tribune*, May 23, 1999, sec. Literary Events, newspapers.com.

63. Julia Watts, "Quare Theory: Some Thoughts on LGBT Appalachian Writing," in *Walk Till the Dogs Get Mean: Meditations on the Forbidden from Contemporary Appalachia*, ed. Adrian Blevins and Karen Salyer McElmurray (Athens: Ohio University Press, 2015), 108.

64. Julia Watts, *Wildwood Flowers* (Tallahassee, FL: Naiad Press, 1996), 7.

65. Watts, 138.

66. Watts, 145.

67. Julia Watts, *Finding H.F.* (New York: Alyson Books, 2001), 110.

68. Watts, 8.

69. Watts, 8, 26, 27.

70. Watts, 4.

71. Cynthia Burack, "Mountain Mann: A Biographical Sketch," *Appalachian Heritage* 34, no. 3 (Summer 2006): 10–12.

72. Jeff Mann, *Loving Mountains, Loving Men* (Athens: Ohio University Press, 2005), xi–xii, xv.

73. Rebecca Baird and Kathryn Staley, "Mountaineer Queer: An Interview with Jeff Mann," *Appalachian Journal* 35, no. 1–2 (Fall 2007/Winter 2008): 61.

74. John C. Inscoe, "Sense of Place, Sense of Being: The Intersection of Geography and Spirit in Recent Appalachian Autobiography: A Review Essay," *Journal of Appalachian Studies* 12, no. 2 (Fall 2006): 161, 162.

75. Dan Vera and Bo Young, "*Loving Mountains, Loving Men*: Dan Vera and Bo Young Speak with the Writer Jeff Mann about Gay Rural Life, Poetry and Food," *White Crane* 68 (2006): 6.

76. Frankie Finley, review of *Loving Mountains, Loving Men*, by Jeff Mann, *Appalachian Journal* 35, no. 1–2 (Fall 2007/Winter 2008): 124.

77. Finley, 126.

78. Marianne Worthington, review of *Loving Mountains, Loving Men*, by Jeff Mann, *Now and Then* 22, no. 1 (Spring 2006): 58; George Brosi, review of *Loving Mountains, Loving Men*, by Jeff Mann, *Appalachian Heritage* 34, no. 1 (Winter 2006): 110.

79. Christopher B. Stewart, review of *Loving Mountains, Loving Men*, by Jeff Mann, *West Virginia History: A Journal of Regional Studies* 2, no. 2 (2008): 127, https://doi.org/10.1353/wvh.0.0019.

80. George Brosi, "Karen Salyer McElmurray: A Biographical Sketch," *Appalachian Heritage* 39, no. 2 (Spring 2011): 13–15.

81. Pam Kingsbury, "Descending into the Darkness: An Interview with Karen Salyer McElmurray," *Southern Scribe: Our Culture of Storytelling*, 2004, http://www.southernscribe.com/zine/authors/McElMurray_Karen.htm.

82. McElmurray refers to Ruth as "the main character" in "In Visions," *Appalachian Heritage* 39, no. 2 (Spring 2011): 21. See Brosi (14–15), who names Ruth as the protagonist. Others characterize this as the story of a family: Brownrigg, "Strangers in Paradise"; Brown, "Adapting to the Light"; McKee, "Coal Dust and Moonshine" (27).

83. Kathryn McKee, "Coal Dust and Moonshine," review of *Strange Birds in the Tree of Heaven*, by Karen Salyer McElmurray, *Women's Review of Books* 17, no. 10/11 (July 2000): 28.

84. Elizabeth Brownrigg, "Strangers in Paradise," review of *Strange Birds in the Tree of Heaven*, by Karen Salyer McElmurray, *Lambda Book Report* 8, no. 7 (February 2000): 16.

85. Danny L. Miller, review of *Strange Birds in the Tree of Heaven*, by Karen Salyer McElmurray, *Journal of Appalachian Studies* 6, nos. 1 and 2 (Spring/Fall 2000): 211.

86. Miller, 211.

87. Miller, 212.

88. George Garrett, "1999: The Year in Fiction—Entry on *Strange Birds in the Tree of Heaven*," in *Dictionary of Literary Biography Yearbook: 1999*, ed. Matthew Bruccoli, Dictionary of Literary Biography Yearbook Series (Detroit: Gale, 2000).

89. Brownrigg, "Strangers in Paradise," 16.

90. Sybil Steinberg, review of *Strange Birds in the Trees* [sic] *of Heaven*, by Karen Salyer McElmurray, *Publishers Weekly* 246, no. 33 (August 16, 1999): 63; Carrie Brown, review of *Strange Birds in the Tree of Heaven*, by Karen Salyer McElmurray, *Chicago Tribune*, January 30, 2000, http://articles.chicagotribune.com/2000-01-30/entertainment/0001300092_1_mining-light-photographers.

91. Denton Loving, "Getting Personal in Your Writing: An Interview with Karen Salyer McElmurray," *Appalachian Heritage* 39, no. 2 (Spring 2011): 24.

92. Karen Salyer McElmurray, "Looking Inside," *Appalachian Heritage* 42, no. 2 (2014): 91.

93. Karen Salyer McElmurray, *Strange Birds in the Tree of Heaven: A Novel* (Athens: University of Georgia Press, 2004), 12, 231.

94. Hillary L. Chute, "An Interview with Alison Bechdel," *MFS Modern Fiction Studies* 52, no. 4 (2006): 1004, https://doi.org/10.1353/mfs.2007.0003.

95. Nisa Donnelly, review of *Fun Home: A Family Tragicomic*, by Alison Bechdel, *Lambda Book Report* (Spring 2006): 14; Christian W. Schneider, "Young Daughter, Old Artificer: Constructing the Gothic *Fun Home*," *Studies in Comics* 1, no. 2 (November 1, 2010): 340, https://doi.org/10.1386/stic.1.2.337_1; Chute, "An Interview with Alison Bechdel," 1004.

96. Bechdel, *Fun Home*, 222, 126.

97. Fiorenzo Iuliano, "Du Côté de *Fun Home*: Alison Bechdel Rewrites Marcel Proust," *Partial Answers: Journal of Literature and the History of Ideas* 13, no. 2 (2015): 299, https://doi.org/10.1353/pan.2015.0016.

98. Schneider, "Young Daughter, Old Artificer," 340.

99. Bechdel, *Fun Home*, 145.

100. Scott Herring, "Queer Infrastructure," in *Another Country: Queer Anti-Urbanism* (New York: New York University Press, 2010), 174.

101. Herring, 174.

102. Herring, 177.

103. Bechdel, *Fun Home*, 8.

104. Bechdel, 111.

105. Bechdel, 128.

106. Loyal Jones, *Appalachian Values* (Ashland, KY: Jesse Stuart Foundation, 1994), 99.

107. Bechdel, *Fun Home*, 30–31.

108. Bechdel, 145.

109. Bechdel, 144.

110. Bechdel, 127.

111. Herring, "Queer Infrastructure," 154, 164.

112. Bechdel, *Fun Home*, 212.

113. Bechdel, 125.

114. Herring, "Queer Infrastructure," 177.

115. Zachary Watterson, "We Fought Them Tooth and Nail: An Interview with Carter Sickels," *Fiction Writers Review* (blog), December 6, 2012, https://fictionwritersreview.com/interview/we-fought-them-tooth-and-nail-an-interview-with-carter-sickels/.

116. See Sickels's essay "Bittersweet: On Transitioning and Finding Home" for more on how his research trips to West Virginia reawakened his feelings of kinship with Appalachia (and his fears for his safety there as a queer man).

117. Carter Sickels, "Johnson City," *Appalachian Heritage*, May 1, 2014, http://appalachianheritage.net/2014/05/01/johnson-city/.

118. Cooper Lee Bombardier, "Carter Sickels: Honesty, Compassion, and Grace," *Lambda Literary* (blog), June 16, 2012, https://www.lambdaliterary.org/features/06/16/carter-sickels-honesty-compassion-and-grace/.

119. Watterson, "We Fought Them Tooth and Nail."

220 | Notes to Chapter 3

120. Bombardier, "Carter Sickels."

121. Josh Inocencio, "*Southernmost* Review: Times Are a-Changin' in Ol' Appalachia," *Spectrum South: The Voice of the Queer South* (blog), May 24, 2018, https://www.spectrumsouth.com/southernmost-review/.

122. Stevens, "Kentucky Writer Silas House on *Southernmost*."

123. Tom Eblen, "'You Don't Ever See a Story about Gay People and Faith.' So Silas House Wrote One," *Lexington Herald-Leader*, June 1, 2018, https://www.kentucky.com/news/local/news-columns-blogs/tom-eblen/article212262719.html.

124. Erin Keane, "Can a Literary Thriller Heal Divides? Silas House's *Southernmost* Isn't Preaching to Either Choir," Salon, June 5, 2018, https://www.salon.com/2018/06/05/can-a-literary-thriller-heal-divides-silas-houses-southernmost-isnt-preaching-to-any-choir/.

125. House, "From the Playwright," 9–10.

126. Octavia Biggs, "Director's Note," in *Program for Silas House's This Is My Heart for You at the Lucille Caudill Little Theatre, 2019* (Morehead, KY: Morehead State University, 2019), bold in original.

Chapter 3. Visibility and Seeing

1. Julia Ballerini, "Photography as a Charitable Weapon: Poor Kids and Self-Representation," *Radical History Review* 69 (1997): 176.

2. Halberstam, *In a Queer Time and Place*, 36–42.

3. Jason Howard, "'Queer Sexual Bodies Are Despised': Garth Greenwell on Writing His Debut Novel and Why Everything Comes Back to Kentucky for Him, 'for Better and for Worse,'" Salon, February 24, 2016, https://www.salon.com/2016/02/24/queer_sexual_bodies_are_despised_garth_greenwell_on_writing_his_debut_novel_and_why_everything_comes_back_to_kentucky_for_him_for_better_and_for_worse/.

4. For more information about the history of photography and the objectification of poor people in Appalachia, see Katherine Henninger, *Ordering the Facade: Photography and Contemporary Southern Women's Writing*, New Directions in Southern Studies (Chapel Hill: University of North Carolina Press, 2007), 139–41, 153.

5. Elizabeth Catte, *What You Are Getting Wrong about Appalachia* (Cleveland, OH: Belt, 2018); Anthony Harkins and Meredith McCarroll, eds., *Appalachian Reckoning: A Region Responds to Hillbilly Elegy*, 1st ed. (Morgantown: West Virginia University Press, 2019).

6. See Watkins, "Why Have There Been No Great Appalachian Photographers?," 21, 23–24; Hawthorne, preface to *The Picture Man*, xiv–xv; and Moltke-Hansen, "Seeing the Highlands, 1900–1939," 25–26. See also Jennifer Baichwal's 2002 documentary film, *The True Meaning of Pictures: Shelby Lee

Adams's Appalachia, for an account of a photographer native to Appalachia whose photographs have generated alternately concern and praise for their portrayals of Appalachians family life.

7. Ballerini, "Photography as a Charitable Weapon," 170.

8. Ballerini, 174, emphasis in original.

9. Roger May, "Overview," Looking at Appalachia, https://lookingatappalachia.org/overview, accessed September 26, 2019,

10. Marianne Hirsch, *Family Frames: Photography, Narrative, and Postmemory* (Cambridge, MA: Harvard University Press, 1997), 6. See also Roland Barthes's *Camera Lucida* and his discussion of family photography and photographs of his mother, 63–75 especially.

11. Hirsch, 8.

12. Richard Meyer, "Queer Photography?," *Aperture*, no. 218 (Spring 2015): 28.

13. Meyer, 28.

14. W. J. T. Mitchell, "Showing Seeing: A Critique of Visual Culture," *Journal of Visual Culture* 1, no. 2 (August 2002): 170.

15. Halberstam, *In a Queer Time and Place*, 6.

16. Halberstam, 4.

17. Carter Sickels, "Photograph, 2007," *Still: The Journal* (Summer 2012), http://www.stilljournal.net/carter-sickels-nonfiction.php. Further quotations in this paragraph are drawn from this source.

18. Sickels. Further quotations in this paragraph are drawn from this source.

19. Sickels, "Johnson City." Further quotations in this paragraph are drawn from this source.

20. Sickels. Further quotations in this paragraph are drawn from this source.

21. Carter Sickels, "Wildlife," *Guernica*, March 16, 2015, https://www.guernicamag.com/wildlife/. Further quotations in this paragraph are drawn from this source.

22. Sickels. Further quotations in this paragraph are drawn from this source.

23. Carter Sickels, *The Prettiest Star* (Spartanburg, SC: Hub City Press, 2020), 87.

24. Sickels, 87.

25. Sickels, 88.

26. Sickels, 285.

27. Sickels, 67.

28. A few reviewers and scholars address Mrs Babcock's lack of a first name (and/or the lack of an independent identity—other than wife/mother—that this omission represents). For more on this issue regarding Mrs Babcock and her name, see Leonard, "Pop Goes the Novel"; Gardiner, "A Wake for Mother," 158; Braendlin, "New Directions in the Contemporary Bildungsroman," 166–67; White.

29. Alther, *Kinflicks*, 9.

30. Alther, 279.

31. Alther, 277.
32. Patricia R. Zimmerman, *Reel Families: A Social History of Amateur Film* (Bloomington: Indiana University Press, 1995), xv.
33. Zimmerman, 123.
34. See Zimmerman chapter 5, "Do-It-Yourself: 1950–1962," 112–42.
35. Alther, *Kinflicks*, 23.
36. Alther, 310.
37. Alther, 310.
38. Charles Alan Watkins, "Why Have There Been No Great Appalachian Photographers?," *Now and Then: The Appalachian Magazine* 14, no. 2 (Summer 1997): 25.
39. Alther, *Kinflicks*, 94.
40. Halberstam, *In a Queer Time and Place*, 1, 2.
41. Alther, *Kinflicks*, 301.
42. Alther, 26.
43. Alther, 26.
44. Alther, 279, 551.
45. Alther, 569.
46. Alther, 23.
47. Alther, 277.
48. Hirsch, *Family Frames*, 22.
49. Hirsch, 22, 23.
50. Alther, *Kinflicks*, 10.
51. Alther, 10, 9, 7.
52. Chute, "An Interview with Alison Bechdel," 1005.
53. Chute, 1006.
54. Bechdel, *Fun Home*, 100.
55. Bechdel, 101.
56. Rachel Dean-Ruzicka, "Mourning and Melancholia in Alison Bechdel's *Fun Home: A Family Tragicomic*," *ImageText: Interdisciplinary Comics Studies* 7, no. 2 (Fall 2013), http://www.english.ufl.edu.marshall.idm.oclc.org/imagetext/archives/v7_2/dean-ruzicka/.
57. K. W. Eveleth, "A Vast 'Network of Transversals': Labyrinthine Aesthetics in *Fun Home*," *South Central Review* 32, no. 3 (2015): 103–04, https://doi.org/10.1353/scr.2015.0031.
58. Salon Staff, "*Fun Home*," Salon, December 12, 2006, https://www.salon.com/2006/12/12/bechdel_int/. For more on photography in *Fun Home*, see also Ariela Freedman, "Drawing on Modernism in Alison Bechdel's *Fun Home*," 130–31; Rachel Deahl, "Family History in Pictures and Prose," *Publisher's Weekly*, June 5, 2006.
59. Bechdel, *Fun Home*, 64.
60. Bechdel, 120.

61. Bechdel, 120.
62. Bechdel, 230.
63. Bechdel, 13.
64. Bechdel, 16.
65. Bechdel, 6.
66. Bechdel, 142.
67. Bechdel, 141.
68. Bechdel, 141.
69. Bechdel, 141.
70. Bechdel, 143.
71. Jared Gardner, "Autography's Biography, 1972–2007," *Biography* 31, no. 1 (2008): 1, 3–4, https://doi.org/10.1353/bio.0.0003.
72. Bechdel, *Fun Home*, 142.
73. Robyn Warhol, "The Space Between: A Narrative Approach to Alison Bechdel's *Fun Home*," *College Literature* 38, no. 3 (2011): 2, https://doi.org/10.1353/lit.2011.0025.
74. Warhol, 10.
75. Bechdel, *Fun Home*, 212.
76. Long and Anderson, "The Spaces Between," 38.
77. Department of Photographs, "Walker Evans (1903–1975)," The Met's Heilbrunn Timeline of Art History, October 2004, https://www.metmuseum.org/toah/hd/evan/hd_evan.htm.
78. Many of the Evans photographs about which Anderson writes—as well as others of his West Virginia photographs—can be viewed online through the websites of the Library of Congress, the Metropolitan Museum of Art, the Museum of Modern Art, and the J. Paul Getty Museum.
79. Maxine Scates, review of *Cold Comfort*, by Maggie Anderson, *Prairie Schooner* 63, no. 1 (1989): 120.
80. Long and Anderson, "The Spaces Between," 39.
81. Long and Anderson, 38.
82. Scates, review of *Cold Comfort*, 120, italics in original.
83. This photo is in the photography collection of the Metropolitan Museum of Art (New York City). As of June 2022, it could be viewed through their website at https://www.metmuseum.org/art/collection/search/276012.
84. Long and Anderson, "The Spaces Between," 39.
85. Henninger, *Ordering the Facade*, 148.
86. Dorothy Allison, "This Is Our World," in *All Out of Faith: Southern Women on Spirituality*, ed. Wendy Reed and Jennifer Horne (Tuscaloosa: University of Alabama Press, 2006), 19.
87. Allison, 21, 23.
88. Megan, "Moving Toward Truth," 73.
89. Henninger, *Ordering the Facade*, 146.

90. Allison, *Bastard Out of Carolina*, 293.
91. Allison, 292.
92. Henninger, *Ordering the Facade*, 146.
93. Allison, *Two or Three Things I Know for Sure*, 33.
94. Allison, 3, italics in original.
95. Allison, 39.
96. Timothy Dow Adams, "Telling Stories in Dorothy Allison's *Two or Three Things I Know for Sure*," *Southern Literary Journal* 36, no. 2 (2004): 92, https://doi.org/10.1353/slj.2004.0001.
97. Henninger, *Ordering the Facade*, 147–48.
98. Allison, *Two or Three Things I Know for Sure*, 90–91.
99. Allison, 92–93, emphasis in original.
100. Hirsch, *Family Frames*, 22, 23.
101. James Agee and Walker Evans, *Let Us Now Praise Famous Men: Three Tenant Families* (Boston: Houghton Mifflin, 1960), 364. Although Katherine Henninger asserts that "Evans photographed his subjects only with their full awareness and consent" (144 of *Ordering the Facade*), both Agee's text—in a number of spots—as well as the photographs available on the American Memory site of the Library of Congress's webpage would suggest that NOT to be true.
102. Agee and Evans, *Let Us Now Praise Famous Men*, 363.
103. Agee and Evans, 367.
104. Agee and Evans, 368.
105. Horace Kephart, *Our Southern Highlanders* (New York: Macmillan, 1921); Muriel Earley Sheppard, *Cabins in the Laurel* (Chapel Hill: University of North Carolina Press, 1935); Allen H. Eaton, *Handicrafts of the Southern Highlands* (New York: Russell Sage Foundation, 1937).
106. Watkins, "Why Have There Been No Great Appalachian Photographers?," 21.
107. Watkins, 24. See also Ann Hawthorne's preface to *The Picture Man: Photographs by Paul Buchanan*, xiv–xv.
108. Watkins, 21.
109. For information on W. R. Trivett, see Ralph E. Lentz II, *W. R. Trivett, Appalachian Pictureman: Photographs of a Bygone Time* (Jefferson, NC: McFarland, 2001). For information on Paul Buchanan, see Ann Hawthorne, ed., *The Picture Man: Photographs by Paul Buchanan* (Chapel Hill: University of North Carolina Press, 1993), especially the introduction by Bruce Morton, 7.
110. Hawthorne, preface to *The Picture Man*, xv; Bruce Morton, introduction to *The Picture Man*, 7.
111. Watkins, "Why Have There Been No Great Appalachian Photographers?," 23.
112. Hawthorne, preface, xiv, my italics.
113. Lentz, *W. R. Trivett, Appalachian Pictureman*, 1.

114. This connection of sexuality and photography is also apparent in Lee Smith's *Oral History*, in which Richard Burlage, the schoolteacher who had impregnated Dory, returns to Hoot Owl Holler years later as an art photographer, eager to capture images of the quaint lives of the mountaineers. See Lee Smith, *Oral History* (New York: Ballantine Books, 1983), 222–34.

115. Fenton Johnson, *Scissors, Paper, Rock* (New York: Pocket Books, 1993), 77.

116. Johnson, 196.
117. Johnson, 202.
118. Johnson, 212.
119. Johnson, 205.
120. Johnson, 222–23, italics in original.
121. Johnson, 206–07.
122. Johnson, 222.
123. McElmurray, *Strange Birds in the Tree of Heaven*, 81.
124. McElmurray, 73.
125. McElmurray, 70.
126. McElmurray, 73.
127. McElmurray, 75.
128. McElmurray, 74.
129. McElmurray, 72, 75.
130. McElmurray, 75.
131. McElmurray, 76.
132. McElmurray, 77–78.
133. McElmurray, 80.
134. McElmurray, 77.
135. McElmurray, 78.
136. McElmurray, 79.
137. McElmurray, 83.
138. McElmurray, 71, italics in original.
139. McElmurray, 80.
140. McElmurray, 82.

Chapter 4. Silences and Storytelling in LGBTQ Appalachian Literature

1. Michel Foucault, *The History of Sexuality* (New York: Pantheon Books, 1985), 27.

2. Foucault, 35, italics in original.

3. Gust A. Yep and Susan B. Shimanoff, "The US Day of Silence: Sexualities, Silences, and the Will to Unsay in the Age of Empire," in *Silence, Feminism,*

Power: Reflections at the Edges of Sound, ed. Sheena Malhotra and Aimee Carrillo Rowe (New York: Palgrave Macmillan, 2013), 141. See 140–42 for an overview of theories of silence and power within communication studies. For more on silence and power, see *Unspoken: A Rhetoric of Silence* (Glenn), *Epistemology of the Closet* (Sedgwick), and *Beyond the Closet: The Transformation of Gay and Lesbian Life* (Seidman).

4. Eve Kosofsky Sedgwick, *Epistemology of the Closet* (Berkeley: University of California Press, 1990), 71.

5. Sedgwick, 71, 3.

6. Loftin, introduction to *Letters to ONE*, 11.

7. Loftin, *Masked Voices*, 1.

8. Loftin, 10; Loftin, *Letters to ONE*, 10, 226.

9. Loftin, *Masked Voices*, 10–11.

10. Steven Seidman, *Beyond the Closet: The Transformation of Gay and Lesbian Life* (New York: Routledge, 2002), 8.

11. Seidman, 9.

12. Seidman, 7.

13. See Loftin, *Masked Voices*, 117–27, for more information on anti-homosexual crusades by postal authorities.

14. Mary L. Gray, *Out in the Country: Youth, Media, and Queer Visibility in Rural America* (New York: New York University Press, 2009), 4. See also 133.

15. Gray, 4.

16. Gray, 3–4.

17. Dorothy Allison, foreword to *Crooked Letter i: Coming Out in the South*, ed. Connie Griffin (Montgomery, AL: NewSouth Books, 2015), 10.

18. Fenton Johnson, "Claiming a Place on Earth: The Conscious Heart of Silas House," *Journal of Appalachian Studies* 20, no. 2 (Fall 2015): 152.

19. Allison, foreword, 11.

20. Elizabeth Craven, "Almost Heaven," in *Crooked Letter i: Coming Out in the South*, ed. Connie Griffin (Montgomery, AL: NewSouth Books, 2015), 29.

21. Mann, *Loving Mountains, Loving Men*, 92.

22. O. James Napier, "Dancing in the Dirt," in *Electric Dirt: A Celebration of Queer Voices and Identities from Appalachia and the South*, ed. The Queer Appalachia / Electric Dirt Collective (Bluefield, WV: Queer Appalachia, 2017), 77.

23. Watts, "Quare Theory," 108.

24. House, "Our Secret Places in the Waiting World," 108, 118.

25. House, 118.

26. Pam McMichael, "The Power of Conversation," *Journal of Appalachian Studies* 20, no. 2 (2014): 145.

27. bell hooks, "Call and Response—Taking a Stand," *Journal of Appalachian Studies* 20, no. 2 (2014): 122.

28. Creadick, "Interview: Fenton Johnson," 164.

29. Lisa Alther, "Border States," in *Bloodroot: Reflections on Place by Appalachian Women Writers*, ed. Joyce Dyer (Lexington: University Press of Kentucky, 1998), 30.

30. davenport, "All This," 88.

31. Silas House, "A Conscious Heart," *Journal of Appalachian Studies* 14, no. 1/2 (Spring 2008): 11.

32. The flowering of LGBTQ Appalachian literature, from the mid-1970s and forward, was simultaneous with what John Alexander Williams has called a "national movement": "The storytelling revival was part of the general shift during the 1970s away from politics and toward the inner frontiers of spirituality and personal growth." *Appalachia: A History* (Chapel Hill: University of North Carolina Press, 2002), 387. In Danny Miller, Sandra Ballard, Robert Herrin, Stephen D. Mooney, Susan Underwood, and Jack Wright's essay "Appalachian Literature," they identify the 1960s and '70s as a period when "attention to folklore, folkways, and the oral tradition in literature grew," in *A Handbook to Appalachia: An Introduction to the Region*, ed. Grace Toney Edwards, JoAnn Aust Asbury, and Ricky L. Cox (Knoxville: University of Tennessee Press, 2006), 208. It is natural that LGBTQ Appalachian authors of this period would pursue their craft with an intensified awareness of the importance of the oral tradition. As Appalachians, they have been immersed in this tradition, and as inhabitants of their cultural moment, they've likewise been privy to this national trend.

33. W. D. Weatherford and Wilma Dykeman, "Literature since 1900," in *The Southern Appalachian Region: A Survey*, ed. Thomas R. Ford (Lexington: University of Kentucky Press, 1967), 260, 261.

34. Jim Wayne Miller, "Appalachian Literature," *Appalachian Journal* 5 (Autumn 1977): 86.

35. Deborah Thompson and Irene Moser, "Appalachian Folklife," in *A Handbook to Appalachia: An Introduction to the Region*, ed. Grace Toney Edwards, JoAnn Aust Asbury, and Ricky L. Cox (Knoxville: University of Tennessee Press, 2006), 154.

36. Tina L. Hanlon, "'Way Back Yonder' but Not So Far Away: Teaching Appalachian Folktales," in *Appalachia in the Classroom: Teaching the Region*, ed. Theresa L. Burriss and Patricia M. Gantt, Series in Race, Ethnicity, and Gender in Appalachia (Athens: Ohio University Press, 2013), 110.

37. Hanlon, 122–24.

38. "Carter Sickels | Bluegrass Writers Studio™ | Eastern Kentucky University," https://creativewriting.eku.edu/carter-sickels, accessed September 28, 2018.

39. Jack Halberstam, in *In a Queer Time and Place*, notes, "While fictional narratives of queer rural life are quite hard to find, some ethnographic work and oral histories did emerge in the 1990s" (42).

40. This play is still occasionally performed at events throughout the region. See Kline's webpage, www.folktalk.org/spoken-histories/glbt-stories/. This material

was also submitted as a research paper ("Pushing On") when Kline was Rockefeller Scholar in Residence at the Center for the Study of Ethnicity and Gender in Appalachia; the paper can be found here, https://www.marshall.edu/csega/files/pushingonappalachianresiliency.pdf, as of June 2022.

41. "Who We Are," Country Queers, https://www.countryqueers.com/who-we-are, accessed June 23, 2022.

42. Rachel Garringer, "Country Queers: About," Country Queers: A Multimedia Oral History Project Documenting the Diverse Experiences of Rural and Small Town LGBTQIA Folks in the U.S.A., June 28, 2013, https://countryqueers.com/about/.

43. "Interview with Rachel Garringer," *Still: The Journal*, http://www.still-journal.net/interview-rachelgarringer.php, accessed November 20, 2018.

44. Dorothy Allison, "Deciding to Live," in *Walk Till the Dogs Get Mean: Meditations on the Forbidden from Contemporary Appalachia*, ed. Adrian Blevins and Karen Salyer McElmurray (Athens: Ohio University Press, 2015), 70.

45. Allison, *Two or Three Things I Know for Sure*, 3.

46. Allison, 3.

47. Allison, "Deciding to Live," 70.

48. Carter Sickels, "Early in My Transition, Two Teenagers Helped Me Embrace My Identity," BuzzFeed, April 22, 2015, https://www.buzzfeed.com/cartersickels/early-in-my-transition-two-teenagers-helped-me-embrace-my-id.

49. Sickels, italics in original.

50. Sickels.

51. Watts, *Finding H.F.*, 5.

52. Watts, 14.

53. Watts, 162.

54. Johnson first wrote about Nick Handley in "Bad Habits," a short story written in 1984 and published in 1987 in the journal *Fiction Network*. It was recently republished in the *Anthology of LGBTQ Fiction and Poetry from Appalachia* (2019), edited by Jeff Mann and Julia Watts.

55. Johnson, *Scissors, Paper, Rock*, 135.

56. Johnson, 135.

57. Johnson, 135–36.

58. The unspoken irony of this chapter is that while Nick's sexuality is unacknowledged, his sister Frances has an ongoing relationship with a monk from the local monastery, Brother Eusebius, whose sexual relationship is in direct violation of his religious vows. This relationship is openly acknowledged by the guests at the Hardins' party, including a discussion of whether Brother Eusebius "can do better" than Frances.

59. Donnelly, review of *Fun Home*, by Alison Bechdel.

60. Deahl, "Family History in Pictures and Prose," 25.

61. Deahl, 26.

62. Bechdel, *Fun Home*, 175.
63. Bechdel, 161.
64. Bechdel, 180.
65. Bechdel, 212.
66. Bechdel, 125, emphasis in original.
67. Bechdel, 117.
68. Avram Finkelstein, *After Silence: A History of AIDS through Its Images* (Oakland: University of California Press, 2018), 46.
69. Mary K. Anglin, "Stories of AIDS in Appalachia," in *Back Talk from Appalachia: Confronting Stereotypes* (Lexington: University Press of Kentucky, 2001), 276.
70. In addition to Anglin's "Stories of AIDS in Appalachia," see "Urbs in Rure" by Verghese et al., *My Own Country* by Verghese, "Finding a Voice" by Houck, and anything on Kentucky writer and activist Belinda Mason. (Recommended resources include obituaries of Mason from the *New York Times* and *Chicago Tribune*, Kate Black's "Kentucky Woman," and the Appalshop short film *Belinda*.)
71. Frank X Walker, "Hummingbird," in *Affrilachia* (Lexington: Old Cove Press, 2000), 22–23.
72. Mann, *Loving Mountains, Loving Men*, 93.
73. Mann, 93.
74. Sickels, *The Prettiest Star*, 7.
75. Sickels, 49.
76. Sickels, 65, italics in original.
77. Sickels, 46.
78. Sickels, 152.
79. See Anglin, 277–78, about *Scissors, Paper, Rock*.
80. Fenton Johnson, *Geography of the Heart: A Memoir* (New York: Washington Square Press, 1996), 92.
81. Unsigned review of *Scissors, Paper, Rock*, 22.
82. Creadick, "Interview: Fenton Johnson," 171.
83. Houck, "Finding a Voice," 203, 191.
84. Johnson, *Scissors, Paper, Rock*, 128.
85. Johnson, 127, 126.
86. Johnson, 128.
87. Johnson, 144.
88. Johnson, 144.
89. Johnson, 161.
90. Johnson, 162.
91. Johnson, 174.
92. Johnson, 175.
93. Maurice Manning, "Strange Birds, Too: A Reflection on the Work of Karen Salyer McElmurray," *Appalachian Heritage* 39, no. 2 (Spring 2011): 40.

230 | Notes to Chapter 4

94. McElmurray, *Strange Birds in the Tree of Heaven: A Novel*, 75.
95. McElmurray, 267.
96. McElmurray, 28.
97. McElmurray, 29.
98. McElmurray, 30.
99. McElmurray, 29.
100. McElmurray, 39.
101. McElmurray, 9.
102. McElmurray, 12.
103. McElmurray, 103, 105.
104. McElmurray, 284.
105. McElmurray, 10.
106. McElmurray, 11.
107. McElmurray, 15.
108. McElmurray, 10.
109. McElmurray, 12.
110. McElmurray, 13.
111. McElmurray, 279.
112. davenport, "All This," 93.
113. davenport, 88.
114. Carson, review of *madness like morning glories*, 77.
115. Janet St. John, review of *Madness Like Morning Glories*, by Doris Davenport, *Booklist* 101, no. 14 (March 15, 2005): 1259. See also Becky Birtha, "Celebrating Themselves: Four Self-Published Black Lesbian Authors," *Off Our Backs* 15, no. 8 (September 1985): 19–21.
116. Miller, "Coming Home to Affrilachia," 103.
117. doris davenport, *Soque Street Poems* (Sautee-Nacoochee, GA: Sautee-Nacoochee Community Association [SNCA], 1995), 2; doris davenport, *madness like morning glories: poems* (Baton Rouge: Louisiana State University Press, 2005).
118. davenport, introduction to *Soque Street Poems*, iv.
119. Denise R. Shaw, "Doris Davenport (1949)," in *Encyclopedia of African American Women Writers* (Westport, CT: Greenwood Press, 2007), 142; Montgomery, "Doris Davenport (1949–)," 157. davenport's first three collections of poetry—*it's like this*, 1980; *eat thunder and drink rain*, 1982; and *voodoo chile / slight return*, 1991—were all self-published. *Soque Street Poems* was published by the Sautee-Nacoochee Community Association, a community arts organization in davenport's home county in Georgia. Only with *madness like morning glories* did davenport find a publishing home with an independent or university press.
120. Melinda Cardozo, "Davenport, Doris Diosa (b. 1949)," in *Encyclopedia of Contemporary LGBTQ Literature of the United States*, ed. Emmanuel S. Nelson (Santa Barbara, CA: Greenwood Press, 2009), 168.
121. Citing Montgomery's 1993 argument about the critical neglect of davenport's work, Shaw claims that, in the intervening fourteen years, davenport

has "gone from scant recognition and rejection by editors to national exposure and publication by a major university press" (142). Although this might have been true in 2007, it is undeniable that all of davenport's subsequent publications have been self-published, and only a handful of scholarly articles have focused on davenport's work since 2007.

122. davenport, "Music in Poetry," 60.
123. davenport, "All This," 88.

Chapter 5. HomePlaceBody

1. Jones, *Appalachian Values*, 99.
2. Jones, 102, 105.
3. Jones, 99.
4. Neema Avashia, *Another Appalachia: Coming Up Queer and Indian in a Mountain Place* (Morgantown: West Virginia University Press, 2022), 57–58.
5. Avashia, 159.
6. Zach Shultz, "Queer Homecoming: On Carter Sickels's *The Prettiest Star*," *Los Angeles Review of Books*, September 12, 2020, https://lareviewofbooks.org/article/queer-homecoming-on-carter-sickelss-the-prettiest-star/.
7. Danny Miller, Sandra Ballard, Roberta Herrin, Stephen D. Mooney, Susan Underwood, and Jack Wright, "Appalachian Literature," in *A Handbook to Appalachia: An Introduction to the Region*, ed. Grace Toney Edwards, JoAnn Aust Asbury, and Ricky L. Cox (Knoxville: University of Tennessee Press, 2006), 204. See also James B. Goode's "The Impact of Coal Mining in the Evolution of Appalachian Kentucky Literature: A Retrospective," *Journal of Kentucky Studies* 31 (2016): 129–38.
8. Maggie Anderson, "The Mountains Dark and Close around Me," in *Bloodroot: Reflections on Place by Appalachian Women Writers*, ed. Joyce Dyer (Lexington: University Press of Kentucky, 1998), 32, 39.
9. Marilou Awiakta, "Following the Deer Trail," in *Selu: Seeking the Corn-Mother's Wisdom* (Golden, CO: Fulcrum, 1993), 32, 33.
10. Marilou Awiakta, "When Earth Becomes an 'It,'" in *Selu: Seeking the Corn-Mother's Wisdom* (Golden, CO: Fulcrum, 1993), 6.
11. Scott Hamilton Suter, "'The Spiritual Energy of the Trees': Nature, Place, and Religion in Silas House's Crow County Trilogy," in *Rough South, Rural South: Region and Class in Recent Southern Literature* (Jackson: University Press of Mississippi, 2016), 183, 186.
12. bell hooks, "Connecting Appalachia to the World Beyond," *Bell Hooks Books* (blog), September 20, 2018, https://bellhooksbooks.com/connecting-appalachia-to-the-world-beyond/.
13. Weatherford and Dykeman, "Literature since 1900," 264.
14. Miller et al., "Appalachian Literature," 200, 199.

15. Jesse Graves, introduction to *The Southern Poetry Anthology: Volume 3 Contemporary Appalachia*, ed. Jesse Graves, Paul Ruffin, and William Wright, The Southern Poetry Anthology (Huntsville: Texas Review Press, 2011), 9.

16. Graves, 9.

17. Sickels, "Johnson City," 19–20.

18. Ralph Waldo Emerson, "Nature," in *The Collected Works of Ralph Waldo Emerson, I: Nature, Addresses, and Lectures* (Cambridge, MA: Belknap Press of Harvard University Press, 1971), 10.

19. Watts, *Finding H.F.*, 8.

20. Watts, 18, italics in original.

21. Watts, 19, 20.

22. Watts, 140.

23. Johnson, *Geography of the Heart: A Memoir*, 211.

24. Johnson, 211.

25. Johnson, 211.

26. Loving, "Getting Personal in Your Writing," 25.

27. McElmurray, *Strange Birds in the Tree of Heaven*, 17–18.

28. McElmurray, 20, italics in original.

29. McElmurray, 20, my italics.

30. McElmurray, 96.

31. McElmurray, 99.

32. McElmurray, 99.

33. McElmurray, 96.

34. McElmurray, 36.

35. McElmurray, 36.

36. McElmurray, 231.

37. McElmurray, 231.

38. McElmurray, 214.

39. McElmurray, 16.

40. McElmurray, 16–17.

41. McElmurray, 17.

42. McElmurray, 287, 288.

43. Loyal Jones, "Appalachian Values," in *Voices from the Hills: Selected Readings in Southern Appalachia*, ed. Robert J. Higgs and Ambrose N. Manning (New York: Frederick Ungar, 1975), 516.

44. Jones, 513.

45. Jones, *Appalachian Values*, 99.

46. Miller et al., "Appalachian Literature," 201.

47. Ted Olson, "Literature," in *High Mountains Rising: Appalachia in Time and Place*, ed. Richard A. Straw and H. Tyler Blethen (Urbana: University of Illinois Press, 2004), 167, 173.

48. Danny L. Miller, "The Appalachian Migratory Experience in Literature," in *Down Home, Downtown: Urban Appalachians Today*, ed. Phillip J. Obermiller (Dubuque, IA: Kendall/Hunt, 1996), 143.

49. This phenomenon has seemed especially powerful as people try to imagine this book project. Whenever I tell someone that I'm working on a book on LGBTQ Appalachian literature, a common response is "IS there any?" I've never pressed further about what in this formulation seems so impossible: LGBTQ people in Appalachia? Writers in Appalachia? Regardless, it appears to boggle the mind.

50. Kath Weston, "Get Thee to a Big City: Sexual Imaginary and the Great Gay Migration," *GLQ: A Journal of Lesbian and Gay Studies* 2 (1995): 256, 262.

51. Weston, 262, 265.

52. Weston, 267.

53. Weston, 274.

54. Gray, *Out in the Country*, 134.

55. Gray, xi.

56. Gray, 4.

57. Gray, 168–69.

58. Gayatri Gopinath, *Impossible Desires: Queer Diasporas and South Asian Public Cultures* (Durham, NC: Duke University Press, 2005), 91.

59. Gopinath, 79.

60. Weston, "Get Thee to a Big City," 270.

61. Jeff Mann, "Appalachian Subculture," *Gay and Lesbian Review* 10, no. 5 (October 2003): 19.

62. Mann, 19.

63. Mann, 21.

64. Watts, "Quare Theory," 108.

65. Watts, 107.

66. Watts, 109.

67. "Lisa Alther: Biography," http://www.lisaalther.com/biography.html, accessed December 12, 2018.

68. Alther, "Border States," 25.

69. "Literary Festival," https://www.ehc.edu/academics/english/literary-festival/, accessed December 12, 2018.

70. Wayne Pond and Lisa Alther, "Healing Laughter: A Conversation," *Iron Mountain Review: Lisa Alther Issue* 17 (Spring 2001): 31, 28.

71. Alther, *Kinflicks*, 35.

72. Alther, 19.

73. Harriette C. Buchanan, "Ambivalence Towards Home and Heritage for Lisa Alther's Appalachian Characters," *Appalachian Heritage* 32, no. 1 (2004): 31, https://doi.org/10.1353/aph.2004.0098.

74. Frederick G. Waage, "Alther and Dillard: The Appalachian Universe," ed. Wilson Somerville, in *Appalachia/America: Proceedings of the 1980 Appalachian Studies Conference*, 1981, 208, italics in original.

75. Michael Shannon Friedman, "Jeff Mann: An Appreciation," *Appalachian Heritage* 34, no. 3 (Summer 2006): 28.

76. Burack, "Mountain Mann," 10.

77. Mann, *Loving Mountains, Loving Men*, 23.

78. Mann, 57.

79. Mann, 57, 59.

80. Emerson, "Nature," 10.

81. Jeff Mann, *Bliss* (Baltimore, MD: Stone Wall, 1998), 33.

82. Mann, 6.

83. Mann, 9.

84. Mann, 10.

85. Mann, 20.

86. Mann, 28.

87. Mann, 17.

88. Mann, 29.

89. Elizabeth Stephens, "Directors' Statement—*Goodbye Gauley Mountain: An Ecosexual Love Story*," https://goodbyegauleymountain.ucsc.edu/directors-statement/, accessed June 20, 2022.

90. See also Annie Sprinkle, Beth Stephens, and Jennie Klein, *Assuming the Ecosexual Position: The Earth as Lover* (Minneapolis: University of Minnesota Press, 2021), 90–102, for Sprinkle and Stephens's account of the inspiration for and making of the film.

91. Elizabeth M. Stephens and Annie M. Sprinkle, "Ecosex Manifesto," SexEcology: Where Art Meets Theory Meets Practice Meets Activism, http://sexecology.org/research-writing/ecosex-manifesto/, accessed June 20, 2022.

92. Sprinkle, Stephens, and Klein, *Assuming the Ecosexual Position*, 14.

93. Stephens and Sprinkle, "Ecosex Manifesto," iv.

94. Stephens and Sprinkle, iv.

95. Theresa L. Burriss, "Ecofeminist Sensibilities and Rural Land Literacies in the Work of Contemporary Appalachian Novelist Ann Pancake," in *Literature and Ecofeminism: Intersectional and International Voices*, 1st ed., ed. Douglas A. Vakoch and Sam Mickey (New York: Routledge, 2018), 99, https://doi.org/10.4324/9781351209755.

96. Burriss, 102. See also Elizabeth S. D. Engelhardt, *The Tangled Roots of Feminism, Environmentalism, and Appalachian Literature* (Athens: Ohio University Press, 2003).

97. Kristen Lillvis, *Posthuman Blackness and the Black Female Imagination* (Athens: University of Georgia Press, 2017), 3.

98. Elizabeth Stephens, "PAR: *Goodbye Gauley Mountain: An Ecosexual Love Story* | Elizabeth Stephens," http://elizabethstephens.org/par-goodbye-gauley-mountain-an-ecosexual-love-story/, accessed October 31, 2018.

99. Stephens.

100. Elizabeth Stephens, "Directors' Statement—*Goodbye Gauley Mountain: An Ecosexual Love Story*," http://goodbyegauleymountain.org/directors-statement/, accessed October 31, 2018.

101. https://goodbyegauleymountain.ucsc.edu/press/.

102. Sprinkle, Stephens, and Klein, *Assuming the Ecosexual Position*, 113, 118–20.

103. Lester Friedman, David Desser, Sarah Kozloff, Martha P. Nochimson, and Stephen Price, *An Introduction to Film Genres* (New York: W.W. Norton, 2014), 122.

104. Stephens, "Directors' Statement."

105. Friedman et al., *Film Genres*, 122.

106. Friedman et al., 136–37; Rick Altman, *A Theory of Narrative* (New York: Columbia University Press, 2008), 55–66.

107. Elizabeth Stephens, "Film Structure," Elizabeth Stephens, September 24, 2011, http://elizabethstephens.org/film-structure/.

108. Stephens, "PAR: *Goodbye Gauley Mountain*."

109. Friedman et al., *Film Genres*, 147.

110. Stephens, "PAR: *Goodbye Gauley Mountain*."

111. davenport, "All This," 89.

112. davenport, 89.

113. davenport, 88.

114. davenport, introduction to *Soque Street Poems*, iv.

115. Birtha, "Celebrating Themselves," 19.

116. Katharine Newman, introduction to *voodoo chile, slight return: poems*, by doris davenport (Charlotte, NC: Soque Street Press, 1991), v.

117. doris davenport, *65 poems* (CreateSpace, 2014).

118. doris davenport, *performance pieces* (CreateSpace, 2016).

Chapter 6. Flight and Food

1. Black and Rhorer, "Out in the Mountains," 25.
2. Burke et al., *Through Their Eyes*.
3. Watts, *Finding H.F.*, 118.
4. Watts, 162.
5. The line initially appeared in "I Gotta Home in Dat Rock," a Negro spiritual popularized by Paul Robeson in the 1920s. Later, the song, with slightly

different lyrics and structure, was transformed into a traditional Appalachian hymn, "God Gave Noah the Rainbow Sign," made famous when it was recorded by the Carter Family.

    6. Watts, *Finding H.F.*, 165.

    7. Beryl Rowland, *Birds with Human Souls: A Guide to Bird Symbolism* (Knoxville: University of Tennessee Press, 1978), xiii–xv; Edward A. Armstrong, *The Life and Lore of the Bird: In Nature, Art, Myth, and Literature* (New York: Crown, 1975), 6, 65.

    8. Armstrong, *Life and Lore of the Bird*, 241; Leonard Lutwack, *Birds in Literature* (Gainesville: University Press of Florida, 1994), xi–xii.

    9. Thomas C. Gannon, *Skylark Meets Meadowlark: Reimagining the Bird in British Romantic and Contemporary Native American Literature* (Lincoln: University of Nebraska Press, 2009), xii, xiv, italics in original.

    10. Lutwack, *Birds in Literature*, 151, 162.

    11. McElmurray, *Strange Birds in the Tree of Heaven*, 3.

    12. McElmurray, 189.

    13. McElmurray, 189.

    14. McElmurray, 31.

    15. McElmurray, 92.

    16. McElmurray, 266, italics in original.

    17. McElmurray, 269, 263.

    18. McElmurray, 265.

    19. McElmurray, 26.

    20. McElmurray, 32.

    21. McElmurray, 275.

    22. McElmurray, 37, 38.

    23. McElmurray, 52.

    24. McElmurray, 277.

    25. McElmurray, 257.

    26. McElmurray, 255.

    27. McElmurray, 260.

    28. Alther, *Kinflicks*, 467.

    29. Alther, 24.

    30. For more on religion in *Kinflicks* and for Alther in general, see Pond and Alther, "Healing Laughter," 29, 33; Hokenson, "Alther, Lisa," 25; and Brosi's 2004 interview with Alther.

    31. Alther, *Kinflicks*, 81.

    32. Alther, 169.

    33. Alther, 400.

    34. Alther, 555.

    35. Larsen, "Reeling through a Daughter's Decade," review of *Kinflicks*, 42.

    36. Joan Lord Hall, "Symbiosis and Separation in Lisa Alther's *Kinflicks*," *Arizona Quarterly* 38, no. 4 (1982): 339.

37. Alther, *Kinflicks*, 190.
38. Alther, 555, 556.
39. Alther, 558.
40. Alther, 558.
41. Alther, 559.
42. Mikhail Bakhtin, *Rabelais and His World*, trans. Helene Iswolsky (Bloomington: Indiana University Press, 1984), 281.
43. Bakhtin, 301, 409.
44. Wendell Berry, "The Pleasures of Eating," in *What Are People For? Essays* (San Francisco: North Point Press, 1990), 145.
45. Berry, 148.
46. Berry, 151.
47. Michael Broderick and Sean Gleason, "We Kill Our Own: Towards a Material Ecology of Farm Life," *Text and Performance Quarterly* 36, no. 4 (October 2016): 254, https://doi.org/10.1080/10462937.2016.1230677.
48. Bakhtin, *Rabelais and His World*, 283.
49. Erica Abrams Locklear, "A Matter of Taste: Reading Food and Class in Appalachian Literature," in *Writing in the Kitchen: Essays on Southern Literature and Foodways*, ed. David A. Davis, Tara Powell, and Jessica B. Harris (Jackson: University Press of Mississippi, 2014), e-book, http://ebookcentral.proquest.com/lib/marshall-ebooks/detail.action?docID=1820913.
50. Jeff Mann, "Southern (LGBT) Living," in *Crooked Letter i: Coming Out in the South* (Montgomery, AL: NewSouth Books, 2015), 48.
51. Mann, 48.
52. Mann, 52–53.
53. Mann, 55–56.
54. Mann, *Loving Mountains, Loving Men*, 160.
55. Mann, 154.
56. Mann, 86.
57. Mann, 70.
58. Ron Mohring, "12 Questions: An Interview with Jeff Mann," *RFD* 30, no. 3 (2004): 12.
59. Mohring, 13.
60. Mohring, 12.
61. Mohring, 12.
62. Mann, *Loving Mountains, Loving Men*, 158, 35–36.
63. Mann, 92.
64. Mann, 158.
65. Mann, 145.
66. Ronni Lundy, introduction to *Cornbread Nation 3: Foods of the Mountain South*, ed. Ronni Lundy (Chapel Hill: University of North Carolina Press, 2005), 1–2.
67. Julia Watts, "Interview with Julia Watts," *Journal of Appalachian Studies* 20, no. 2 (Fall 2014): 179.

68. Mark F. Sohn, *Appalachian Home Cooking: History, Culture, and Recipes* (Lexington: University Press of Kentucky, 2005), 2, 5.

69. See Allison E. Carey, "Food in *Finding H.F.* and *Secret City* by Julia Watts: The Food of Home and the Food of the Big City," *Journal of Appalachian Studies* 20, no. 2 (Fall 2014): 170–80, https://doi.org/10.5406/jappastud.20.2.0170.

70. Julia Watts, *The Kind of Girl I Am* (Midway, FL: Spinsters Ink, 2007), 44–45.

71. Watts, 53.

72. Julia Watts, *Phases of the Moon* (Tallahassee, FL: Naiad Press, 1997), 39.

73. Watts, 63–64.

74. Watts, 64–65.

75. Watts, 67.

76. Sickels, "Johnson City."

77. Bakhtin, *Rabelais and His World*, 283.

78. Bakhtin, 282–83, 281.

79. Bakhtin, 291.

80. Johnson, *Scissors, Paper, Rock*, 140.

81. Johnson, 141.

82. Johnson, 141.

83. Johnson, 168.

84. Johnson, 168.

85. Bakhtin, *Rabelais and His World*, 169.

86. Johnson, *Scissors, Paper, Rock*, 170.

Conclusion

1. House, "Conscious Heart, Continued," 119.

2. House, 118.

3. Christopher Ingraham, "In the Modern History of Mass Shootings in America, Orlando Is the Deadliest," *Washington Post*, June 12, 2016, https://www.washingtonpost.com/news/wonk/wp/2016/06/12/in-the-modern-history-of-mass-shootings-in-america-orlando-is-the-absolute-worst/; "New FBI Hate Crimes Report Shows Increases in Anti-LGBTQ Attacks," HRC, https://www.hrc.org/press-releases/new-fbi-hate-crimes-report-shows-increases-in-anti-lgbtq-attacks, accessed May 27, 2021.

4. Of course, in the time since November 2016, the frequency of hate crimes has also increased, for LGBTQ Americans, Muslim Americans, immigrants, and many other groups. Not that things were perfect before November 2016, as Silas House's recitation of hate crimes in his 2014 ASA keynote, "Our Secret Places in the Waiting World: Or, A Conscious Heart, Continued," makes clear. My point here about overall improvement is not meant to ignore the many individual and institutionalized acts of injustice and hate that persist.

5. *Dobbs v. Jackson*, 597 U.S. 2 (2022).

6. "Fireside Industries," *The University Press of Kentucky* (blog), https://www.kentuckypress.com/fireside-industries/, accessed May 27, 2021.

7. "Appalachian Futures: Black, Native, and Queer Voices," The University Press of Kentucky, https://www.kentuckypress.com/appalachian-futures-black-native-and-queer-voices/, accessed May 27, 2021.

8. Claire Kirch, "Author Julia Watts Disinvited from Teen Lit Festival," PublishersWeekly.com, September 2019, https://www.publishersweekly.com/pw/by-topic/childrens/childrens-authors/article/81097-author-julia-watts-disinvited-from-teen-lit-festival.html.

Bibliography

"2 Smith Teachers Held in Vice Case." *New York Times*, September 4, 1960.

"About the Appalachian Region." Appalachian Regional Commission. https://www.arc.gov/about-the-appalachian-region/. Accessed June 9, 2022.

Adams, Alice. "Endjokes," review of *Kinflicks*, by Lisa Alther. *Harper's Magazine*, May 1976, 94, 98.

Adams, Timothy Dow. "Telling Stories in Dorothy Allison's *Two or Three Things I Know for Sure*." *Southern Literary Journal* 36, no. 2 (2004): 82–99. https://doi.org/10.1353/slj.2004.0001.

Agee, James, and Walker Evans. *Let Us Now Praise Famous Men: Three Tenant Families*. Boston: Houghton Mifflin, 1960.

Allison, Dorothy. *Bastard Out of Carolina*. New York: Dutton, 1992.

———. "A Conversation with Dorothy Allison." Interview by Mary Flinn and Randy Marshall. *Blackbird: An Online Journal of Literature and the Arts* 16, no. 2 (Fall 2017). https://blackbird.vcu.edu/v16n2/features/allison-d/conversation_page.shtml.

———. "Deciding to Live." In *Walk Till the Dogs Get Mean: Meditations on the Forbidden from Contemporary Appalachia*, edited by Adrian Blevins and Karen Salyer McElmurray, 65–70. Athens: Ohio University Press, 2015.

———. Foreword to *Crooked Letter i: Coming Out in the South*, edited by Connie Griffin, 9–11. Montgomery, AL: NewSouth Books, 2015.

———. "This Is Our World." In *All Out of Faith: Southern Women on Spirituality*, edited by Wendy Reed and Jennifer Horne. Tuscaloosa: University of Alabama Press, 2006.

———. *Two or Three Things I Know for Sure*. New York: Penguin, 1995.

Alther, Lisa. "Border States." In *Bloodroot: Reflections on Place by Appalachian Women Writers*, edited by Joyce Dyer, 22–30. Lexington: University Press of Kentucky, 1998.

———. *Kinflicks*. London: Virago, 1999. Originally published 1976.

Altman, Rick. *A Theory of Narrative*. New York: Columbia University Press, 2008.

Anderson, Maggie. *Cold Comfort*. Pitt Poetry Series. Pittsburgh, PA: University of Pittsburgh Press, 1986.

———. *The Great Horned Owl*. Riderwood, MD: Icarus Press, 1979.

———. "House and Graveyard, Rowlesburg, West Virginia, 1935." In *Cold Comfort*, 23–24. Pitt Poetry Series. Pittsburgh, PA: University of Pittsburgh Press, 1986.

———. "The Mountains Dark and Close around Me." In *Bloodroot: Reflections on Place by Appalachian Women Writers*, edited by Joyce Dyer, 31–39. Lexington: University Press of Kentucky, 1998.

———. *A Space Filled with Moving*. Pittsburgh, PA: University of Pittsburgh Press, 1992.

———. "Two Rivers." In *Liberating Memory: Our Work and Our Working-Class Consciousness*, edited by Janet Zandy, 144–51. New Brunswick, NJ: Rutgers University Press, 1995.

Anglin, Mary K. "AIDS in Appalachia: Medical Pathologies and the Problem of Identity." *Journal of Appalachian Studies* 3, no. 2 (1997): 171–87.

———. "Stories of AIDS in Appalachia." In *Back Talk from Appalachia: Confronting Stereotypes*, 267–80. Lexington: University Press of Kentucky, 2001.

Annichiarico, Mark, and Barbara Hoffert. "Best Books of 1992." *Library Journal*, January 1, 1993.

"Appalachian Futures: Black, Native, and Queer Voices." The University Press of Kentucky. https://www.kentuckypress.com/appalachian-futures-black-native-and-queer-voices/. Accessed May 27, 2021.

Ardrian, Sheela. "Bright and Dark." *Lesbian Review of Books* 7, no. 1 (Fall 2000): 14–15.

"Arresting Dress: A Timeline of Anti-Cross-Dressing Laws in the United States." *PBS NewsHour*, May 31, 2015. https://www.pbs.org/newshour/nation/arresting-dress-timeline-anti-cross-dressing-laws-u-s.

Armstrong, Edward A. *The Life and Lore of the Bird: In Nature, Art, Myth, and Literature*. New York: Crown, 1975.

Avashia, Neema. *Another Appalachia: Coming Up Queer and Indian in a Mountain Place*. Morgantown: West Virginia University Press, 2022.

Awiakta, Marilou. *Selu: Seeking the Corn-Mother's Wisdom*. Golden, CO: Fulcrum, 1993.

Baird, Rebecca, and Kathryn Staley. "Mountaineer Queer: An Interview with Jeff Mann." *Appalachian Journal* 35, no. 1–2 (Fall 2007/Winter 2008): 58–75.

Bakhtin, Mikhail. *Rabelais and His World*. Translated by Helene Iswolsky. Bloomington: Indiana University Press, 1984.

Ballerini, Julia. "Photography as a Charitable Weapon: Poor Kids and Self-Representation." *Radical History Review* 69 (1997): 160–88.

Barthes, Roland. *Camera Lucida: Reflections on Photography*. Translated by Richard Howard. New York: Hill and Wang, 1981.

Bechdel, Alison. *Fun Home: A Family Tragicomic*. New York: Houghton Mifflin, 2006.
Beer, Patricia. "Sickbed Humor," review of *Kinflicks*, by Lisa Alther. *The Listener* (August 26, 1976): 253–54.
Berry, Wendell. "The Pleasures of Eating." In *What Are People For? Essays*, 145–52. San Francisco: North Point Press, 1990.
Biggs, Octavia. "Director's Note." In *Program for Silas House's This Is My Heart for You at the Lucille Caudill Little Theatre, 2019*. Morehead, KY: Morehead State University, 2019.
Birtha, Becky. "Celebrating Themselves: Four Self-Published Black Lesbian Authors." *Off Our Backs* 15, no. 8 (September 1985): 19–21.
Black, Kate. "Kentucky Woman." POZ, September 1, 2000. https://www.poz.com/article/Kentucky-Woman-10169-4008.
———. Review of *Through Their Eyes: Stories of Gays and Lesbians in the Mountains*, by Burke, Caudill, Cupp, and Rowlette. *Journal of Appalachian Studies* 6, nos. 1, 2 (2000): 250–52.
Black, Kate, and Marc A. Rhorer. "Out in the Mountains: Exploring Lesbian and Gay Lives." *Journal of the Appalachian Studies Association* 7 (1995): 18–28.
Boggess, Carol. Afterword to *Chinaberry*, by James Still, edited by Silas House, 143–53. Lexington: University Press of Kentucky, 2011.
———. *James Still: A Life*. Lexington: University Press of Kentucky, 2017.
Bombardier, Cooper Lee. "Carter Sickels: Honesty, Compassion, and Grace." *Lambda Literary* (blog), June 16, 2012. https://www.lambdaliterary.org/features/06/16/carter-sickels-honesty-compassion-and-grace/.
Brady, Maureen, and Judith McDaniel. "Lesbians in the Mainstream: Images of Lesbians in Recent Commercial Fiction." *Conditions* 6 (1979): 82–105.
Braendlin, Bonnie Hoover. "New Directions in the Contemporary Bildungsroman: Lisa Alther's *Kinflicks*." *Women and Literature* 1 (1980): 160–71.
Broderick, Michael, and Sean Gleason. "We Kill Our Own: Towards a Material Ecology of Farm Life." *Text and Performance Quarterly* 36, no. 4 (October 2016): 250–64. https://doi.org/10.1080/10462937.2016.1230677.
Brosi, George. "Karen Salyer McElmurray: A Biographical Sketch." *Appalachian Heritage* 39, no. 2 (Spring 2011): 13–15.
———. Review of *James Still: A Life*, by Carol Boggess. *Appalachian Journal* 45, no. 3/4 (2018): 788–91. https://doi.org/10.2307/j.ctt1tg5p23.
———. Review of *Loving Mountains, Loving Men*, by Jeff Mann. *Appalachian Heritage* 34, no. 1 (Winter 2006): 110.
Brown, Carrie. "Adapting to the Light," review of *Strange Birds in the Tree of Heaven*, by Karen Salyer McElmurray. *Chicago Tribune*, January 30, 2000, http://articles.chicagotribune.com/2000-01-30/entertainment/0001300092_1_mining-light-photographers.

Brownrigg, Elizabeth. "Strangers in Paradise," review of *Strange Birds in the Tree of Heaven*, by Karen Salyer McElmurray. *Lambda Book Report* 8, no. 7 (February 2000): 16–17.

Bruck, Julie. "Novel of Rare Compassion from AIDS Era." *The Gazette*, September 4, 1993.

Buchanan, Harriette C. "Ambivalence Towards Home and Heritage for Lisa Alther's Appalachian Characters." *Appalachian Heritage* 32, no. 1 (2004): 31–34. https://doi.org/10.1353/aph.2004.0098.

Burack, Cynthia. "Mountain Mann: A Biographical Sketch." *Appalachian Heritage* 34, no. 3 (Summer 2006): 10–12.

Burke, Danielle, April Caudill, Charles Cupp, and Brittany Rowlette. *Through Their Eyes: Stories of Gays and Lesbians in the Mountains*. Appalachian Media Institute/Appalshop, 1999. https://scholarworks.moreheadstate.edu/appalachian_kentucky_video_archives/50/.

Burriss, Theresa L. "Ecofeminist Sensibilities and Rural Land Literacies in the Work of Contemporary Appalachian Novelist Ann Pancake." In *Literature and Ecofeminism: Intersectional and International Voices*, edited by Douglas A. Vakoch and Sam Mickey, 1st ed., 99–114. New York: Routledge, 2018. https://doi.org/10.4324/9781351209755.

Cardozo, Melinda. "Davenport, Doris Diosa (b. 1949)." In *Encyclopedia of Contemporary LGBTQ Literature of the United States*, edited by Emmanuel S. Nelson, Volume 1: A-L: 168–69. Santa Barbara, CA: Greenwood Press, 2009.

Carey, Allison E. "Food in *Finding H.F.* and *Secret City* by Julia Watts: The Food of Home and the Food of the Big City." *Journal of Appalachian Studies* 20, no. 2 (Fall 2014): 170–80. https://doi.org/10.5406/jappastud.20.2.0170.

Carson, Warren J. Review of *madness like morning glories*, by Doris Davenport. *Appalachian Heritage* 33, no. 2 (2005): 77–78. https://doi.org/10.1353/aph.2005.0102.

"Carter Sickels | Bluegrass Writers Studio™ | Eastern Kentucky University." https://creativewriting.eku.edu/carter-sickels. Accessed September 28, 2018.

Catte, Elizabeth. *What You Are Getting Wrong about Appalachia*. Cleveland, OH: Belt, 2018.

Charles, Douglas M. *Hoover's War on Gays: Exposing the FBI's "Sex Deviates" Program*. Lawrence: University Press of Kansas, 2015.

Christensen, Jessica. " 'There's Been Blood Shed a-Plenty': Female Vengeance in River of Earth." *KPA Bulletin* 30 (2015): 75–86.

Chute, Hillary L. "An Interview with Alison Bechdel." *MFS Modern Fiction Studies* 52, no. 4 (2006): 1004–13. https://doi.org/10.1353/mfs.2007.0003.

Clark, Jim. Introduction to *Fable in the Blood: The Selected Poems of Byron Herbert Reece*, by Byron Herbert Reece, edited by Jim Clark, xi–xlii. Athens: University of Georgia Press, 2002.

Cohen, Charles E. "Painful Homecomings," review of *Scissors, Paper, Rock*, by Fenton Johnson. *San Francisco Examiner*, July 25, 1993.

Cook, Raymond A. "Byron Herbert Reece: Ten Years After." *Georgia Review* 22, no. 1 (1968): 74–89.

———. *Mountain Singer: The Life and the Legacy of Byron Herbert Reece*. Rpt. ed. Atlanta, GA: Cherokee, 1980.

Craven, Elizabeth. "Almost Heaven." In *Crooked Letter i: Coming Out in the South*, edited by Connie Griffin, 19–29. Montgomery, AL: NewSouth Books, 2015.

Creadick, Anna. "Interview: Fenton Johnson." *Appalachian Journal* 22, no. 2 (Winter 1995): 160–73.

Cross, Carlyle. "Cross, Carlyle." *James Still Correspondence Database*. https://stillbib.omeka.net/items/show/64623. Accessed July 11, 2022.

Cumming, Robert B. "Resonance across Time and Cultures: An Introduction to George Scarbrough's Han-Shan Poems." In *Under the Lemon Tree*, by George Scarbrough, edited by Rebecca Passmore Mobbs and Robert B. Cumming, 15–22. Oak Ridge, TN: Iris Press, 2011.

Cvetkovich, Ann. *An Archive of Feelings: Trauma, Sexuality, and Lesbian Public Cultures*. Durham, NC: Duke University Press, 2003.

Daly, Mary Ann. "Roses Grown for Their Thorns," review of *Two or Three Things I Know for Sure*, by Dorothy Allison. *Lambda Book Report* 4, no. 12 (October 1995): 25–26.

davenport, doris diosa. *65 poems*. CreateSpace, 2014.

———. "All This, and Honeysuckles Too." In *Bloodroot: Reflections on Place by Appalachian Women Writers*, edited by Joyce Dyer, 87–97. Lexington: University Press of Kentucky, 1998.

———. Introduction to *Soque Street Poems*, iv–vi. Sautee-Nacoochee, GA: Sautee-Nacoochee Community Association (SNCA), 1995.

———. *madness like morning glories: poems*. Baton Rouge: Louisiana State University Press, 2005.

———. "Music in Poetry: If You Can't Feel It / You Can't Fake It." *Mid-American Review* 10, no. 2 (1990): 57–64.

———. *Performance Pieces*. CreateSpace, 2016.

———. *Soque Street Poems*. Sautee-Nacoochee, GA: Sautee-Nacoochee Community Association (SNCA), 1995.

Deahl, Rachel. "Family History in Pictures and Prose." *Publisher's Weekly*, June 5, 2006.

Dean-Ruzicka, Rachel. "Mourning and Melancholia in Alison Bechdel's *Fun Home: A Family Tragicomic*." *ImageText: Interdisciplinary Comics Studies* 7, no. 2 (Fall 2013). http://www.english.ufl.edu.marshall.idm.oclc.org/imagetext/archives/v7_2/dean-ruzicka/.

Department of Photographs. "Walker Evans (1903–1975)." The Met's Heilbrunn Timeline of Art History, October 2004. https://www.metmuseum.org/toah/hd/evan/hd_evan.htm.

Dickstein, Lore. "An Easy Lay, Spiritually Speaking." *Ms.* 4, no. 12 (June 1976): 90–91.

Donnelly, Nisa. Review of *Fun Home: A Family Tragicomic*, by Alison Bechdel. *Lambda Book Report* (Spring 2006): 14.

"Doris Davenport, Ph.D." LinkedIn. https://www.linkedin.com/in/davenportpoetprofessor/. Accessed October 31, 2018.

Dyer, Joyce. "Confluences: Fluidity in the Art and Vision of Maggie Anderson." *Iron Mountain Review* 21 (2005): 27–34.

Eaton, Allen H. *Handicrafts of the Southern Highlands*. New York: Russell Sage Foundation, 1937.

Eblen, Tom. " 'You Don't Ever See a Story about Gay People and Faith.' So Silas House Wrote One." *Lexington Herald-Leader*, June 1, 2018. https://www.kentucky.com/news/local/news-columns-blogs/tom-eblen/article212262719.html.

Emerson, Ralph Waldo. "Nature." In *The Collected Works of Ralph Waldo Emerson, I: Nature, Addresses, and Lectures*, 3–45. Cambridge, MA: Belknap Press of Harvard University Press, 1971.

Engelhardt, Elizabeth S. D. *The Tangled Roots of Feminism, Environmentalism, and Appalachian Literature*. Athens: Ohio University Press, 2003.

Enszer, Julie R. "doris davenport's *it's like this*." *Huffington Post* (blog), September 25, 2013. https://www.huffingtonpost.com/julie-r-enszer/doris-davenport-its-like-this_b_3972323.html.

Eveleth, K. W. "A Vast 'Network of Transversals': Labyrinthine Aesthetics in *Fun Home*." *South Central Review* 32, no. 3 (2015): 88–109. https://doi.org/10.1353/scr.2015.0031.

"Executive Orders." National Archives, August 15, 2016. https://www.archives.gov/federal-register/codification/executive-order/10450.html.

"Fiction Book Review: *Clay's Quilt* by Silas House." *Publisher's Weekly*, March 1, 2001. https://www.pubishersweekly.com/9781565123076.

Finkelstein, Avram. *After Silence: A History of AIDS through Its Images*. Oakland: University of California Press, 2018.

Finley, Frankie. Review of *Loving Mountains, Loving Men*, by Jeff Mann. *Appalachian Journal* 35, no. 1–2 (Fall 2007/Winter 2008): 123–26.

"Fireside Industries." *The University Press of Kentucky* (blog). https://www.kentuckypress.com/fireside-industries/. Accessed May 27, 2021.

Foucault, Michel. *The History of Sexuality*. New York: Pantheon Books, 1985.

Francis, Robert. *The Trouble with Francis: An Autobiography*. Amherst: University of Massachusetts Press, 1971.

Freedman, Ariela. "Drawing on Modernism in Alison Bechdel's *Fun Home*." *Journal of Modern Literature* 32, no. 4 (July 2009): 125–40. https://doi.org/10.2979/JML.2009.32.4.125.

Friedman, Lester, David Desser, Sarah Kozloff, Martha P. Nochimson, and Stephen Prince. *An Introduction to Film Genres*. New York: W.W. Norton, 2014.

Friedman, Michael Shannon. "Jeff Mann: An Appreciation." *Appalachian Heritage* 34, no. 3 (Summer 2006): 28–31.

Gannon, Thomas C. *Skylark Meets Meadowlark: Reimagining the Bird in British Romantic and Contemporary Native American Literature*. Lincoln: University of Nebraska Press, 2009.

Gardiner, Judith Kegan. "A Wake for Mother: The Maternal Deathbed in Women's Fiction." *Feminist Studies* 4, no. 2 (June 1978): 146. https://doi.org/10.2307/3177465.

Gardner, Jared. "Autography's Biography, 1972–2007." *Biography* 31, no. 1 (2008): 1–26. https://doi.org/10.1353/bio.0.0003.

Garrett, George. "1999: The Year in Fiction—Entry on *Strange Birds in the Tree of Heaven*." In *Dictionary of Literary Biography Yearbook: 1999*, edited by Matthew Bruccoli, 32. Dictionary of Literary Biography Yearbook Series. Detroit: Gale, 2000.

Garringer, Rachel. "Country Queers: About." Country Queers: A Multimedia Oral History Project Documenting the Diverse Experiences of Rural and Small Town LGBTQIA Folks in the U.S.A., June 28, 2013. https://countryqueers.com/about/.

Glenn, Cheryl. *Unspoken: A Rhetoric of Silence*. Carbondale: Southern Illinois University Press, 2004. https://www.amazon.com/Unspoken-Rhetoric-Silence-Cheryl-Glenn/dp/0809325845/ref=sr_1_1?keywords=unspoken+cheryl+glenn&qid=1580330809&sr=8-1.

"Goodbye Gauley Mountain: An Ecosexual Love Story | Home." http://goodbyegauleymountain.org/. Accessed October 31, 2018.

Goode, James B. "The Impact of Coal Mining in the Evolution of Appalachian Kentucky Literature: A Retrospective." *Journal of Kentucky Studies* 31 (2016): 129–38.

Gopinath, Gayatri. *Impossible Desires: Queer Diasporas and South Asian Public Cultures*. Durham, NC: Duke University Press, 2005.

Graves, Jesse. Introduction to *The Southern Poetry Anthology: Volume 3 Contemporary Appalachia*, edited by Jesse Graves, Paul Ruffin, and William Wright, 8–10. The Southern Poetry Anthology. Huntsville, TX: Texas Review Press, 2011.

Gray, Mary L. *Out in the Country: Youth, Media, and Queer Visibility in Rural America*. New York: New York University Press, 2009.

Griffith, E. V. "Byron Herbert Reece: A Personal Memoir with Letters." *Georgia Review* 19, no. 2 (1965): 131–68.

Halberstam, Jack. *In a Queer Time and Place: Transgender Bodies, Subcultural Lives*. New York: New York University Press, 2005.

Hall, Joan Lord. "Symbiosis and Separation in Lisa Alther's *Kinflicks*." *Arizona Quarterly* 38, no. 4 (1982): 336–46.

Hanlon, Tina L. "'Way Back Yonder' but Not So Far Away: Teaching Appalachian Folktales." In *Appalachia in the Classroom: Teaching the Region*, edited by Theresa L. Burriss and Patricia M. Gantt, 109–28. Series in Race, Ethnicity, and Gender in Appalachia. Athens: Ohio University Press, 2013.

Harkins, Anthony, and Meredith McCarroll, eds. *Appalachian Reckoning: A Region Responds to Hillbilly Elegy*. 1st ed. Morgantown: West Virginia University Press, 2019.

Harlan, Jennifer. "Theater: Play Examines Homosexuality and Harassment in Appalachia: Author Silas House Takes on Homosexuality and Harassment in Appalachia." *LEO Weekly*, January 8, 2014, sec. Arts & Culture. https://www.leoweekly.com/2014/01/theater-play-examines-homosexuality-and-harassment-in-appalachia/.

Hawthorne, Ann. Preface to *The Picture Man: Photographs by Paul Buchanan*, edited by Ann Hawthorne, xi–xxii. Chapel Hill: University of North Carolina Press, 1993.

Henninger, Katherine. *Ordering the Facade: Photography and Contemporary Southern Women's Writing*. New Directions in Southern Studies. Chapel Hill: University of North Carolina Press, 2007.

Henricks, Robert G. Introduction to *The Poetry of Han-Shan: A Complete, Annotated Translation of Cold Mountain*, 3–26. Albany: State University of New York Press, 1990.

Herring, Scott. "Queer Infrastructure." In *Another Country: Queer Anti-Urbanism*, 149–80. New York: New York University Press, 2010.

Hirsch, Marianne. *Family Frames: Photography, Narrative, and Postmemory*. Cambridge, MA: Harvard University Press, 1997.

Hogeland, Lisa Maria. *Feminism and Its Fictions: The Consciousness-Raising Novel and the Women's Liberation Movement*. Philadelphia: University of Pennsylvania Press, 1998.

Hokenson, Jan. "Alther, Lisa." In *Gay and Lesbian Literature*, edited by Tom Pendergast and Sara Pendergast, 4–7. Detroit: St. James Press, 1994.

hooks, bell. "Call and Response—Taking a Stand." *Journal of Appalachian Studies* 20, no. 2 (2014): 122–23.

———. "Connecting Appalachia to the World Beyond." *Bell Hooks Books* (blog), September 20, 2018. https://bellhooksbooks.com/connecting-appalachia-to-the-world-beyond/.

Hoppenthaler, John. "Maggie Anderson Interview with John Hoppenthaler." ConnotationPress—An Online Artifact, March 2019. https://www.connotationpress.com/hoppenthaler-s-congeries/2017/november-2017/3128-maggie-anderson-poetry.

Houck, James. "Finding a Voice: Affirming Religious Coping as a Strength among Disenfranchised Appalachians." *Journal of Appalachian Studies* 18, nos. 1, 2 (2012): 189–205.

House, Silas. "A Conscious Heart." *Journal of Appalachian Studies* 14, no. 1/2 (Spring 2008): 7–19.

———. "From the Playwright." In *This Is My Heart for You*, by Silas House, 7–11. Berea, KY: Loyal Jones Appalachian Center, 2014.

———. Introduction to *Chinaberry*, by James Still, edited by Silas House, ix–xvii. Lexington: University Press of Kentucky, 2011.

———. "Kentucky County Gets Media Attention over Clerk's Stand on Marriage." Interview by Steve Inskeep. NPR, September 3, 2015. https://www.npr.org/2015/09/03/437132849/kentucky-county-gets-media-attention-over-clerks-stand-on-marriage.

———. "Looking in the Mirror." BookBrowse.com, June 1, 2018. https://www.bookbrowse.com/author_interviews/full/index.cfm/author_number/3103/silas-house.

———. "The Masterpiece Decision Isn't Harmless." *New York Times*, June 5, 2018, sec. Opinion. https://www.nytimes.com/2018/06/05/opinion/masterpiece-cakeshop-decision-kentucky.html.

———. "The Other in an Othered Culture: LGBTQ Writers in Appalachia." Panel convened at the Appalachian Studies Association Conference, Cincinnati, OH, April 2018.

———. "Our Secret Places in the Waiting World: Or, A Conscious Heart, Continued." *Journal of Appalachian Studies* 20, no. 2 (Fall 2014): 103–21.

———. *Southernmost*. New York: Algonquin Books, 2018.

———. *This Is My Heart for You*. Berea, KY: Loyal Jones Appalachian Center, 2014.

Howard, Jason Kyle. "Creative Process Blog Tour." *Jason Kyle Howard* (blog), August 19, 2014. http://www.jason-howard.com/blog.html.

———. "'Queer Sexual Bodies Are Despised': Garth Greenwell on Writing His Debut Novel and Why Everything Comes Back to Kentucky for Him, 'for Better and for Worse.'" Salon, February 24, 2016. https://www.salon.com/2016/02/24/queer_sexual_bodies_are_despised_garth_greenwell_on_writing_his_debut_novel_and_why_everything_comes_back_to_kentucky_for_him_for_better_and_for_worse/.

Ingraham, Christopher. "In the Modern History of Mass Shootings in America, Orlando Is the Deadliest." *Washington Post*, June 12, 2016. https://www.washingtonpost.com/news/wonk/wp/2016/06/12/in-the-modern-history-of-mass-shootings-in-america-orlando-is-the-absolute-worst/.

Inness, Sherrie A. "Alther, Lisa (b. 1944)." In *The Gay and Lesbian Literary Heritage: A Reader's Companion to the Writers and Their Works, from Antiquity to the Present*, edited by Claude J. Summers, 21. New York: Routledge, 2002. https://search-ebscohost-com.marshall.idm.oclc.org/login.aspx?direct=true&db=nlebk&AN=707852&site=ehost-live.

Inocencio, Josh. "Identity, Family, Belief: Novelist Silas House Chats Writing about Appalachia." *Spectrum South: The Voice of the Queer South* (blog), July 31, 2017. https://www.spectrumsouth.com/novelist-silas-house/.

———. "*Southernmost* Review: Times Are a-Changin' in Ol' Appalachia." *Spectrum South: The Voice of the Queer South* (blog), May 24, 2018. https://www.spectrumsouth.com/southernmost-review/.

Inscoe, John C. "Sense of Place, Sense of Being: The Intersection of Geography and Spirit in Recent Appalachian Autobiography: A Review Essay." *Journal of Appalachian Studies* 12, no. 2 (Fall 2006): 156–68.

"Interview with Rachel Garringer." *Still: The Journal*. http://www.stilljournal.net/interview-rachelgarringer.php. Accessed November 20, 2018.

Iuliano, Fiorenzo. "Du Côté de *Fun Home*: Alison Bechdel Rewrites Marcel Proust." *Partial Answers: Journal of Literature and the History of Ideas* 13, no. 2 (2015): 287–309. https://doi.org/10.1353/pan.2015.0016.

Johnson, David K. *The Lavender Scare: The Cold War Persecution of Gays and Lesbians in the Federal Government*. Chicago: University of Chicago Press, 2004.

Johnson, Fenton. "Claiming a Place on Earth: The Conscious Heart of Silas House." *Journal of Appalachian Studies* 20, no. 2 (Fall 2014): 151–53. https://doi.org/10.5406/jappastud.20.2.0151.

———. *Geography of the Heart: A Memoir*. New York: Washington Square Press, 1996.

———. *Scissors, Paper, Rock*. New York: Pocket Books, 1993.

Jones, Rodney. "Entering *Tellico Blue*." In *Tellico Blue*, 2nd ed., vii–ix. Oak Ridge, TN: Iris Press, 1999.

Jones, Loyal. "Appalachian Values." In *Voices from the Hills: Selected Readings in Southern Appalachia*, edited by Robert J. Higgs and Ambrose N. Manning, 507–17. New York: Frederick Ungar, 1975.

———. *Appalachian Values*. Ashland, KY: Jesse Stuart Foundation, 1994.

Justus, Michelle. "Patriarchal Trauma in Appalachian Literature," 2016. Open Dissertations. https://search.ebscohost.com/login.aspx?direct=true&db=ddu&AN=D1F86287F95E5712&site=ehost-live.

Keane, Erin. "Can a Literary Thriller Heal Divides? Silas House's *Southernmost* Isn't Preaching to Either Choir." Salon, June 5, 2018. https://www.salon.com/2018/06/05/can-a-literary-thriller-heal-divides-silas-houses-southernmost-isnt-preaching-to-any-choir/.

Kenan, Randall. "Sorrow's Child." *Nation*, December 28, 1992.

Kephart, Horace. *Our Southern Highlanders*. New York: Macmillan, 1921.

Kingsbury, Pam. "Descending into the Darkness: An Interview with Karen Salyer McElmurray." *Southern Scribe: Our Culture of Storytelling*, 2004. http://www.southernscribe.com/zine/authors/McElmurray_Karen.htm.

Kirch, Claire. "Author Julia Watts Disinvited from Teen Lit Festival." *Publisher's Weekly*, September 2019. https://www.publishersweekly.com/pw/by-topic/childrens/childrens-authors/article/81097-author-julia-watts-disinvited-from-teen-lit-festival.html.

Kobersmith, Kim. "Clay's Legacy." *Kentucky Monthly*, September 30, 2021. http://www.kentuckymonthly.com/api/content/21188b28-21e5-11ec-a885-12f1225286c6/.

Kumbier, Alana. *Ephemeral Material: Queering the Archive*. Series on Gender and Sexuality in Information Studies 5. Sacramento, CA: Litwin Books, 2014.

Lang, John. "The Editor's Page." *Iron Mountain Review* 17 (Spring 2001): 2.

Larsen, Anne. "Reeling through a Daughter's Decade," review of *Kinflicks*, by Lisa Alther. *Village Voice*, March 8, 1976.

Lentz, Ralph E., II. *W. R. Trivett, Appalachian Pictureman: Photographs of a Bygone Time*. Contributions to Southern Appalachian Studies 4. Jefferson, NC: McFarland, 2001.

Leonard, John. "Pop Goes the Novel," review of *Kinflicks*, by Lisa Alther. *New York Times Book Review*, March 14, 1976.

Lillvis, Kristen. *Posthuman Blackness and the Black Female Imagination*. Athens: University of Georgia Press, 2017.

"Lisa Alther: Biography." http://www.lisaalther.com/biography.html. Accessed December 12, 2018.

"Literary Events." *Chicago Tribune*, May 23, 1999, sec. Literary Events. Newspapers.com.

"Literary Festival." https://www.ehc.edu/academics/english/literary-festival/. Accessed December 12, 2018.

Locklear, Erica Abrams. "A Matter of Taste: Reading Food and Class in Appalachian Literature." In *Writing in the Kitchen: Essays on Southern Literature and Foodways*, edited by David A. Davis, Tara Powell, and Jessica B. Harris, e-book. Jackson: University Press of Mississippi, 2014. http://ebookcentral.proquest.com/lib/marshall-ebooks/detail.action?docID=1820913.

Loftin, Craig M. Introduction to *Letters to ONE: Gay and Lesbian Voices from the 1950s and 1960s*, edited by Craig M. Loftin, 1–12. Queer Politics and Cultures. Albany: State University of New York Press, 2012.

———, ed. *Letters to ONE: Gay and Lesbian Voices from the 1950s and 1960s*. Queer Politics and Cultures. Albany: State University of New York Press, 2012.

———. *Masked Voices: Gay Men and Lesbians in Cold War America*. Queer Politics and Cultures. Albany: State University of New York Press, 2012.

Long, Kate, and Maggie Anderson. "The Spaces Between: A Conversation." *Iron Mountain Review* 21 (2005): 35–42.

Loving, Denton. "Getting Personal in Your Writing: An Interview with Karen Salyer McElmurray." *Appalachian Heritage* 39, no. 2 (Spring 2011): 24–27.

Luckenbill, Dan. "ONE, Inc., Is Founded." In *LGBTQ Events: 1, 1848–1983*, edited by Robert C. Evans, 102–05. Great Events from History. Salem Press/Grey House, 2018. Gale eBooks. https://link.gale.com/apps/doc/CX7241200054/GVRL?u=hunt91316&sid=GVRL&xid=e9de1d02.

Lundegaard, Erik. "Books in Brief: Fiction and Poetry." *New York Times*, July 15, 2001, sec. Books. https://www.nytimes.com/2001/07/15/books/books-in-brief-fiction-poetry.html.

Lundy, Ronni. Introduction to *Cornbread Nation 3: Foods of the Mountain South*, edited by Ronni Lundy, 1–6. Chapel Hill: University of North Carolina Press, 2005.

Lutwack, Leonard. *Birds in Literature*. Gainesville: University Press of Florida, 1994.

MacKenzie, Joy. "Harrowing Tales from a Hard Life," review of *Two or Three Things I Know for Sure*, by Dorothy Allison. *Sunday Star-Times*, April 28, 1996, A edition, sec. Features—Books. Newspaper Source Plus.

Mackin, Randy. *George Scarbrough, Appalachian Poet: A Biographical and Literary Study with Unpublished Writings*. Contributions to Southern Appalachian Studies 29. Jefferson, NC: McFarland, 2011.

Mann, Jeff. "Appalachian Subculture." *Gay and Lesbian Review* 10, no. 5 (October 2003): 19–21.

———. *Bliss*. Baltimore, MD: Stone Wall, 1998.

———. *Loving Mountains, Loving Men*. Athens: Ohio University Press, 2005.

———. "Southern (LGBT) Living." In *Crooked Letter i: Coming Out in the South*, 46–62. Montgomery, AL: NewSouth Books, 2015.

———. "Stonewall and Matewan: Some Thoughts on Gay Life in Appalachia." *Journal of Appalachian Studies* 5, no. 2 (Fall 1999): 207–14.

Mann, Jeff, and Julia Watts, eds. *LGBTQ Fiction and Poetry from Appalachia*. Morgantown: West Virginia University Press, 2019.

Manning, Maurice. "Strange Birds, Too: A Reflection on the Work of Karen Salyer McElmurray." *Appalachian Heritage* 39, no. 2 (Spring 2011): 40–43.

Manoff, Marlene. "Theories of the Archive from across the Disciplines." *Portal: Libraries and the Academy* 4, no. 1 (January 2004): 9–25. https://doi.org/10.1353/pla.2004.0015.

May, Roger. "Overview." Looking at Appalachia. https://lookingatappalachia.org/overview. Accessed September 26, 2019.

McCoy, Karissa. "Re-Writing Region, Re-Constructing Whiteness: Appalachia and the 'Place' of Whiteness in American Culture, 1930–2003." Dissertation, Vanderbilt University, 2004.

McElmurray, Karen Salyer. "In Visions." *Appalachian Heritage* 39, no. 2 (Spring 2011): 16–22.

———. "Looking Inside." *Appalachian Heritage* 42, no. 2 (2014): 85–102.

———. *Strange Birds in the Tree of Heaven: A Novel*. Athens: University of Georgia Press, 2004.

McKee, Kathryn. "Coal Dust and Moonshine," review of *Strange Birds in the Tree of Heaven*, by Karen Salyer McElmurray. *Women's Review of Books* 17, no. 10/11 (July 2000): 27–28.

McMichael, Pam. "The Power of Conversation." *Journal of Appalachian Studies* 20, no. 2 (2014): 142–45.

Meeker, Martin. "One." In *Encyclopedia of Lesbian, Gay, Bisexual and Transgender History in America*, edited by Marc Stein, 2:358–60. New York: Charles Scrib-

ner's Sons, 2004. https://link.gale.com/apps/doc/CX3403600373/GVRL?u=hunt91316&sid=GVRL&xid=57758e06.
Megan, Carolyn A. "Moving Toward Truth: An Interview with Dorothy Allison." *Kenyon Review* 16, no. 4 (Fall 1994): 71–83.
Meyer, Richard. Preface to *Art and Queer Culture*, by Catherine Lord and Richard Meyer, 9–12. New York: Phaidon Press, 2013.
———. "Queer Photography?" *Aperture*, no. 218 (Spring 2015): 28–29.
Miller, Danny, Sandra Ballard, Roberta Herrin, Stephen D. Mooney, Susan Underwood, and Jack Wright. "Appalachian Literature." In *A Handbook to Appalachia: An Introduction to the Region*, edited by Grace Toney Edwards, JoAnn Aust Asbury, and Ricky L. Cox, 199–216. Knoxville: University of Tennessee Press, 2006.
Miller, Danny L. "The Appalachian Migratory Experience in Literature." In *Down Home, Downtown: Urban Appalachians Today*, edited by Phillip J. Obermiller, 143–56. Dubuque, IA: Kendall/Hunt, 1996.
———. "Homosexuality in Appalachian Literature." Paper presented at the Appalachian Studies Association Conference, Helen, GA, March 30, 1996.
———. Review of *Strange Birds in the Tree of Heaven*, by Karen Salyer McElmurray. *Journal of Appalachian Studies* 6, nos. 1, 2 (Spring/Fall 2000): 211–12.
Miller, James A. "Coming Home to Affrilachia: The Poems of Doris Davenport." In *Her Words: Diverse Voices in Contemporary Appalachian Women's Poetry*, 96–106. Knoxville: University of Tennessee Press, 2002.
Miller, Jim Wayne. "Appalachian Literature." *Appalachian Journal* 5 (Autumn 1977): 82–91.
———. " 'Daring to Look in the Well': A Conversation." In *James Still in Interviews, Oral Histories and Memoirs*, edited by Ted Olson, 44–57. Contributions to Southern Appalachian Studies 23. Jefferson, NC: McFarland, 2009.
———. "Jim Dandy: James Still at Eighty." In *James Still: Critical Essays on the Dean of Appalachian Literature*, edited by Ted Olson and Kathy H. Olson, 209–21. Contributions to Southern Appalachian Studies 17. Jefferson, NC: McFarland, 2007.
Mitchell, W. J. T. "Showing Seeing: A Critique of Visual Culture." *Journal of Visual Culture* 1, no. 2 (August 2002): 165–81. https://doi.org/10.1177/147041290200100202.
Mohring, Ron. "12 Questions: An Interview with Jeff Mann." *RFD* 30, no. 3 (2004): 11–13.
Moltke-Hansen, David. "Seeing the Highlands, 1900–1939: Southwestern Virginia through the Lens of T. R. Phelps." *Southern Cultures* 1, no. 1 (Fall 1994): 23–49. https://doi.org/10.1353/scil1994.0013.
Montgomery, Helena Louise. "Doris Davenport (1949–)." In *Contemporary Lesbian Writers of the United States*, 155–59. London: Greenwood Press, 1993.

Morton, Bruce. Introduction to *The Picture Man: Photographs by Paul Buchanan*, edited by Ann Hawthorne, 1–8. Chapel Hill: University of North Carolina Press, 1993.

Napier, O. James. "Dancing in the Dirt." In *Electric Dirt: A Celebration of Queer Voices and Identities from Appalachia and the South*, edited by The Queer Appalachia / Electric Dirt Collective, 74–77. Bluefield, WV: Queer Appalachia, 2017.

"New FBI Hate Crimes Report Shows Increases in Anti-LGBTQ Attacks." HCR. https://www.hrc.org/press-releases/new-fbi-hate-crimes-report-shows-increases-in-anti-lgbtq-attacks. Accessed May 27, 2021.

Newman, Katharine. Introduction to *voodoo chile, slight return: poems*, by doris davenport, iv–vi. Charlotte, NC: Soque Street Press, 1991.

Olson, Ted. "Literature." In *High Mountains Rising: Appalachia in Time and Place*, edited by Richard A. Straw and H. Tyler Blethen, 165–78. Urbana: University of Illinois Press, 2004.

Polk's Augusta (Richmond County, GA.) City Directory 1970. Richmond, VA: R. L. Polk, 1970.

Pond, Wayne, and Lisa Alther. "Healing Laughter: A Conversation." *Iron Mountain Review: Lisa Alther Issue* 17 (Spring 2001): 28–36.

"Program of the 1995 Appalachian Studies Association Conference." Morgantown: West Virginia University, 1995.

Reece, Byron Herbert. *Ballad of the Bones and Other Poems*. New York: E. P. Dutton, 1945.

———. *Fable in the Blood: The Selected Poems of Byron Herbert Reece*. Edited by Jim Clark. Athens: University of Georgia Press, 2002.

Reynolds, David. "White Trash in Your Face: The Literary Descent of Dorothy Allison." *Appalachian Journal* 20, no. 4 (Summer 1993): 355–66.

Reynolds, Teresa Perry. "James Still: Alabamian, Transplanted Knott Countian." *Appalachian Heritage* 38, no. 4 (Fall 2010): 48–51. https://doi.org/10.1353/aph.2010.0036.

Rohy, Valerie. "In the Queer Archive." *GLQ: A Journal of Lesbian and Gay Studies* 16, no. 3 (June 1, 2010): 341–61. https://doi.org/10.1215/10642684-2009-034.

Rowland, Beryl. *Birds with Human Souls: A Guide to Bird Symbolism*. Knoxville: University of Tennessee Press, 1978.

Ruppersburg, Hugh. Foreword to *The Hawk and the Sun*, by Byron Herbert Reece, ix–xviii. Athens, GA: Brown Thrasher Books, 1994.

Salon Staff. "*Fun Home*." Salon, December 12, 2006. https://www.salon.com/2006/12/12/bechdel_int/.

Satterwhite, Emily. *Dear Appalachia: Readers, Identity, and Popular Fiction since 1878*. Lexington: University Press of Kentucky, 2011.

Scarbrough, George. "Love in the Afternoon." In *In Homage to Priapus*, edited by E. V. Griffith, 31–32. Greenleaf Classic GL152. San Diego, CA: Greenleaf Classics, 1970.

———. "Revenant." *Poetry*, July 2000, 207.

———. "Something of a Bio and an Itinerary: September 13, 1992." In *George Scarbrough, Appalachian Poet*, by Randy Mackin, 183–88. Contributions to Southern Appalachian Studies 29. Jefferson, NC: McFarland, 2011.

———. "Sunday Shopping." *Poetry*, February 1997, 283.

———. *Under the Lemon Tree*. Edited by Robert B. Cumming and Rebecca Passmore Mobbs. Oak Ridge, TN: Iris Press, 2011.

Scates, Maxine. Review of *Cold Comfort*, by Maggie Anderson. *Prairie Schooner* 63, no. 1 (1989): 118–23.

Schafer, William J. "The Bridges of Fenton Johnson." *Appalachian Journal* 22, no. 2 (1995): 154–59.

Schneider, Christian W. "Young Daughter, Old Artificer: Constructing the Gothic Fun Home." *Studies in Comics* 1, no. 2 (November 1, 2010): 337–58. https://doi.org/10.1386/stic.1.2.337_1.

Schwartz, Patricia Roth. "Profound Pitt Poets." *Lambda Book Report* 9, no. 2 (September 2000): 21.

Sedgwick, Eve Kosofsky. *Epistemology of the Closet*. Berkeley: University of California Press, 1990.

Seidman, Steven. *Beyond the Closet: The Transformation of Gay and Lesbian Life*. New York: Routledge, 2002.

Sellers, Bettie. *The Bitter Berry: The Life of Byron Herbert Reece*. Southern Literature Series. Atlanta: Georgia Humanities Council, 1992.

Shaw, Denise R. "Doris Davenport (1949)." In *Encyclopedia of African American Women Writers*. Westport, CT: Greenwood Press, 2007.

Sheppard, Muriel Earley. *Cabins in the Laurel*. Chapel Hill: University of North Carolina Press, 1935.

Shultz, Zach. "Queer Homecoming: On Carter Sickels's *The Prettiest Star*." *Los Angeles Review of Books*, September 12, 2020. https://lareviewofbooks.org/article/queer-homecoming-on-carter-sickelss-the-prettiest-star/.

Shurbutt, Sylvia Bailey, ed. *Silas House: Exploring an Appalachian Writer's Work*. Lexington: University Press of Kentucky, 2021.

Sickels, Carter. "Bittersweet: On Transitioning and Finding Home." In *Walk Till the Dogs Get Mean: Meditations on the Forbidden from Contemporary Appalachia*, edited by Adrian Blevins and Karen Salyer McElmurray, 73–79. Athens: Ohio University Press, 2015.

———. "Early in My Transition, Two Teenagers Helped Me Embrace My Identity." BuzzFeed, April 22, 2015. https://www.buzzfeed.com/cartersickels/early-in-my-transition-two-teenagers-helped-me-embrace-my-id.

———. "Johnson City." *Appalachian Heritage*, May 1, 2014. http://appalachianheritage.net/2014/05/01/johnson-city/.

———. "Photograph, 2007." *Still: The Journal* (Summer 2012). http://www.still-journal.net/carter-sickels-nonfiction.php.

———. *The Prettiest Star*. Spartanburg, SC: Hub City Press, 2020.

---. "Silas House: On Capturing the Rural South and Loving in a Fraught . . ." *Lambda Literary* (blog), June 14, 2018. https://www.lambdaliterary.org/interviews/06/14/silas-house/.

---. "Wildlife." *Guernica*, March 16, 2015. https://www.guernicamag.com/wildlife/.

Sledge, John. "Posthumous Novel *Chinaberry* Adds to James Still's Legacy." *Press-Register*. April 3, 2011. https://www.al.com/entertainment-press-register/2011/04/posthumous_novel_chinaberry_ad.html.

Smith, Joan. "AIDS and the American Heartland: Local Writer's Newest Work Echoes Kentucky Memories of Love, Family Life." *San Francisco Examiner*, July 11, 1993.

Smith, Lee. *Oral History*. New York: Ballantine Books, 1983.

Sohn, Mark F. *Appalachian Home Cooking: History, Culture, and Recipes*. Lexington: University Press of Kentucky, 2005.

Spriggs, Bianca Lynne, and Jeremy Paden. Introduction to *Black Bone: 25 Years of the Affrilachian Poets*, edited by Bianca Lynne Spriggs and Jeremy Paden, 17–19. Lexington: *pluck! The Journal of Affrilachian Arts and Culture*, rpt. University Press of Kentucky, 2018.

Sprinkle, Annie, Beth Stephens, and Jennie Klein. *Assuming the Ecosexual Position: The Earth as Lover*. Minneapolis: University of Minnesota Press, 2021.

St. John, Janet. Review of *Madness Like Morning Glories*, by Doris Davenport. *Booklist* 101, no. 14 (March 15, 2005): 1259.

Stambuk, Andrew. *The Man Who Is and Is Not There: The Poetry and Prose of Robert Francis*. Amherst: University of Massachusetts Press, 2011.

Staten, Vince. "Who'd Want to Read a Novel about Growing Up in Kingsport?" *Kingsport Times-News*, June 5, 1976. newspapers.com.

Steinberg, Sybil. Review of *Strange Birds in the Trees [sic] of Heaven*, by Karen Salyer McElmurray. *Publisher's Weekly* 246, no. 33 (August 16, 1999): 63.

Stephens, Elizabeth. "Directors' Statement—*Goodbye Gauley Mountain: An Ecosexual Love Story*." https://goodbyegauleymountain.ucsc.edu/directors-statement/. Accessed June 20, 2022.

---. "Film Structure." Elizabeth Stephens, September 24, 2011. http://elizabethstephens.org/film-structure/.

---. "PAR: *Goodbye Gauley Mountain: An Ecosexual Love Story* | Elizabeth Stephens." http://elizabethstephens.org/par-goodbye-gauley-mountain-an-ecosexual-love-story/. Accessed October 31, 2018.

Stephens, Elizabeth M., and Annie M. Sprinkle. "Ecosex Manifesto." SexEcology: Where Art Meets Theory Meets Practice Meets Activism. http://sexecology.org/research-writing/ecosex-manifesto/. Accessed October 31, 2018, and June 20, 2022.

Stevens, Ashlie. "Kentucky Writer Silas House on *Southernmost*, Sexuality and His Faith Journey." WFPL, June 4, 2018. https://wfpl.org/kentucky-writer-silas-house-on-southernmost-sexuality-and-his-faith-journey/.

Stewart, Christopher B. Review of *Loving Mountains, Loving Men*, by Jeff Mann. *West Virginia History: A Journal of Regional Studies* 2, no. 2 (2008): 127–28. https://doi.org/10.1353/wvh.0.0019.

Still, James. *Chinaberry*. Edited by Silas House. Lexington: University Press of Kentucky, 2011.

———. "Mountain Heritage." *New Republic* 85, no. 1098 (December 18, 1935): 170.

———. *River of Earth*. Lexington: University Press of Kentucky, 1978.

Stuart, Jesse. "Byron Herbert Reece: In Memoriam, I." *Georgia Review* 12 (1958): 359–62.

Suter, Scott Hamilton. "'The Spiritual Energy of the Trees': Nature, Place, and Religion in Silas House's Crow County Trilogy." In *Rough South, Rural South: Region and Class in Recent Southern Literature*, 182–90. Jackson: University Press of Mississippi, 2016.

Switzer, Ann. "Kingsport Skin Shows through in *Kinflicks*." *Kingsport Times-News*, March 14, 1976. newspapers.com.

Thompson, Deborah, and Irene Moser. "Appalachian Folklife." In *A Handbook to Appalachia: An Introduction to the Region*, edited by Grace Toney Edwards, JoAnn Aust Asbury, and Ricky L. Cox, 143–62. Knoxville: University of Tennessee Press, 2006.

Thompson, Lawrance, and R. H. Winnick. *Robert Frost: The Later Years, 1938–1963*. New York: Holt, Rinehart and Winston, 1976.

Todd, Richard. "Two Good Old-Fashioned Young Novelists." *Atlantic Monthly* 237, no. 5 (May 1976): 104–07.

Unsigned review of *Chinaberry*, by James Still. *Publishers Weekly* 258, no. 7 (February 14, 2011): 38–39.

Unsigned review of *Scissors, Paper, Rock*, by Fenton Johnson. *Virginia Quarterly Review* 71, no. 1 (Winter 1994): 22.

Unsigned review of *A Space Filled with Moving*, by Maggie Anderson. *Publisher's Weekly* 239, no. 17 (April 6, 1992): 58.

Vera, Dan, and Bo Young. "*Loving Mountains, Loving Men*: Dan Vera and Bo Young Speak with the Writer Jeff Mann about Gay Rural Life, Poetry and Food." *White Crane* 68 (2006): 5–8.

Verghese, Abraham. *My Own Country: A Doctor's Story of a Town and Its People in the Age of AIDS*. New York: Simon & Schuster, 1994.

Verghese, Abraham, Steven L. Berk, and Felix Sarubbi. "Urbs in Rure: Human Immunodeficiency Virus Infection in Rural Tennessee." *Journal of Infectious Diseases* 160, no. 6 (December 1, 1989): 1051–55. https://doi.org/10.1093/infdis/160.6.1051.

Waage, Frederick G. "Alther and Dillard: The Appalachian Universe." Edited by Wilson Somerville. *Appalachia/America: Proceedings of the 1980 Appalachian Studies Conference*, 1981, 200–208.

Walker, Frank X. *Affrilachia*. Lexington: Old Cove Press, 2000.

Warhol, Robyn. "The Space Between: A Narrative Approach to Alison Bechdel's *Fun Home.*" *College Literature* 38, no. 3 (2011): 1–20. https://doi.org/10.1353/lit.2011.0025.

Watkins, Charles Alan. "Why Have There Been No Great Appalachian Photographers?" *Now and Then: The Appalachian Magazine* 14, no. 2 (Summer 1997): 21–25.

Watterson, Zachary. "We Fought Them Tooth and Nail: An Interview with Carter Sickels." *Fiction Writers Review* (blog), December 6, 2012. https://fictionwritersreview.com/interview/we-fought-them-tooth-and-nail-an-interview-with-carter-sickels/.

Watts, Julia. *Finding H.F.* New York: Alyson Books, 2001.

———. "Interview with Julia Watts." *Journal of Appalachian Studies* 20, no. 2 (Fall 2014): 177–80.

———. *The Kind of Girl I Am.* Midway, FL: Spinsters Ink, 2007.

———. *Phases of the Moon.* Tallahassee, FL: Naiad Press, 1997.

———. "Quare Theory: Some Thoughts on LGBT Appalachian Writing." In *Walk Till the Dogs Get Mean: Meditations on the Forbidden from Contemporary Appalachia*, edited by Adrian Blevins and Karen Salyer McElmurray, 105–09. Athens: Ohio University Press, 2015.

———. *Wildwood Flowers.* Tallahassee, FL: Naiad Press, 1996.

Weatherford, W. D., and Wilma Dykeman. "Literature since 1900." In *The Southern Appalachian Region: A Survey*, edited by Thomas R. Ford, 259–70. Lexington: University of Kentucky Press, 1967.

Wells, Betty Jean. "Wells, Betty Jean." *James Still Correspondence Database.* https://stillbib.omeka.net/items/show/64831. Accessed July 11, 2022.

Werth, Barry. *The Scarlet Professor—Newton Arvin: A Literary Life Shattered by Scandal.* Rpt. ed. New York: Anchor Books, 2002. Kindle.

Weston, Kath. "Get Thee to a Big City: Sexual Imaginary and the Great Gay Migration." *GLQ: A Journal of Lesbian and Gay Studies* 2 (1995): 253–77.

White, Gwen. "The Dutiful-Mother Syndrome in Lisa Alther's *Kinflicks.*" *Border States: Journal of the Kentucky-Tennessee American Studies Association* 9 (1993): 6.

"Who We Are." Country Queers. https://www.countryqueers.com/who-we-are. Accessed June 23, 2022.

Williams, John Alexander. *Appalachia: A History.* Chapel Hill: University of North Carolina Press, 2002.

Williamson, Jerry, and George Scarbrough. "The County and Beyond: A Conversation." *Iron Mountain Review* 16 (Spring 2000): 31–38.

Wise, Manfred [Pratt Dickson]. *What Is It the Mountains Say?* London: Brookside Press, 1958.

Worthington, Marianne. Review of *Loving Mountains, Loving Men*, by Jeff Mann. *Now and Then* 22, no. 1 (Spring 2006): 58.

Yep, Gust A., and Susan B. Shimanoff. "The US Day of Silence: Sexualities, Silences, and the Will to Unsay in the Age of Empire." In *Silence, Feminism, Power: Reflections at the Edges of Sound*, edited by Sheena Malhotra and Aimee Carrillo Rowe, 139–56. New York: Palgrave Macmillan, 2013.

Zimmerman, Patricia R. *Reel Families: A Social History of Amateur Film*. Bloomington: Indiana University Press, 1995.

Index

Page numbers in *italics* indicate illustrations.

abortion, 196–97
ACT UP, 129–30
Adams, Timothy Dow, 109
Affrilachian poets, 3, 59, 64, 216n58; davenport as, 61, 138–43; Spriggs as, 176; Walker and, 64, 138, 141
Agee, James, 103, 110–11, 224n101
AIDS/HIV, 59–61, 151; Johnson on, 10, 60–61, 113–14, 130–34, 192, 196; Sickels on, 88–89; "silence = death" and, 129–34
Aleichem, Sholom, 19
Allison, Dorothy, 3, 13, 55–58; Adams on, 109; Bechdel and, 58; coming out experience of, 122; Daly on, 56; film about, 58; Garringer and, 125; Henninger on, 108, 109; Kenan on, 56; photography and, 106–10
Allison, Dorothy, works of: *Bastard Out of Carolina*, 5, 55–58, 106–8; "Deciding to Live," 126; *Trash*, 55; *Two or Three Things I Know for Sure*, 56–57, 83, 106–10, 126
Alther, Lisa, 2, 3, 11, 13; on heteronormativity, 89–96; Lessing on, 50; on storytelling, 124; Vermont home of, 158–59. See also *Kinflicks*

Alzheimer's disease, 85
Anderson, Maggie, 2, 10, 52–55; Dyer on, 55; photography and, 102–6, *105*
Anderson, Maggie, works of: *Cold Comfort*, 52–53, 102–6, *105*; *The Great Horned Owl*, 52; "The Mountains Dark and Close around Me," 147; *A Space Filled with Moving*, 53; *Windfall*, 52–54; *Years That Answer*, 52
Anglin, Mary, 60, 129–30
Anzaldúa, Gloria E., 61
Appalachian epistemology, 96–102
Appalachian studies, 18–19, 123–24. See also LGBTQ Appalachian literature
Appalachian Values (Jones), 74, 145, 154
Arnow, Harriette, 184
Arvin, Newton, 16–17, 22
Avashia, Neema, 146
Awiakta, Marilou, 147–48

Bakhtin, Mikhail, 173, 182–83, 191–93
Baldwin, James, 56
Ball, Ron, 31

Ballerini, Julia, 82
Barthes, Roland, 221n10
Bechdel, Alison, 3, 72–75, 96–102; Allison and, 58; awards of, 72; Chute on, 72; coming out experience of, 102, 123; *Fun Home*, 10, 13, 72–75, 83, 96–102, 128–29; Herring on, 73–75; on LGBTQ labeling, 99; Warhol on, 102
Belinda (film), 60
Berea College: davenport at, 170; House at, 1, 8; Still at, 9, 28, 31
Berry, Wendell, 183
Bevin, Matt, 203n28
Biggs, Octavia, 78
birds in LGBTQ Appalachian literature, 173–82; in Alther, 179–82; in McElmurray, 175–79
Birtha, Becky, 170
Black, Kate, 4–6, 60, 125, 174
Blevins, Adrian, 70
Bloodroot: Reflections on Place by Appalachian Women Writers, 64, 138, 147
Bluegrass Writers Studio, 75
Boggess, Carol, 18–27, 207n77
Brady, Maureen, 51
Broderick, Michael, 183
Brosi, George, 18–19, 21–22, 69
Brown, Mayme, 19
Brown, Nickole, 3
Brownrigg, Elizabeth, 70–71
Buchanan, Harriette C., 159
Buchanan, Paul, 112
Burriss, Theresa L., 164
Bush, George H. W., 60
Butler, Judith, 4

Cadle, Dean, 32
Capote, Truman, 14
Cardozo, Melinda, 142
Carson, Warren J., 64, 139

Cherokee, 147
Chute, Hillary, 72
Civil Service Commission (CSC), 17
Clark, Jim, 45
closeted experiences, 6–7, 13–14, 19–22, 118–25, 146, 198; in "Appalachian Subculture," 157; in "Early in My Transition...," 126–27; in *Finding H. F.*, 127; in *Fun Home*, 128–29; in "Love in the Afternoon," 38–40; in *Loving Mountains, Loving Men*, 68, 161–62; in "Quare Theory," 157–58; in *Scissors, Paper, Rock*, 127–28; in *Strange Birds in the Tree of Heaven*, 135–38; in *Two or Three Things I Know for Sure*, 126
coming out experiences, 13, 120; of Allison, 122; of Bechdel, 102, 123; of Craven, 122; of House, 34; of Mann, 122, 154; of Napier, 122; of Scarbrough, 198; of Sickels, 76; of Watts, 123
Cook, Raymond A., 52
Corcoran, Jonathan, 2, 197
Country Queers (organization), 125
Craven, Elizabeth, 122
Cross, Carlyle, 27–34, 207n77
Cruz, Ted, 203n28
cuisine, Appalachian, 12, 59, 173–74, 182–94
Cvetkovich, Ann, 14–15

Daly, Mary Ann, 56
davenport, doris, 13, 61–64, 138–43; Birtha on, 170; Miller on, 62; performance poetry of, 11, 160, 167–71, 199–200; on slavery, 169; spelling of name of, 216n54; on storytelling, 124
davenport, doris, works of: *eat thunder and drink rain*, 170;

it's like this, 62; *madness like morning glories*, 11, 61–64, 138–43; *performance pieces*, 171; *65 poems*, 170–71; *Soque Street Poems*, 10, 11, 61–64, 138–43, 168–69
Davis, Kim, 8, 203n28
Depta, Victor, 3
Dickey, James, 35
Dickson, Edward Pratt, 43–45
Dobbs v. Jackson (2022), 196–97
dogs, 55, 70, 153, 167, 197
Dunbar, Paul Laurence, 142
Dyer, Joyce, 55
Dykeman, Wilma, 124, 148

An Early Frost (film), 130
ecocriticism, 175
"Ecosex Manifesto" (Stephens and Sprinkle), 163–66
Eisenhower, Dwight D., 15
Emerson, Ralph Waldo, 149–50, 160, 161
Emory & Henry Literary Festival, 54, 159
Enszer, Julie R., 64
Evans, Walker, 102–6, *105*, 110–11, 224n101
Eveleth, K. W., 97

Faulkner, William, 56
Federal Bureau of Investigation (FBI), 14–16, 44, 212n153
Fellows, Will, 4
Finley, Frankie, 68–69
Fitzgerald, Zelda, 98
food, Appalachian, 12, 59, 173–74, 182–94
Foucault, Michel, 119–20
Fox, John, Jr., 148
Francis, Robert, 22–24
Frazier, Thomas, 31
Friedman, Lester, 165–67

Frost, Robert, 18, 23–24
Fugitive Poets, 35
Fun Home (Bechdel), 10, 13, 72–75, 83, 96–102, 128–29

Gannon, Thomas C., 175
Gardner, Jared, 101
Garringer, Rae, 125
Gay and Lesbian Literary Heritage, 51–52
gay rights movement, 15–17; Don't Ask Don't Tell policy and, 120; marriage equality and, 8, 196–97; Mattachine Society and, 44–45, 212n153; Stonewall Uprising and, 17. *See also* LGBTQ
Giardina, Denise, 58, 184
Gleason, Sean, 183
"God Gave Noah the Rainbow Sign" (hymn), 174–75, 235n5
Goodbye Gauley Mountain (film), 160, 163–67, 234n89
Gopinath, Gayatri, 156–57
Graves, Jesse, 148
Gray, Mary L., 121–22, 125, 156, 158
Griffith, E. V., 38–43
Griswold v. Connecticut (1965), 197

Halberstam, Jack, 155; *In a Queer Time and Place*, 84–85, 92, 227n39; on "metronormativity," 3–4, 81–82
Hall, Wade, 209n107
Han-Shan (poet), 36–37, 210nn118–19
Hanlon, Tina L., 124
Haraway, Donna, 164
hate crimes, 196, 238nn3–4. *See also* homophobia
Hawthorne, Ann, 112
Heidegger, Martin, 93
Henninger, Katherine, 106–9
Herring, Scott, 73–75

heteronormativity: Alther on, 89–96; Bechdel on, 96–102; Halberstam on, 84–85; Hirsch on, 83, 95, 106; Sickels on, 84–87. *See also* "metronormativity"
Hillbilly Elegy (film), 82
Hindman Settlement School, 197
Hirsch, Marianne, 83, 95, 106, 110
Hogeland, Lisa Maria, 51
home movies, 89–91, 93–96
homeplace, 11, 20, 68, 145, 154–60. *See also* love of place
homophobia, 118; davenport and, 142; hate crimes and, 196, 238nn3–4; House and, 14, 77–78; Lavender Scare and, 6, 15, 17, 22, 42, 46; Mann on, 68, 161, 186; Scarbrough and, 35–36, 40; Watts on, 150
hooks, bell, 123, 148
House, Silas, 1–3, 7–9, 76–79; on coming out, 34; Garringer and, 125; homophobia and, 14, 78; hooks and, 123; on LGBTQ literary studies, 123, 174, 195, 238n4; on love of place, 148; partner of, 8; on Still's *Chinaberry*, 27; on storytelling, 124
House, Silas, works of: *Clay's Quilt*, 7; *Southernmost*, 8, 10, 76–77; *This Is My Heart for You*, 7, 9, 77–79
Hovious, Darrell, 31
Howard, Jason, 2, 8, 82
Howard, Ron, 82
Howell, Rebecca Gayle, 2
Huckabee, Mike, 203n28
Hudson, Rock, 14
Hughes, Langston, 142
Hurston, Zora Neale, 142
Huston, Anjelica, 58

In Homage to Priapus (Griffith), 38, 39
In a Queer Time and Place (Halberstam), 84–85, 92, 227n39
Inscoe, John C., 68
Inskeep, Steve, 8
Iuliano, Fiorenzo, 72–73

Johnson, David K., 17
Johnson, Fenton, 2, 3, 13, 58–61; *Geography of the Heart*, 132–33, 151; *The Man Who Loved Birds*, 197–98; partner of, 132, 151; photography and, 113–15; on "silence or flight," 122; on storytelling, 124. *See also Scissors, Paper, Rock*
Jones, Loyal, 148–49; *Appalachian Values*, 74, 145, 154
Jong, Erica, 50, 51

Keats, John, 187
Kephart, Horace, 111
Kinflicks (Alther), 2, 10, 49–52, 83, 198; birds in, 179–82; home movies and, 89–91, 93–96; religious beliefs in, 173–75, 179–80; satire of, 159
Kline, Carrie, 125, 227n40
Ku Klux Klan, 78, 174
Kumbier, Alana, 15

Larsen, Anne, 181
Lavender Scare, 6, 15, 17, 22, 42, 46. *See also* homophobia
Lawrence v. Texas (1963), 197
Lentz, Ralph E., II, 112
Lessing, Doris, 50
LGBTQ, 14–15; "conversion therapy" and, 22; definitions of, 4–5; labeling of, 46, 53–54, 99; queer photography and, 83–84; rainbow flag of, 174–75; transgender people and, 75–76, 86–88, 196. *See also* gay rights movement

LGBTQ Appalachian literature, 52, 126–29, 233n49; anthologies of, 65, 69, 122, 147, 185–86, 197; beginnings of, 13–14, 34; birds in, 173–82; cuisine in, 182–94; religious beliefs in, 66, 76–77, 173–75, 177–80; storytelling traditions in, 124–25; transcendence in, 173–75; Williams on, 227n32. *See also specific authors*
Liberace, 14
Locklear, Erica Abrams, 183–84
Loftin, Craig M., 6, 16, 17, 44, 120–21
Long, Kate, 104
Lord, Catherine, 4
Lorde, Audre, 123
love of place, 74, 76, 145–46, 148; nature as refuge and, 147–54. *See also* homeplace
Lundy, Ronni, 189

Mackin, Randy, 35–37, 40
Mann, Jeff, 11, 13, 20, 59; on Appalachian cuisine, 182, 184–88; coming out experience of, 122, 154; on double erasure, 146; Inscoe on, 68; on Keats, 187; Miller and, 201n12; on natural world, 160–61; partner of, 67
Mann, Jeff, works of: "Appalachian Subculture," 157; *Bliss*, 67–68, 161–63; "Civilization Comes to Summers County," 188; "Dilly Beans," 186; "Fried Chicken and Spoon Bread," 130–31, 187; "Gathering Green Tomatoes in the Rain," 187; *Loving Mountains, Loving Men*, 67–69, 130–31, 160–61, 163; "Regional Oddities," 187–88; "Saving What We Can," 186, 187; "Southern (LGBT) Living," 185–86; "Stonewall and Matewan," 5–6, 67, 157; "Yellow-Eye Beans," 184–85, 187
Maren, Mesha, 2, 197
marriage equality, 8, 196–97. *See also* gay rights movement
Mason, Belinda, 60
Masterpiece Cakeshop v. Colorado Civil Rights Commission (2018), 196, 203n29
Mattachine Society, 43–45, 212n153
May, Roger, 82–83
McCarthy, Cormac, 57
McCarthyism, 6, 15. *See also* Lavender Scare
McCoy, Karissa, 57
McCrumb, Sharyn, 124
McDaniel, Judith, 51
McDonald's restaurants, 188
McElmurray, Karen Salyer, 3, 11, 69–71, 115–18. See also *Strange Birds in the Tree of Heaven*
McKee, Kathryn, 70
McMichael, Pam, 123
Mehta, Rahul, 2
Melville, Herman, 17
memento mori, 85, 95
"metronormativity," 3–4, 75, 76, 81–82. *See also* heteronormativity
Metropolitan Community Church, 66, 174–75
Meyer, Richard, 4, 83
Miller, Danny L., 147, 148; "Homosexuality in Appalachian Literature," 5, 31, 57–58; Mann and, 201n12; on McElmurray, 71; on urban Appalachia, 154–55
Miller, James A., 139
Miller, Jim Wayne, 124
Milton, John, 175
Minick, Jim, 68
Mitchell, W. J. T., 84
Mooney, Stephen D., 227n32

266 | Index

Moraga, Cherríe, 61
Morehead State College (KY), 24–25, 28, 78–79
Moser, Irene, 124
Murfree, Mary Noailles, 69, 148

Napier, O. James, 122
nature as refuge, 11, 147–54. *See also* love of place
Newman, Katherine, 170

Obergefell v. Hodges (2015), 196, 197, 203n28
O'Connor, Flannery, 56
Olson, Ted, 155
ONE: The Homosexual Magazine, 16, 43–44
oral tradition, 119–25, 227n32. *See also* storytelling

Paden, Jeremy, 59
Pancake, Ann, 3, 164
Perrin, Al, 32–33
photography, 81–84, 111–12; Allison and, 106–10; Alther and, 89–96; Anderson and, 102–6, *105*; Ballerini on, 82; Barthes on, 221n10; Bechdel on, 96–102; davenport on, 141–42; Evans and, 102–6, *105*, 110–11, 224n101; Eveleth on, 97; Hirsch on, 83, 95, 106; Johnson and, 113–15; Loyal Jones and, 145; May on, 82–83; McElmurray and, 115–18; as *memento mori*, 85, 95; Meyer on, 83; queer, 83–84; Sickels and, 83–89
Porter, Katherine Anne, 18
posthumanism, 164, 166, 167, 175
"poverty porn," 82
pronoun choice, 86, 101–2, 126–27, 149
Proust, Marcel, 98

queer photography, 83–84

queer time, 84–85, 92; definition of, 84; Halberstam on, 84–85

Radway, Leon, 46
Rawlings, Marjorie Kinnan, 18
Reece, Byron Herbert, 9, 14, 41–47, 198; awards of, 41; biographers of, 42, 43, 44; death of, 17–18; Lavender Scare and, 42
Reece, Byron Herbert, works of: *The Ballad of the Bones*, 41, 45; *Bow Down in Jericho*, 44; *Fable in the Blood*, 45; *The Hawk and the Sun*, 44, 45; "If Only Lovers," 20
Reed, John Shelton, 159
religious beliefs, 66, 76–77, 173–75, 177–80
Rhorer, Marc A., 4–5, 125
Rohy, Valerie, 15
Rose, Larry, 132, 151
Ruppersburg, Hugh, 45

Satterwhite, Emily, 7
Scarbrough, George, 2, 9, 14, 34–40; biographer of, 37, 40; family of, 35, 198; Griffith and, 38, 40–41; homophobic reactions to, 35–36, 40; Reece and, 41–43
Scarbrough, George, works of: *The Course Is Upward*, 34; "Love in the Afternoon," 38, 40; *Summer So-Called*, 34; *Tellico Blue*, 34; *Under the Lemon Tree*, 36–37
Scates, Maxine, 103, 105
Schafer, William J., 59
Schwartz, Delmore, 18
Scissors, Paper, Rock (Johnson): AIDS in, 10, 60–61, 113–14, 130–34, 192, 196; Appalachian cuisine in, 12, 59, 182, 191–94; closeted experiences in, 127–28; photographer in, 112–15
Sedgwick, Eve Kosofsky, 120, 164

Seidman, Steven, 121
Sellers, Bettie, 42, 44
Shaw, Denise R., 142, 230n121
Shimanoff, Susan B., 120
Shultz, Zach, 146
Sickels, Carter, 2, 10, 11, 20, 75–76; on coming out, 76; on heteronormativity, 84–87; on photography, 83–89; on pronouns, 86, 126–27, 149; on storytelling, 124–25
Sickels, Carter, works of: "Early in My Transition...," 126–27; *The Evening House*, 75–76; "Johnson City," 84, 86–87, 149, 182, 191; "Photograph, 2007," 84–86, 148–49; *The Prettiest Star*, 88–89, 130, 131–32, 198; "Wildlife," 84, 86–88
"silence = death," 129–34. *See also* AIDS/HIV
Sipple, Savannah, 2, 197
Smith, Lee, 124, 225n114
Snyder, Gary, 210n118
Society for the Study of the Multi-Ethnic Literature of the United States, 170
Sohn, Mark, 189, 193
Southern Agrarians, 35
Spriggs, Bianca Lynne, 59, 176
Sprinkle, Annie, 160, 163–67
St. John, Janet, 139
Stambuk, Andrew, 24
Stein, Gertrude, 53
Steinbeck, John, 19
Stephens, Elizabeth "Beth," 2, 3, 11, 163–67, 234n89
Stewart, Albert, 20–21, 24–25
Stewart, Christopher B., 69
Still, James, 9–10, 13–14, 17–34; archives of, 28; Arvin and, 22; awards of, 18, 19; biographer of, 18–19; Central American trip of, 29–32; Cross and, 27–34, 207n77; Francis and, 22–24; Frost and, 18, 23–24; Steinbeck and, 19; Stewart and, 20–21, 24–25; Wells and, 26–29, 32, 33
Still, James, works of: *Appalachian Mother Goose*, 25; *Chinaberry*, 9, 26–27, 34, 206n57; *Jack and the Wonder Beans*, 23; *Pattern of a Man and Other Stories*, 30; *River of Earth*, 18, 19, 25–26, 34, 124; *Rusties and Riddles*, 25
Stonewall Uprising (1969), 17
storytelling, 119–25, 227n32; Alther on, 124; doris davenport on, 124, 139; Foucault on, 119–20; House on, 124; Johnson on, 124
Strange Birds in the Tree of Heaven (McElmurray), 10–12, 69–71, 112, 115–18; Appalachian cuisine in, 182; hearing voices in, 135–38; natural world in, 151–54; winged things in, 177–79
Stuart, Jesse, 21, 41
Swem, Gregg, 209n107

Thompson, Deborah, 124
Thoreau, Henry David, 160, 162
Through Their Eyes (film), 6, 125, 174
transgender people, 75–76, 84, 86–88, 196. *See also* LGBTQ
Trivett, W. R., 111–12

Ulmann, Doris, 111
urban Appalachia, 154–55

Vance, J. D., 82
Vera, Dan, 68
Verghese, Abraham, 60
voodoo, 139, 169

Waage, Frederick G., 159
Walker, Frank X, 64, 130, 138, 141, 216n58. *See also* Affrilachian poets
Walls, Jeannette, 68

Warhol, Robyn, 102
Watkins, Charles Alan, 112
Watts, Julia, 11, 20, 65–67; on Appalachian cuisine, 182, 189; coming out experience of, 123; on double erasure, 146
Watts, Julia, works of: *Finding H.F.*, 1, 66–67, 127, 150–51, 174–75; *The Kind of Girl I Am*, 189–190; *Phases of the Moon*, 190–91; "Quare Theory," 65, 123, 157–58; *Quiver*, 198; *Wildwood Flowers*, 65–66
Weatherford, W. D., 124, 148
Wells, Betty Jean "B. J.," 26–29, 32, 33
West, Don, 21
Weston, Kath, 155, 157
Wiggington, Eliot, 209n107
Wilde, Oscar, 14, 46, 120, 128
Williams, Alexander, 227n32
Williams, Tennessee, 56
Wise, Manfred (pseud. of Edward Pratt Dickson), 43–45
Wolfe, Thomas, 71, 154, 158
Wootten, Bayard, 111, 112
Worthington, Marianne, 69

Yep, Gust A., 120
Young, Bo, 68

Zimmerman, Patricia, 90

www.ingramcontent.com/pod-product-compliance
Lightning Source LLC
Chambersburg PA
CBHW030531230426
43665CB00010B/847